Vol. 10

Story & Art by
Ao Mimori

Contents

The Story Thus Far...

Ryoko falls hard for Ryunosuke, the quiet, bespectacled cutie who sits next to her in class. Then she learns that he moonlights as a host—a guy who dates women for money! Soft-spoken bookworm by day, aggressive ladies' man by night, Ryu may be more than the inexperienced Ryoko can handle. But she can't seem to get him out of her head...or her heart...

Ryunosuke has to take after-school classes to keep from dropping out, which leaves Ryoko alone in the evenings. Kurama, a shy guy with a crush on Ryoko, invites her to a club to hear his band. Ryoko decides not to go, but Kurama's friend Shu forces her onto his motorcycle. Meanwhile, Miss Izumi finds Kurama's invitation, shows it to Ryunosuke and offers to take him to the club to investigate. They arrive just in time to see Kurama grab the mic and ask Ryoko to be his girlfriend!

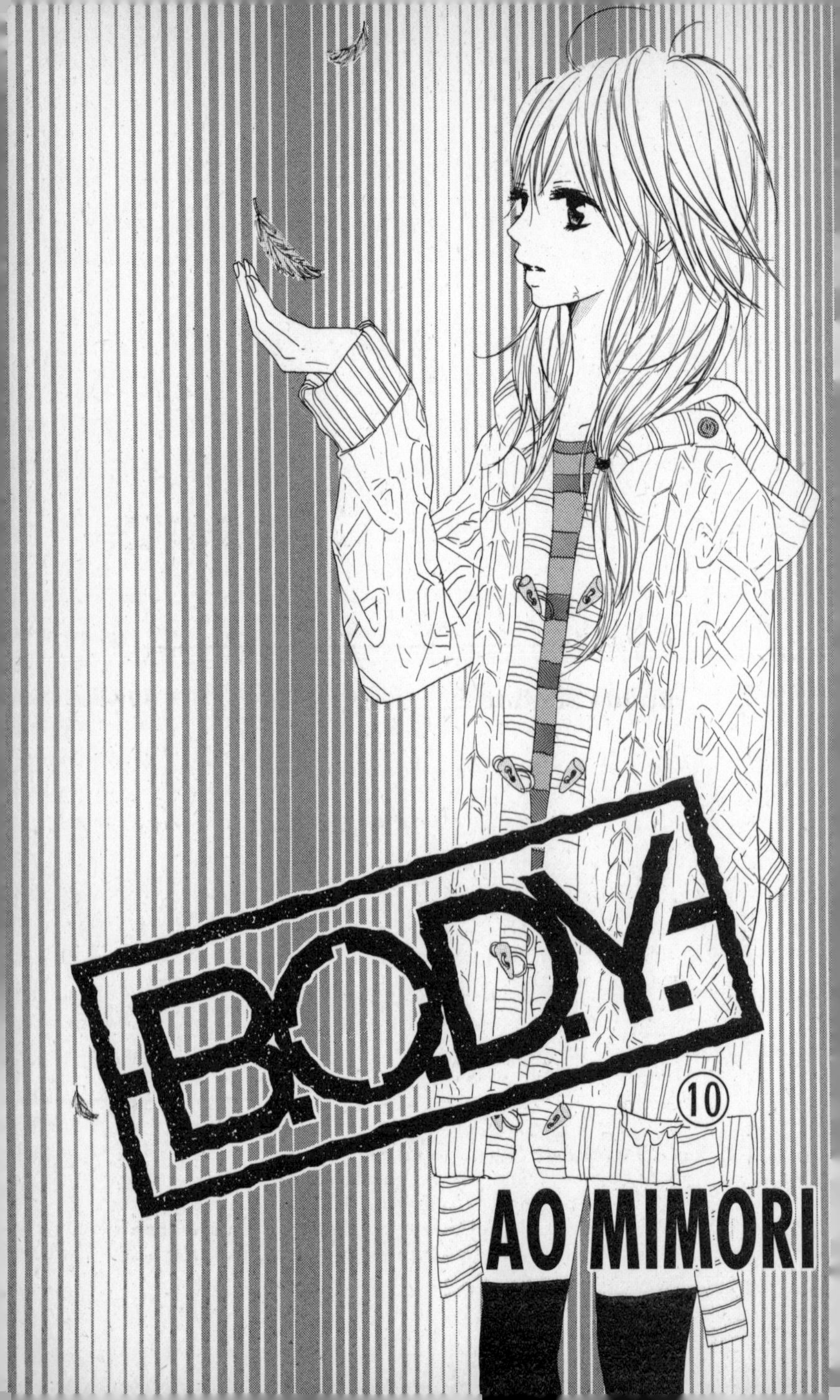
B.O.D.Y.
10
AO MIMORI

Hello, everybody!

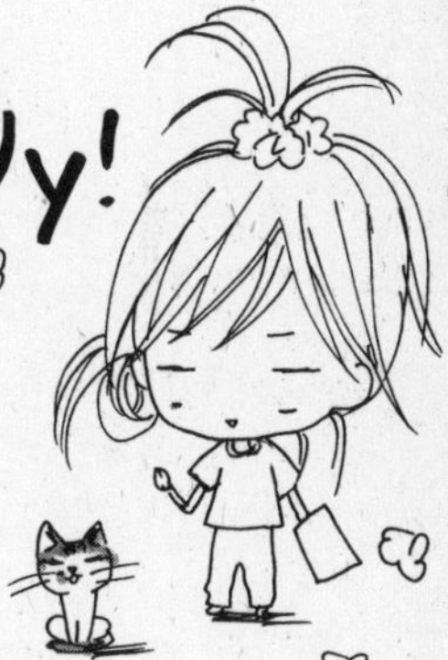

It's been a while!! How've you been?
Volume 10 is finally out!!! I'm happy and kind of embarrassed at the same time!!! Who knew it would go on this long? I don't think anybody did.
Thanks, everyone!!!

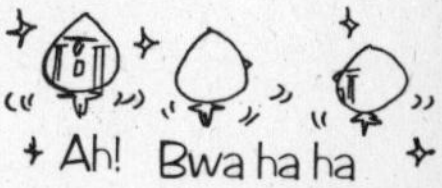
Ah!
Bwa ha ha

To celebrate the tenth volume, I did a color poster of all the characters. The story's getting pretty turbulent, but everyone looks like they're getting along on the poster.

As usual, there are some totally useless bonus pages at the end. Hope you enjoy them!

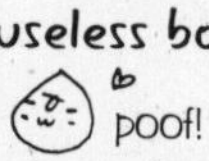
poof!

I received a lot of letters after volume 9 asking what was going to happen between those two. Um... well...
All I can say is, "read on!!"

See you!

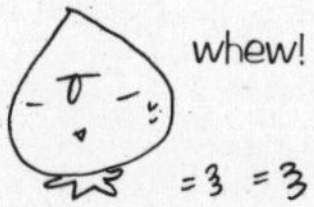
whew!

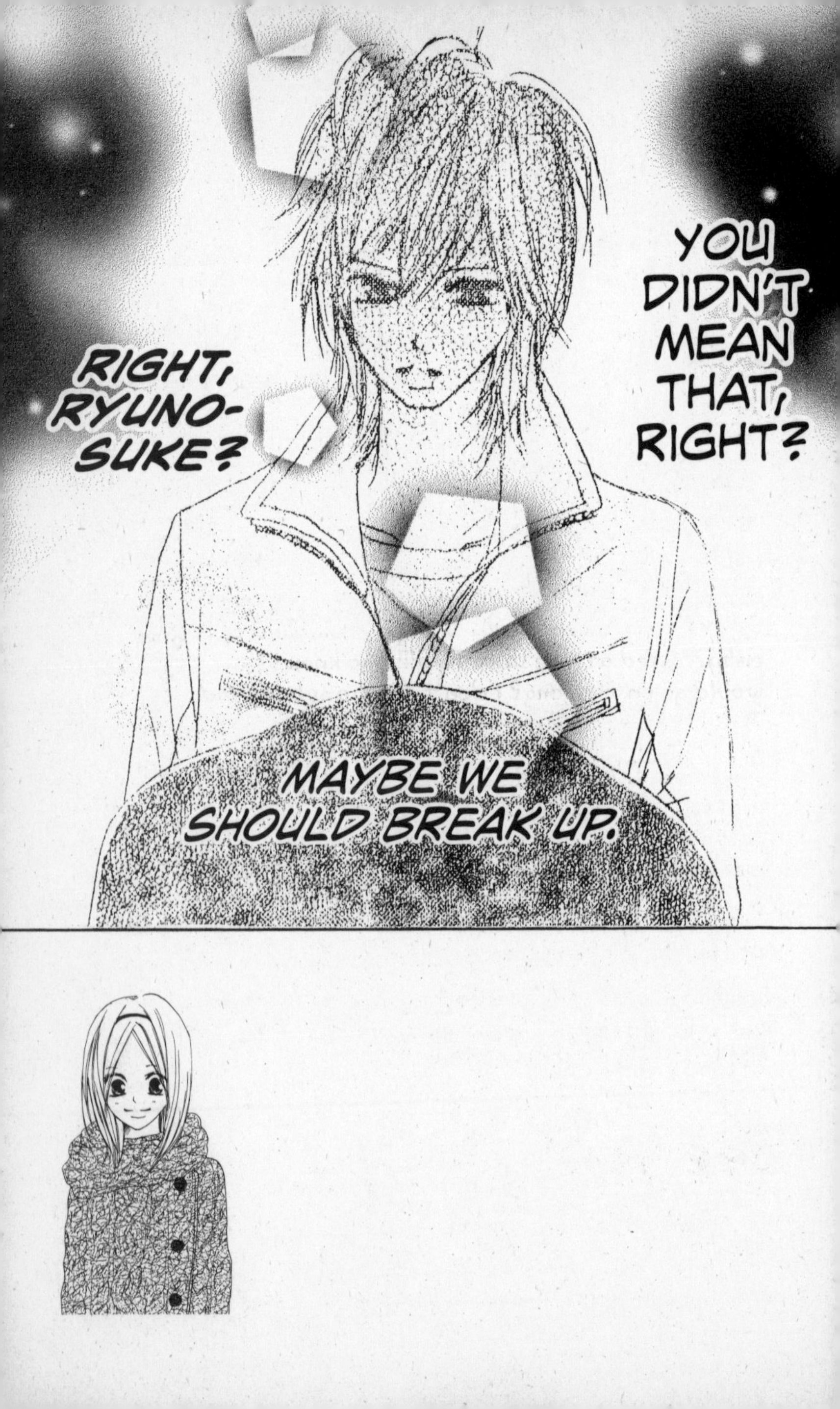
YOU DIDN'T MEAN THAT, RIGHT?
RIGHT, RYUNO-SUKE?
MAYBE WE SHOULD BREAK UP.

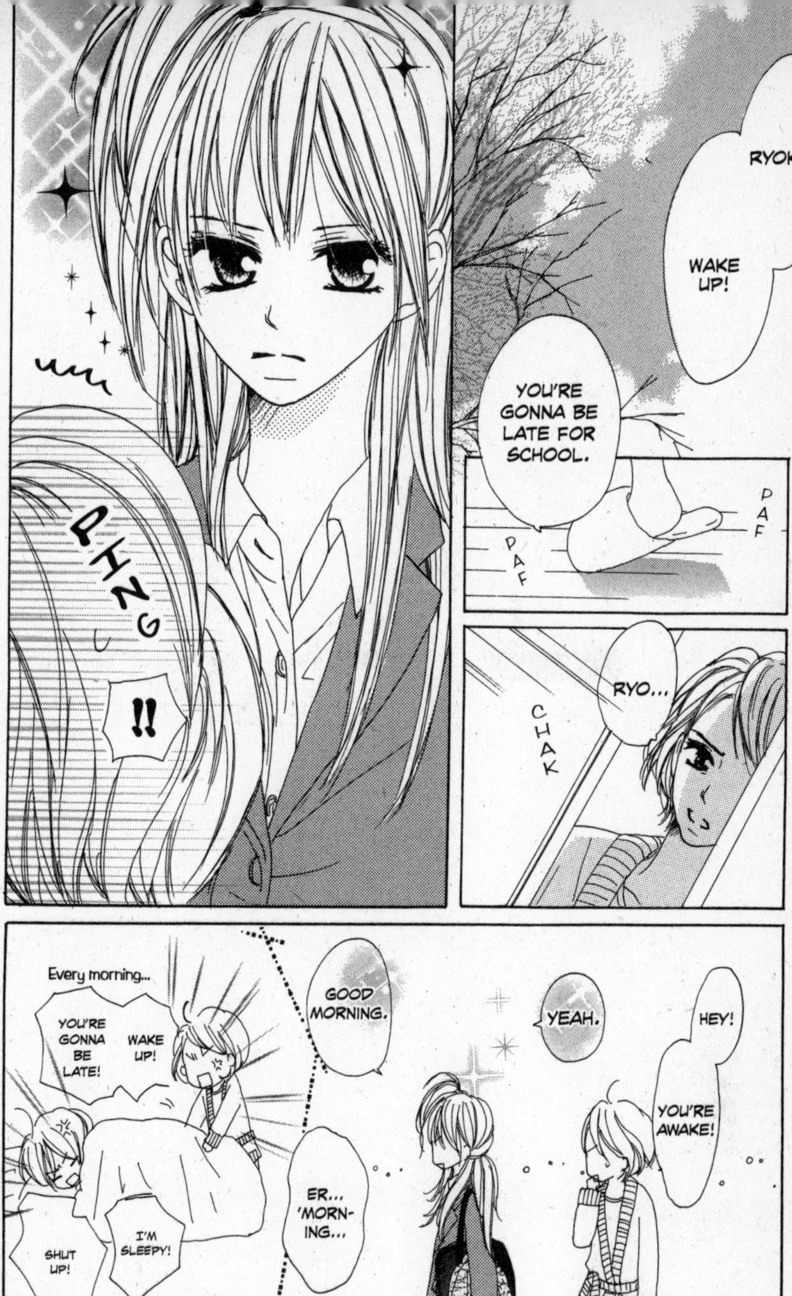
RYOKO!
WAKE UP!
YOU'RE GONNA BE LATE FOR SCHOOL.
PAF
PAF
PAF
PAF
RYO...
CHAK
PING
!!
HEY!
YOU'RE AWAKE!
YEAH.
GOOD MORNING.
ER... 'MORNING...
Every morning...
WAKE UP!
YOU'RE GONNA BE LATE!
I'M SLEEPY!
SHUT UP!

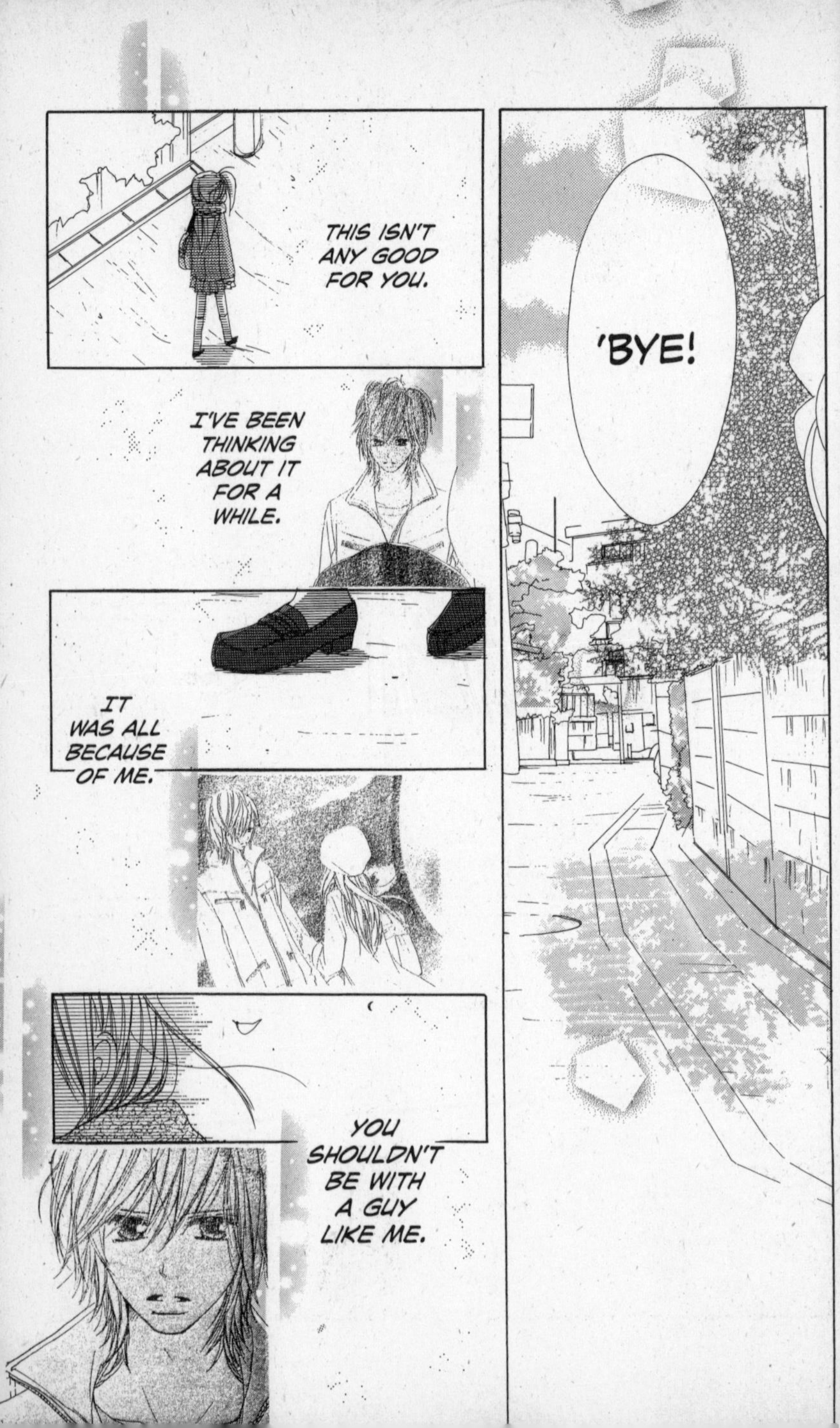
'BYE!
THIS ISN'T ANY GOOD FOR YOU.
I'VE BEEN THINKING ABOUT IT FOR A WHILE.
IT WAS ALL BECAUSE OF ME.
YOU SHOULDN'T BE WITH A GUY LIKE ME.

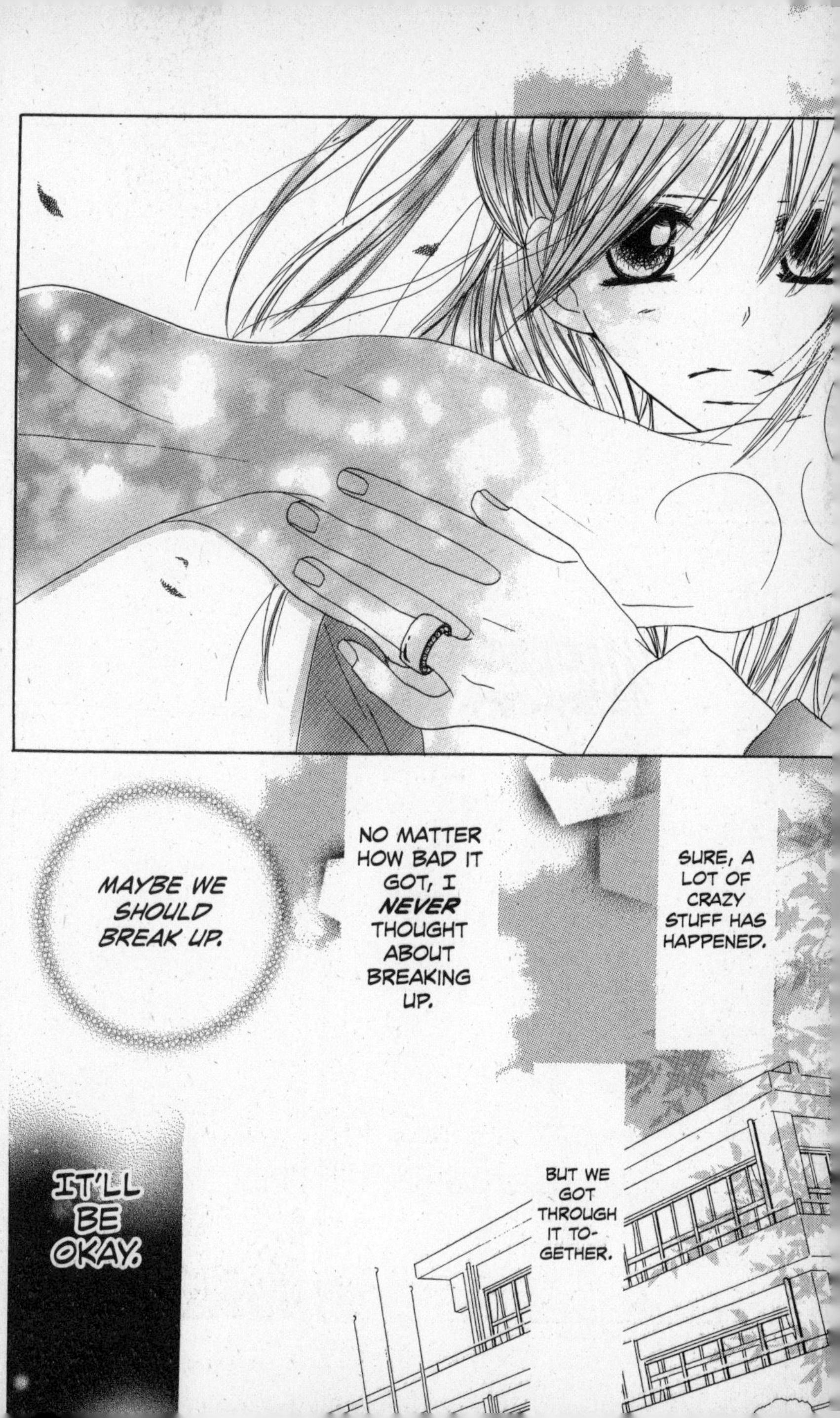
SURE, A LOT OF CRAZY STUFF HAS HAPPENED.
BUT WE GOT THROUGH IT TO-GETHER.
NO MATTER HOW BAD IT GOT, I **NEVER** THOUGHT ABOUT BREAKING UP.
MAYBE WE SHOULD BREAK UP.
IT'LL BE OKAY.

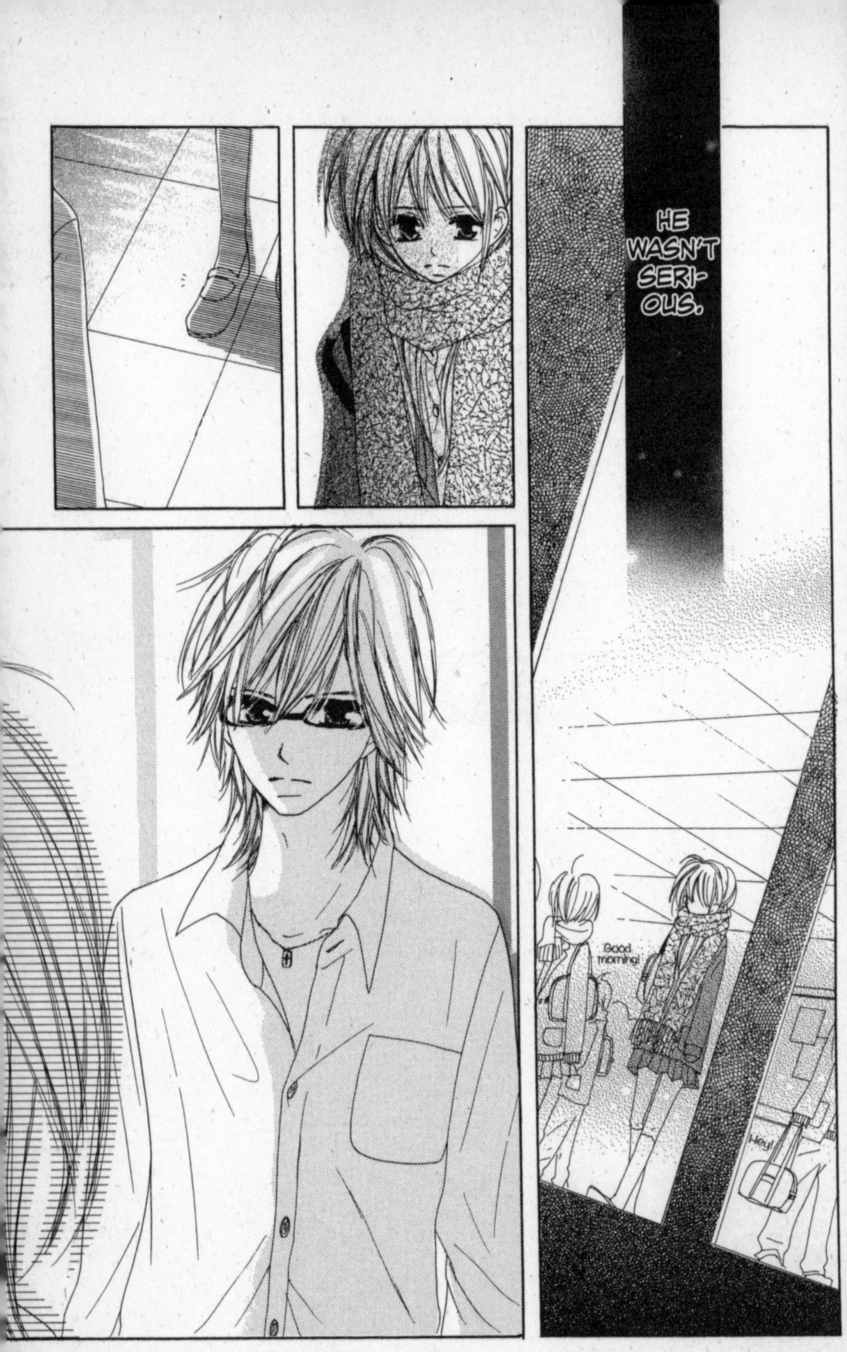
HE WASN'T SERI-OUS.
Good morning!
Hey!

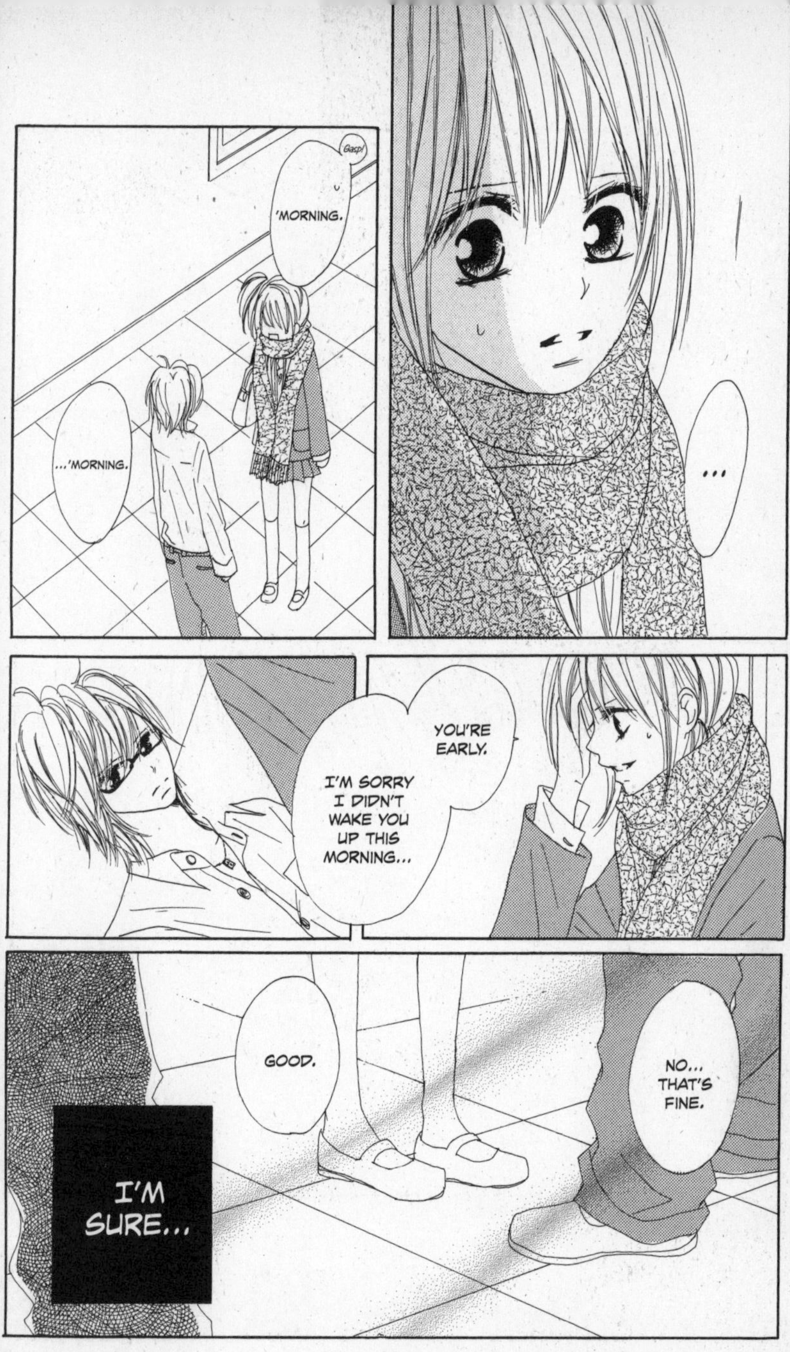
...
Gasp!
'MORNING.
...'MORNING.
YOU'RE EARLY.
I'M SORRY I DIDN'T WAKE YOU UP THIS MORNING...
NO... THAT'S FINE.
GOOD.
I'M SURE...

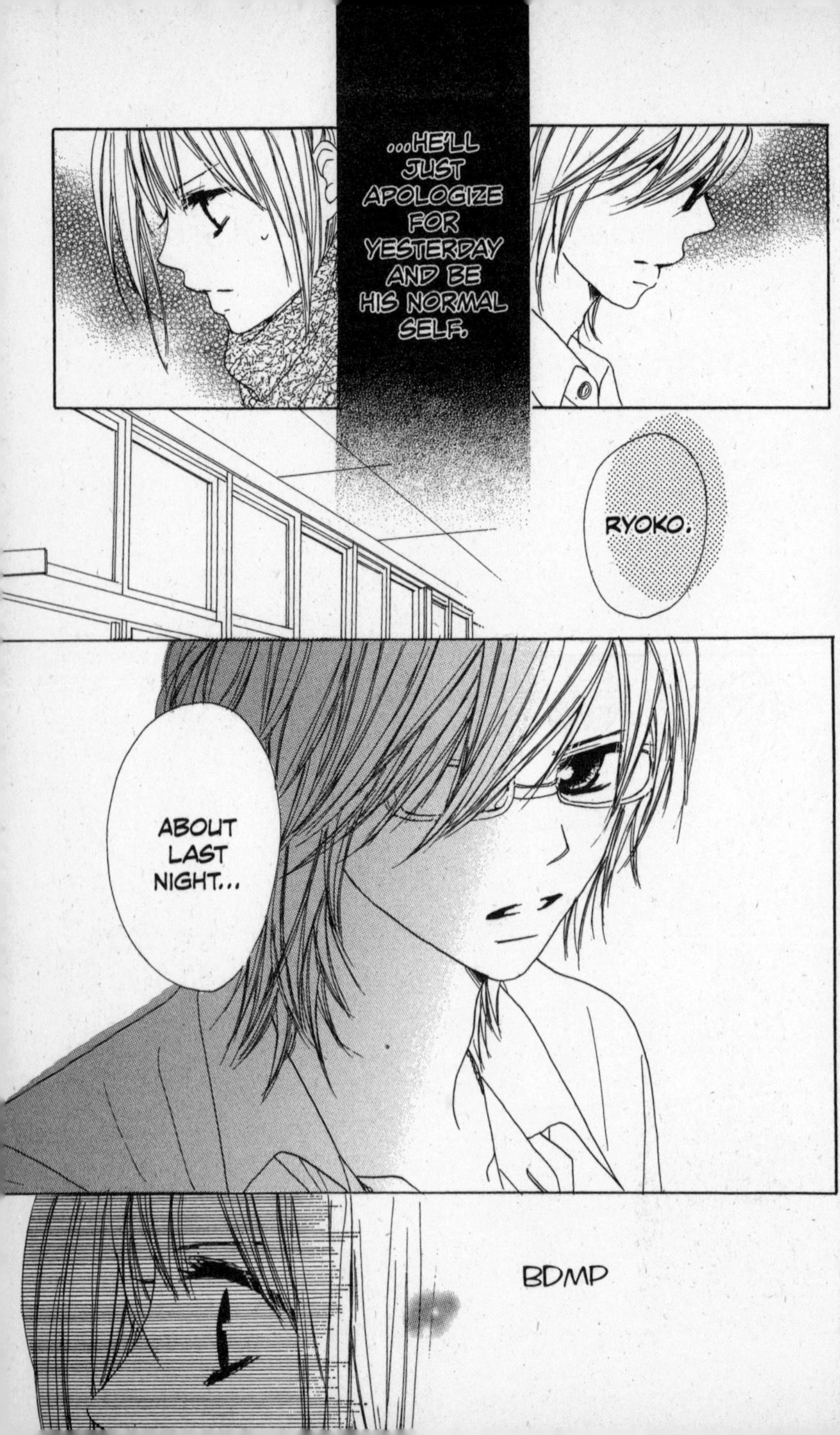
...HE'LL JUST APOLOGIZE FOR YESTERDAY AND BE HIS NORMAL SELF.
RYOKO.
ABOUT LAST NIGHT...
BDMP

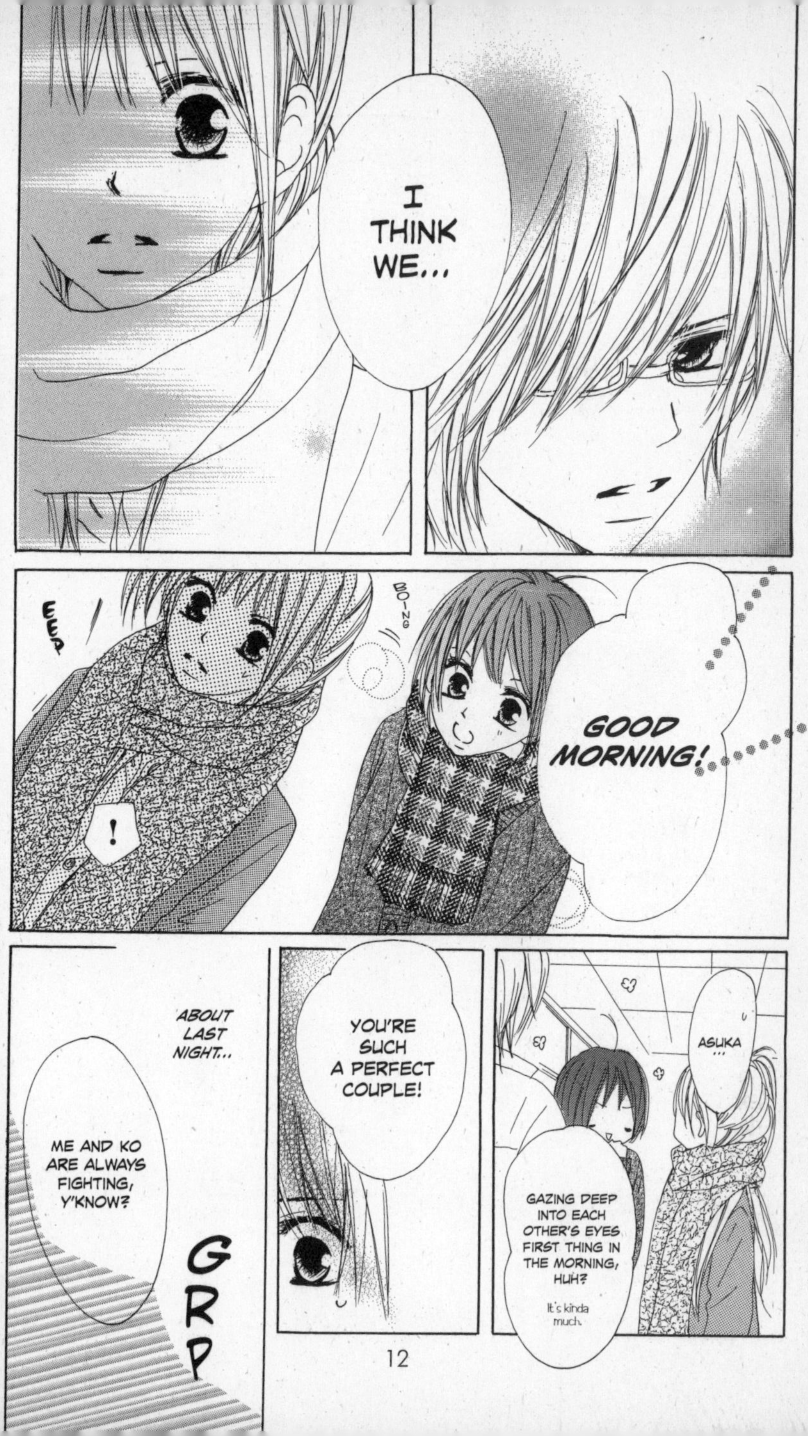
I THINK WE...
GOOD MORNING!
BOING
!
EEP
ASUKA ...
GAZING DEEP INTO EACH OTHER'S EYES FIRST THING IN THE MORNING, HUH?
It's kinda much.
YOU'RE SUCH A PERFECT COUPLE!
ABOUT LAST NIGHT...
ME AND KO ARE ALWAYS FIGHTING, Y'KNOW?
GRP

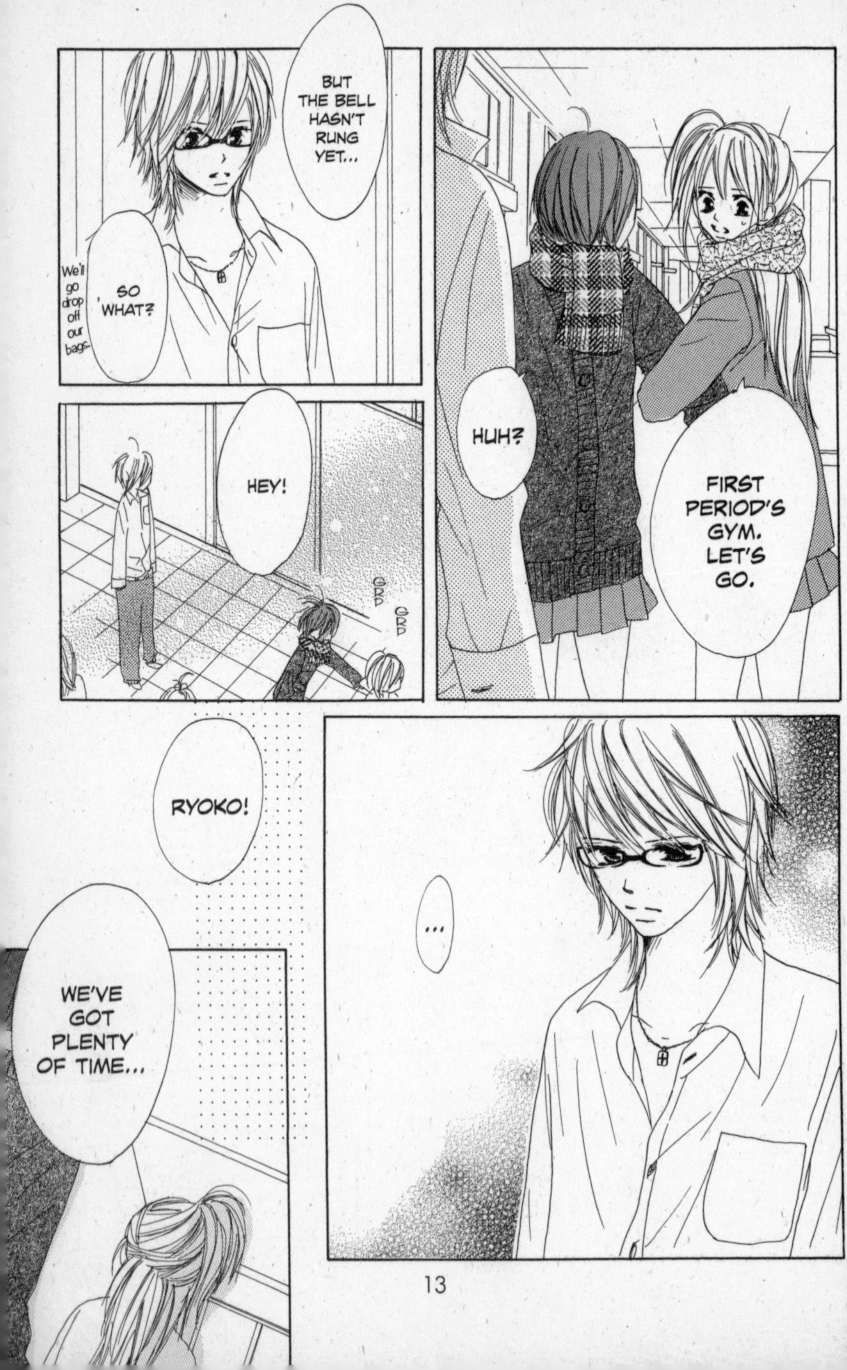
FIRST PERIOD'S GYM. LET'S GO.
HUH?
BUT THE BELL HASN'T RUNG YET...
SO WHAT?
We'll go drop off our bags.
HEY!
GRP
GRP
...
RYOKO!
WE'VE GOT PLENTY OF TIME...

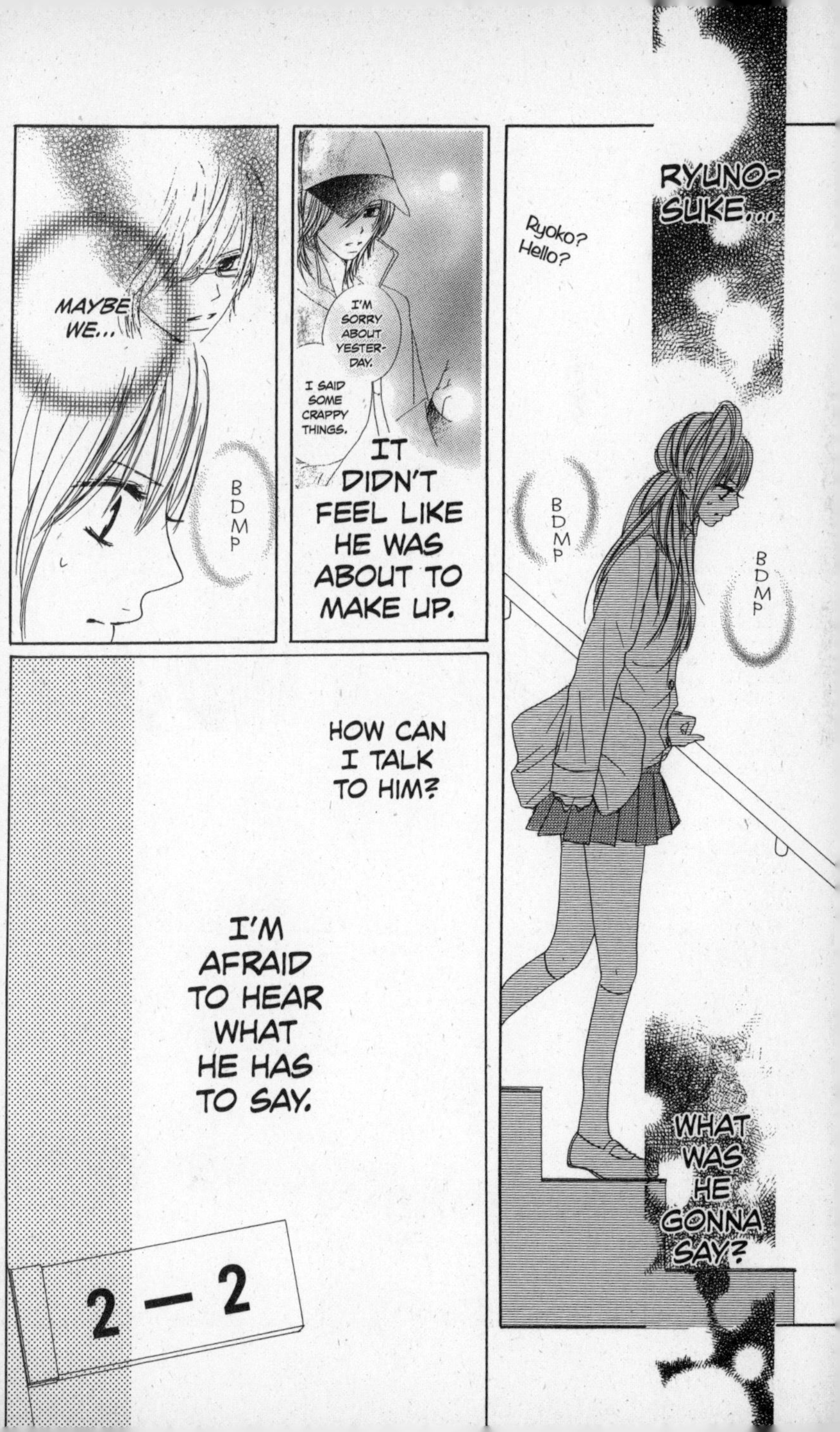
RYUNO-SUKE...
Ryoko? Hello?
BDMP
BDMP
WHAT WAS HE GONNA SAY?
I'M SORRY ABOUT YESTER-DAY.
I SAID SOME CRAPPY THINGS.
IT DIDN'T FEEL LIKE HE WAS ABOUT TO MAKE UP.
MAYBE WE...
BDMP
HOW CAN I TALK TO HIM?
I'M AFRAID TO HEAR WHAT HE HAS TO SAY.
2 — 2

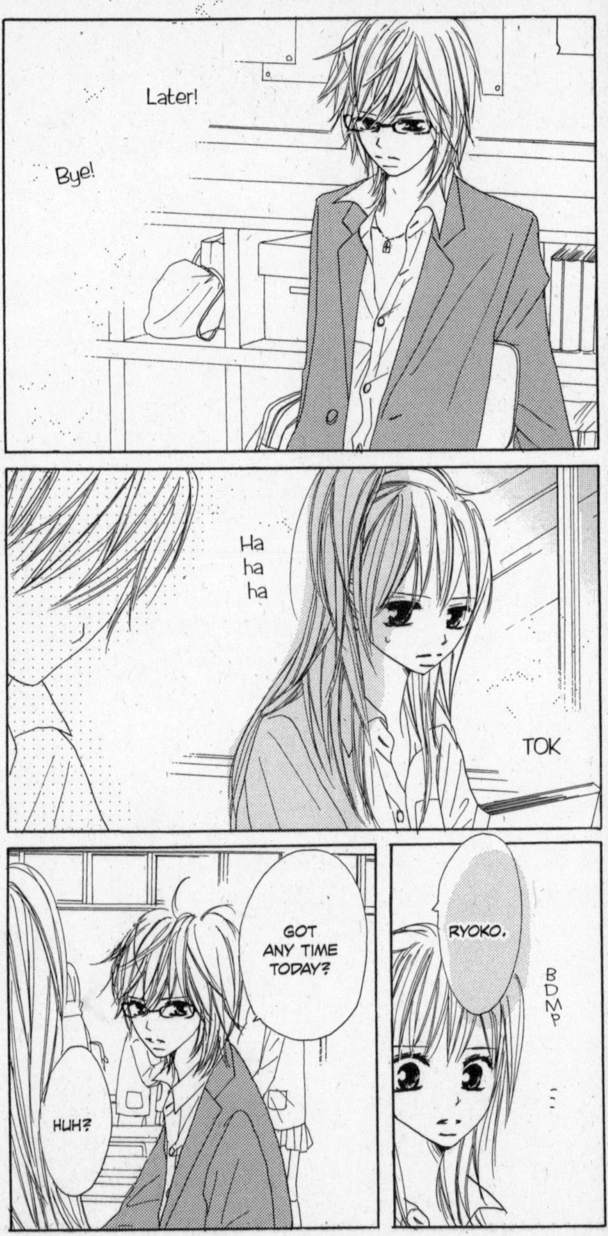
Later!
Bye!
Ha ha ha
TOK
RYOKO.
BDMP
GOT ANY TIME TODAY?
HUH?

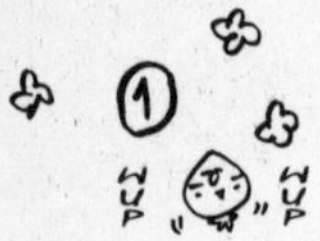
1
WUP WUP

Hello again!! Ao Mimori here. I'll be freestyling it through these side notes again!! Only those interested in my personal life should keep reading.

We got a lot of responses to the stuff I wrote about Animal Crossing in the last volume, but a few readers also responded to my affinity for foreign TV shows. That made me so happy!

In fact, I recently subscribed to J:COM so I can get American TV on cable. It's a storm of shows from FOX and AXN!!! EEK!♥

I've been watching ANIMAX and FOX and AXN and the Discovery Channel and music channels.♥ Bliss.♥ I love anime too... Oh, and I forgot to mention in the last volume that I watch Lost!! There's nobody I'm particularly rooting for on the show. I just wanna find out what happens next. Oh, but I hate that one guy...

(2) To be continued...

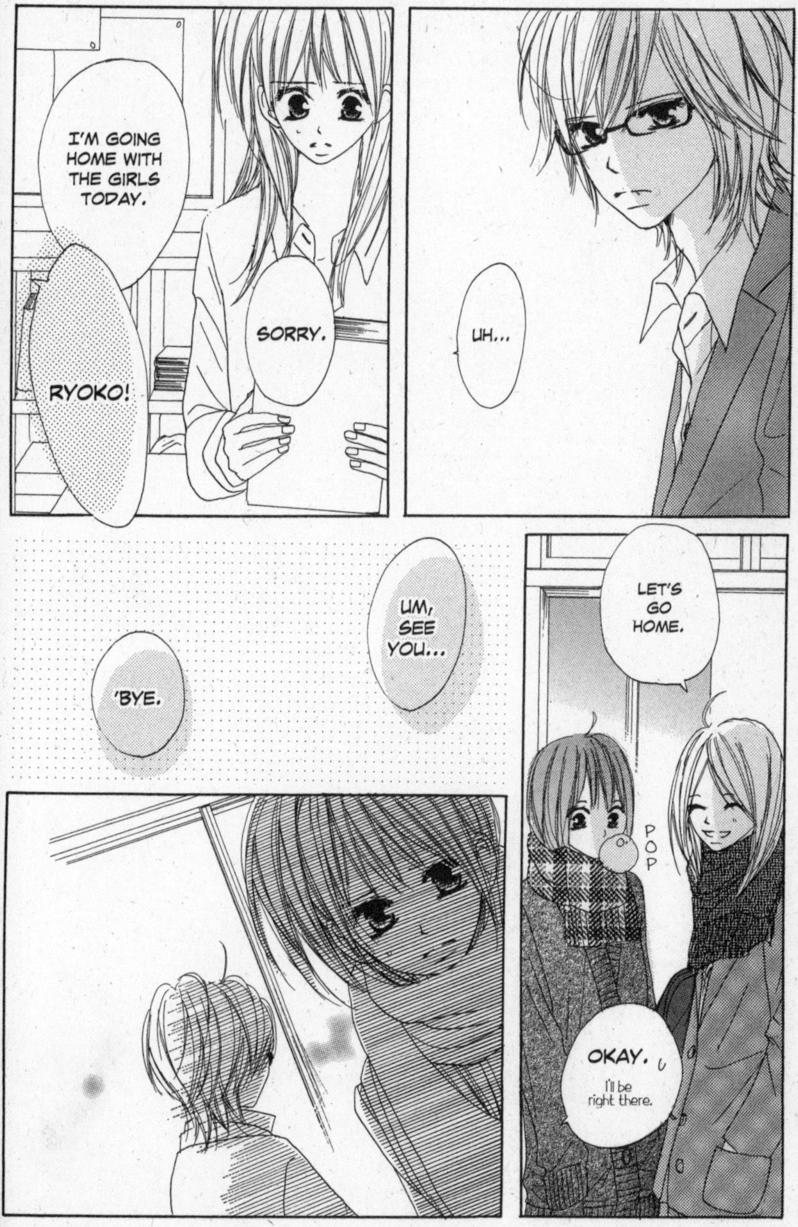
UH...
I'M GOING HOME WITH THE GIRLS TODAY.
SORRY.
RYOKO!
LET'S GO HOME.
POP
OKAY.
I'll be right there.
UM, SEE YOU...
'BYE.

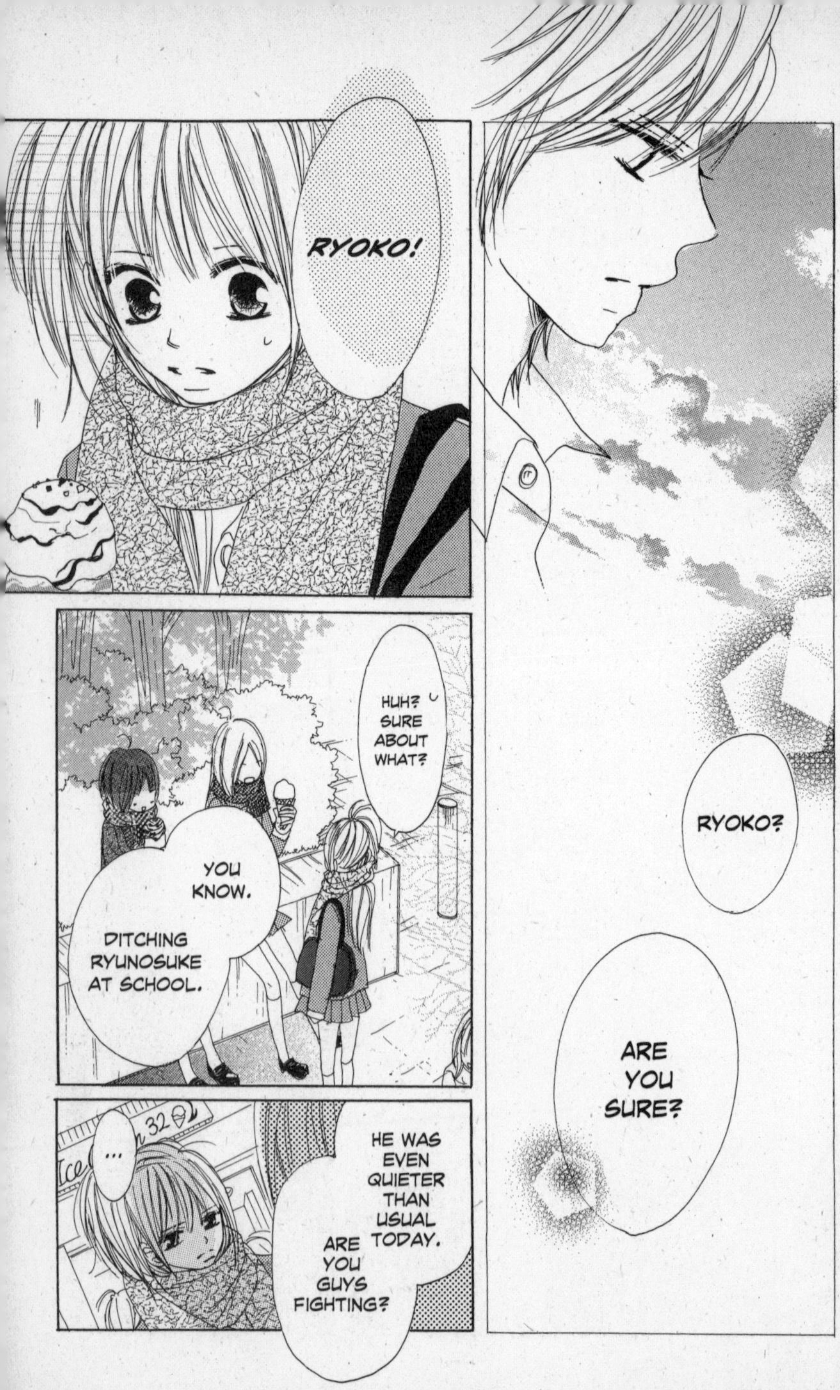
RYOKO?
ARE YOU SURE?
RYOKO!
HUH? SURE ABOUT WHAT?
YOU KNOW.
DITCHING RYUNOSUKE AT SCHOOL.
HE WAS EVEN QUIETER THAN USUAL TODAY.
ARE YOU GUYS FIGHTING?
...

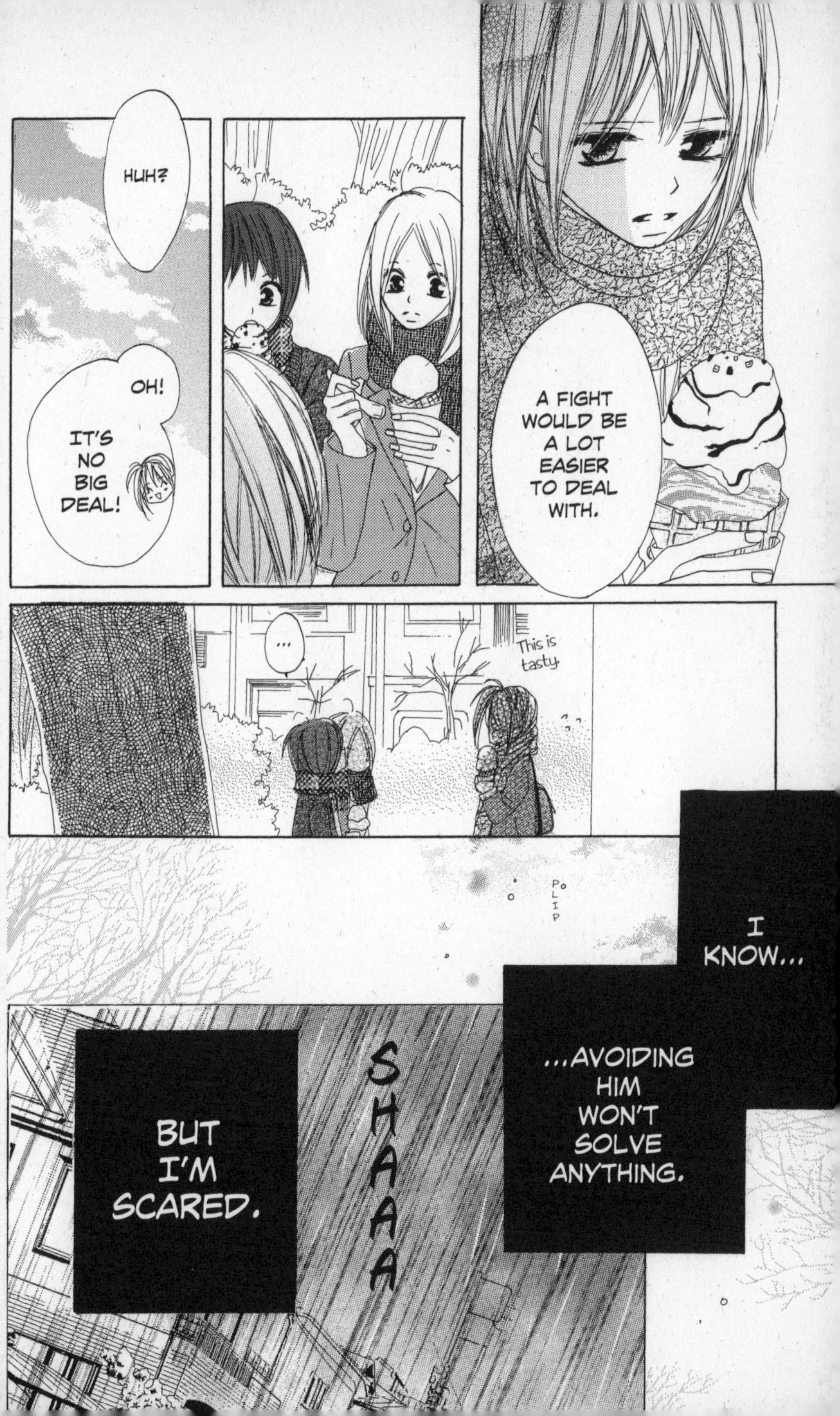
A FIGHT WOULD BE A LOT EASIER TO DEAL WITH.
HUH?
OH!
IT'S NO BIG DEAL!
This is tasty.
...
PLIP
I KNOW...
...AVOIDING HIM WON'T SOLVE ANYTHING.
SHAAAA
BUT I'M SCARED.

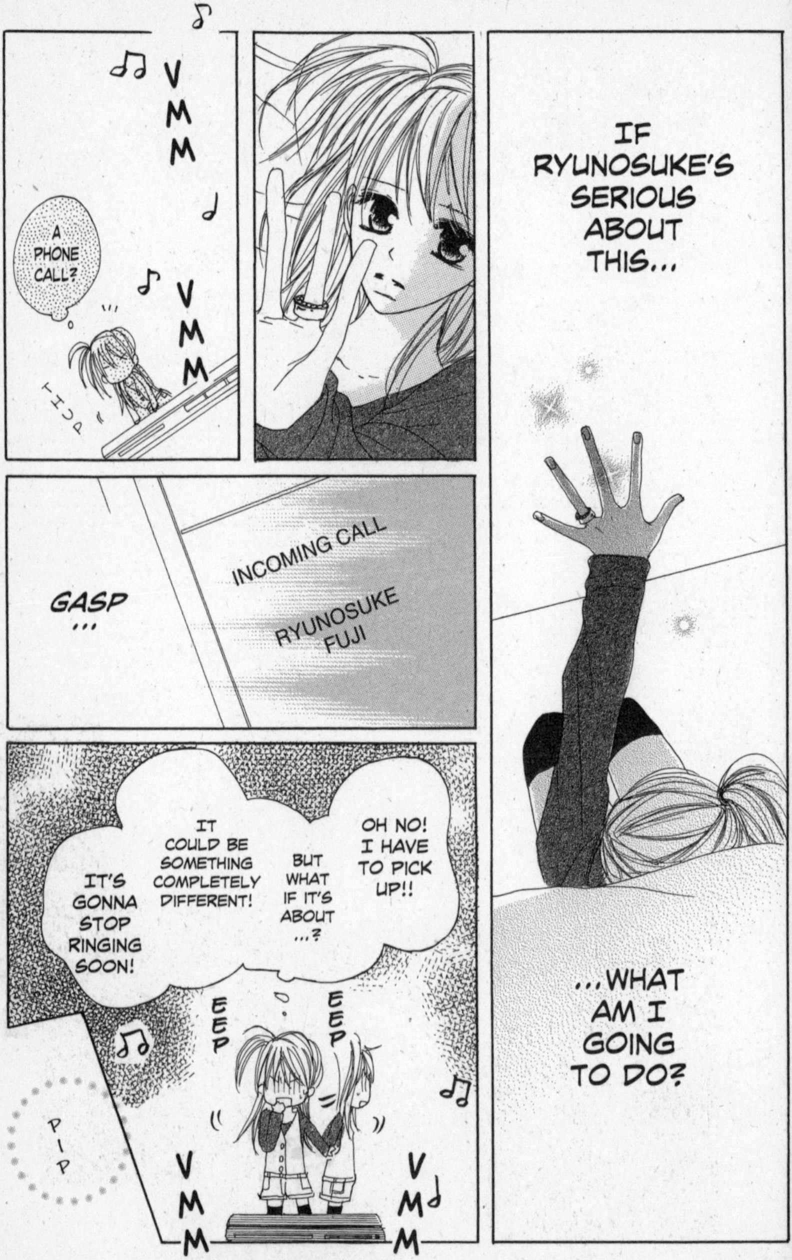
IF RYUNOSUKE'S SERIOUS ABOUT THIS...
...WHAT AM I GOING TO DO?
VMM
A PHONE CALL?
VMM
INCOMING CALL
RYUNOSUKE FUJI
GASP...
OH NO! I HAVE TO PICK UP!!
BUT WHAT IF IT'S ABOUT ...?
IT COULD BE SOMETHING COMPLETELY DIFFERENT!
IT'S GONNA STOP RINGING SOON!
EEP
EEP
VMM
VMM
PIP

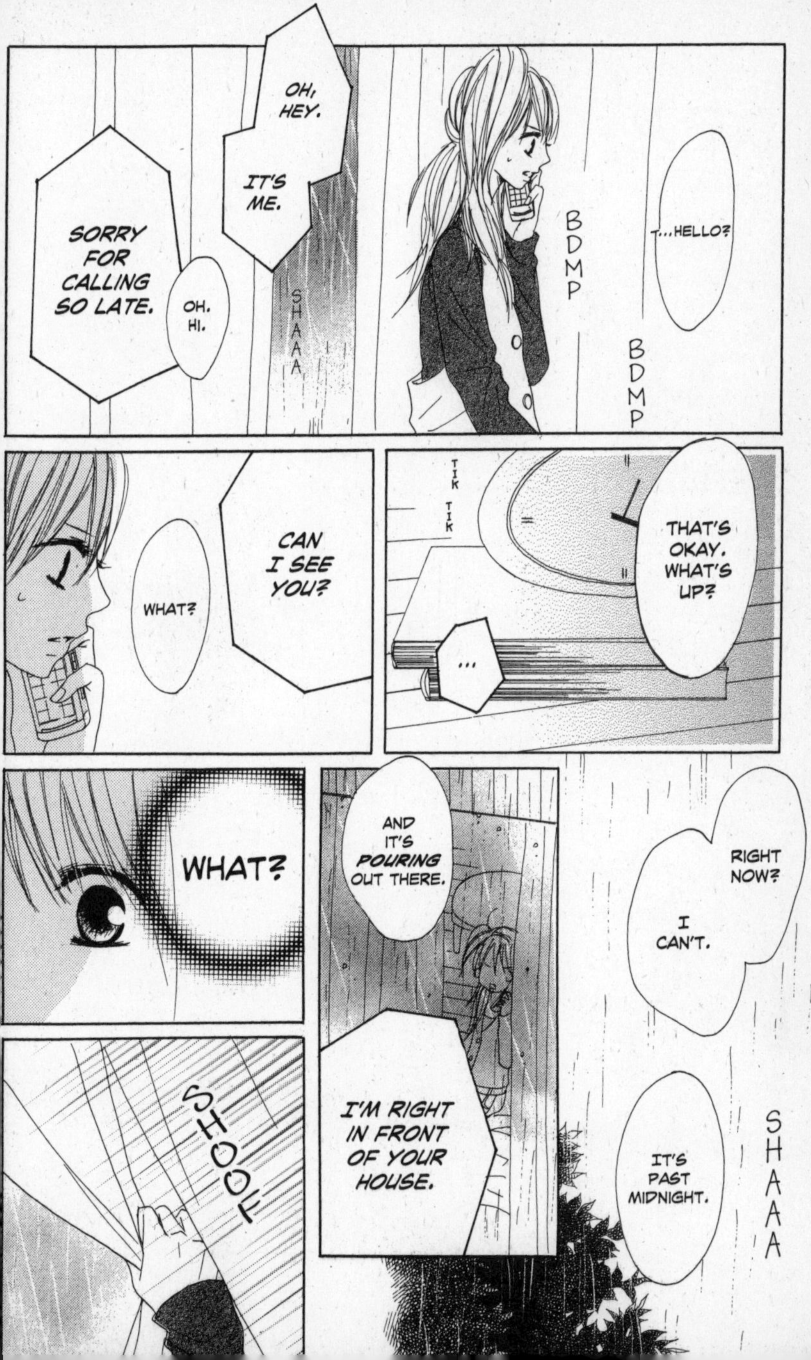
...HELLO?
BDMP
BDMP
OH, HEY.
IT'S ME.
SHAAA
OH. HI.
SORRY FOR CALLING SO LATE.
TIK TIK
THAT'S OKAY. WHAT'S UP?
...
CAN I SEE YOU?
WHAT?
RIGHT NOW?
I CAN'T.
IT'S PAST MIDNIGHT.
SHAAA
AND IT'S *POURING* OUT THERE.
I'M RIGHT IN FRONT OF YOUR HOUSE.
WHAT?
SHOOF

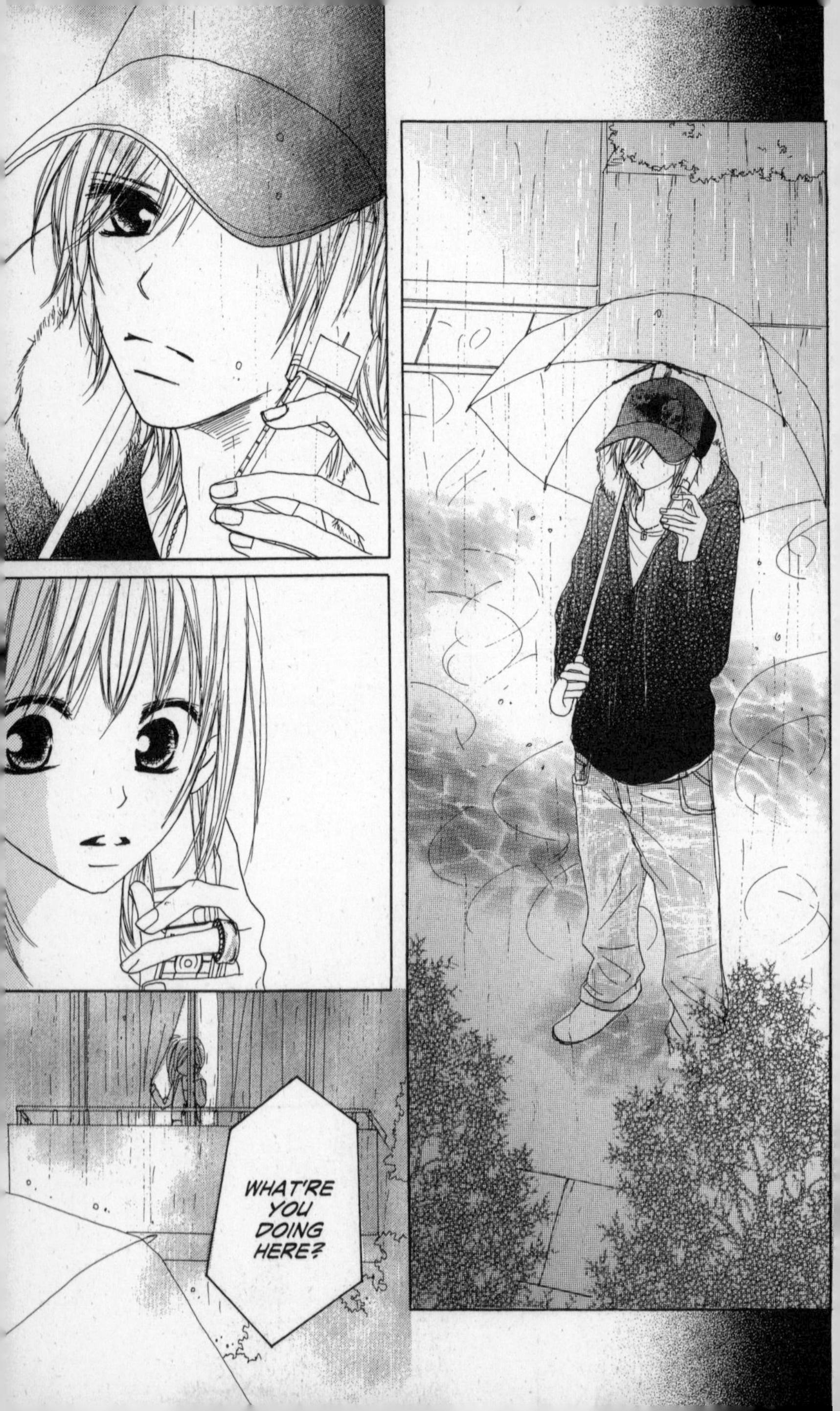
WHAT'RE YOU DOING HERE?

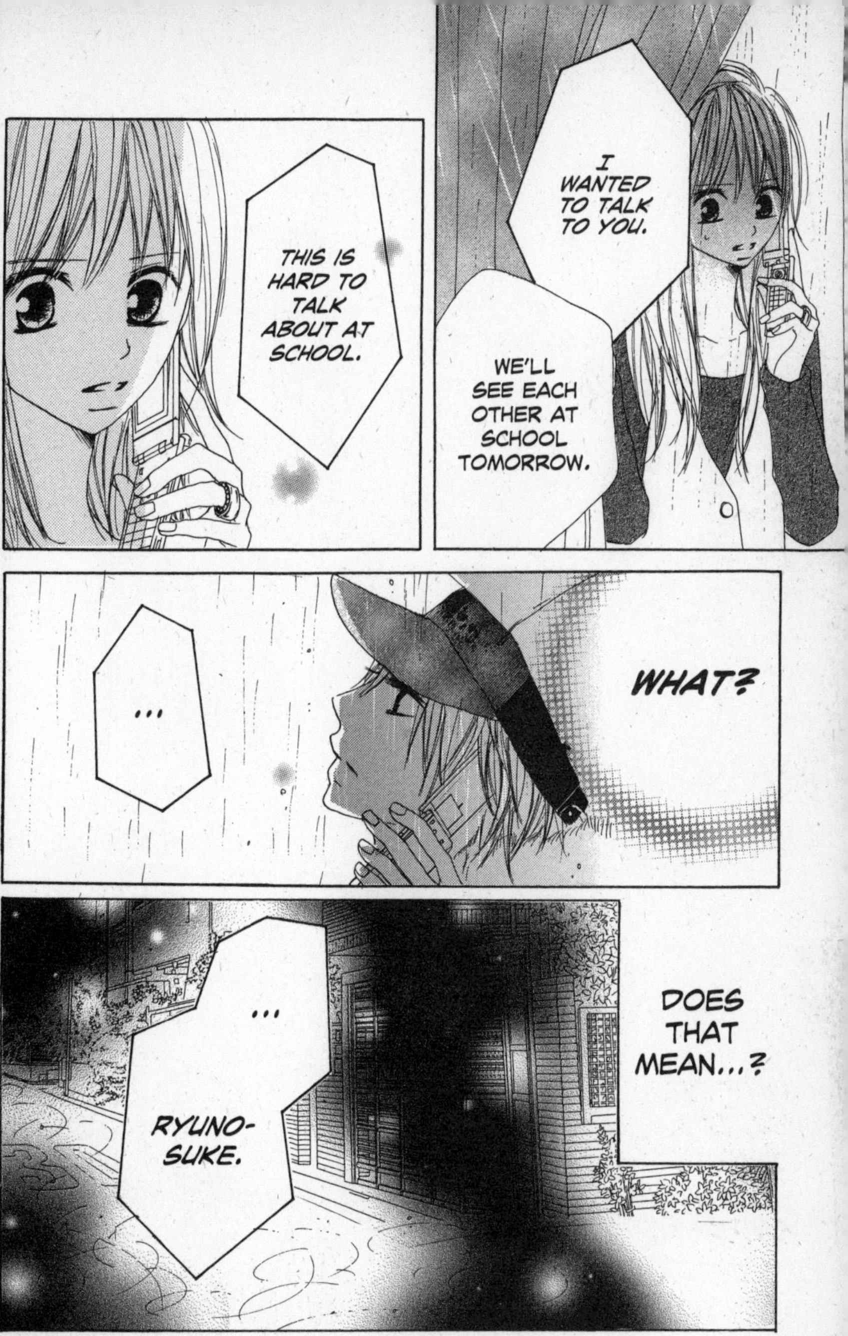
I WANTED TO TALK TO YOU.
WE'LL SEE EACH OTHER AT SCHOOL TOMORROW.
THIS IS HARD TO TALK ABOUT AT SCHOOL.
WHAT?
...
DOES THAT MEAN...?
... RYUNO-SUKE.

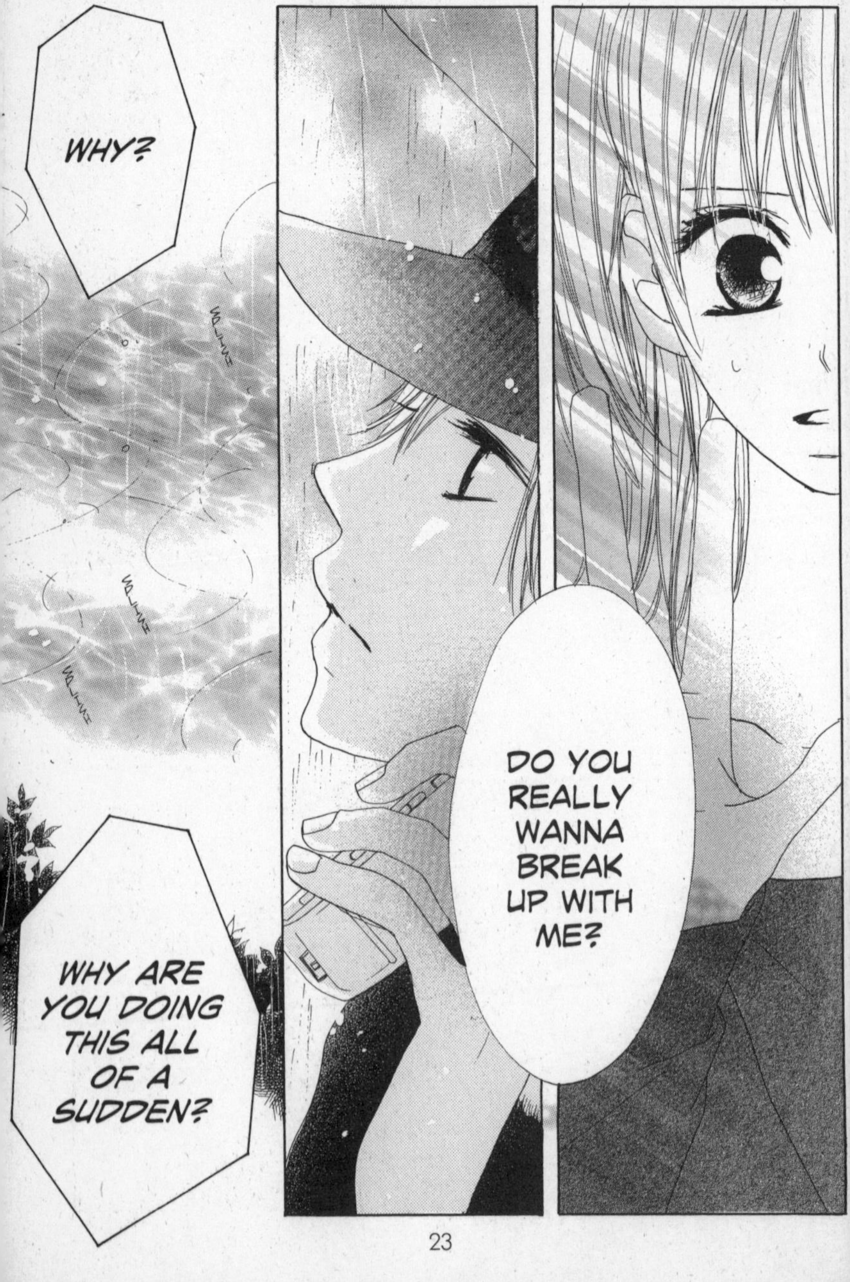
DO YOU REALLY WANNA BREAK UP WITH ME?
WHY?
WHY ARE YOU DOING THIS ALL OF A SUDDEN?

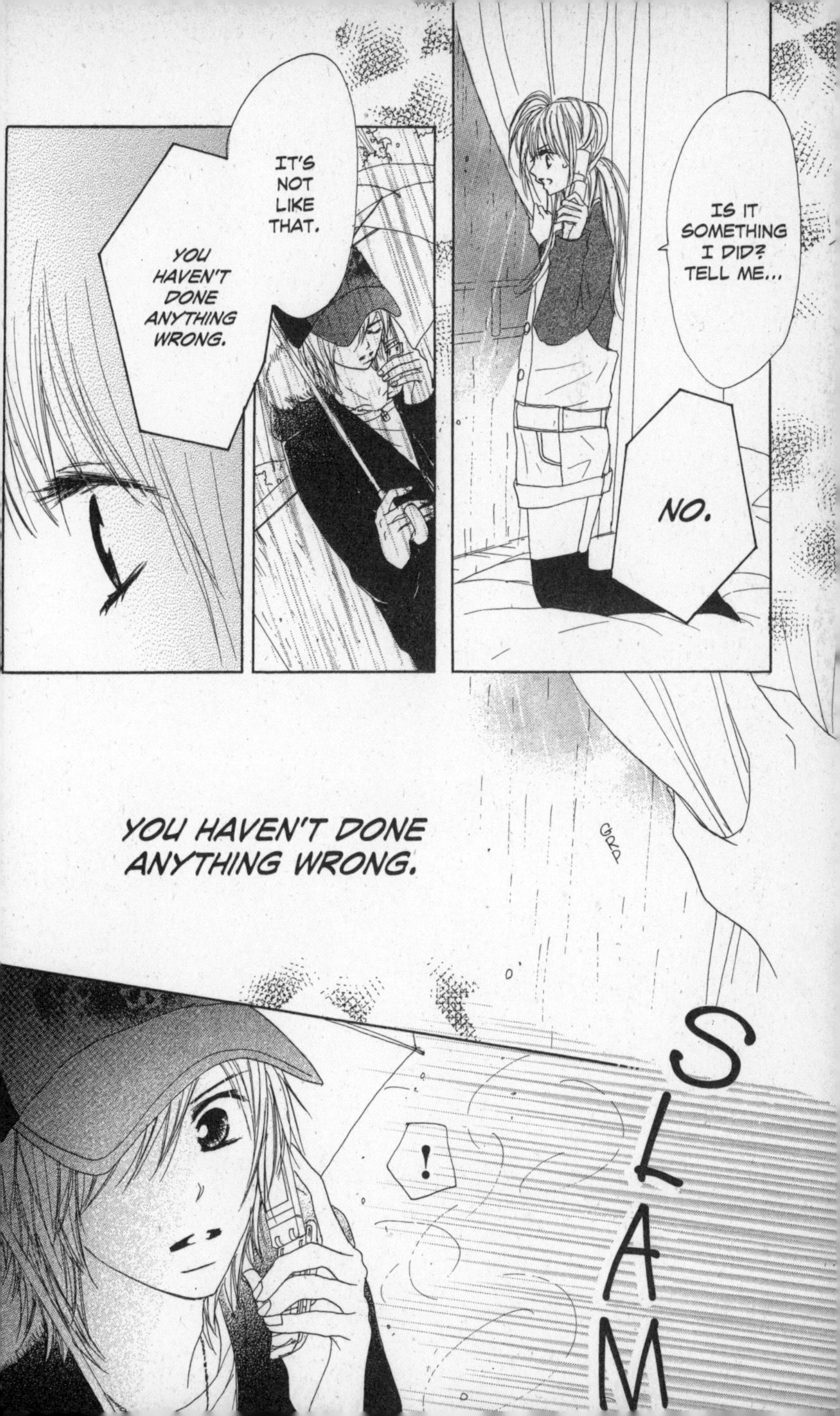
IS IT SOMETHING I DID? TELL ME...
NO.
IT'S NOT LIKE THAT.
YOU HAVEN'T DONE ANYTHING WRONG.
YOU HAVEN'T DONE ANYTHING WRONG.
!
SLAM

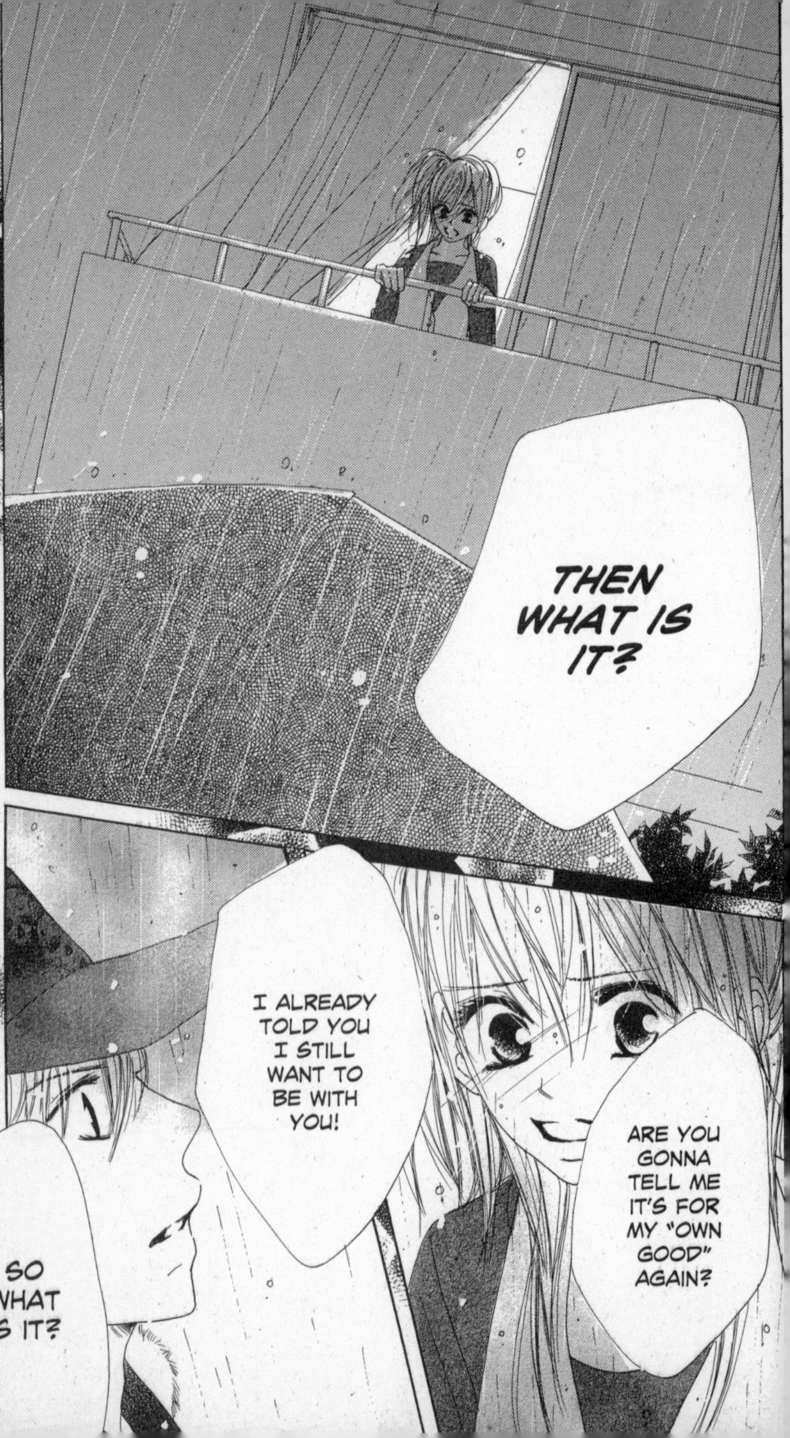
THEN WHAT IS IT?
ARE YOU GONNA TELL ME IT'S FOR MY "OWN GOOD" AGAIN?
I ALREADY TOLD YOU I STILL WANT TO BE WITH YOU!
SO WHAT IS IT?

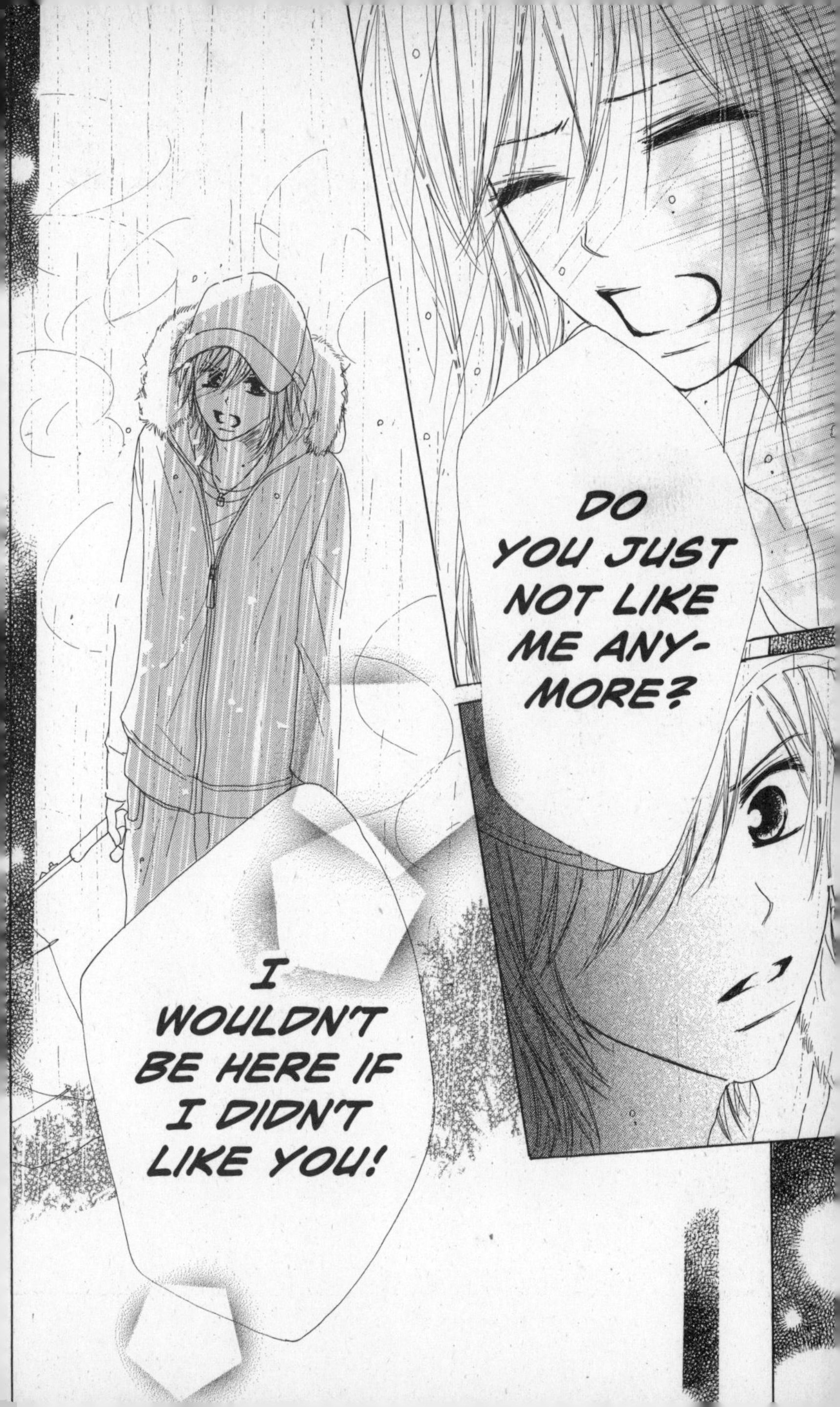
DO YOU JUST NOT LIKE ME ANY-MORE?
I WOULDN'T BE HERE IF I DIDN'T LIKE YOU!

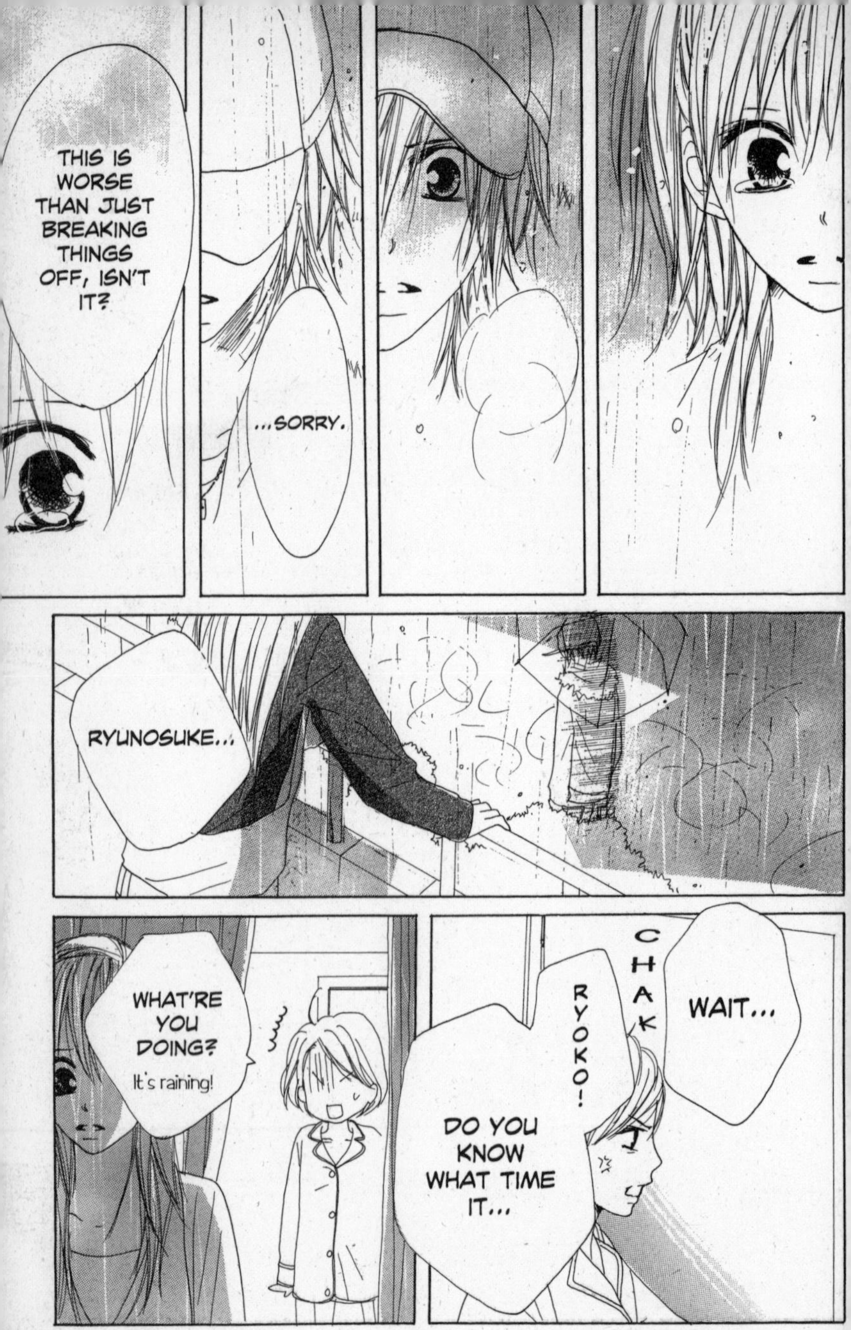
...SORRY.
THIS IS WORSE THAN JUST BREAKING THINGS OFF, ISN'T IT?
RYUNOSUKE...
WAIT...
CHAK
RYOKO!
DO YOU KNOW WHAT TIME IT...
WHAT'RE YOU DOING?
It's raining!

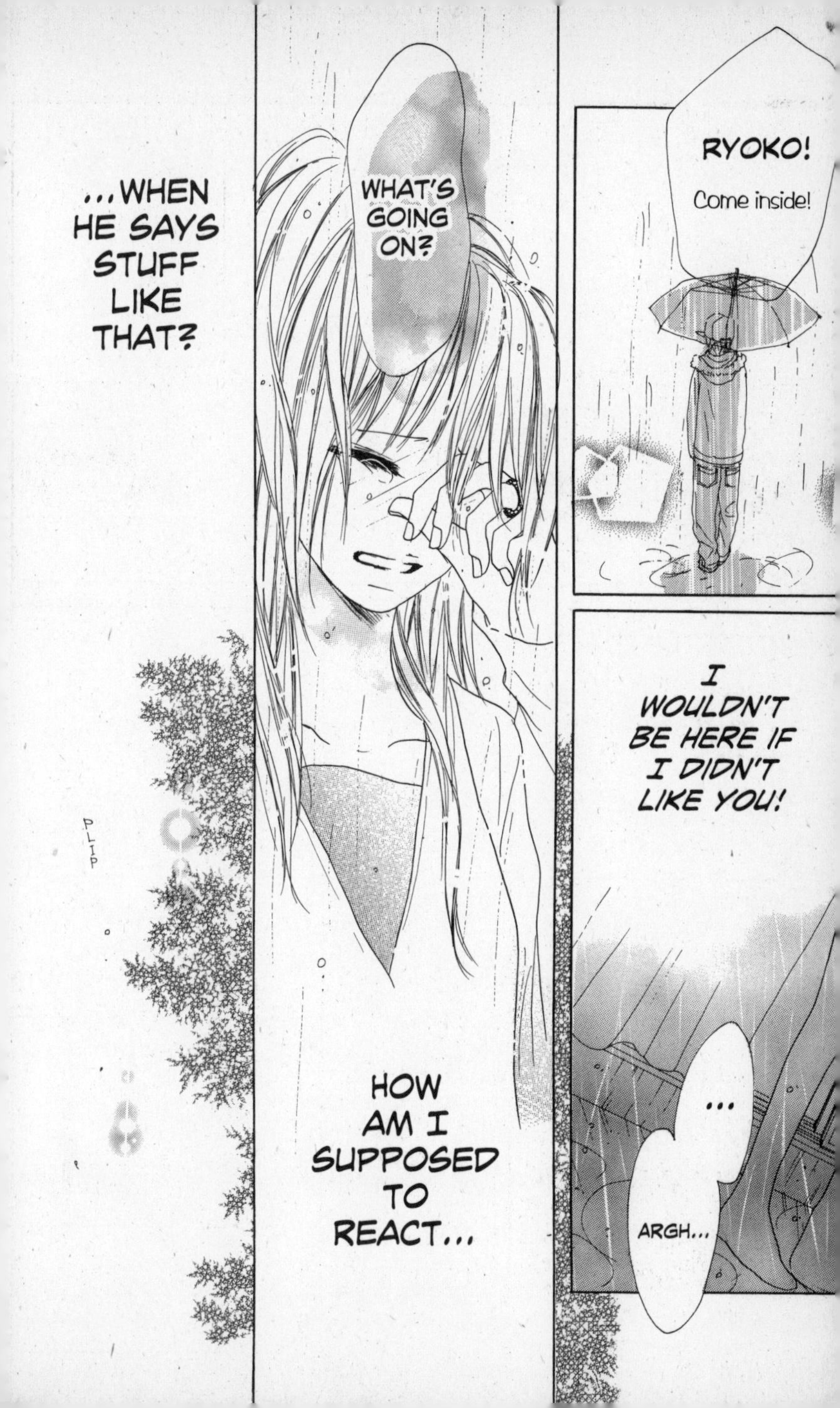
RYOKO!
Come inside!
I WOULDN'T BE HERE IF I DIDN'T LIKE YOU!
...
ARGH...
WHAT'S GOING ON?
HOW AM I SUPPOSED TO REACT...
...WHEN HE SAYS STUFF LIKE THAT?
PLIP

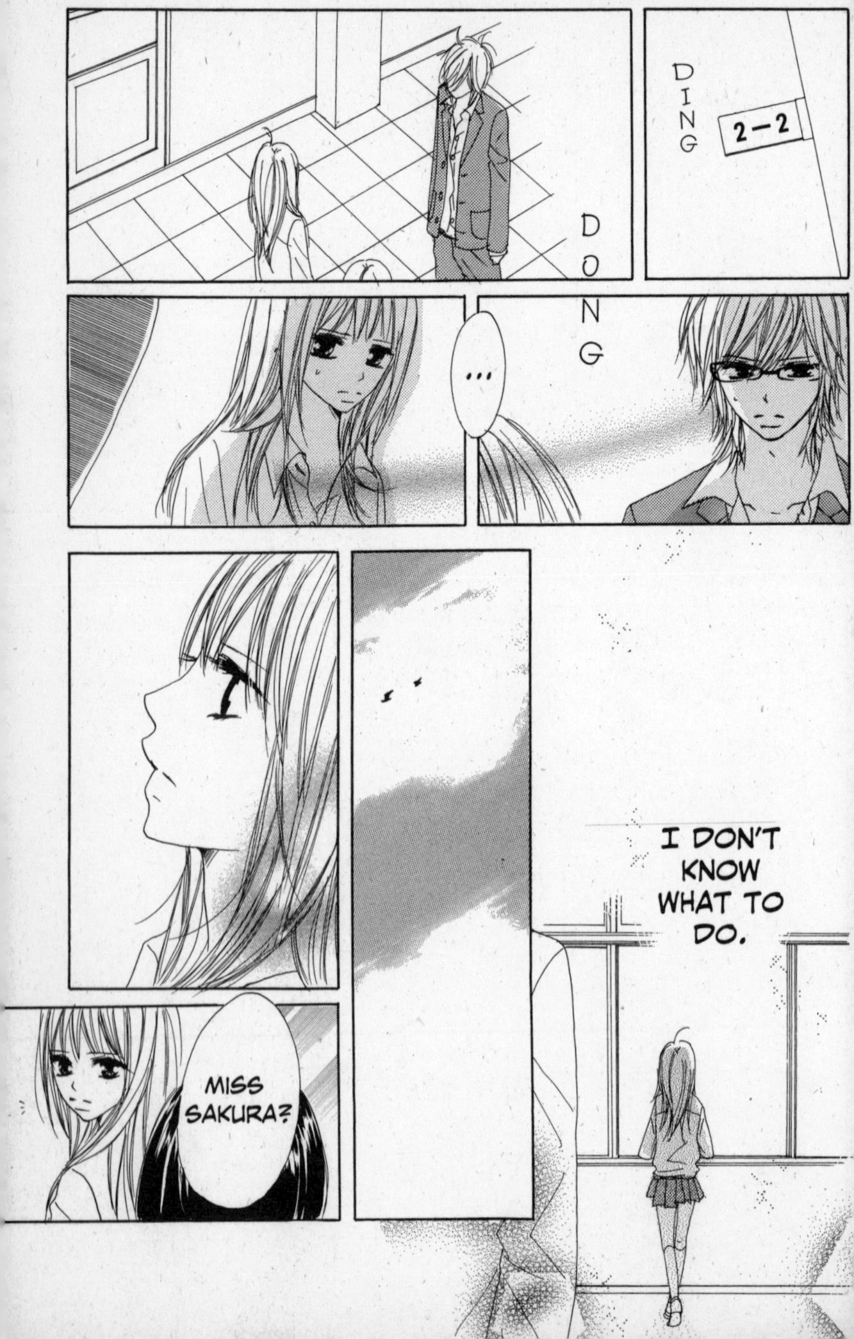
2-2
DING
DONG
...
I DON'T KNOW WHAT TO DO.
MISS SAKURA?

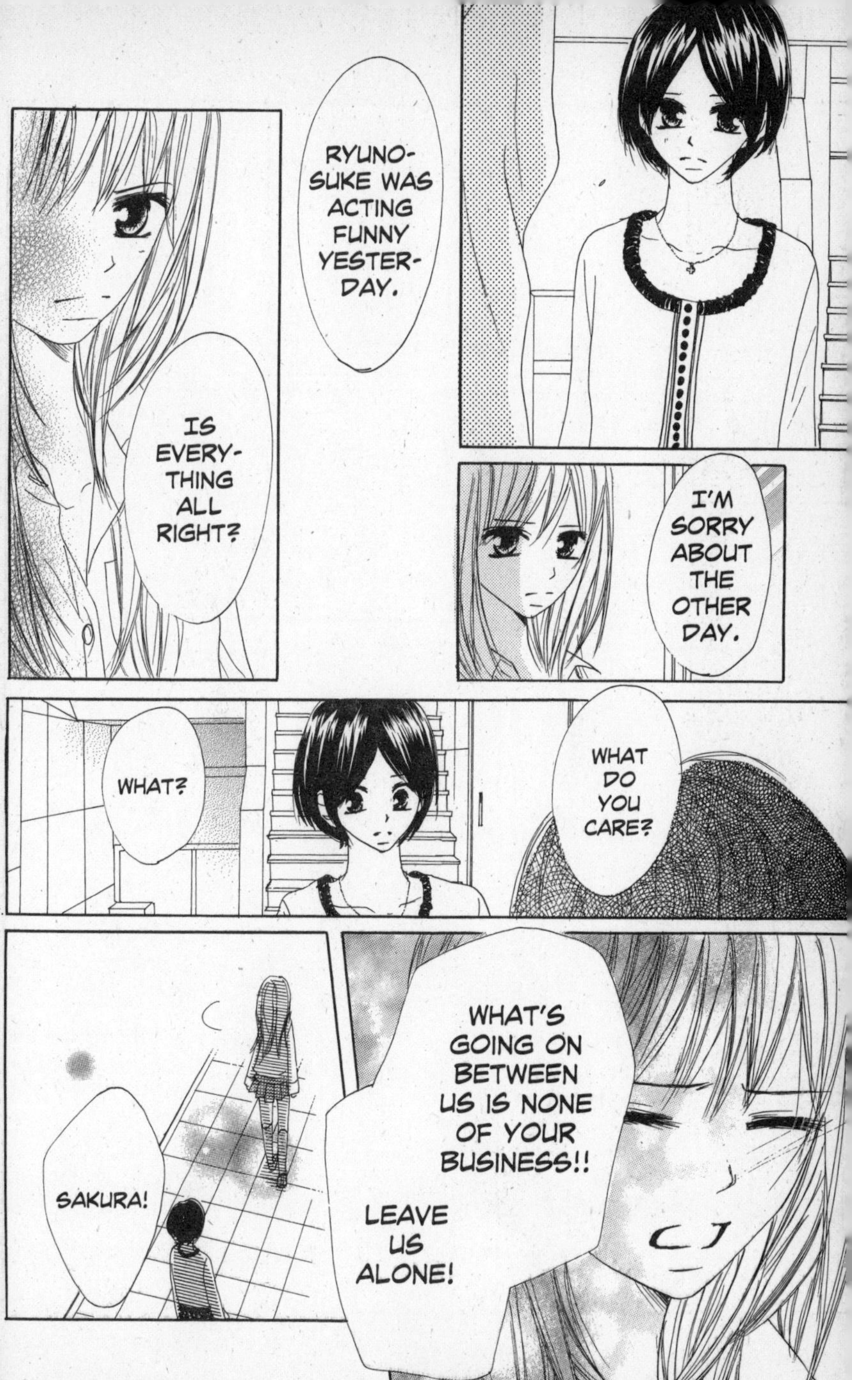
RYUNO-SUKE WAS ACTING FUNNY YESTER-DAY.
I'M SORRY ABOUT THE OTHER DAY.
IS EVERY-THING ALL RIGHT?
WHAT DO YOU CARE?
WHAT?
WHAT'S GOING ON BETWEEN US IS NONE OF YOUR BUSINESS!!
LEAVE US ALONE!
SAKURA!

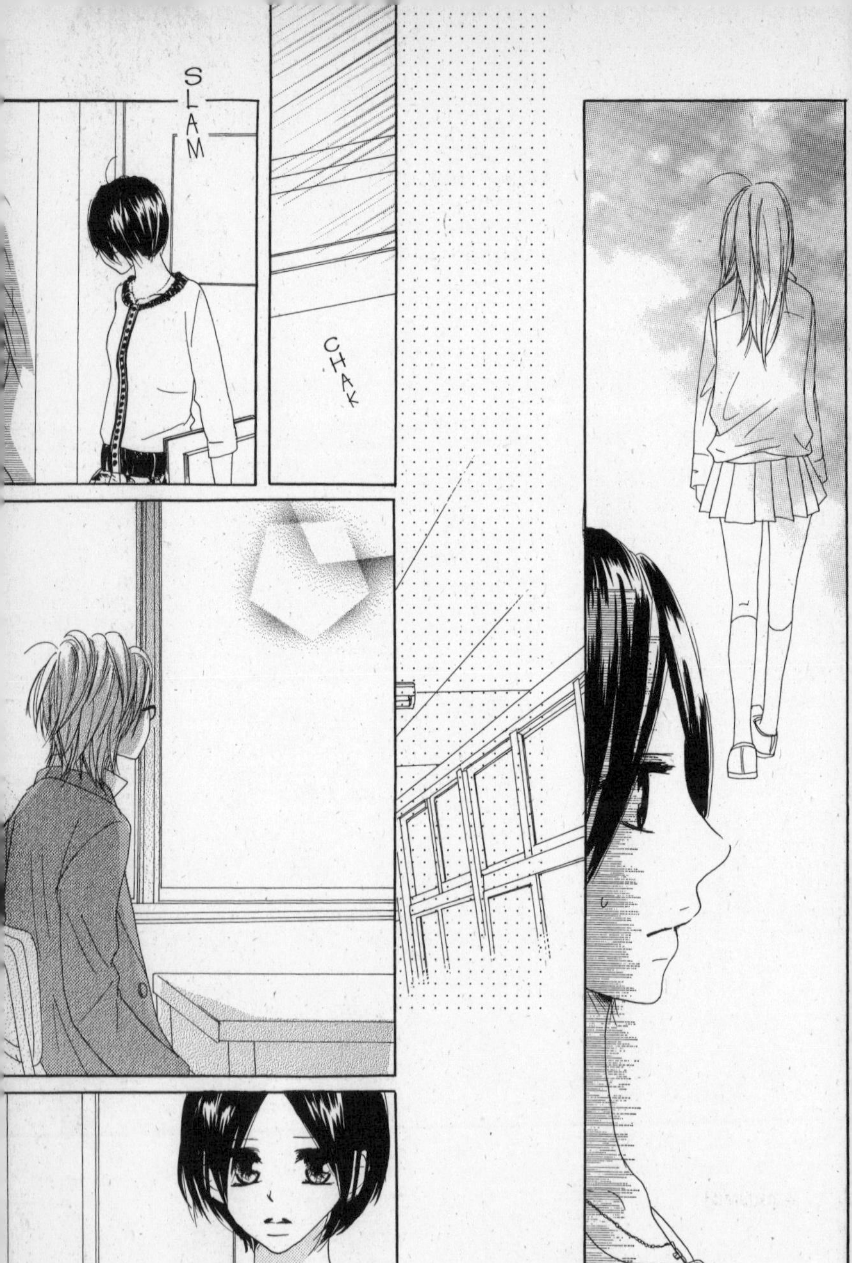
CHAK
SLAM

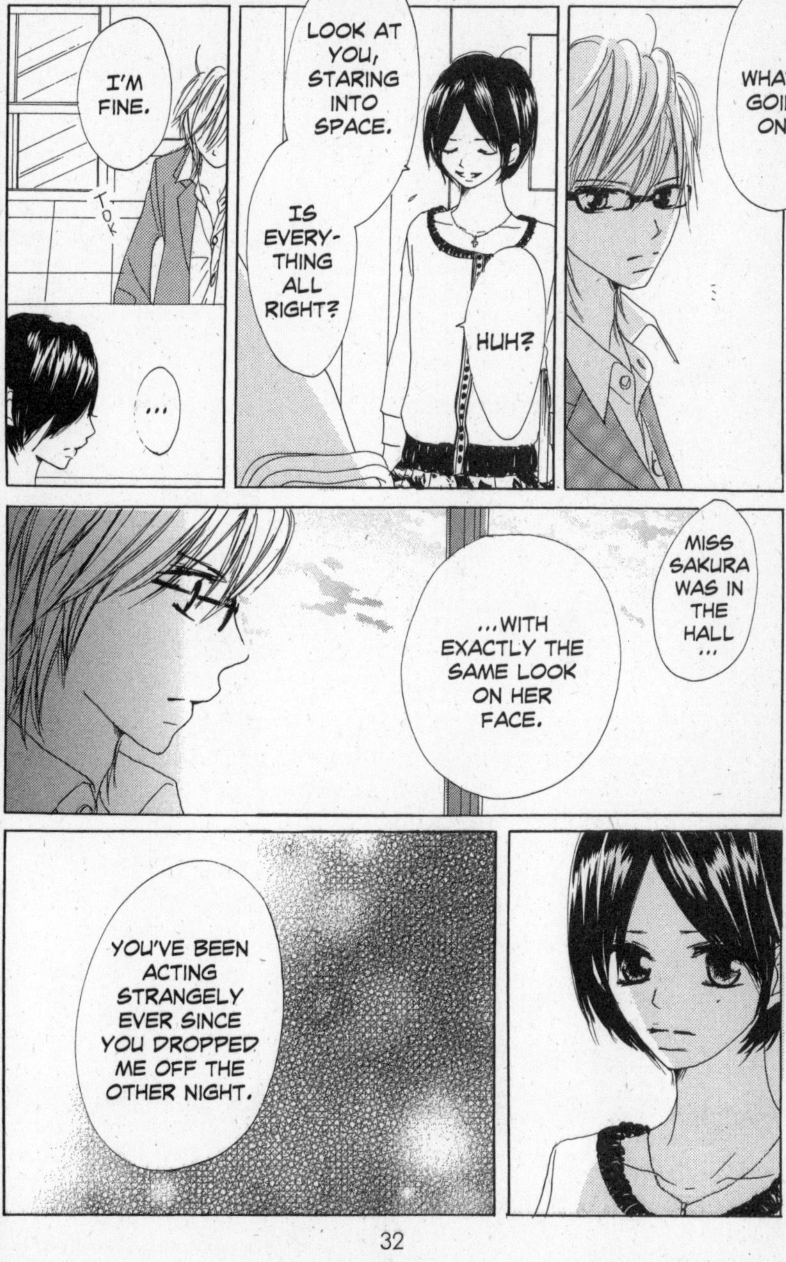
WHAT'S GOING ON?
LOOK AT YOU, STARING INTO SPACE.
IS EVERYTHING ALL RIGHT?
HUH?
I'M FINE.
TOK
...
MISS SAKURA WAS IN THE HALL...
...WITH EXACTLY THE SAME LOOK ON HER FACE.
YOU'VE BEEN ACTING STRANGELY EVER SINCE YOU DROPPED ME OFF THE OTHER NIGHT.

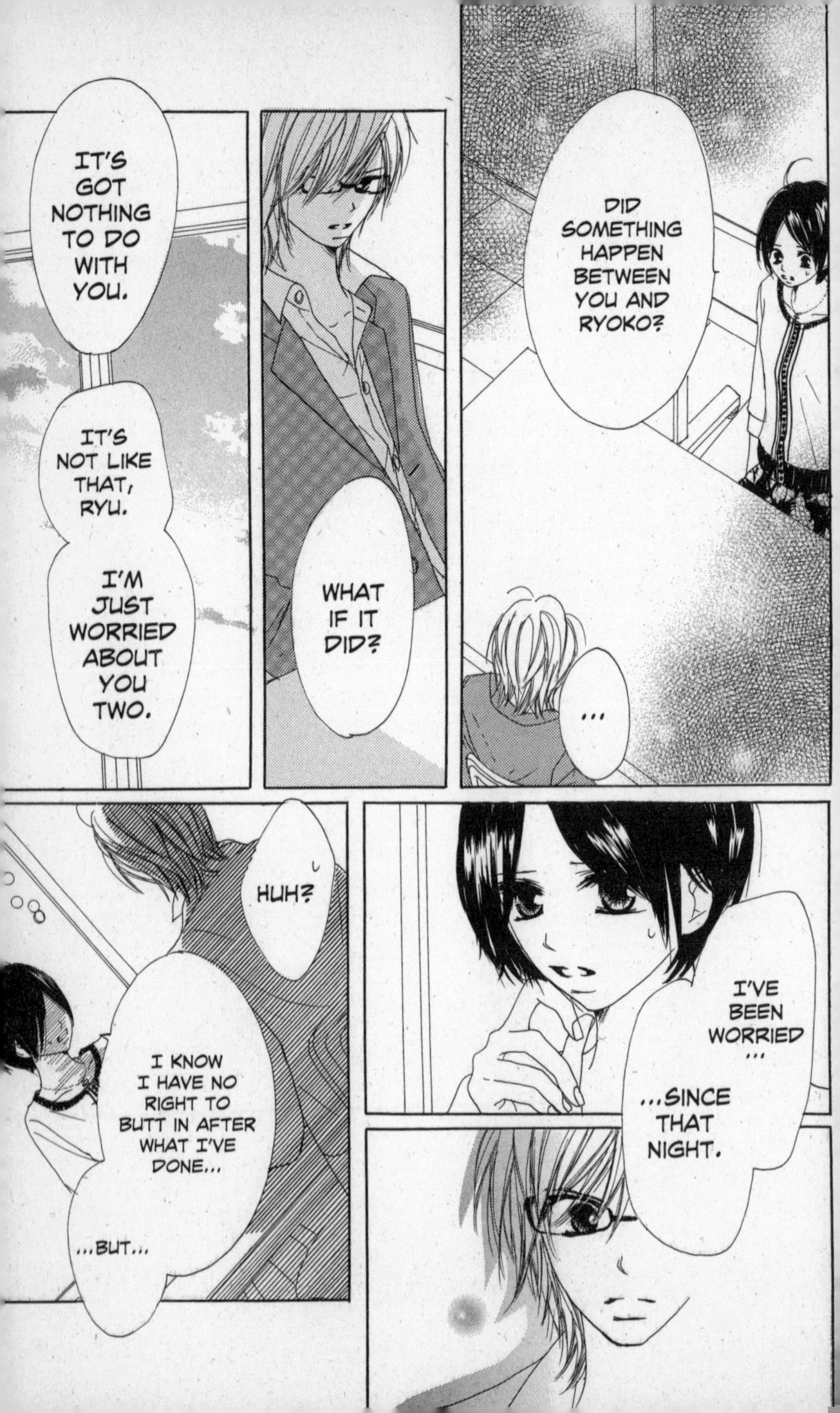
DID SOMETHING HAPPEN BETWEEN YOU AND RYOKO?
...
WHAT IF IT DID?
IT'S GOT NOTHING TO DO WITH YOU.
IT'S NOT LIKE THAT, RYU.
I'M JUST WORRIED ABOUT YOU TWO.
I'VE BEEN WORRIED...
...SINCE THAT NIGHT.
HUH?
I KNOW I HAVE NO RIGHT TO BUTT IN AFTER WHAT I'VE DONE...
...BUT...

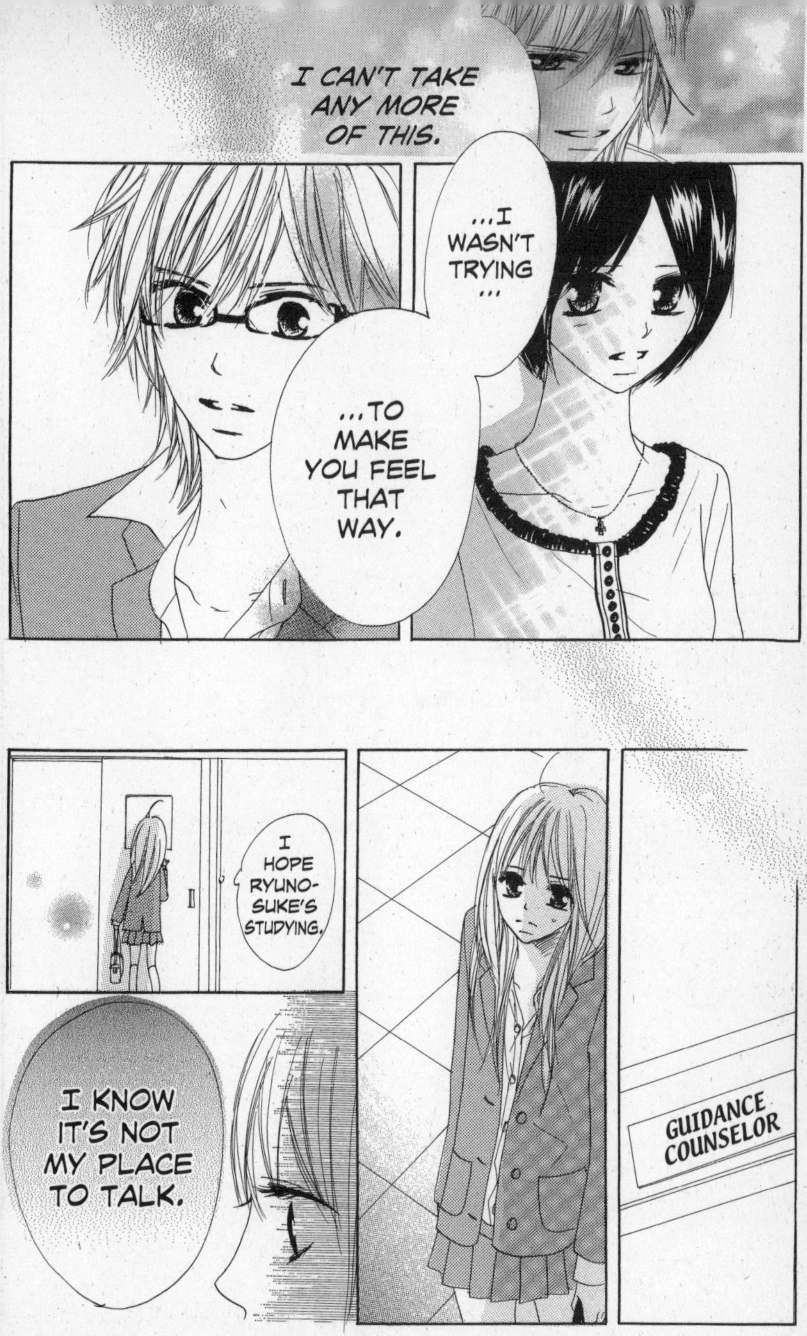
I CAN'T TAKE ANY MORE OF THIS.
...I WASN'T TRYING ...
...TO MAKE YOU FEEL THAT WAY.
GUIDANCE COUNSELOR
I HOPE RYUNO-SUKE'S STUDYING.
I KNOW IT'S NOT MY PLACE TO TALK.

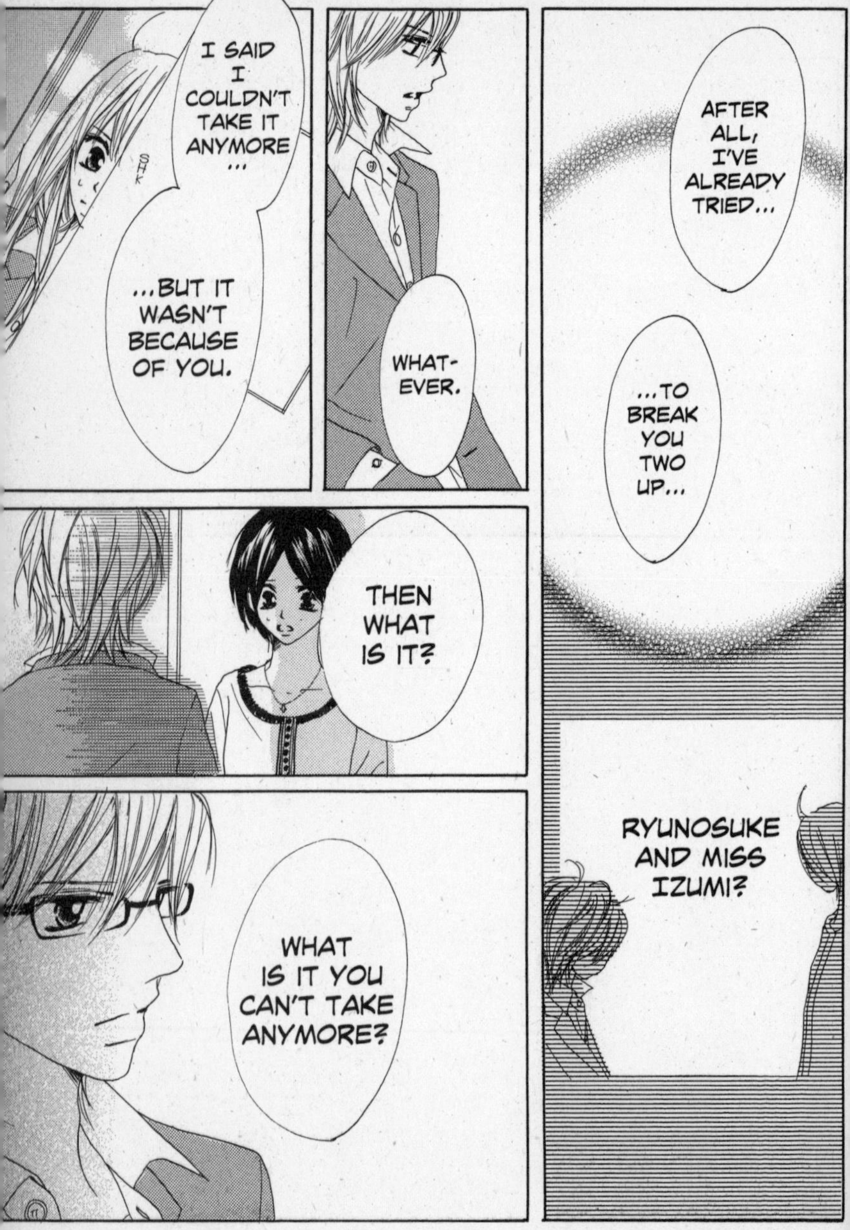
AFTER ALL, I'VE ALREADY TRIED...
...TO BREAK YOU TWO UP...
RYUNOSUKE AND MISS IZUMI?
WHAT-EVER.
I SAID I COULDN'T TAKE IT ANYMORE...
SHK
...BUT IT WASN'T BECAUSE OF YOU.
THEN WHAT IS IT?
WHAT IS IT YOU CAN'T TAKE ANYMORE?

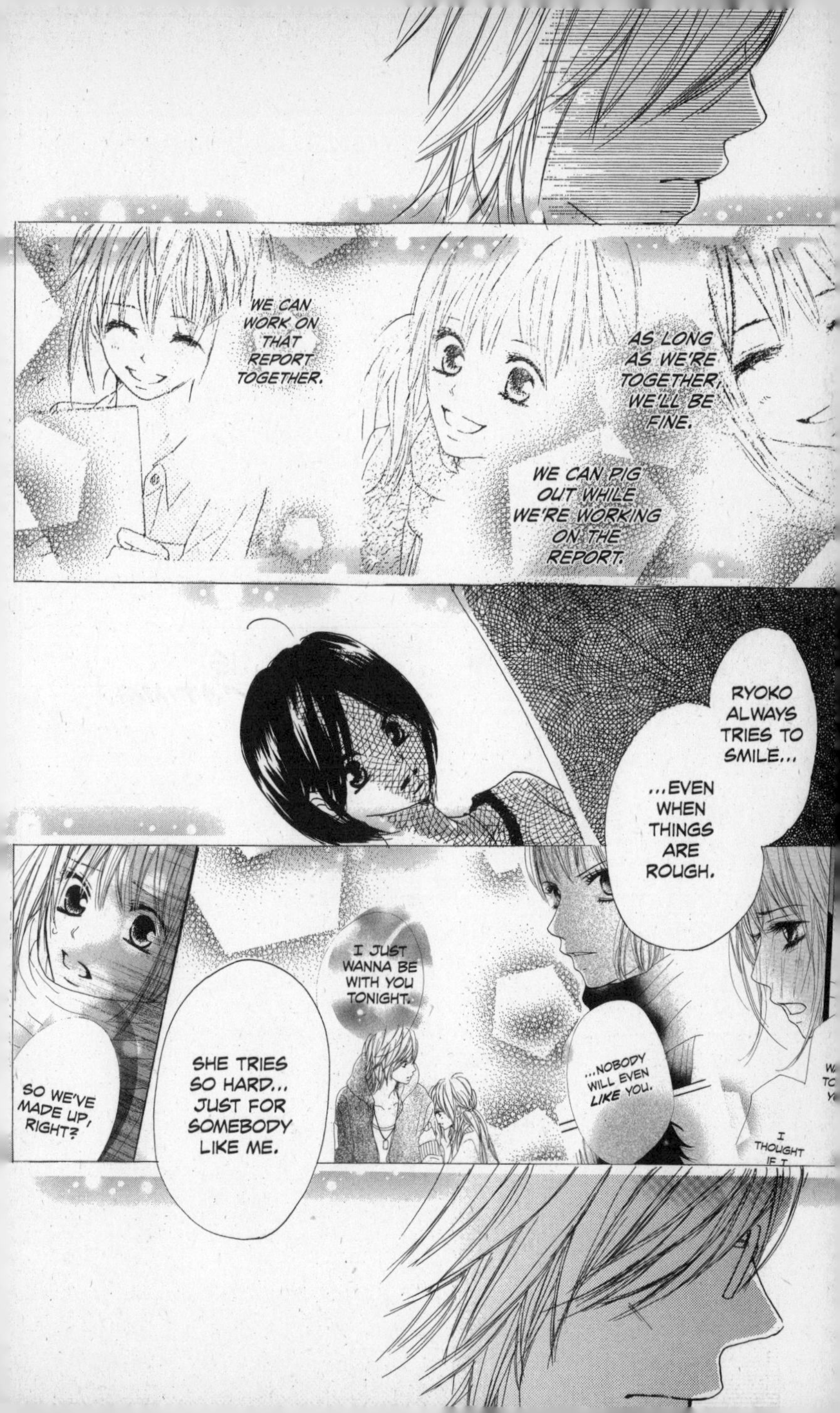
AS LONG AS WE'RE TOGETHER, WE'LL BE FINE.
WE CAN PIG OUT WHILE WE'RE WORKING ON THE REPORT.
WE CAN WORK ON THAT REPORT TOGETHER.
RYOKO ALWAYS TRIES TO SMILE...
...EVEN WHEN THINGS ARE ROUGH.
I THOUGHT
...NOBODY WILL EVEN *LIKE* YOU.
I JUST WANNA BE WITH YOU TONIGHT.
SHE TRIES SO HARD... JUST FOR SOMEBODY LIKE ME.
SO WE'VE MADE UP, RIGHT?

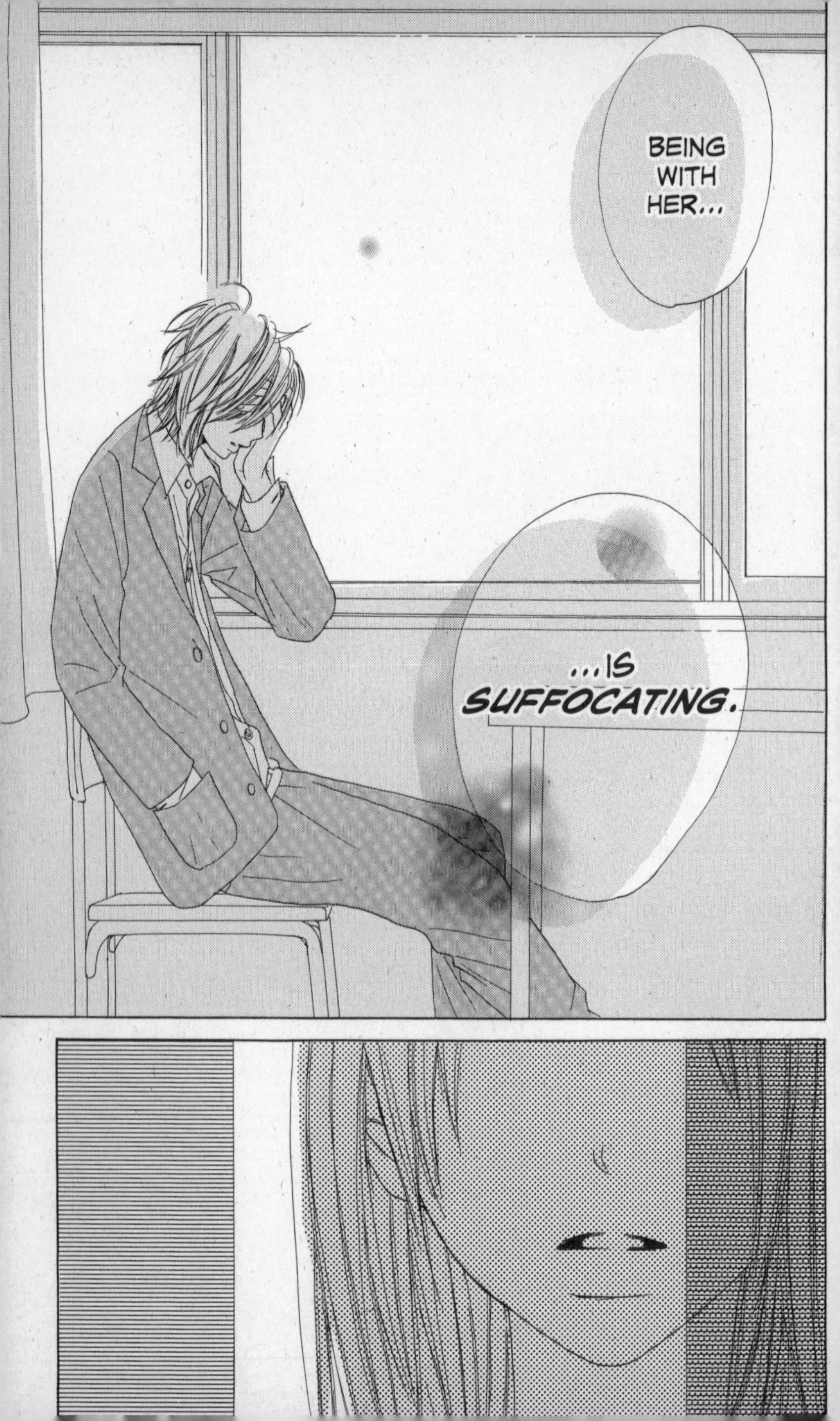
BEING WITH HER...
...IS SUFFOCATING.

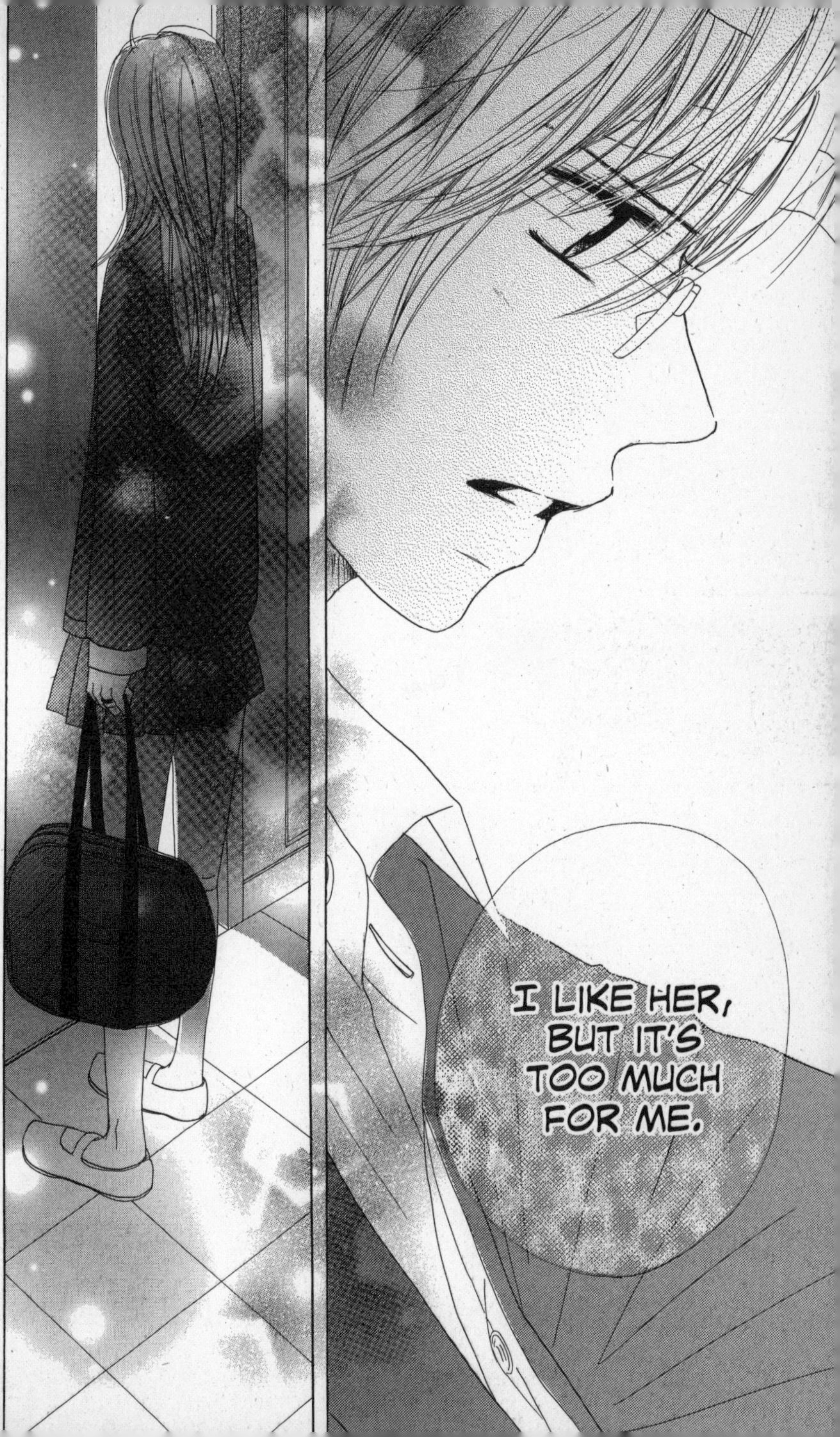
I LIKE HER, BUT IT'S TOO MUCH FOR ME.

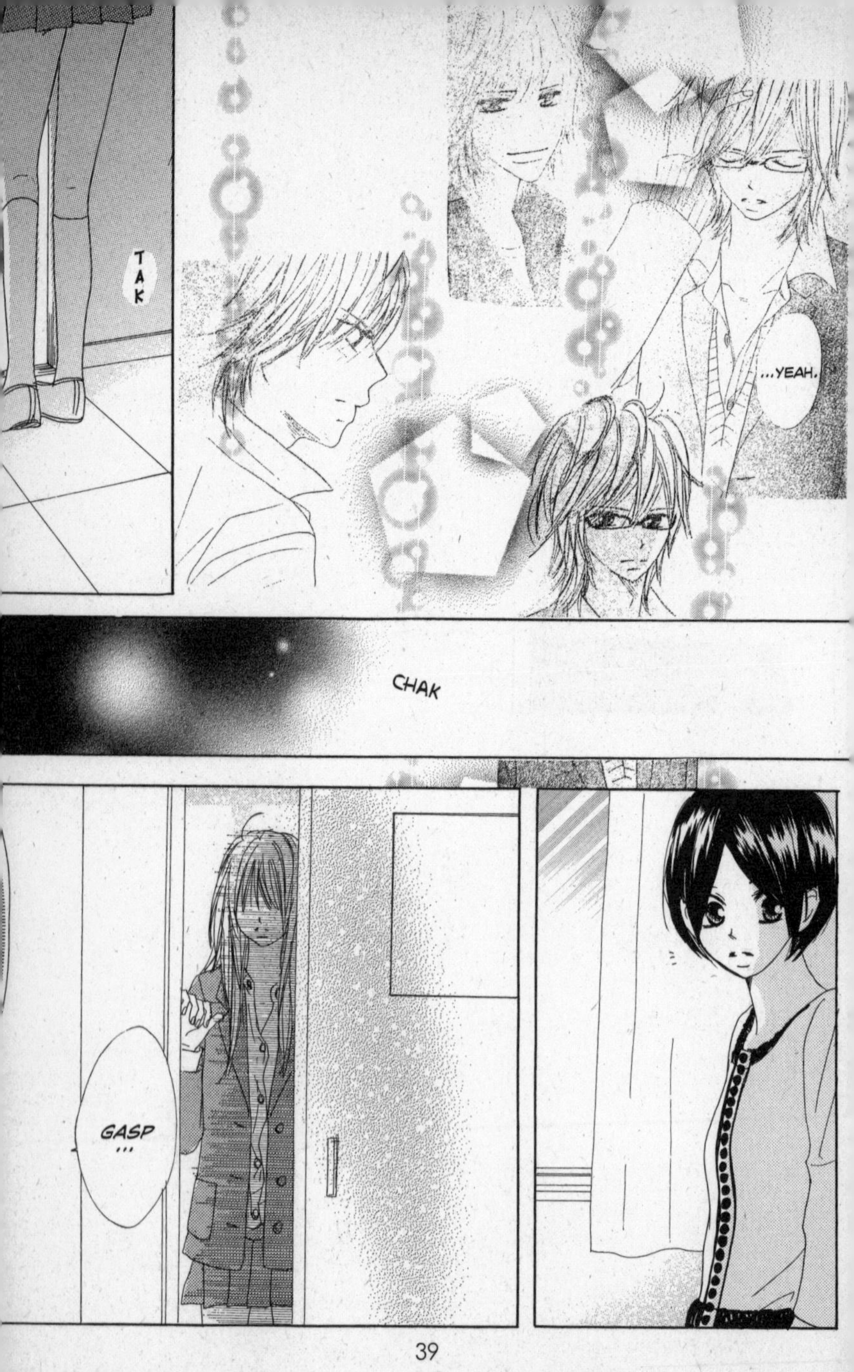
...YEAH.
TAK
CHAK
GASP ...

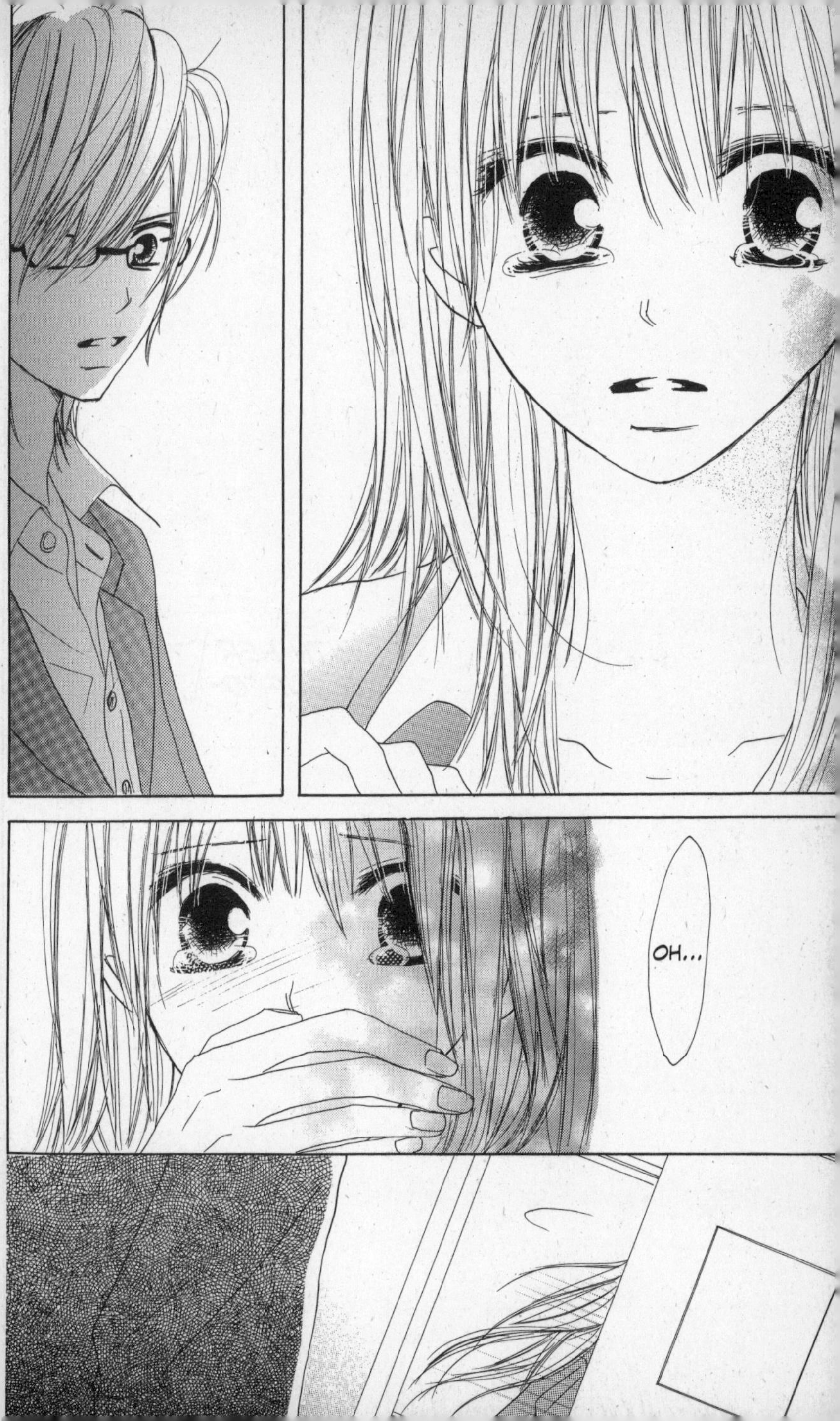
OH...

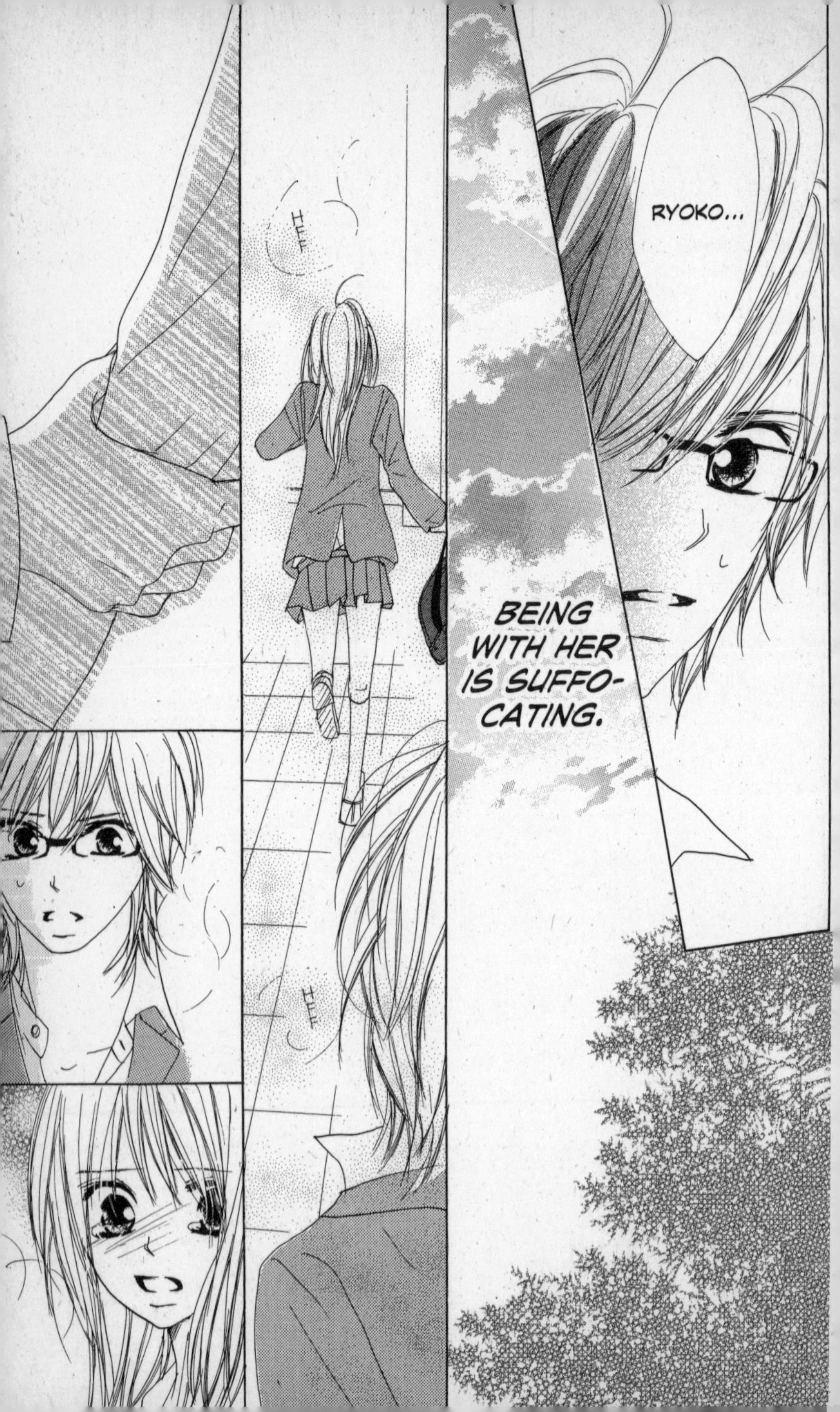
RYOKO...
BEING WITH HER IS SUFFO-CATING.
HEF
HEF

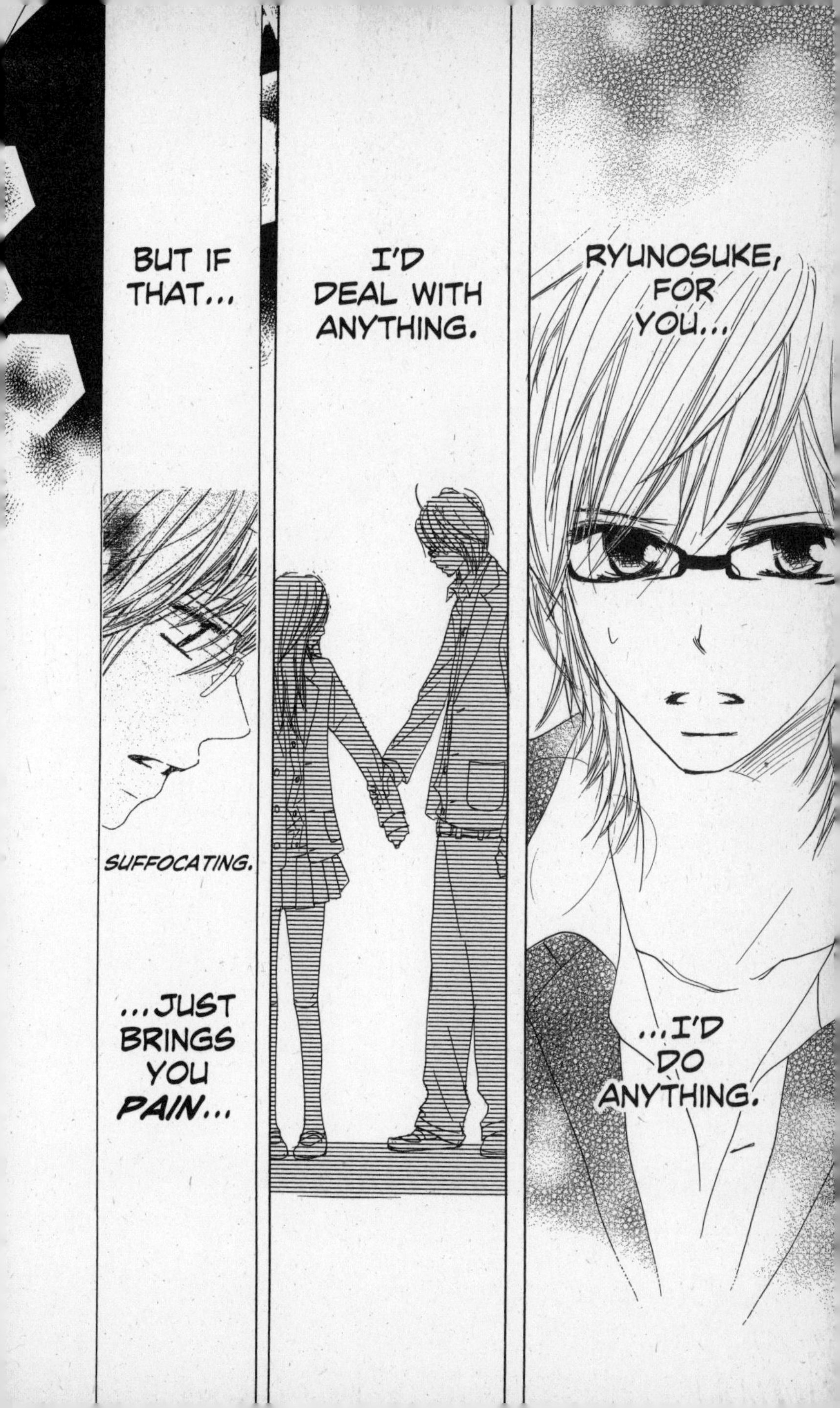
RYUNOSUKE, FOR YOU...
...I'D DO ANYTHING.
I'D DEAL WITH ANYTHING.
BUT IF THAT...
SUFFOCATING.
...JUST BRINGS YOU PAIN...

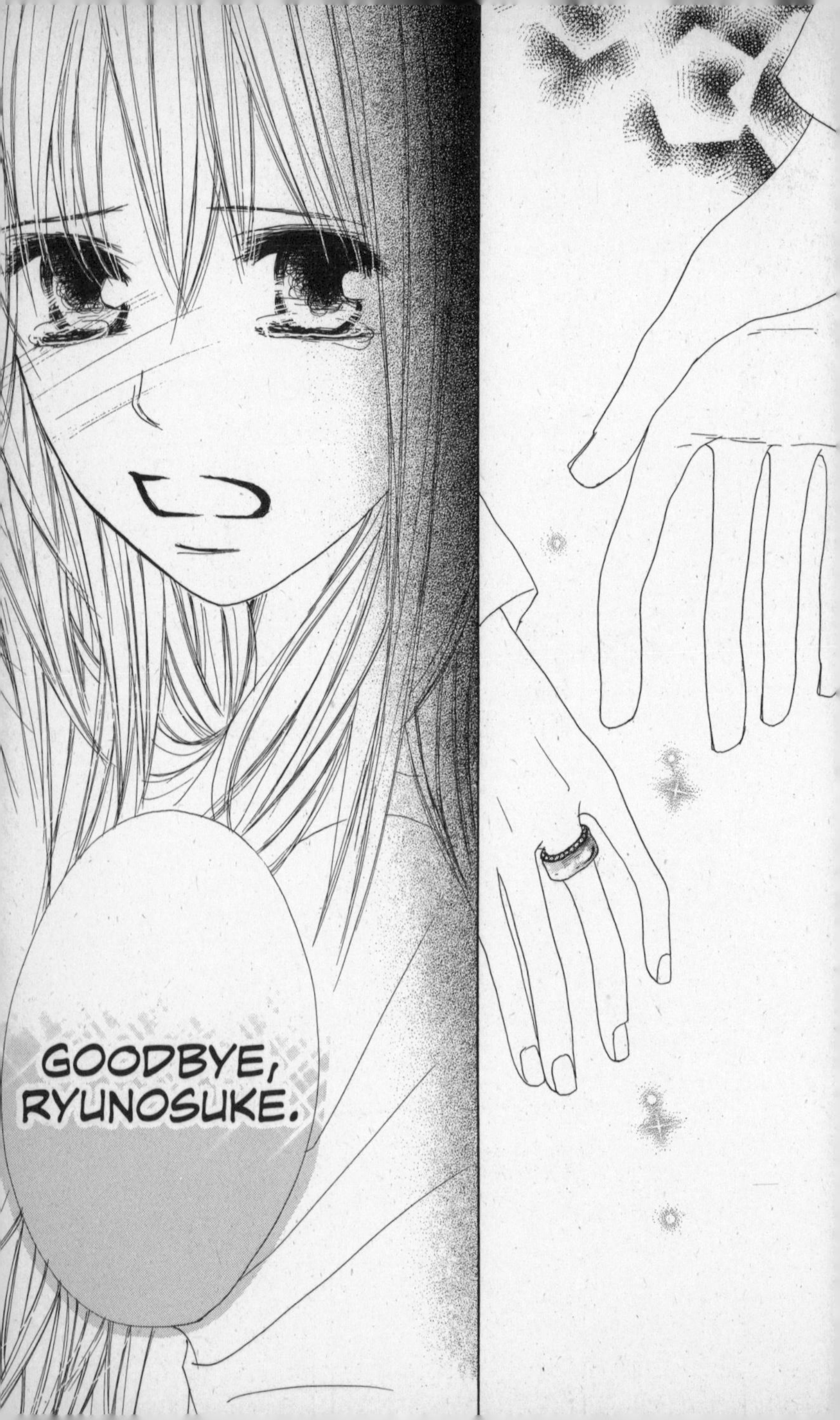
GOODBYE, RYUNOSUKE.

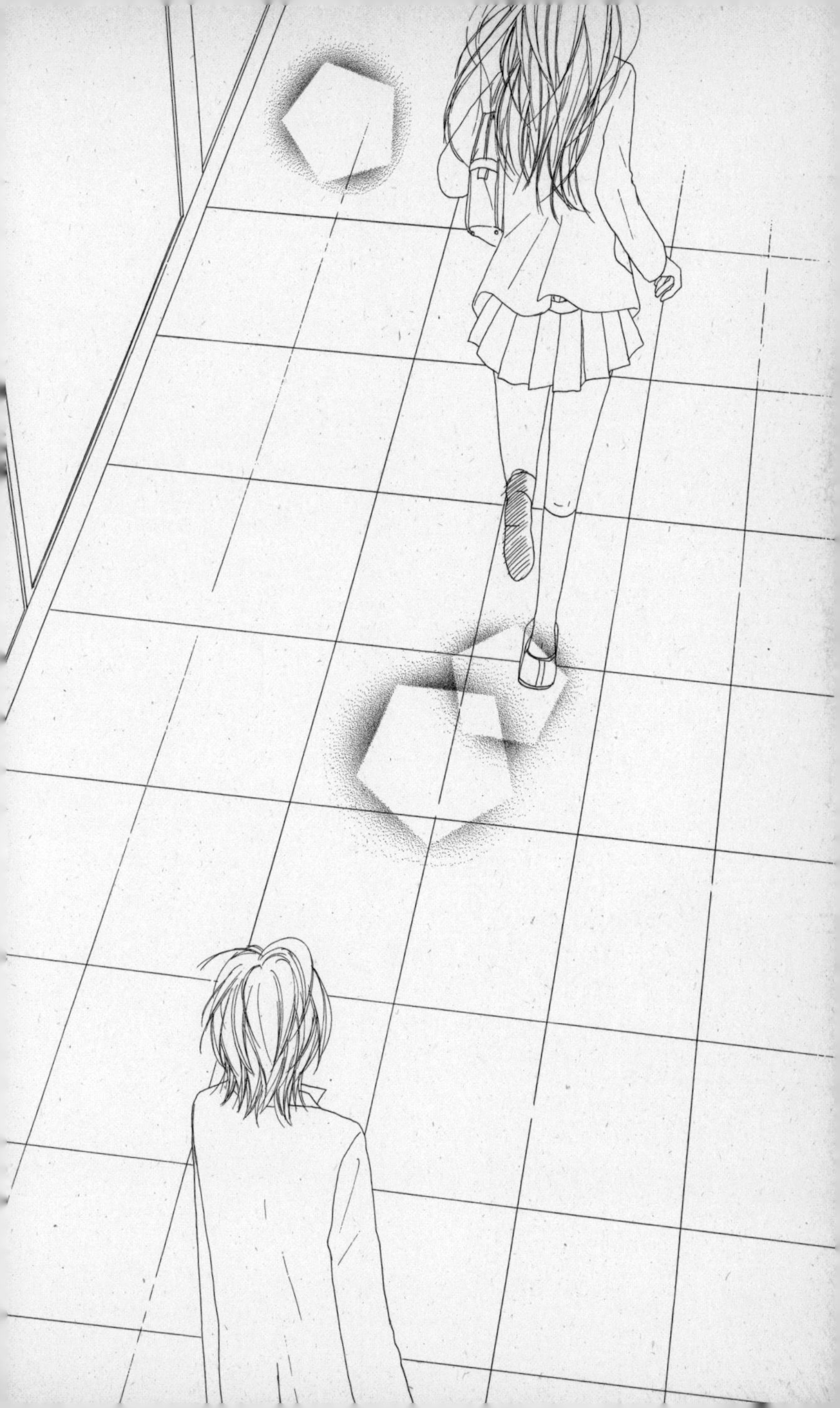

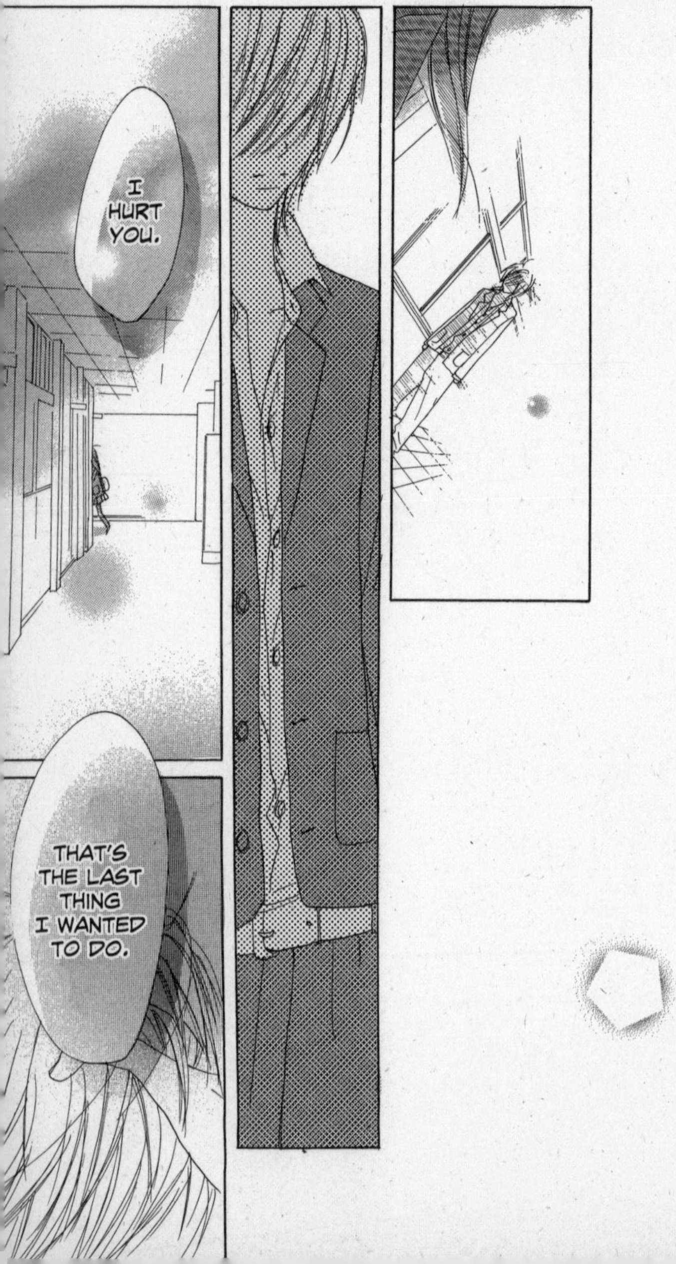
I HURT YOU.
THAT'S THE LAST THING I WANTED TO DO.

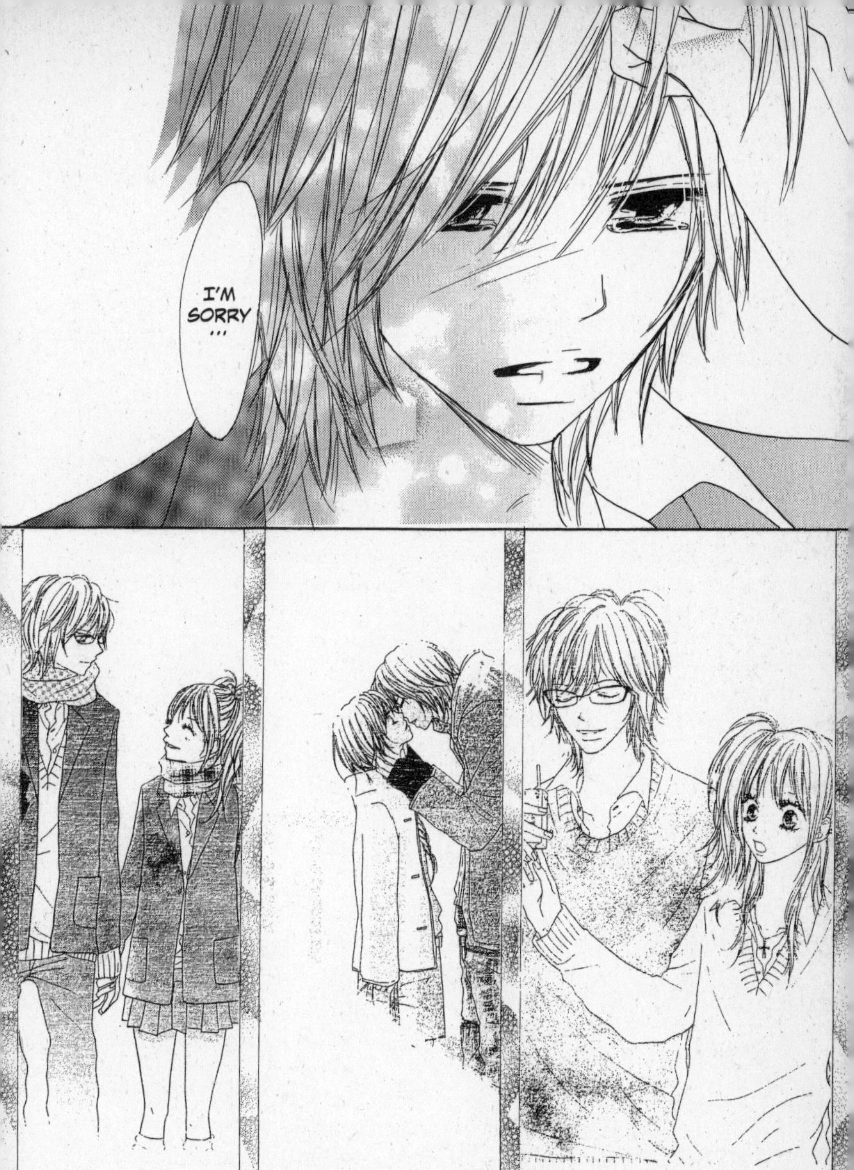
I'M SORRY ...

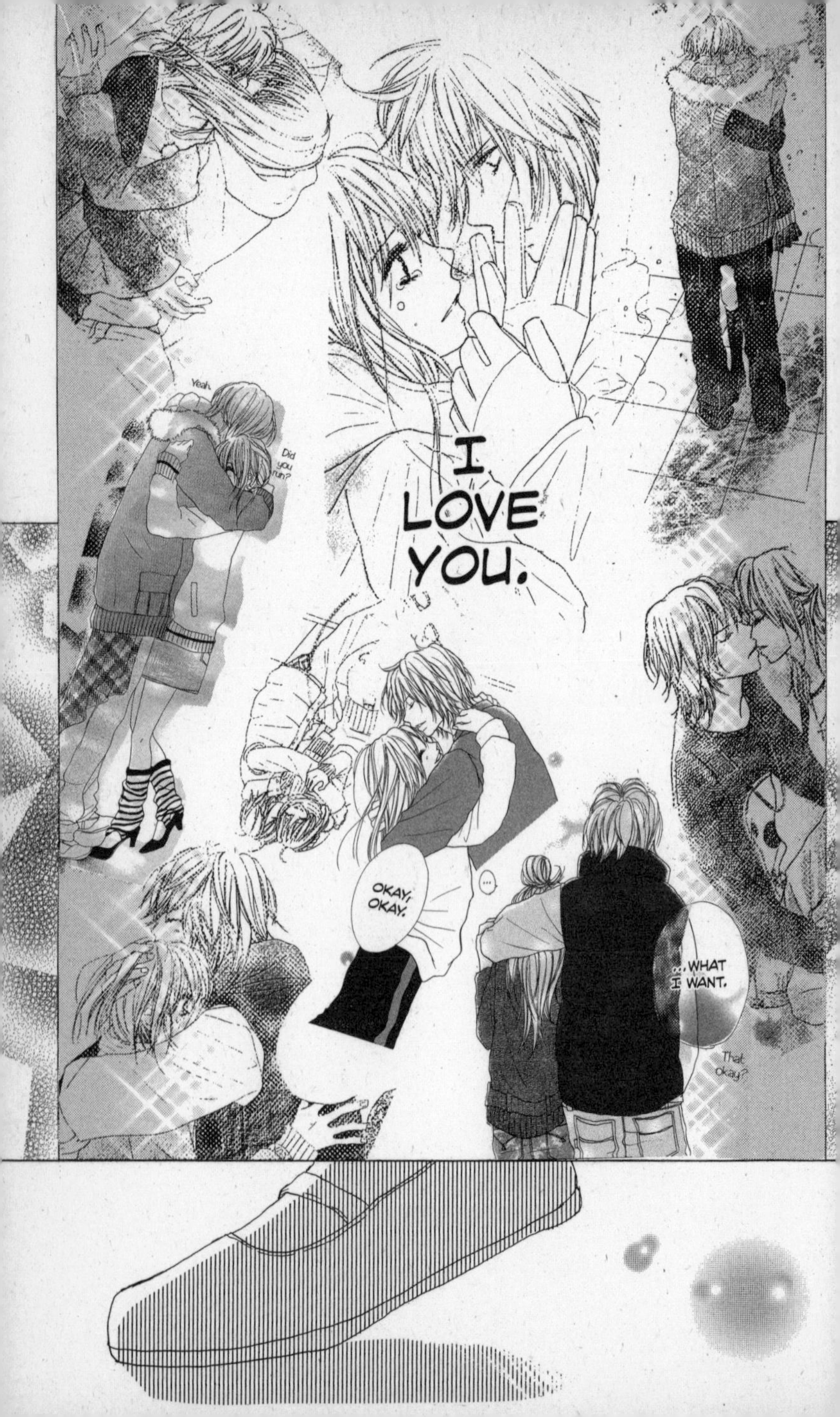
I LOVE YOU.
Yeah.
Did you run?
...WHAT I WANT.
That okay?
...
OKAY, OKAY.

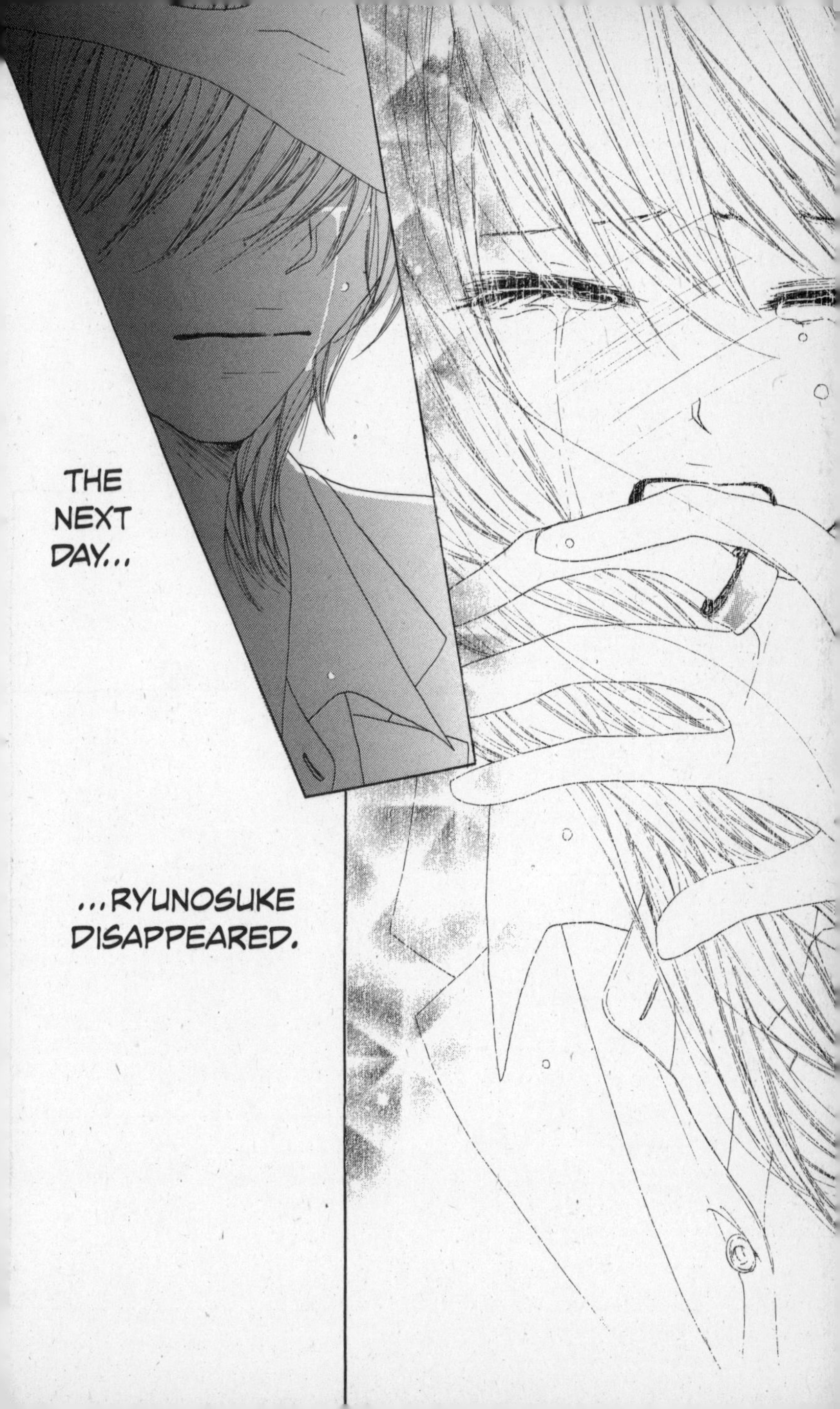
THE NEXT DAY...
...RYUNOSUKE DISAPPEARED.

The Animal Crossing bonus segment in volume 9 was surprisingly popular. I got responses like, "It was better than the actual story," "Tell me more about the forest," and so on.

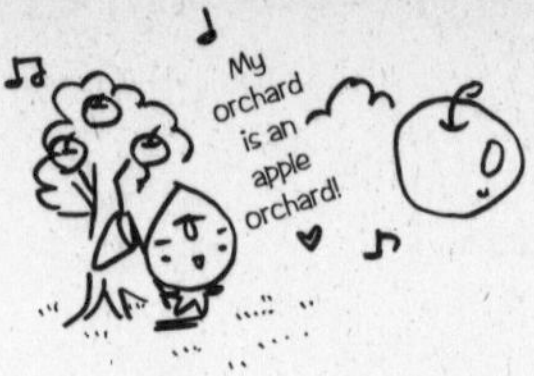
My orchard is an apple orchard!

Animal Crossing and Me, Part 2

I'd like to share one memorable story.

Those not interested can skip it.

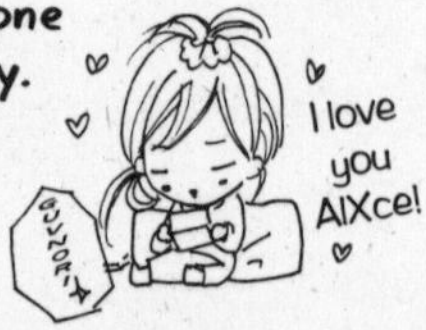
I love you AlXce!
Guvnor!

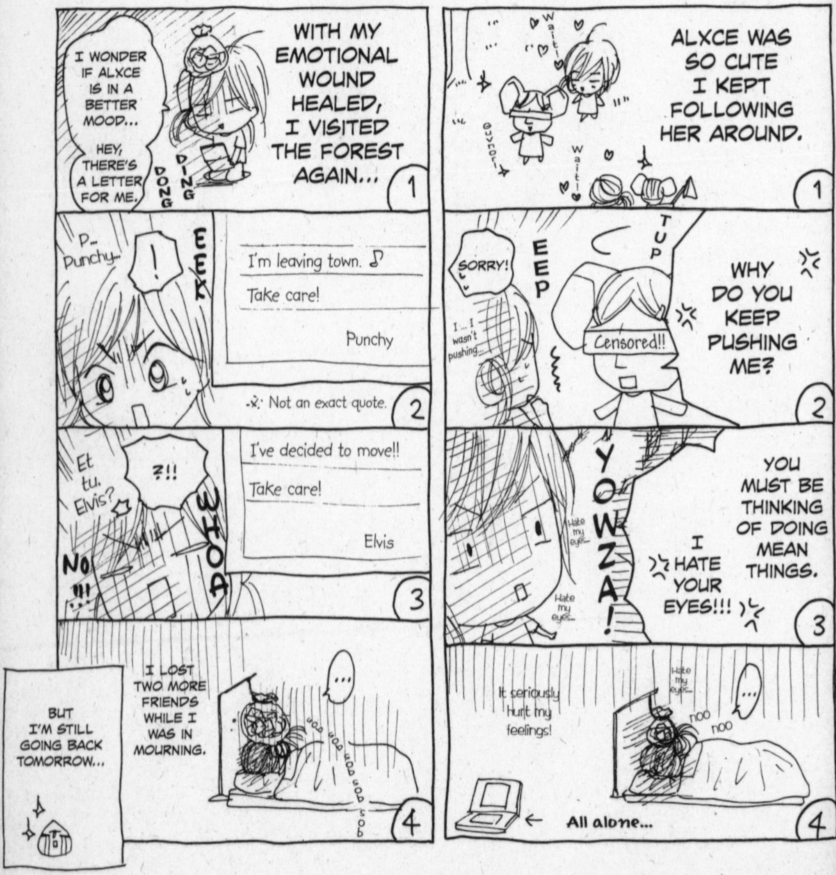
ALXCE WAS SO CUTE I KEPT FOLLOWING HER AROUND.
Wait!
Guvnor!
Wait!
TUP
WHY DO YOU KEEP PUSHING ME?
Censored!!
EEP
SORRY!
I... I wasn't pushing...
YOU MUST BE THINKING OF DOING MEAN THINGS.
I HATE YOUR EYES!!!
YOWZA!
Hate my eyes...
Hate my eyes...
Hate my eyes...
...
noo noo
It seriously hurt my feelings!
All alone...
WITH MY EMOTIONAL WOUND HEALED, I VISITED THE FOREST AGAIN...
I WONDER IF ALXCE IS IN A BETTER MOOD...
DING DONG
HEY, THERE'S A LETTER FOR ME.
I'm leaving town. ♪
Take care!
Punchy
EEK
!
P... Punchy...
※ Not an exact quote.
I've decided to move!!
Take care!
Elvis
WHOA
?!!
Et tu, Elvis?
NO!!!...
I LOST TWO MORE FRIENDS WHILE I WAS IN MOURNING.
...
SOB SOB SOB SOB SOB
BUT I'M STILL GOING BACK TOMORROW...

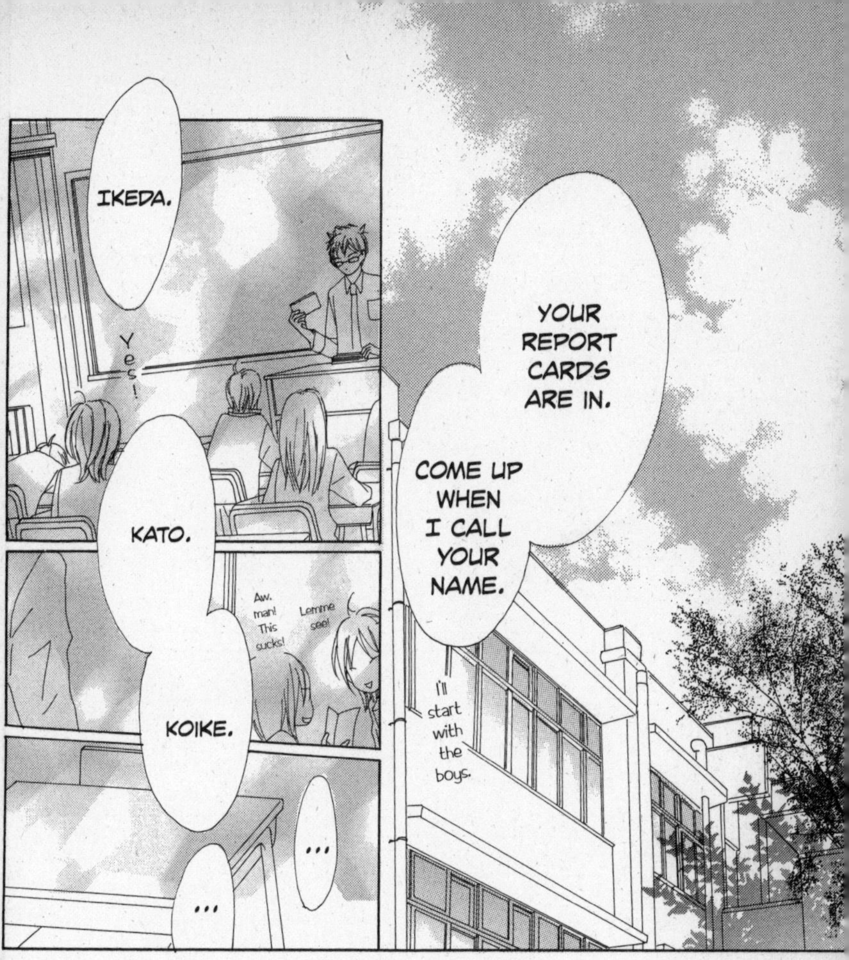
YOUR REPORT CARDS ARE IN.
COME UP WHEN I CALL YOUR NAME.
I'll start with the boys.
IKEDA.
Yes!
KATO.
Lemme see!
Aw. man! This sucks!
KOIKE.
...
...

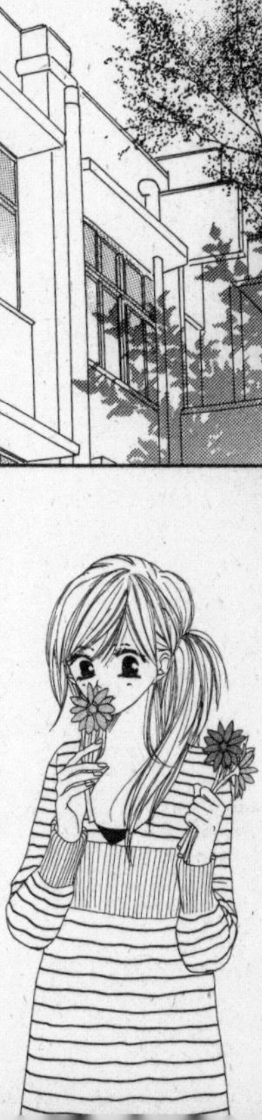

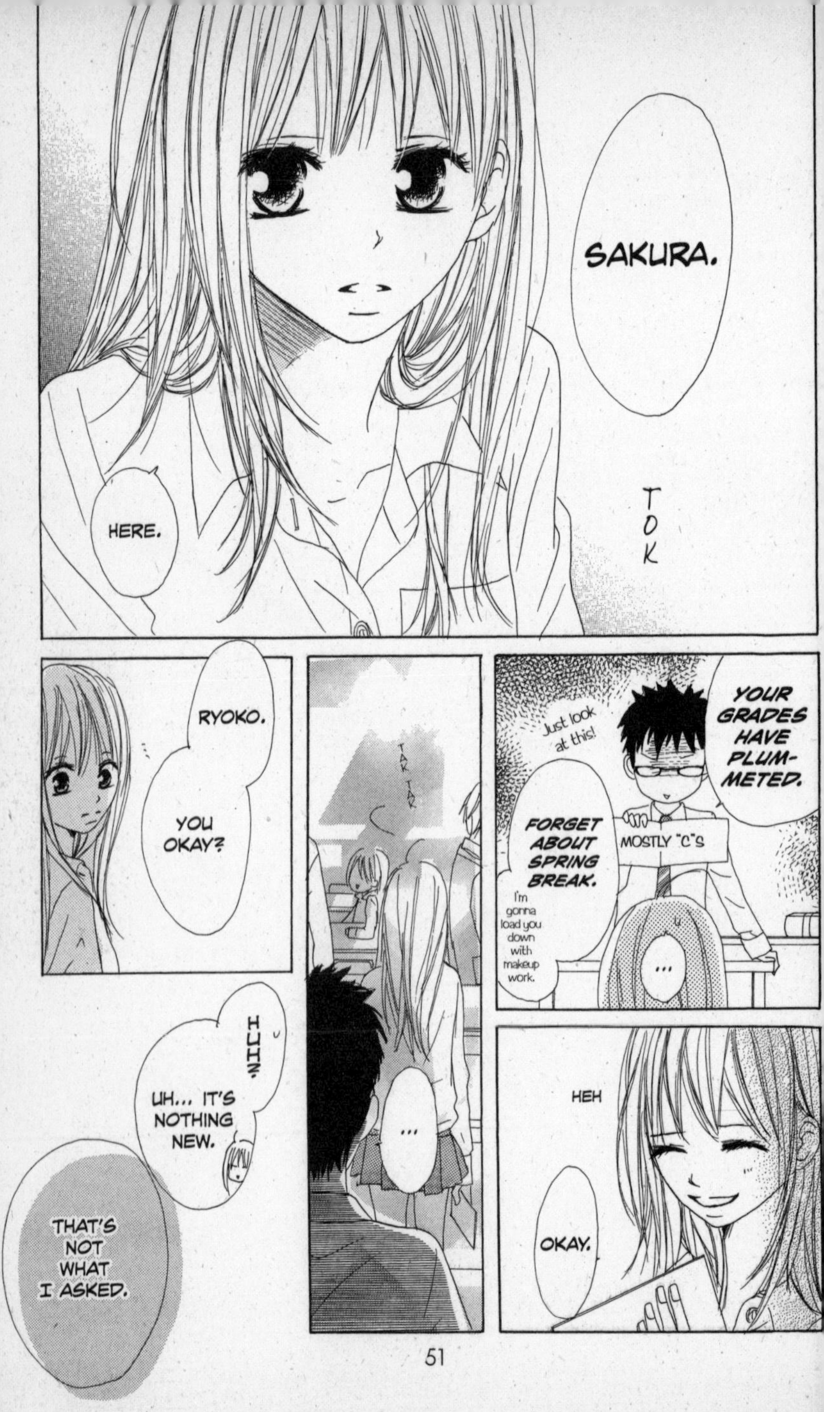
SAKURA.
TOK
HERE.
YOUR GRADES HAVE PLUM-METED.
Just look at this!
MOSTLY "C"S
FORGET ABOUT SPRING BREAK.
I'm gonna load you down with makeup work.
...
HEH
OKAY.
TAK TAK
...
RYOKO.
YOU OKAY?
HUH?
UH... IT'S NOTHING NEW.
THAT'S NOT WHAT I ASKED.

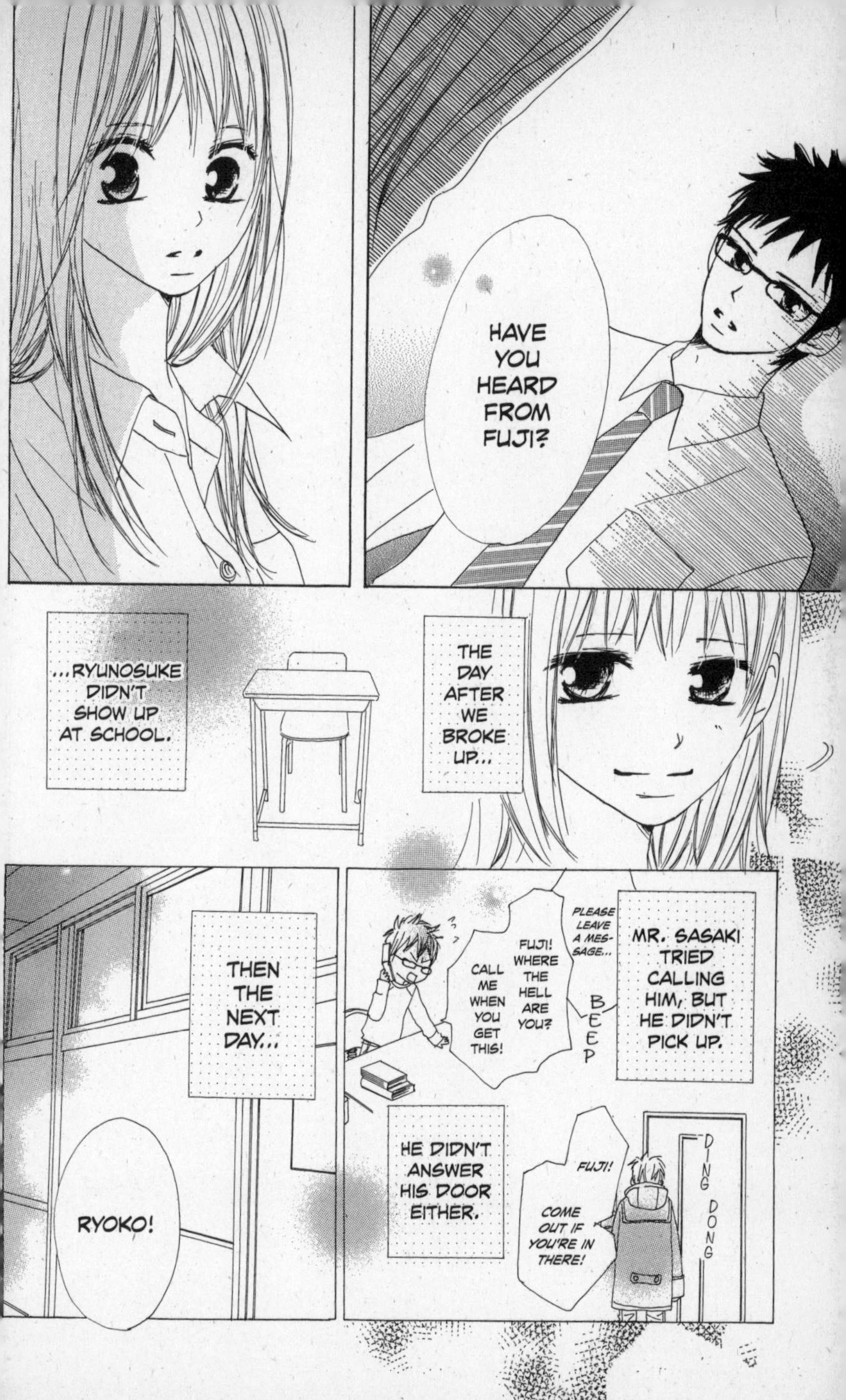
HAVE YOU HEARD FROM FUJI?
THE DAY AFTER WE BROKE UP...
...RYUNOSUKE DIDN'T SHOW UP AT SCHOOL.
MR. SASAKI TRIED CALLING HIM, BUT HE DIDN'T PICK UP.
PLEASE LEAVE A MES-SAGE...
BEEP
FUJI! WHERE THE HELL ARE YOU?
CALL ME WHEN YOU GET THIS!
HE DIDN'T ANSWER HIS DOOR EITHER.
DING DONG
FUJI!
COME OUT IF YOU'RE IN THERE!
THEN THE NEXT DAY...
RYOKO!

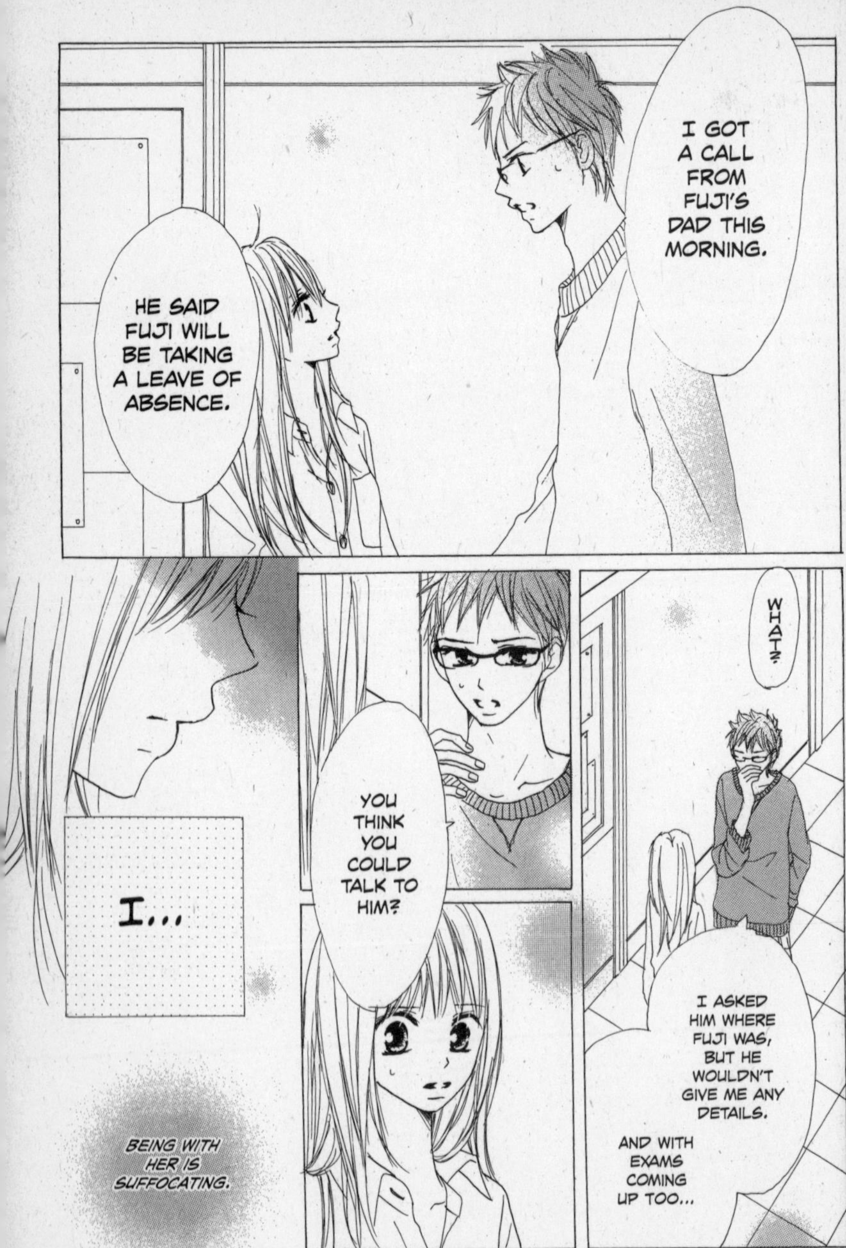
I GOT A CALL FROM FUJI'S DAD THIS MORNING.
HE SAID FUJI WILL BE TAKING A LEAVE OF ABSENCE.
WHAT?
I ASKED HIM WHERE FUJI WAS, BUT HE WOULDN'T GIVE ME ANY DETAILS.
AND WITH EXAMS COMING UP TOO...
YOU THINK YOU COULD TALK TO HIM?
I...
BEING WITH HER IS SUFFOCATING.

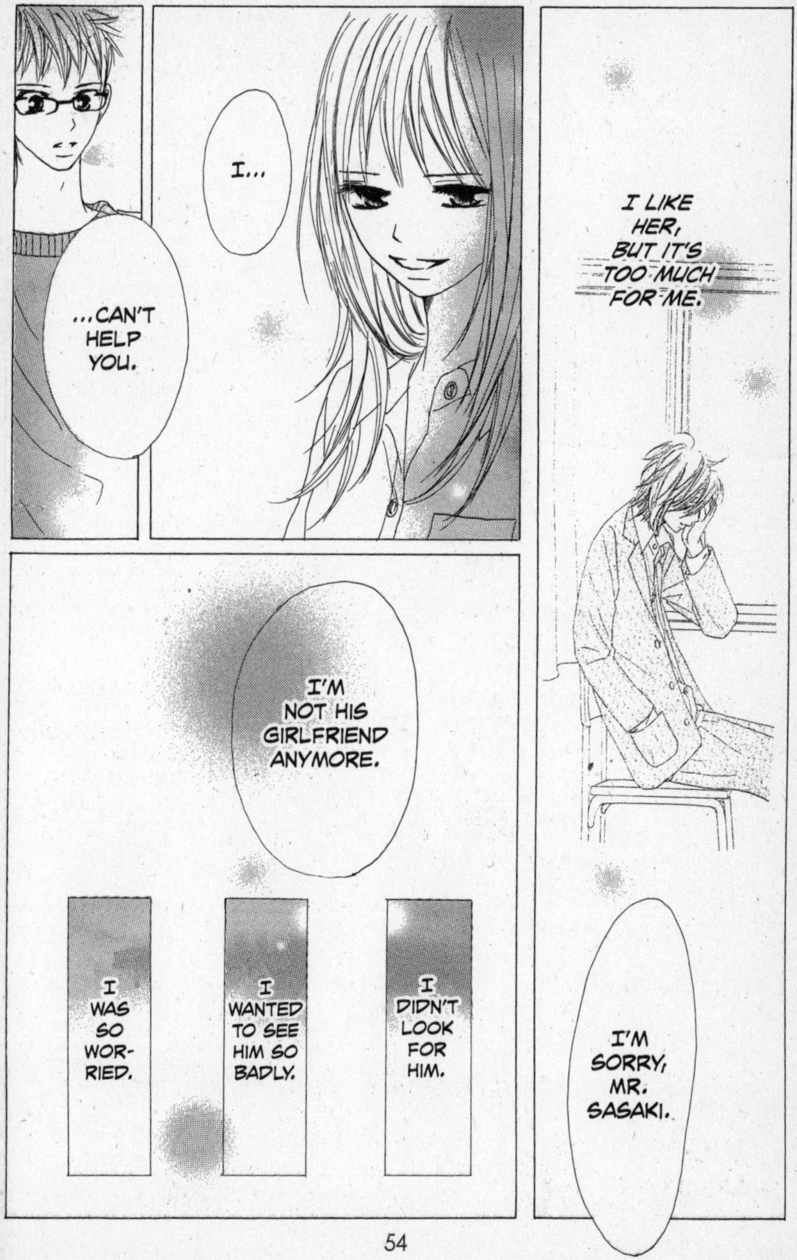
I LIKE HER, BUT IT'S TOO MUCH FOR ME.
I'M SORRY, MR. SASAKI.
I...
...CAN'T HELP YOU.
I'M NOT HIS GIRLFRIEND ANYMORE.
I DIDN'T LOOK FOR HIM.
I WANTED TO SEE HIM SO BADLY.
I WAS SO WOR-RIED.

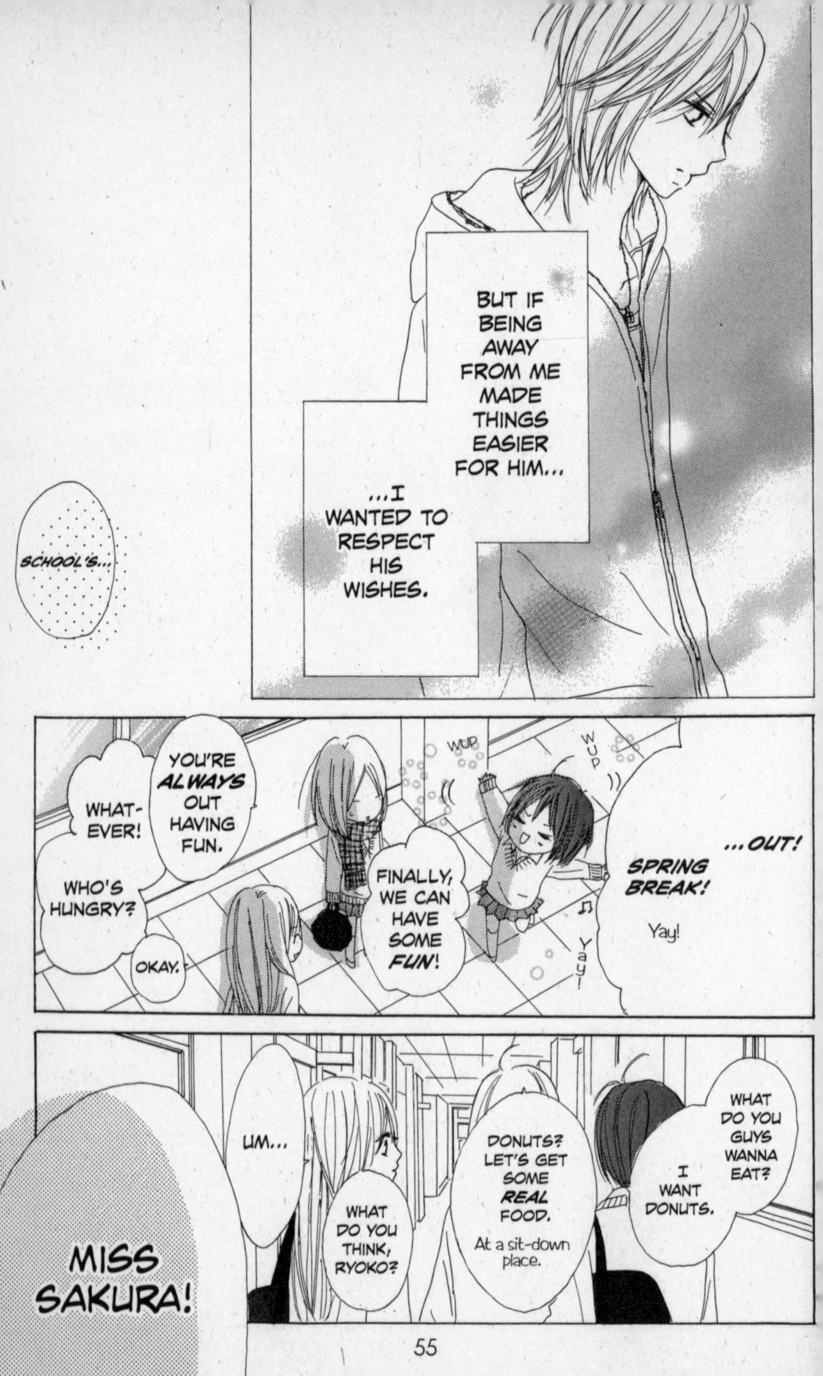
BUT IF BEING AWAY FROM ME MADE THINGS EASIER FOR HIM...
...I WANTED TO RESPECT HIS WISHES.
SCHOOL'S...
...OUT!
SPRING BREAK!
Yay!
WUP
WUP
Yay!
FINALLY, WE CAN HAVE SOME FUN!
YOU'RE ALWAYS OUT HAVING FUN.
WHAT-EVER!
WHO'S HUNGRY?
OKAY.
WHAT DO YOU GUYS WANNA EAT?
I WANT DONUTS.
DONUTS? LET'S GET SOME REAL FOOD.
At a sit-down place.
WHAT DO YOU THINK, RYOKO?
UM...
MISS SAKURA!

...

H FF

H FF

H FF

I'M...

...SORRY
...

WAIT!

HAVE YOU HEARD
...

...FROM RYU?

I was just wondering...

I'LL
...

...LOOK FOR HIM OVER SPRING BREAK!

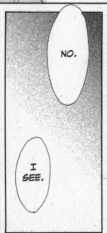

NO.

I SEE.

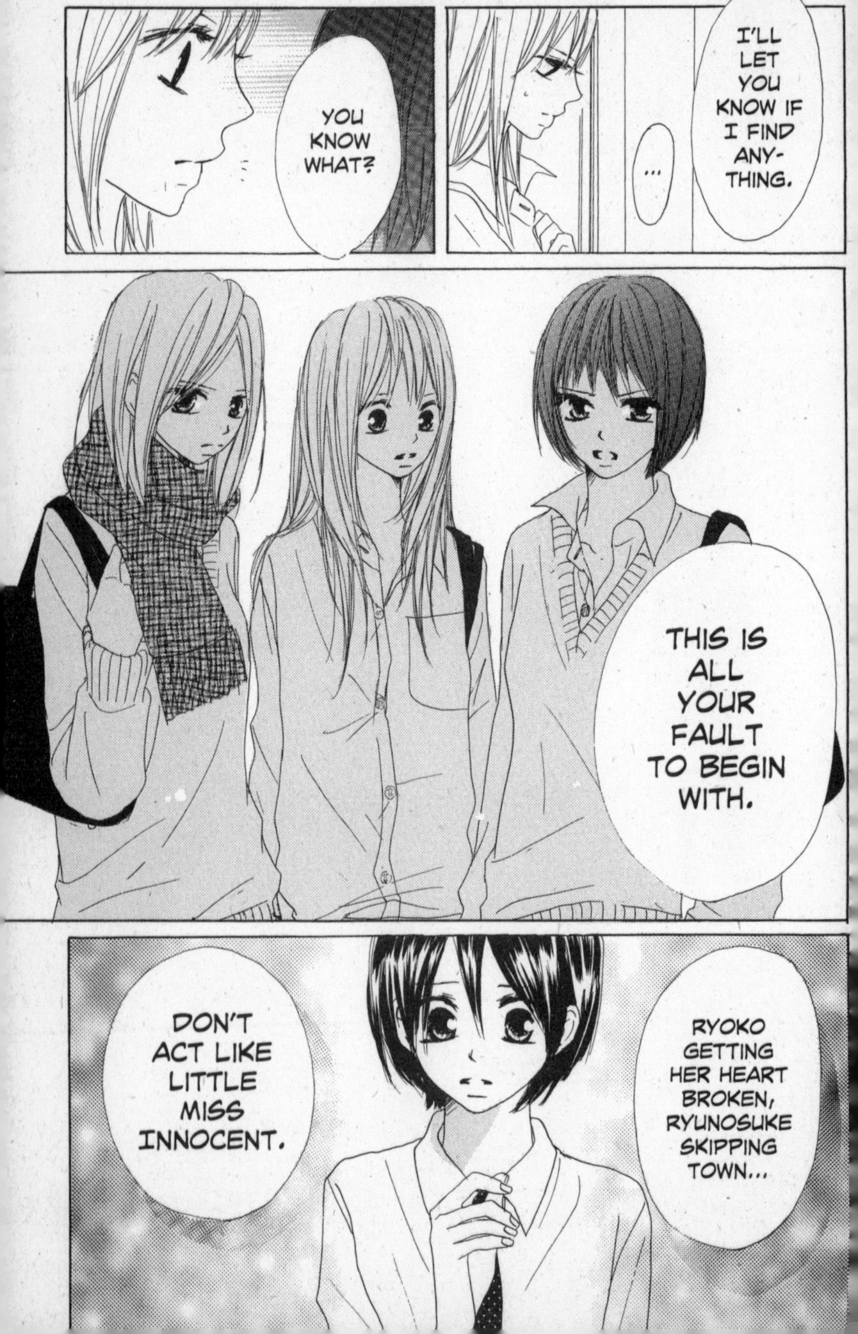
I'LL LET YOU KNOW IF I FIND ANYTHING.
...
YOU KNOW WHAT?
THIS IS ALL YOUR FAULT TO BEGIN WITH.
RYOKO GETTING HER HEART BROKEN, RYUNOSUKE SKIPPING TOWN...
DON'T ACT LIKE LITTLE MISS INNOCENT.

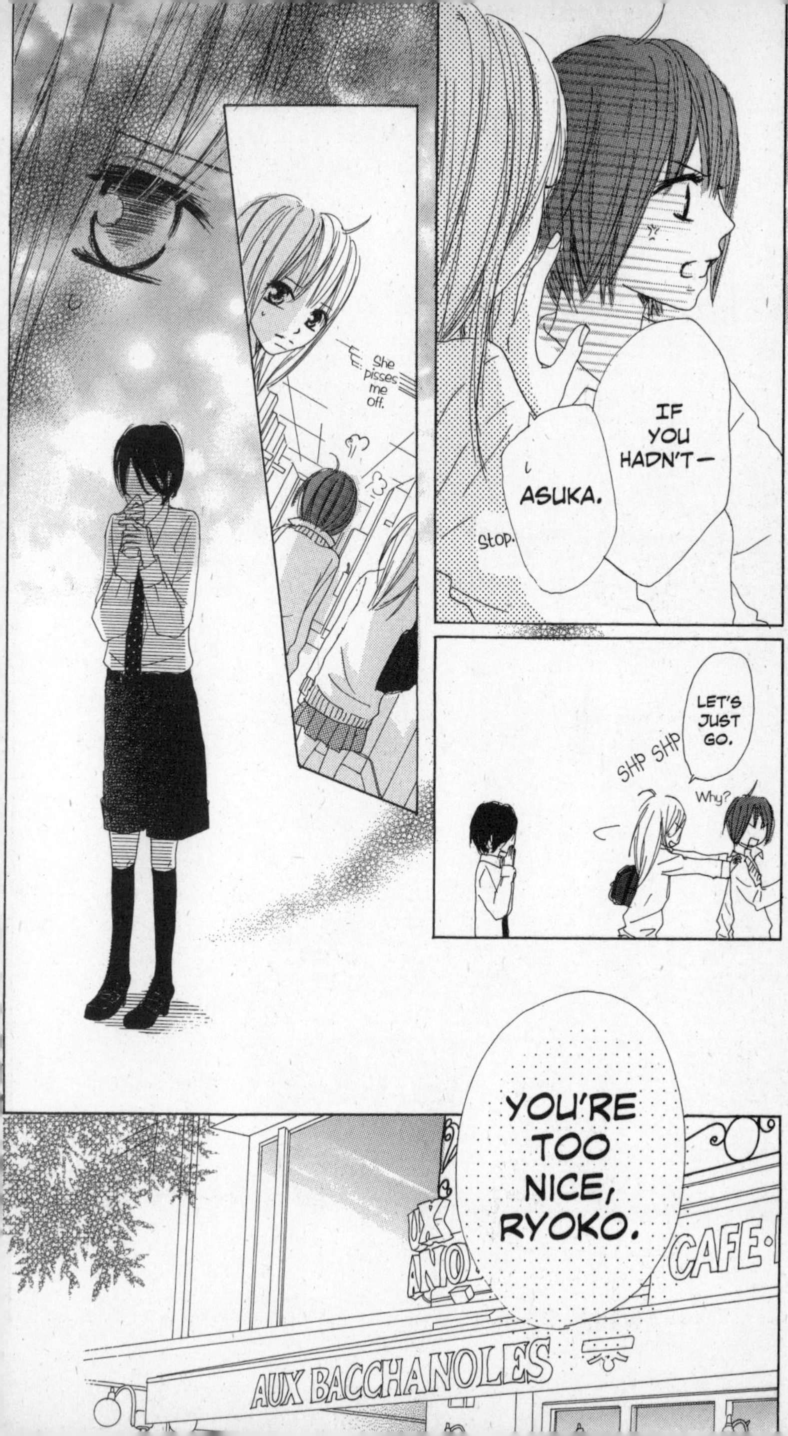
IF YOU HADN'T—
ASUKA.
Stop.
LET'S JUST GO.
SHP SHP
Why?
She pisses me off.
YOU'RE TOO NICE, RYOKO.
AUX BACCHANOLES

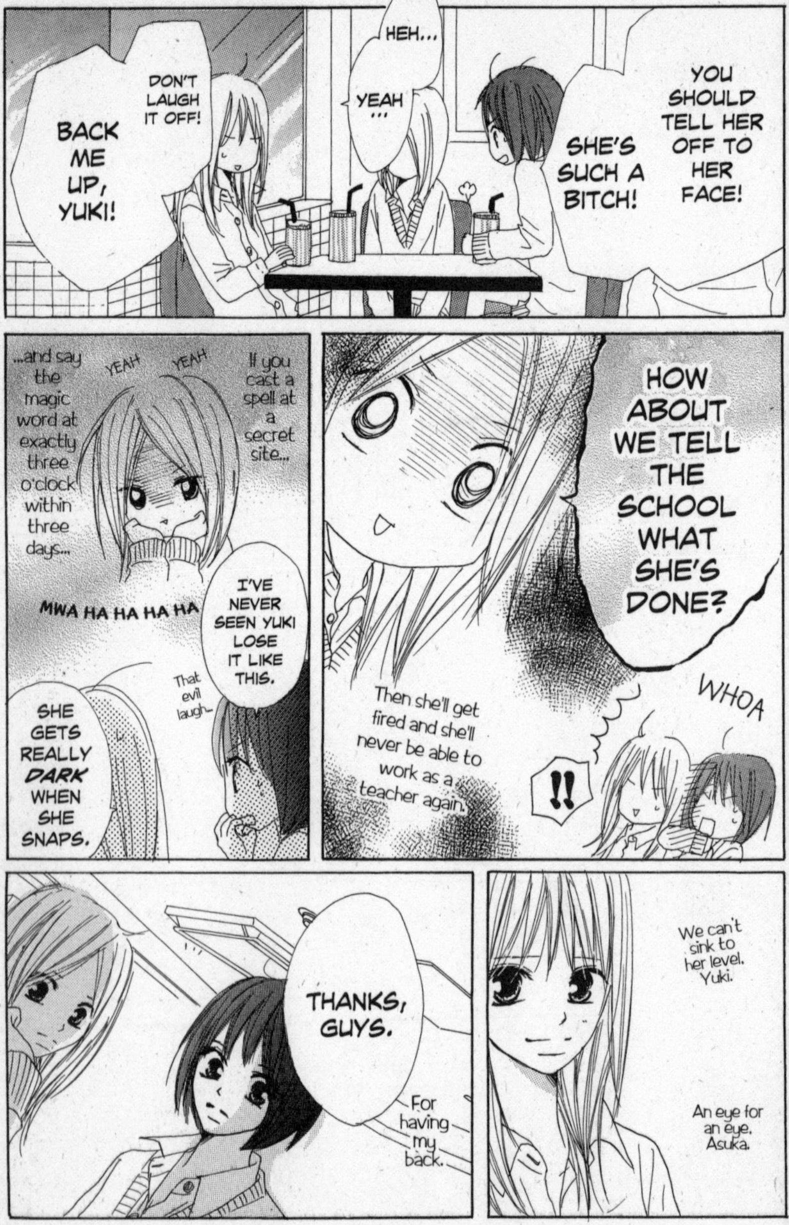

YOU SHOULD TELL HER OFF TO HER FACE!
SHE'S SUCH A BITCH!
HEH...
YEAH...
DON'T LAUGH IT OFF!
BACK ME UP, YUKI!
HOW ABOUT WE TELL THE SCHOOL WHAT SHE'S DONE?
WHOA
Then she'll get fired and she'll never be able to work as a teacher again.
!!
If you cast a spell at a secret site...
YEAH YEAH
...and say the magic word at exactly three o'clock within three days...
MWA HA HA HA HA
I'VE NEVER SEEN YUKI LOSE IT LIKE THIS.
That evil laugh...
SHE GETS REALLY *DARK* WHEN SHE SNAPS.
We can't sink to her level. Yuki.
An eye for an eye. Asuka.
THANKS, GUYS.
For having my back.

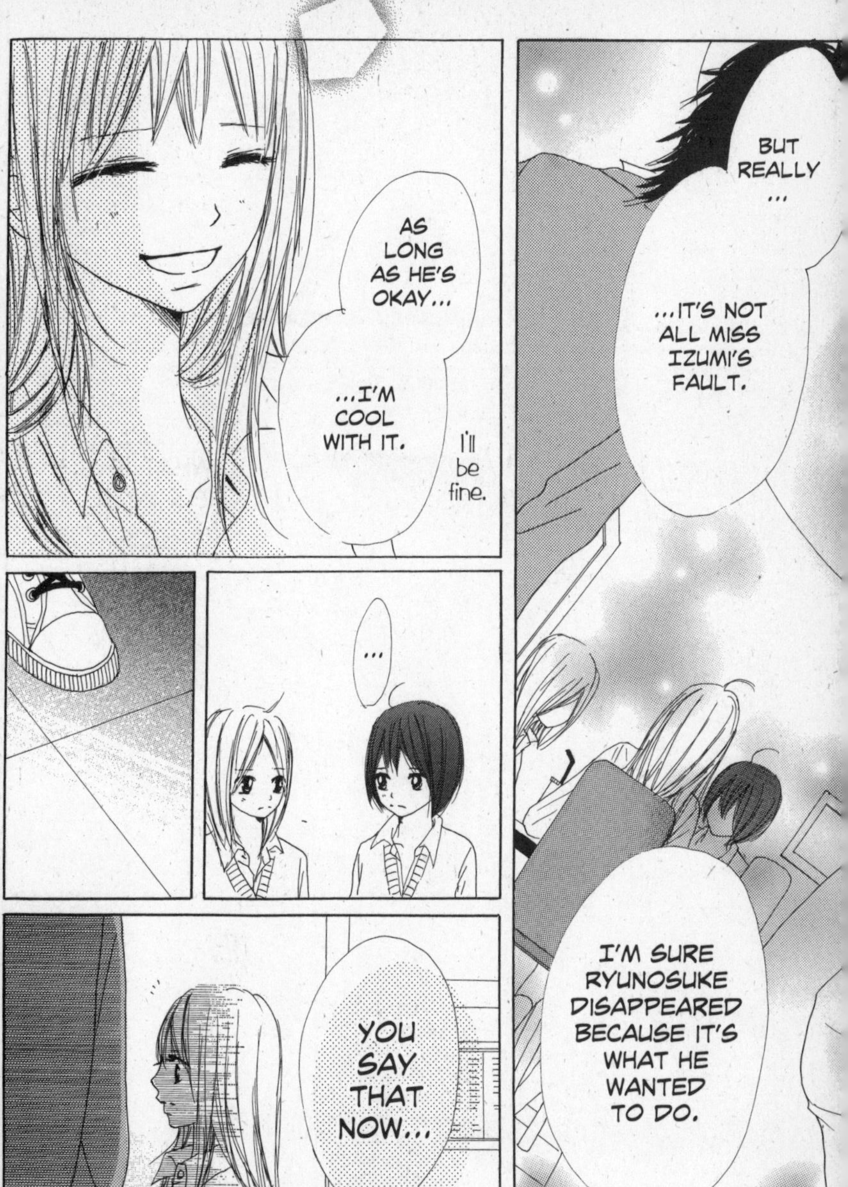
BUT REALLY ...
...IT'S NOT ALL MISS IZUMI'S FAULT.
I'M SURE RYUNOSUKE DISAPPEARED BECAUSE IT'S WHAT HE WANTED TO DO.
AS LONG AS HE'S OKAY...
...I'M COOL WITH IT.
I'll be fine.
...
YOU SAY THAT NOW...

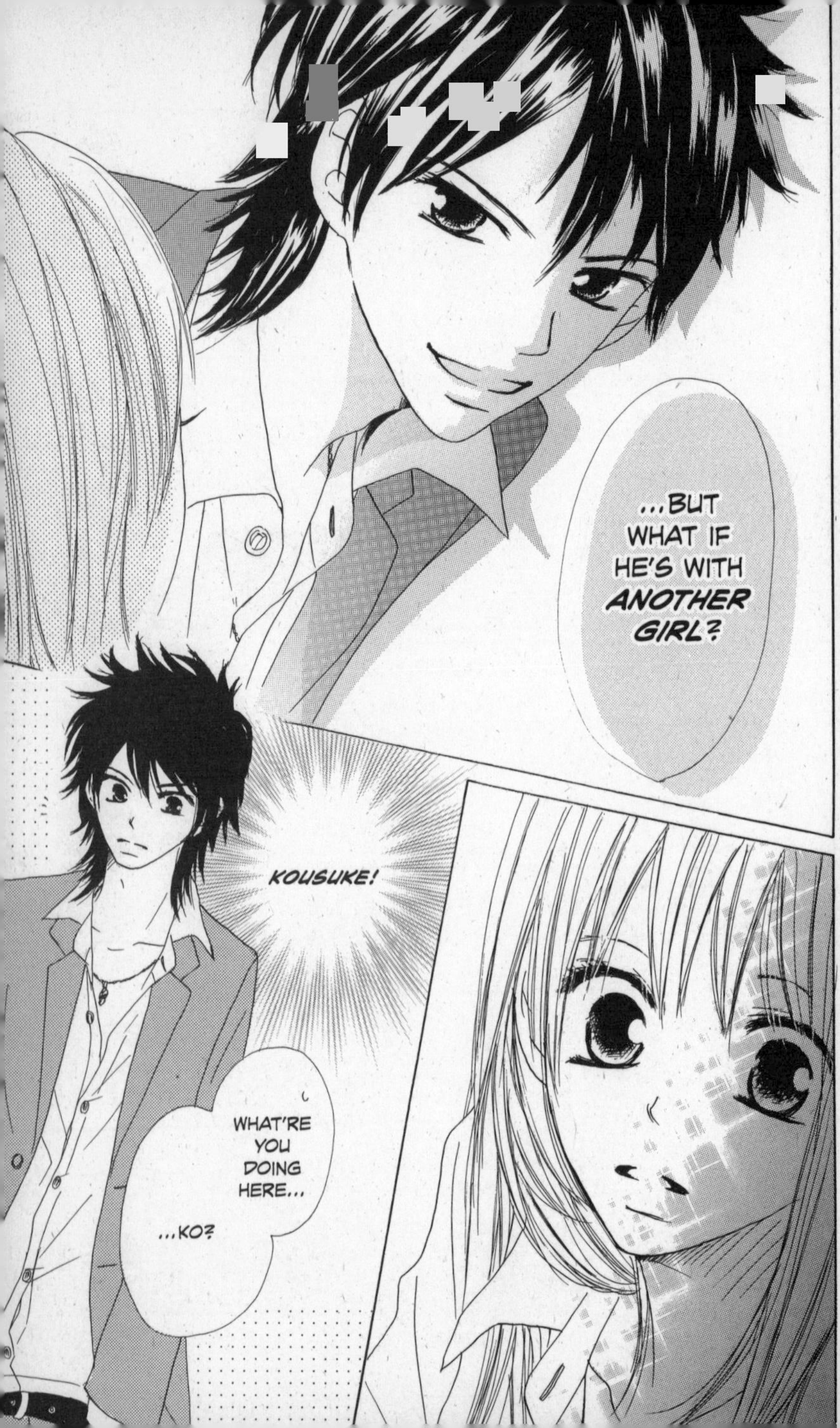
...BUT WHAT IF HE'S WITH ANOTHER GIRL?
KOUSUKE!
WHAT'RE YOU DOING HERE...
...KO?

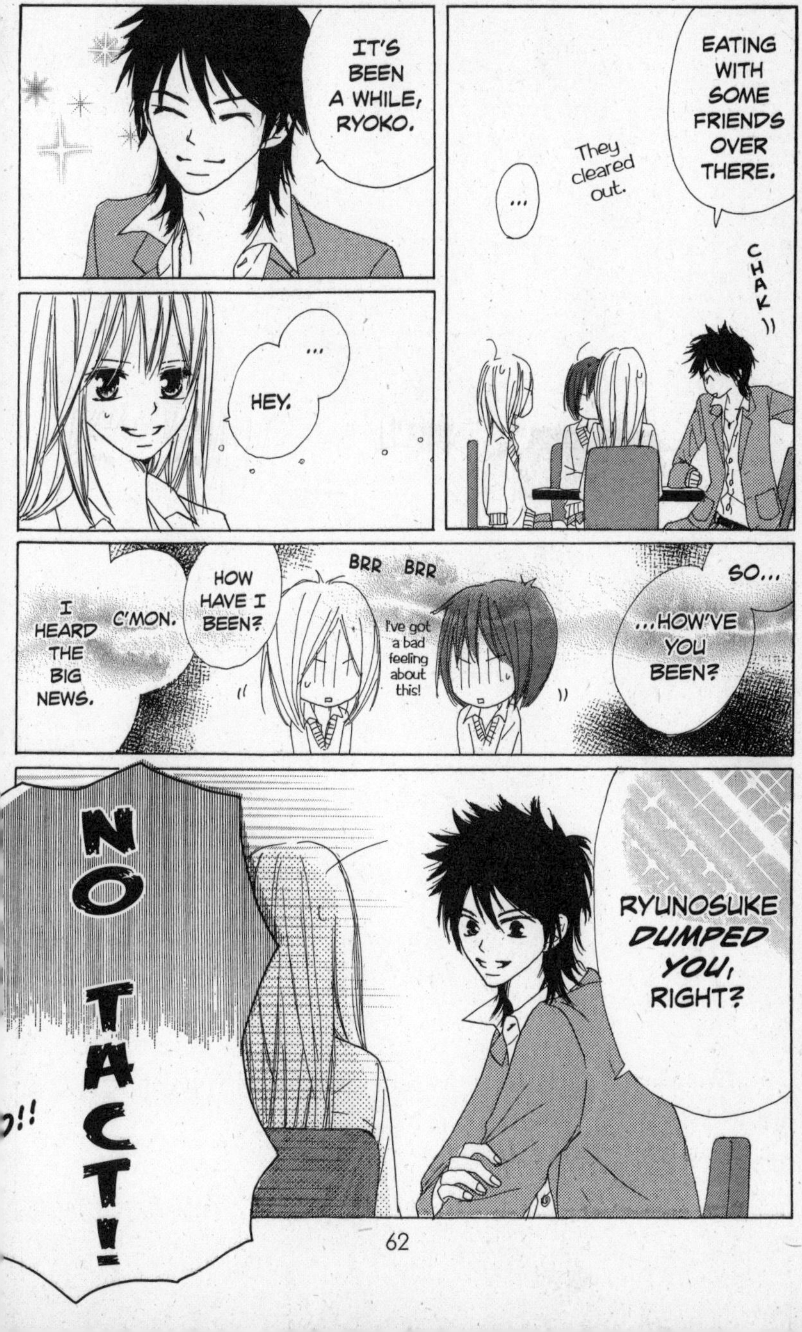
EATING WITH SOME FRIENDS OVER THERE.
They cleared out.
...
CHAK
IT'S BEEN A WHILE, RYOKO.
...
HEY.
SO...
...HOW'VE YOU BEEN?
BRR BRR
I've got a bad feeling about this!
HOW HAVE I BEEN?
C'MON.
I HEARD THE BIG NEWS.
RYUNOSUKE DUMPED YOU, RIGHT?
NO TACT!

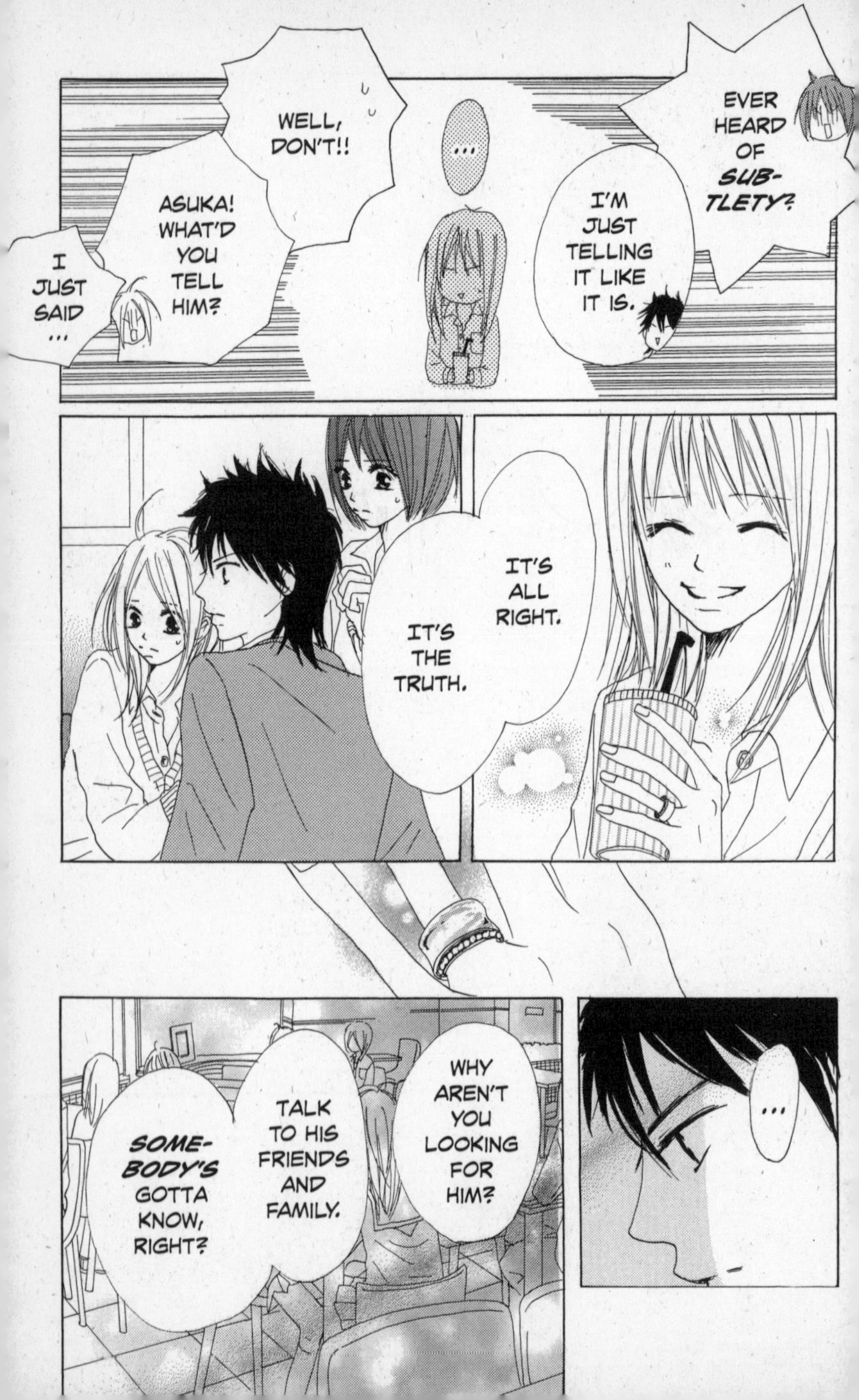
EVER HEARD OF SUBTLETY?
I'M JUST TELLING IT LIKE IT IS.
...
WELL, DON'T!!
ASUKA! WHAT'D YOU TELL HIM?
I JUST SAID ...
IT'S ALL RIGHT.
IT'S THE TRUTH.
...
WHY AREN'T YOU LOOKING FOR HIM?
TALK TO HIS FRIENDS AND FAMILY.
SOMEBODY'S GOTTA KNOW, RIGHT?

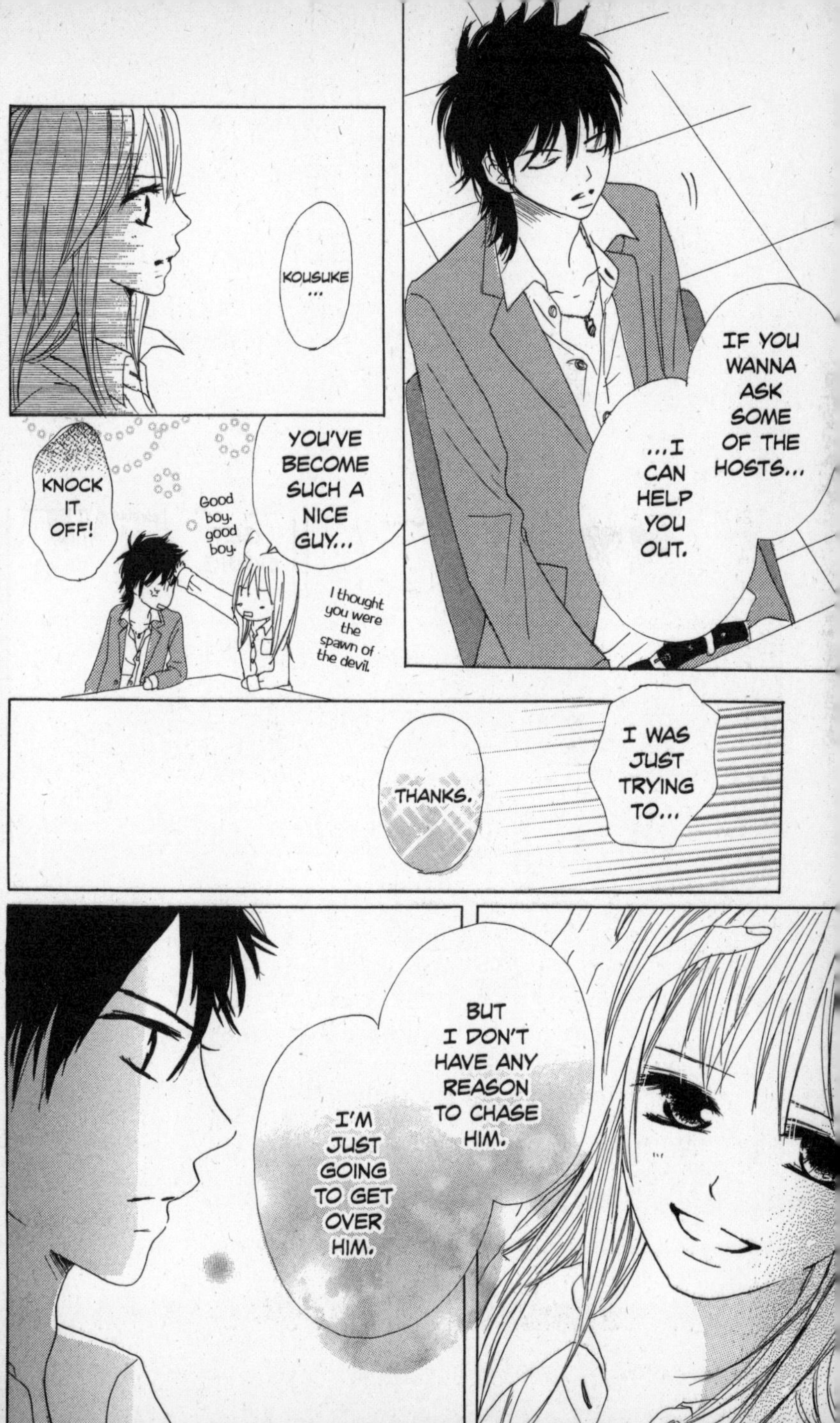
IF YOU WANNA ASK SOME OF THE HOSTS...
...I CAN HELP YOU OUT.
KOUSUKE...
YOU'VE BECOME SUCH A NICE GUY...
Good boy, good boy.
I thought you were the spawn of the devil.
KNOCK IT OFF!
I WAS JUST TRYING TO...
THANKS.
BUT I DON'T HAVE ANY REASON TO CHASE HIM.
I'M JUST GOING TO GET OVER HIM.

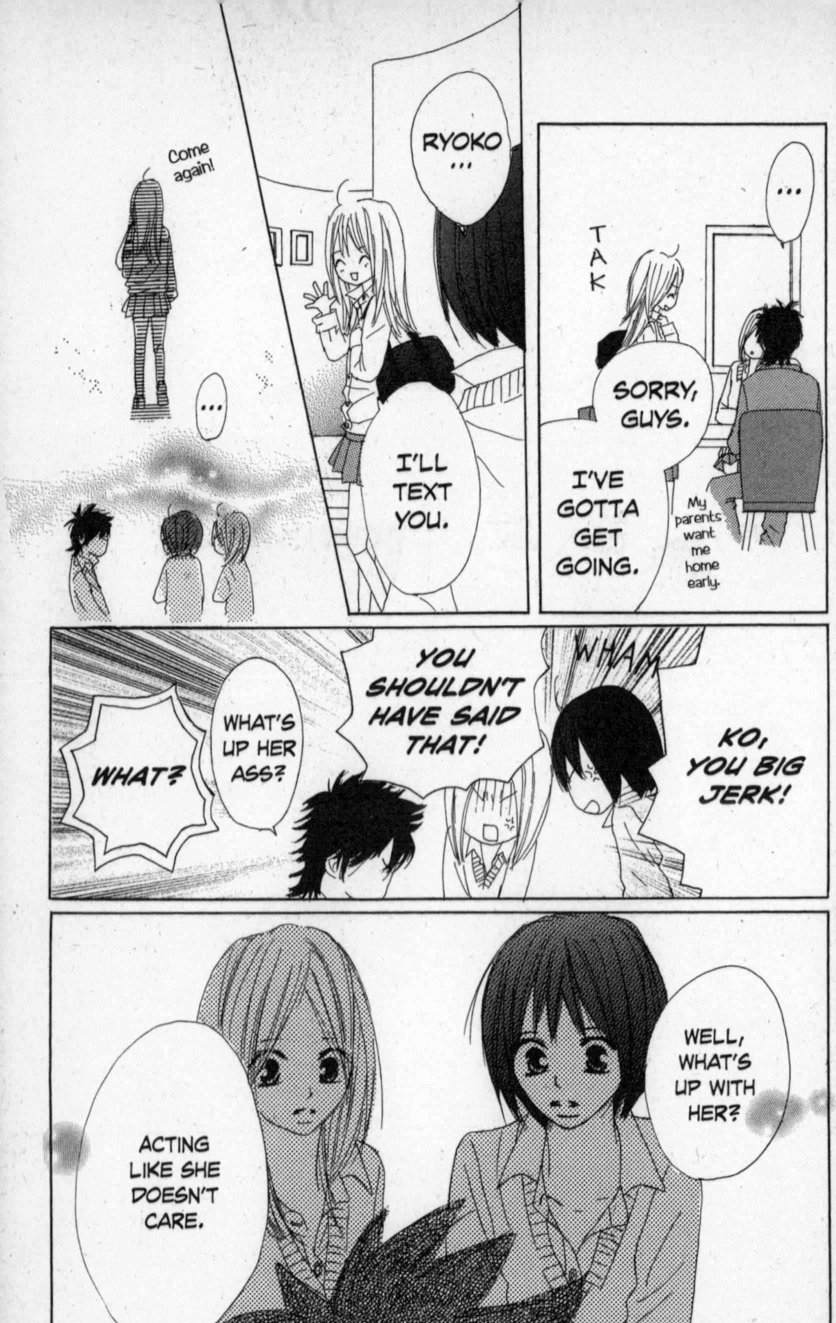
...
TAK
SORRY, GUYS.
I'VE GOTTA GET GOING.
My parents want me home early.
RYOKO ...
I'LL TEXT YOU.
Come again!
...
KO, YOU BIG JERK!
WHAM
YOU SHOULDN'T HAVE SAID THAT!
WHAT'S UP HER ASS?
WHAT?
WELL, WHAT'S UP WITH HER?
ACTING LIKE SHE DOESN'T CARE.

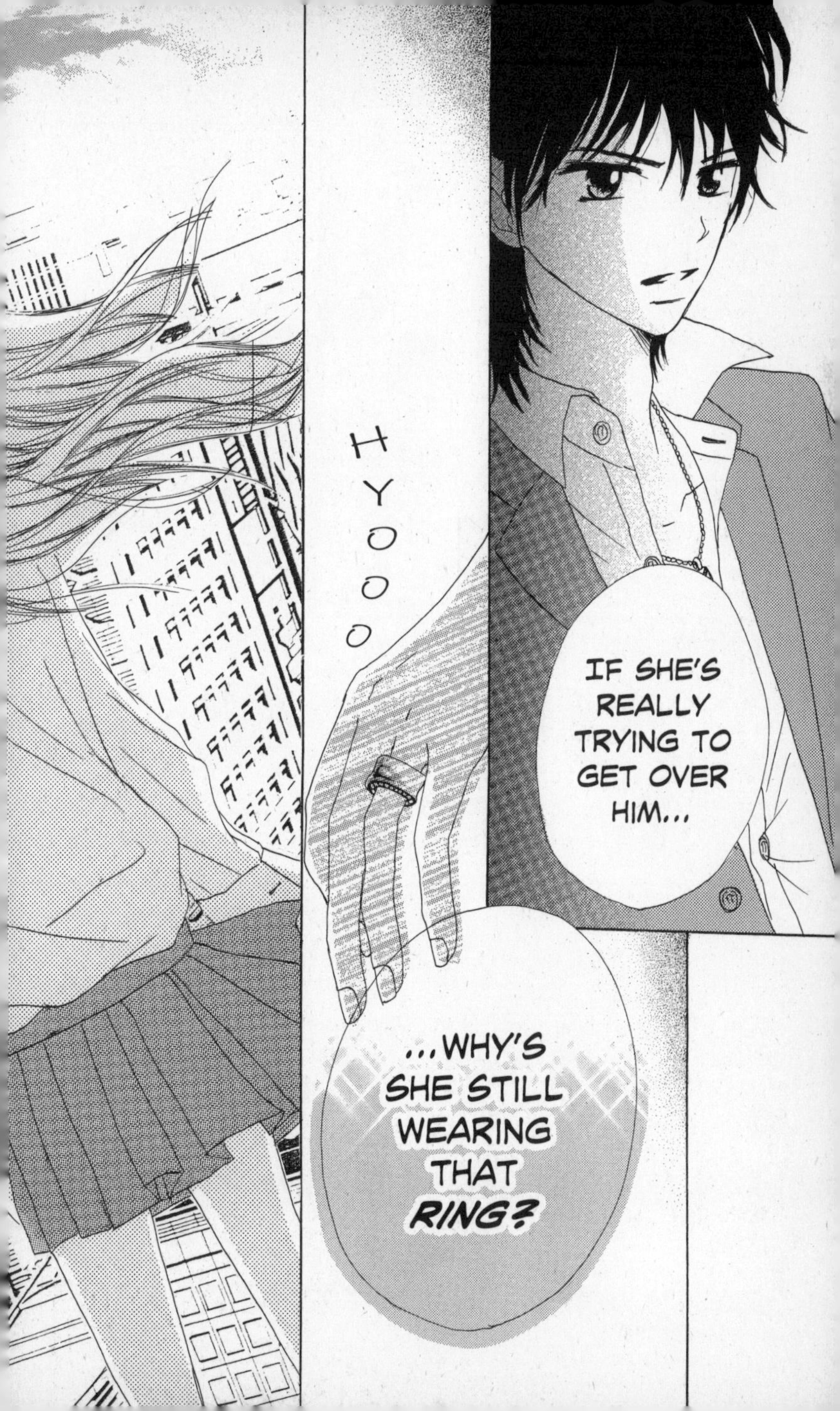
IF SHE'S REALLY TRYING TO GET OVER HIM...
HYOOO
...WHY'S SHE STILL WEARING THAT *RING?*

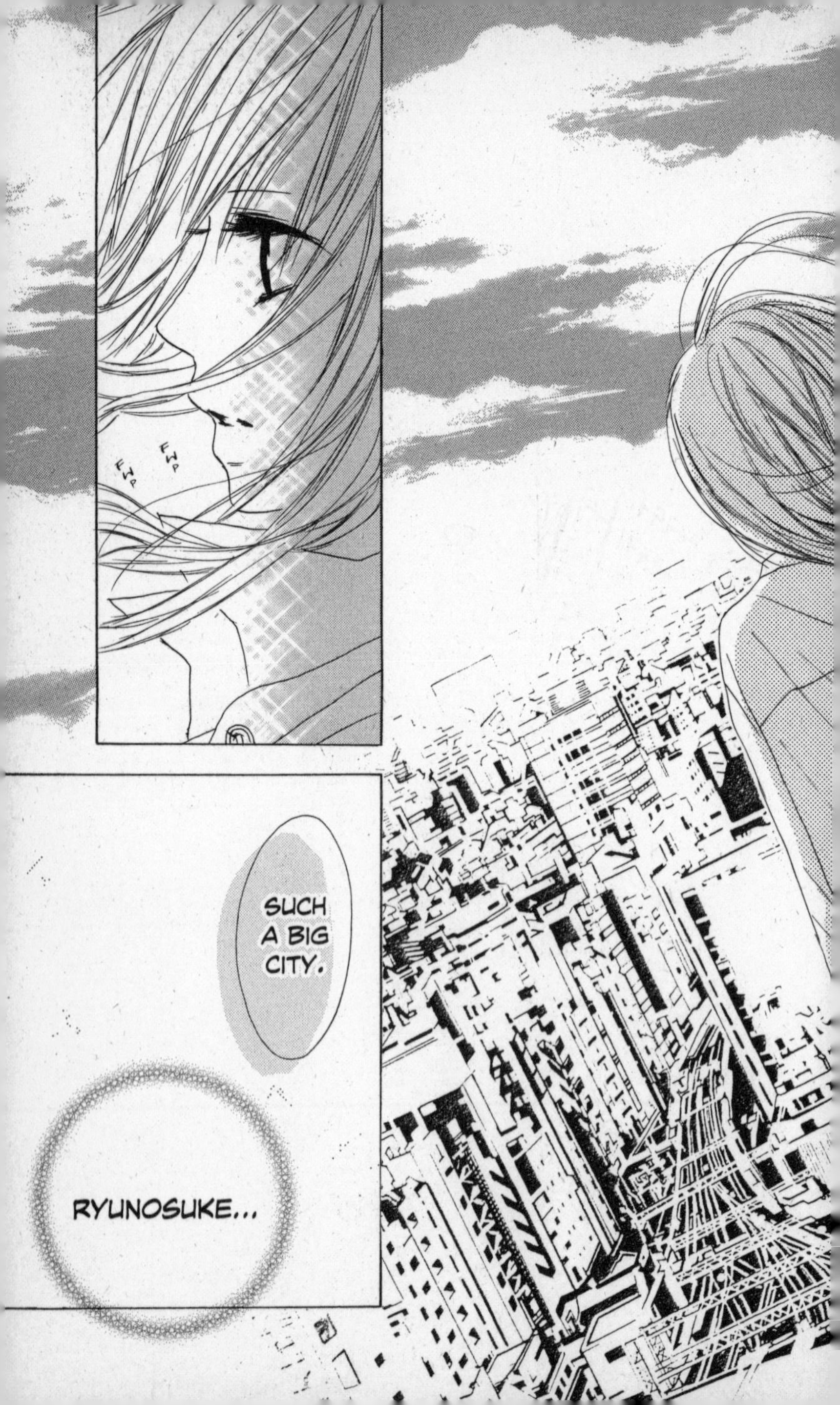
FWP
FWP
SUCH A BIG CITY.
RYUNOSUKE...

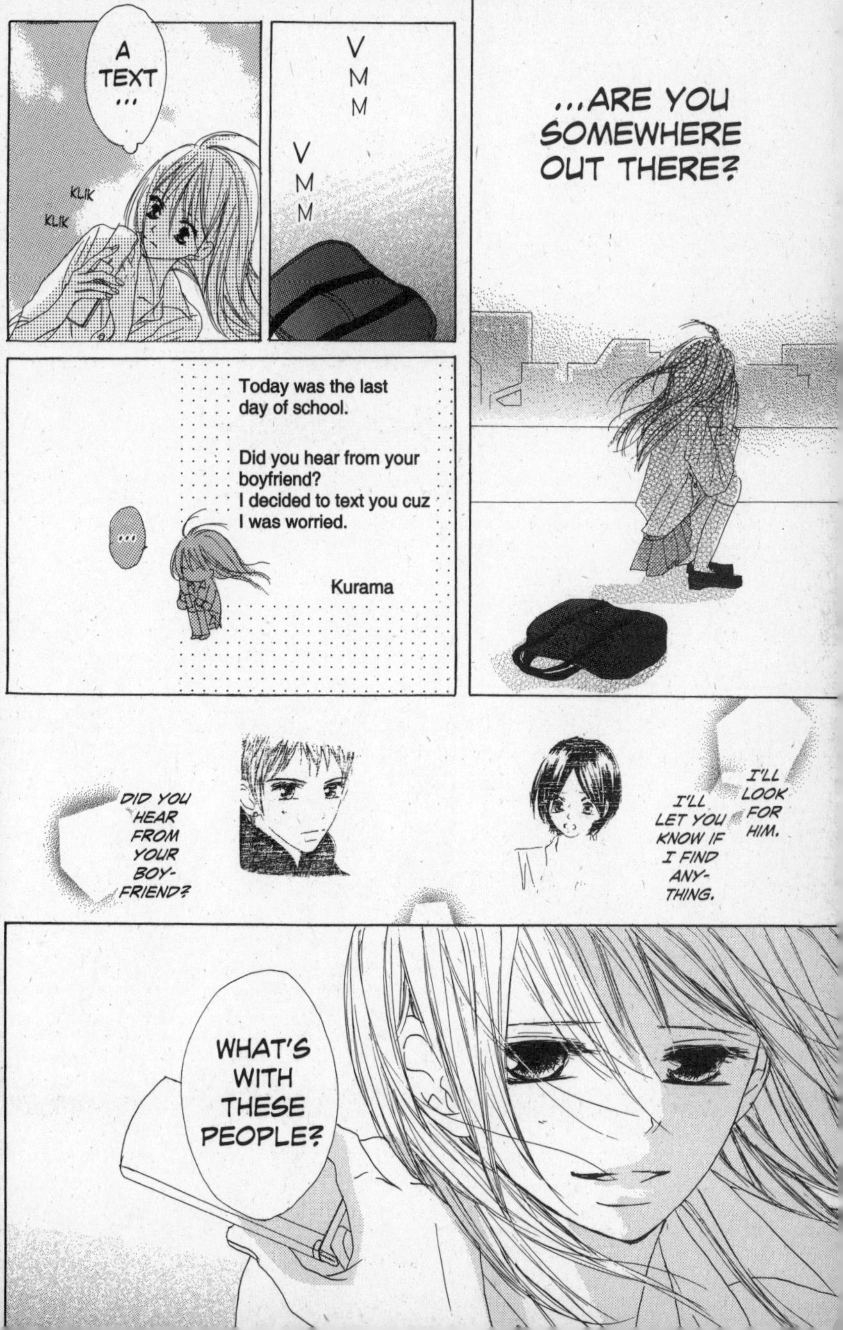
...ARE YOU SOMEWHERE OUT THERE?
VMM
VMM
A TEXT...
KLIK
KLIK
Today was the last day of school.
Did you hear from your boyfriend?
I decided to text you cuz I was worried.
Kurama
...
I'LL LOOK FOR HIM.
I'LL LET YOU KNOW IF I FIND ANYTHING.
DID YOU HEAR FROM YOUR BOYFRIEND?
WHAT'S WITH THESE PEOPLE?

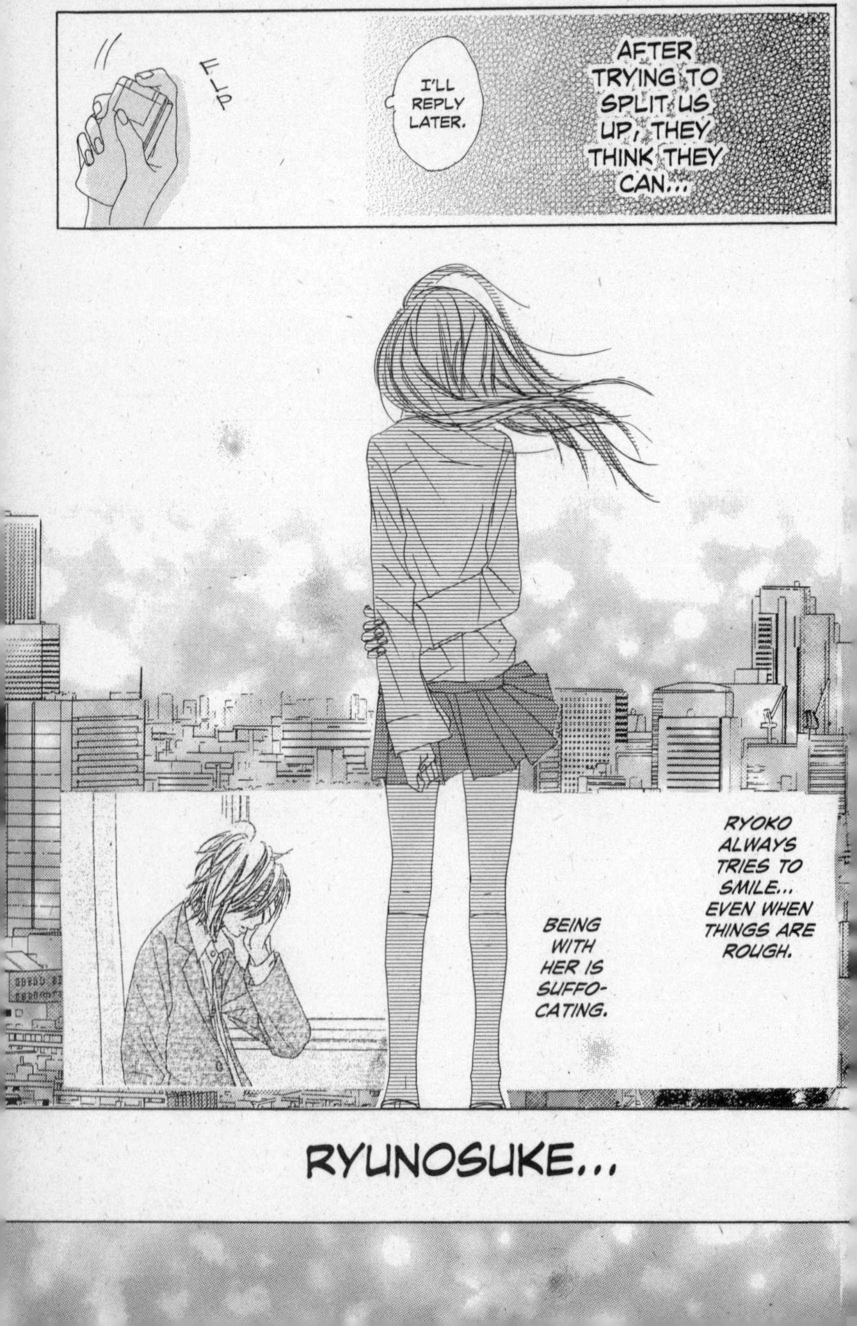
AFTER TRYING TO SPLIT US UP, THEY THINK THEY CAN...
I'LL REPLY LATER.
FLP
RYOKO ALWAYS TRIES TO SMILE... EVEN WHEN THINGS ARE ROUGH.
BEING WITH HER IS SUFFO-CATING.
RYUNOSUKE...

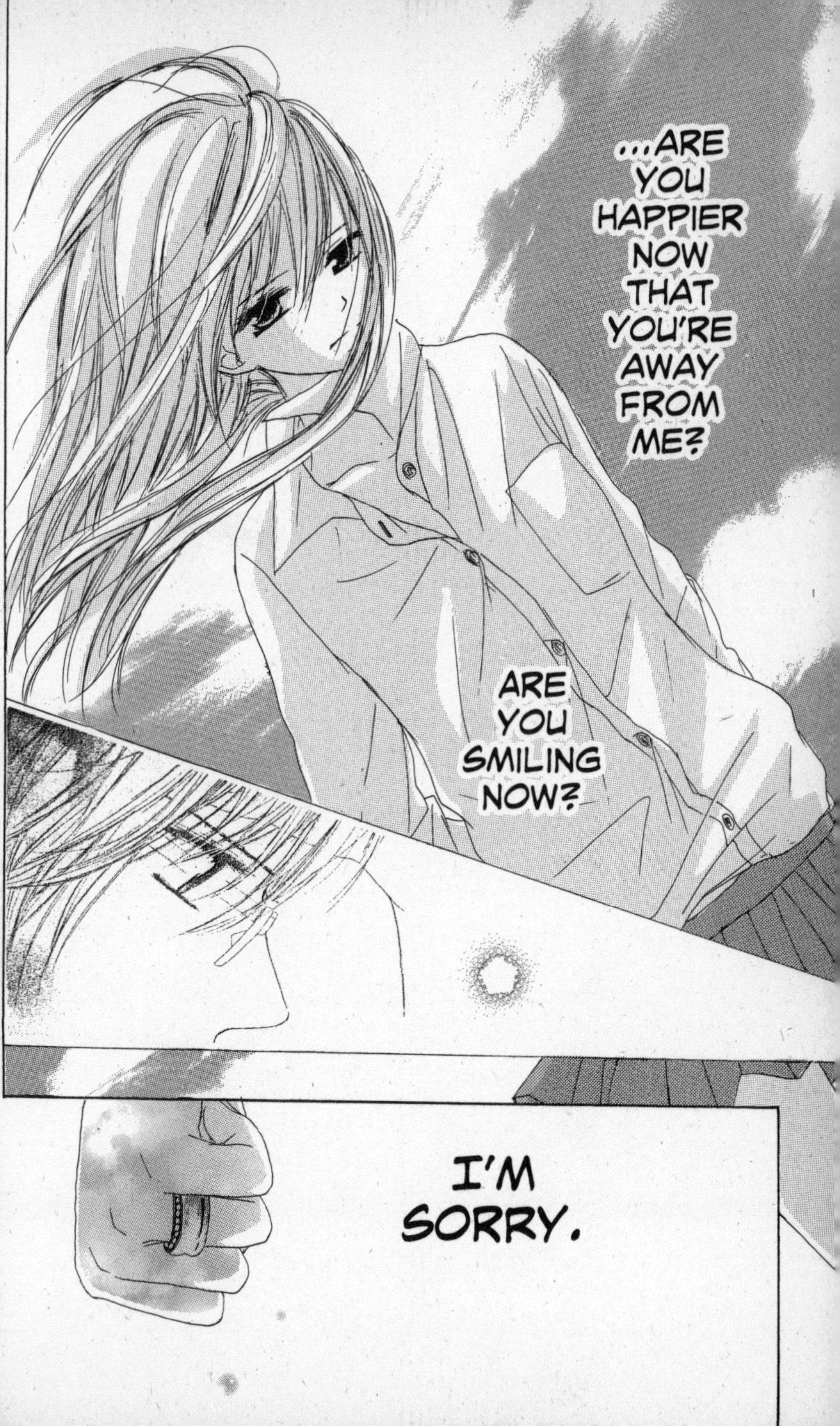
...ARE YOU HAPPIER NOW THAT YOU'RE AWAY FROM ME?
ARE YOU SMILING NOW?
I'M SORRY.

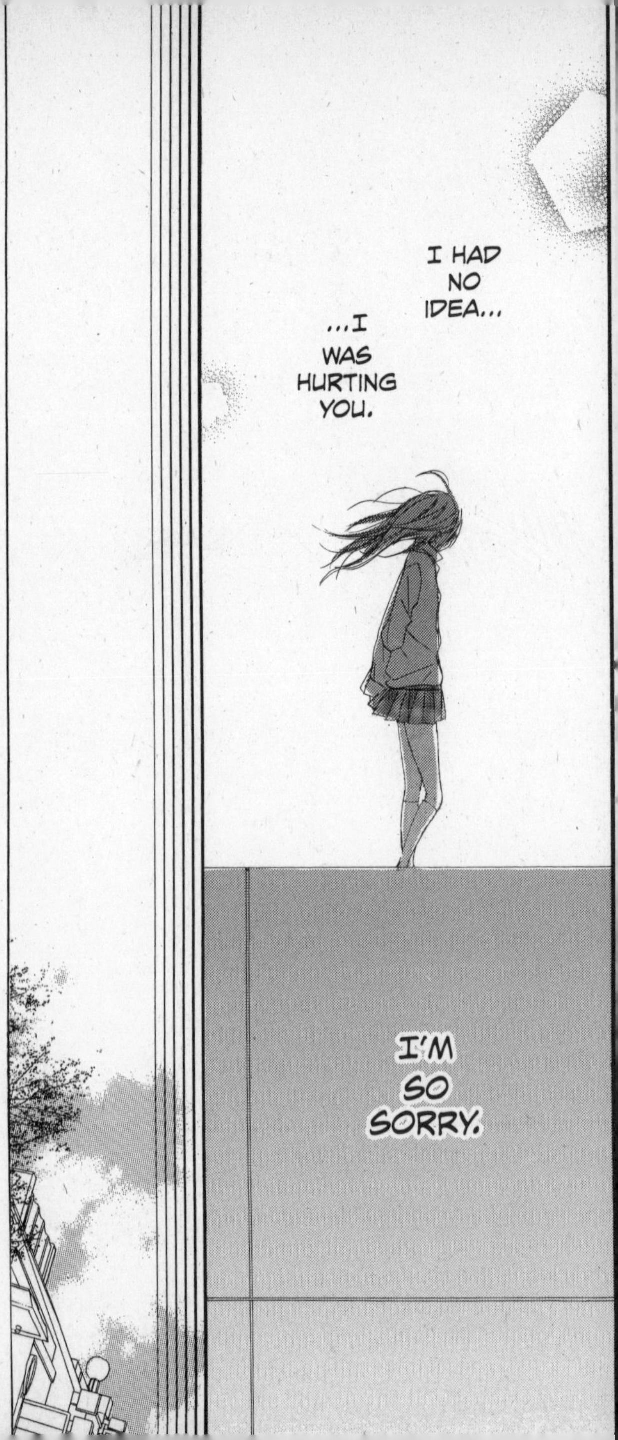
I HAD NO IDEA...
...I WAS HURTING YOU.
I'M SO SORRY.

(2) Continued... HEH

Walt's dad!

I felt the urge to kill while watching season 2!! Grrr!!

To those who haven't seen it yet, I won't go into details...but when you get the chance, please watch *Lost*. I highly recommend it.

I've been watching *Alias* recently too. I didn't pay much attention to it at first...

TV

I've never heard of...

...this show before!

...but after a while I was hooked. I couldn't miss an episode. I'm intrigued by the subtle cosplay element.

But it's tough to have all these TV shows available, because I wanna watch all of them! I turn them off while I'm working, and before I know it I've missed a bunch of my favorite shows. I should just record them... but it's such a pain.

I mostly watch the *Sgt. Frog* anime while I'm working. It soothes my soul. I like Tamama a lot these days... All the little frogs... they're so cute.

(3) To be continued...

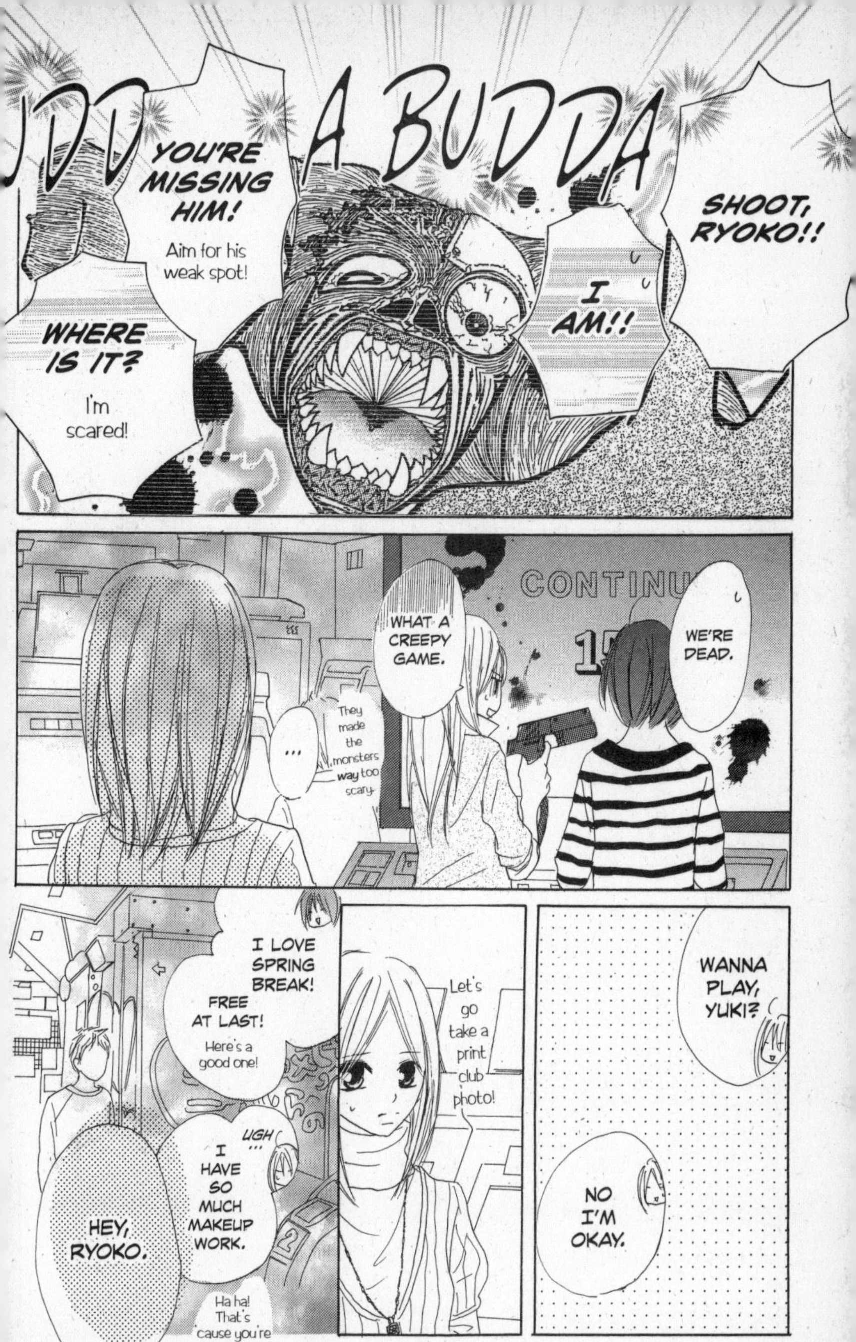

DD
A BUDDA
SHOOT, RYOKO!!
I AM!!
YOU'RE MISSING HIM!
Aim for his weak spot!
WHERE IS IT?
I'm scared!
WE'RE DEAD.
WHAT A CREEPY GAME.
They made the monsters way too scary.
...
CONTINU
WANNA PLAY, YUKI?
NO I'M OKAY.
Let's go take a print club photo!
I LOVE SPRING BREAK!
FREE AT LAST!
Here's a good one!
UGH...
I HAVE SO MUCH MAKEUP WORK.
HEY, RYOKO.
Ha ha! That's cause you're so dumb!

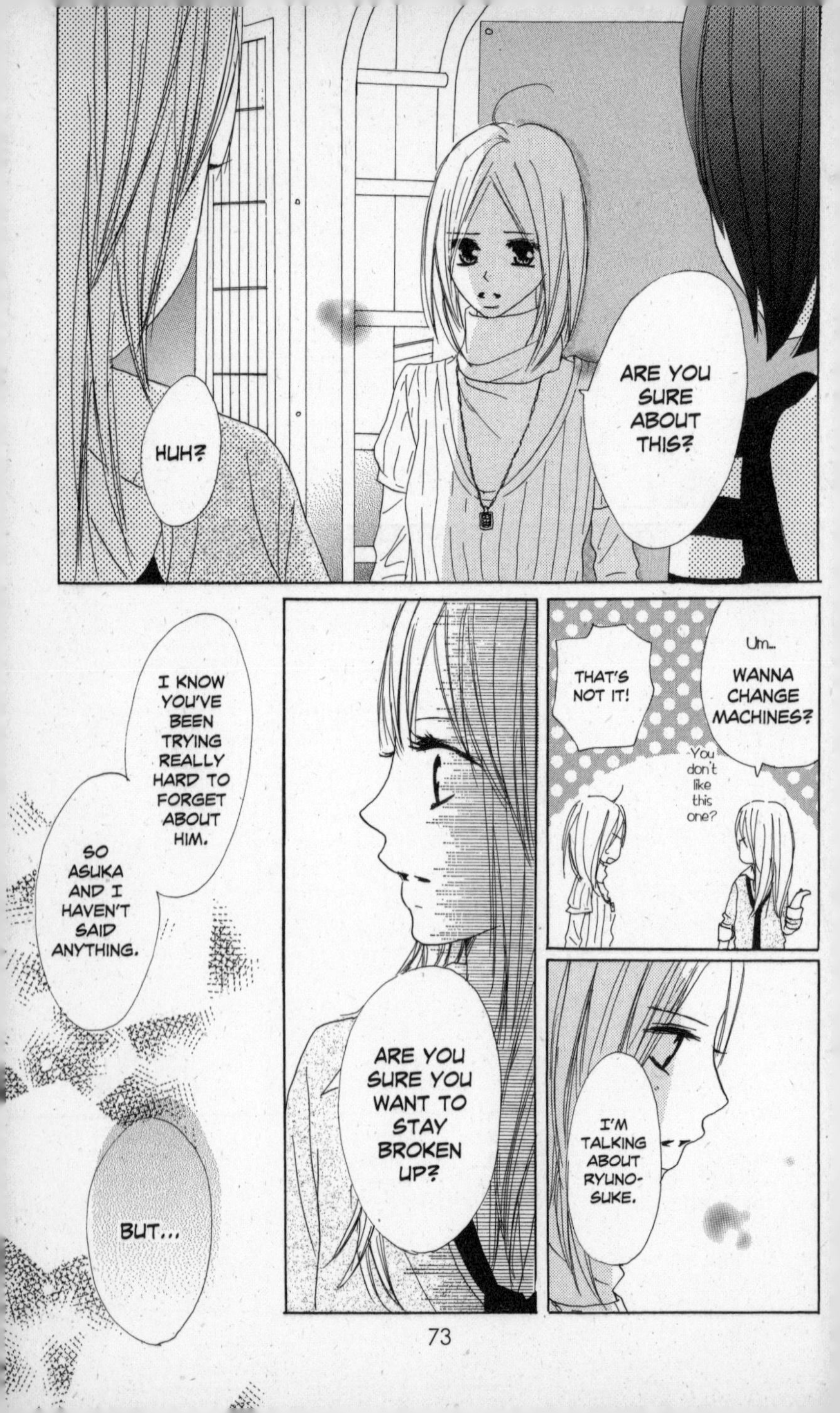
ARE YOU SURE ABOUT THIS?
HUH?
Um... WANNA CHANGE MACHINES?
You don't like this one?
THAT'S NOT IT!
I'M TALKING ABOUT RYUNO-SUKE.
ARE YOU SURE YOU WANT TO STAY BROKEN UP?
I KNOW YOU'VE BEEN TRYING REALLY HARD TO FORGET ABOUT HIM.
SO ASUKA AND I HAVEN'T SAID ANYTHING.
BUT...

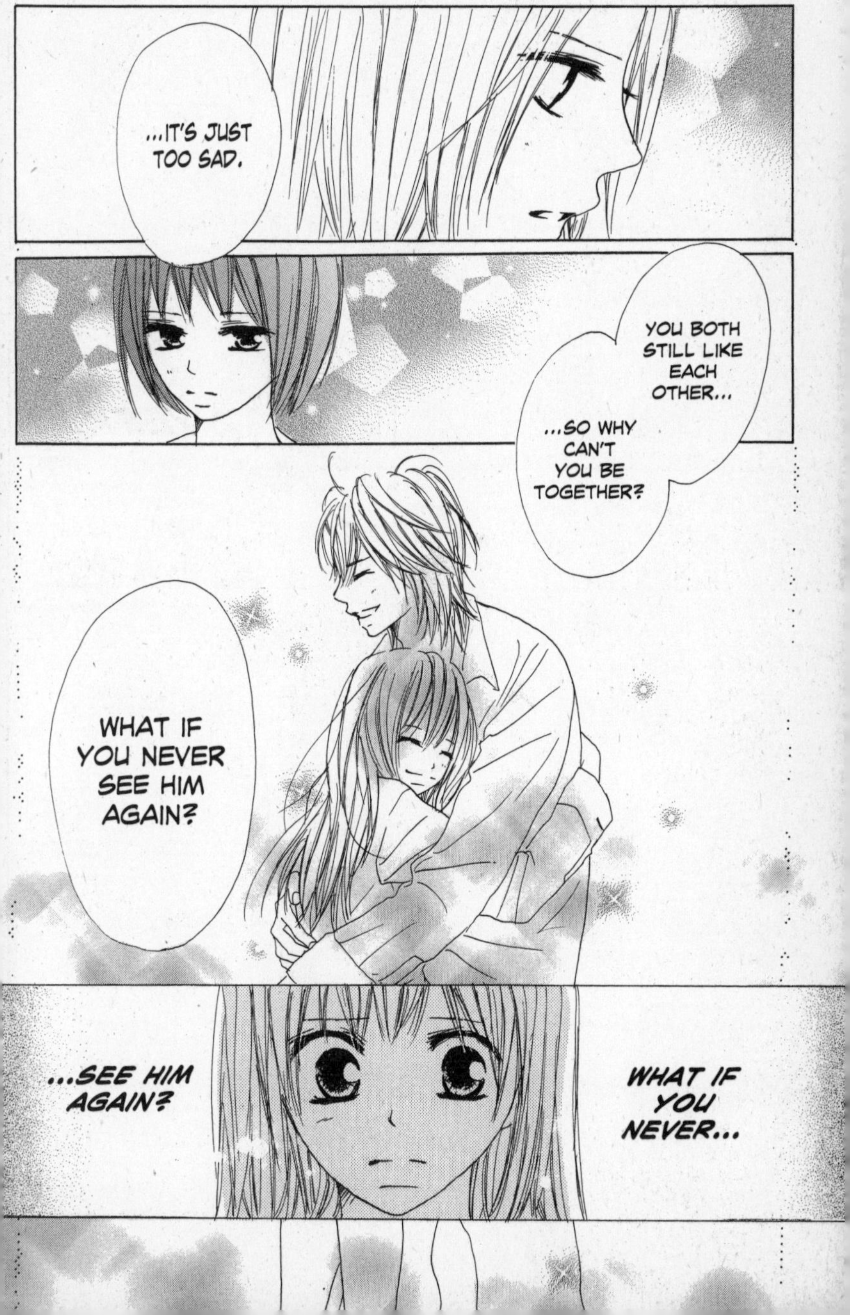
...IT'S JUST TOO SAD.
YOU BOTH STILL LIKE EACH OTHER...
...SO WHY CAN'T YOU BE TOGETHER?
WHAT IF YOU NEVER SEE HIM AGAIN?
WHAT IF YOU NEVER...
...SEE HIM AGAIN?

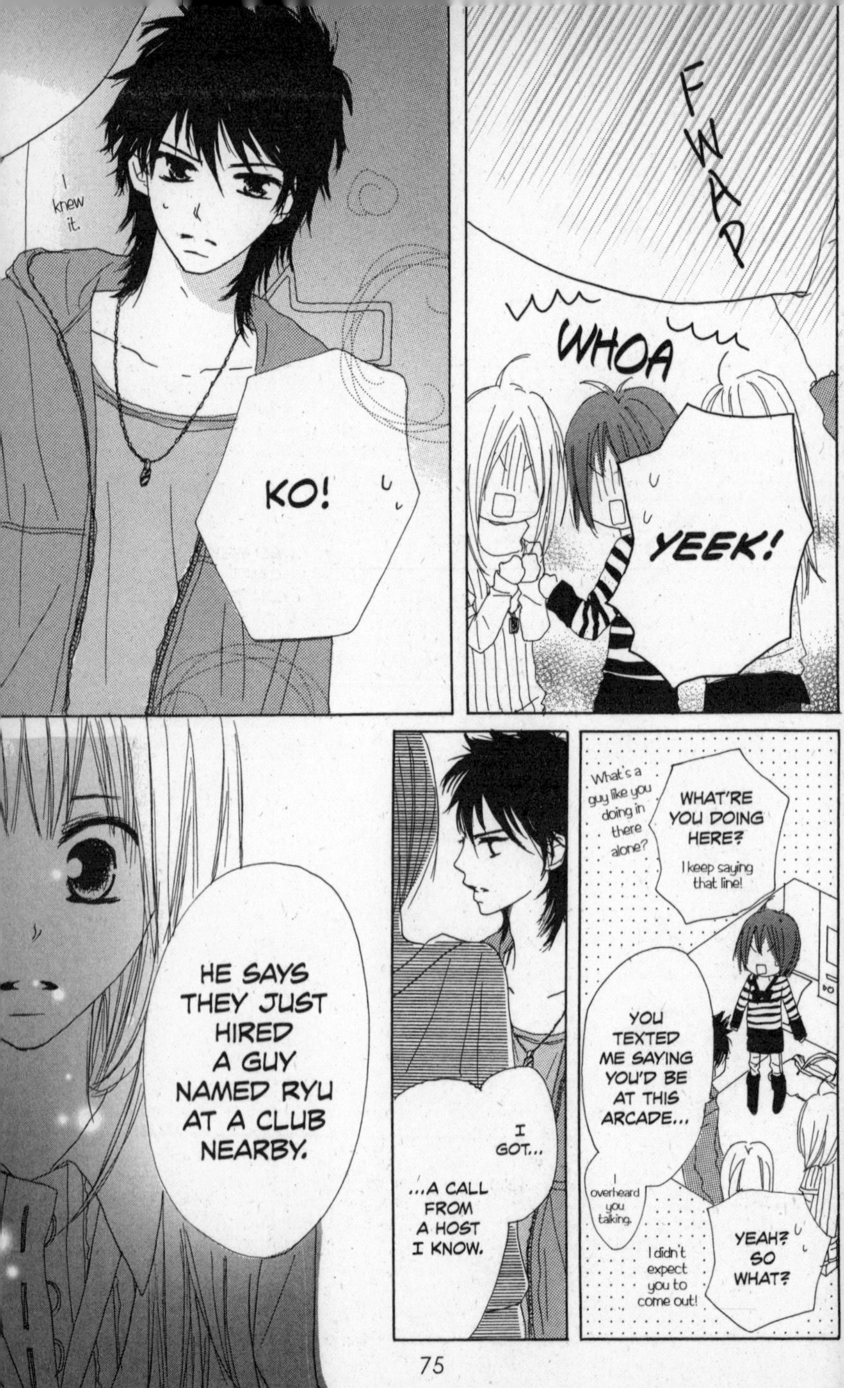
FWAP
WHOA
YEEK!
I knew it.
KO!
WHAT'RE YOU DOING HERE?
I keep saying that line!
What's a guy like you doing in there alone?
YOU TEXTED ME SAYING YOU'D BE AT THIS ARCADE...
I overheard you talking.
YEAH? SO WHAT?
I didn't expect you to come out!
I GOT...
...A CALL FROM A HOST I KNOW.
HE SAYS THEY JUST HIRED A GUY NAMED RYU AT A CLUB NEARBY.

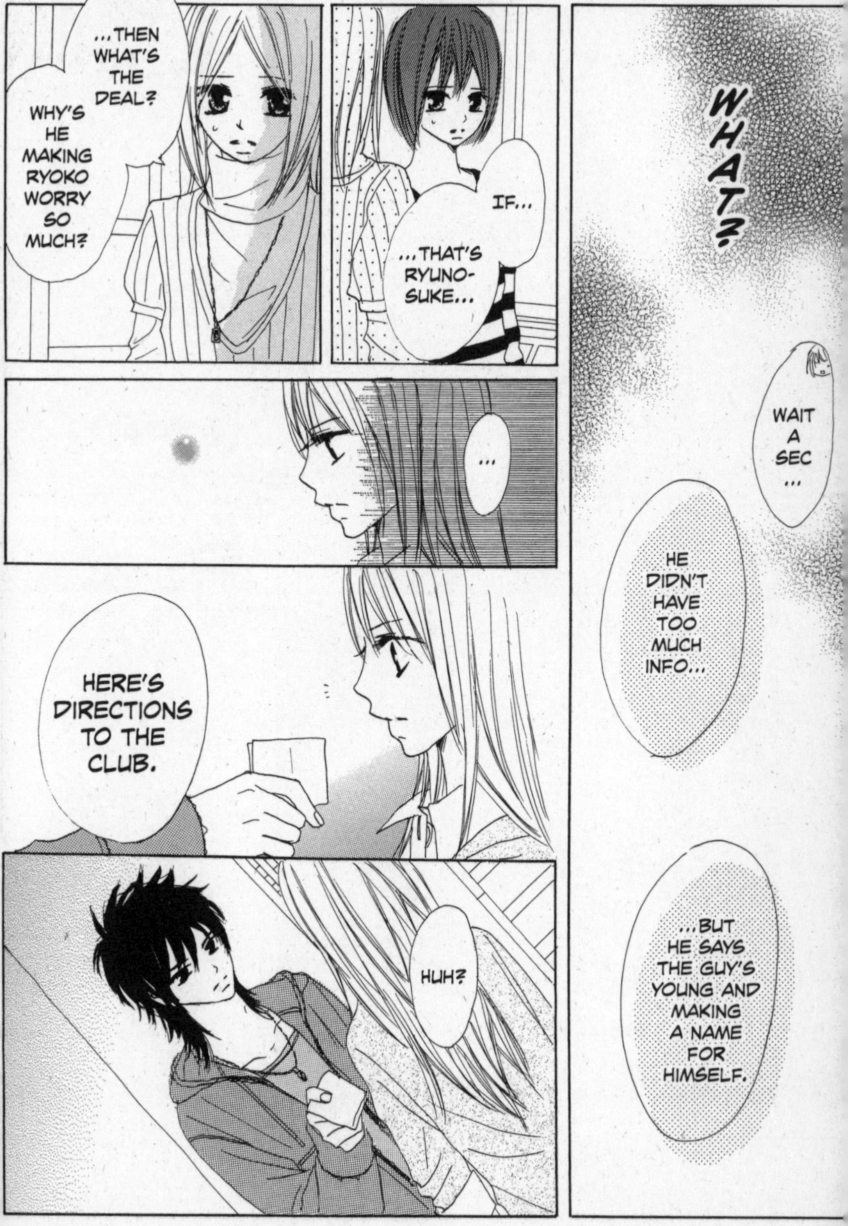
WHAT?!
WAIT A SEC...
HE DIDN'T HAVE TOO MUCH INFO...
...BUT HE SAYS THE GUY'S YOUNG AND MAKING A NAME FOR HIMSELF.
IF...
...THAT'S RYUNO-SUKE...
...THEN WHAT'S THE DEAL?
WHY'S HE MAKING RYOKO WORRY SO MUCH?
...
HERE'S DIRECTIONS TO THE CLUB.
HUH?

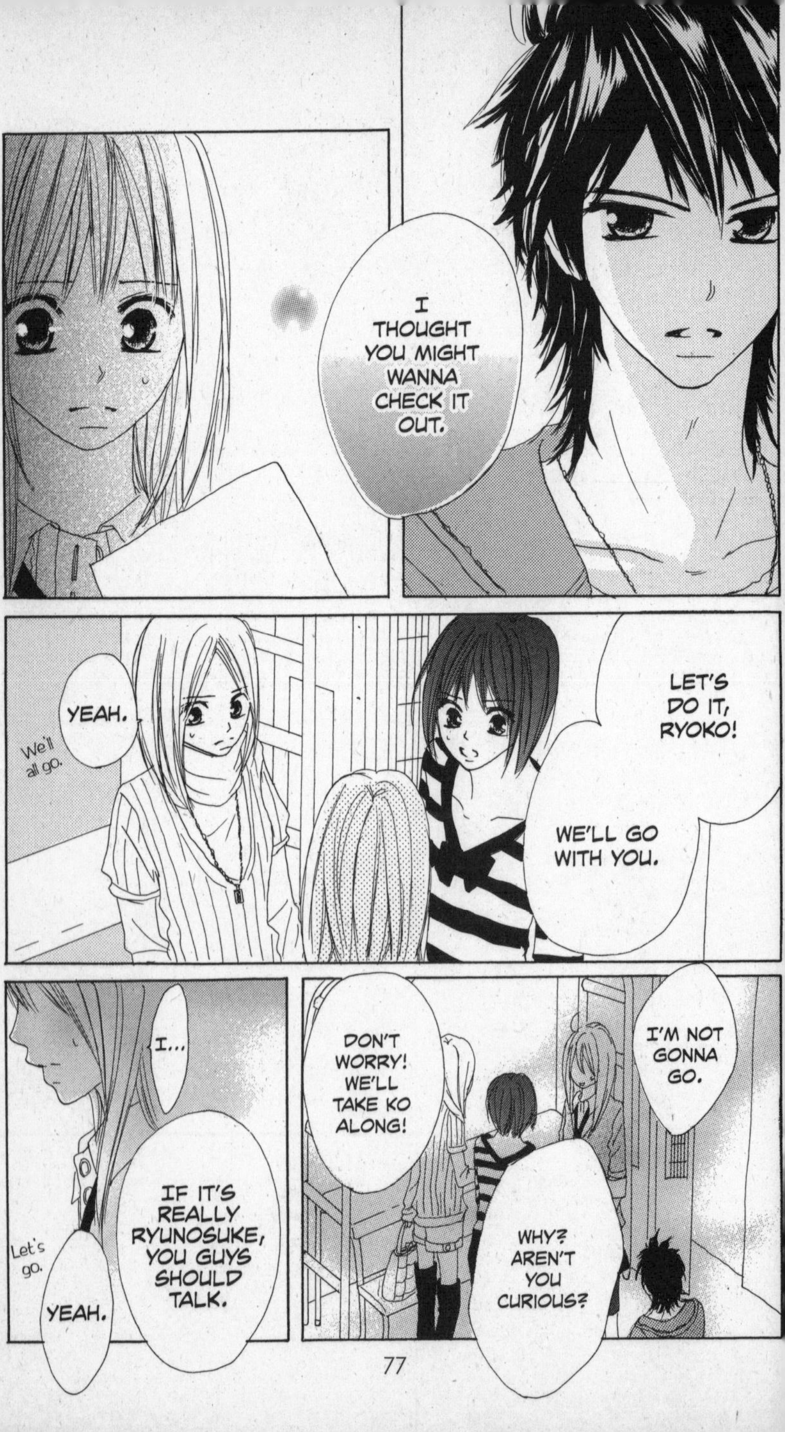
I THOUGHT YOU MIGHT WANNA CHECK IT OUT.
LET'S DO IT, RYOKO!
WE'LL GO WITH YOU.
YEAH.
We'll all go.
I'M NOT GONNA GO.
DON'T WORRY! WE'LL TAKE KO ALONG!
WHY? AREN'T YOU CURIOUS?
I...
IF IT'S REALLY RYUNOSUKE, YOU GUYS SHOULD TALK.
Let's go.
YEAH.

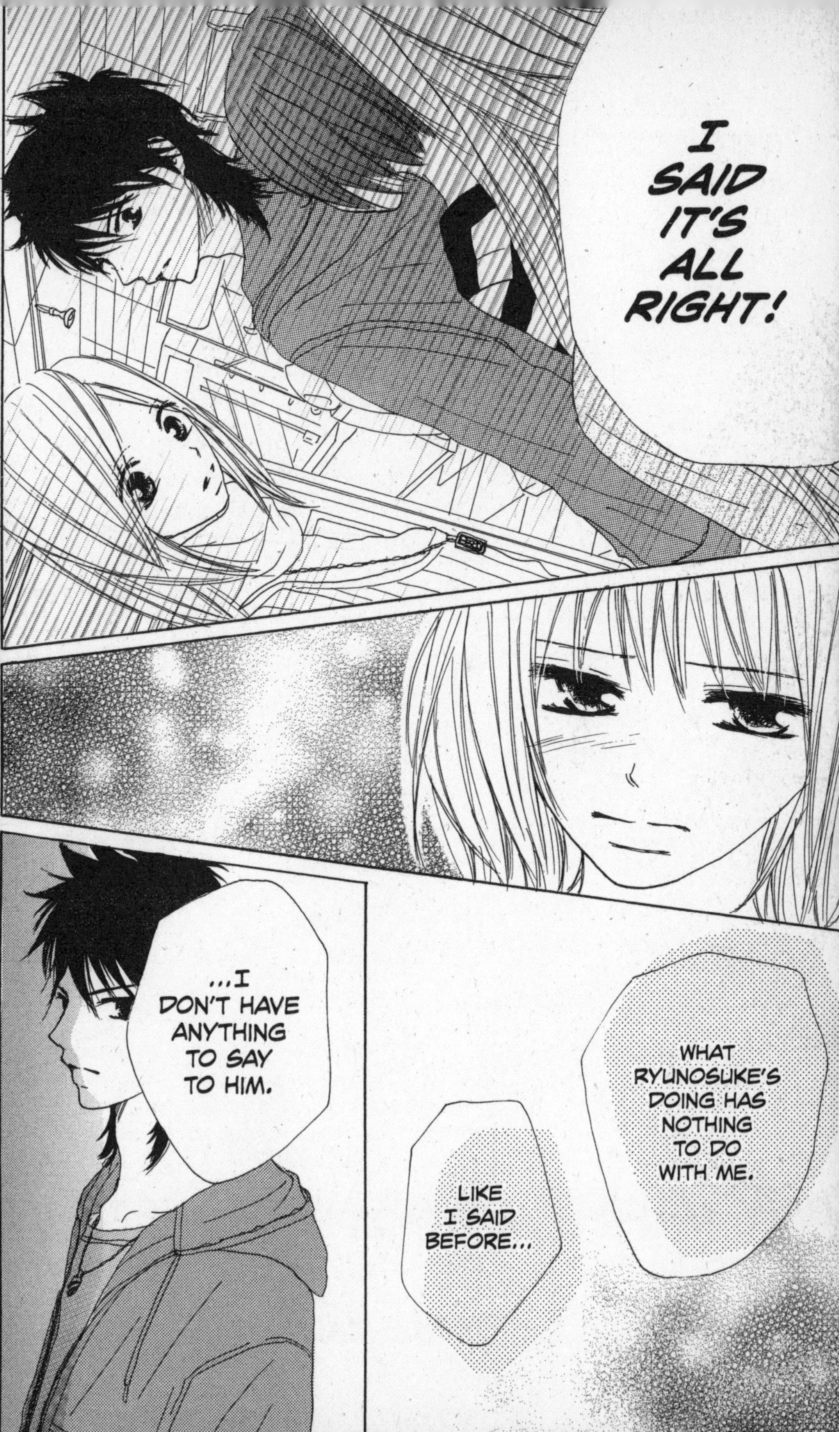
I SAID IT'S ALL RIGHT!
WHAT RYUNOSUKE'S DOING HAS NOTHING TO DO WITH ME.
LIKE I SAID BEFORE...
...I DON'T HAVE ANYTHING TO SAY TO HIM.

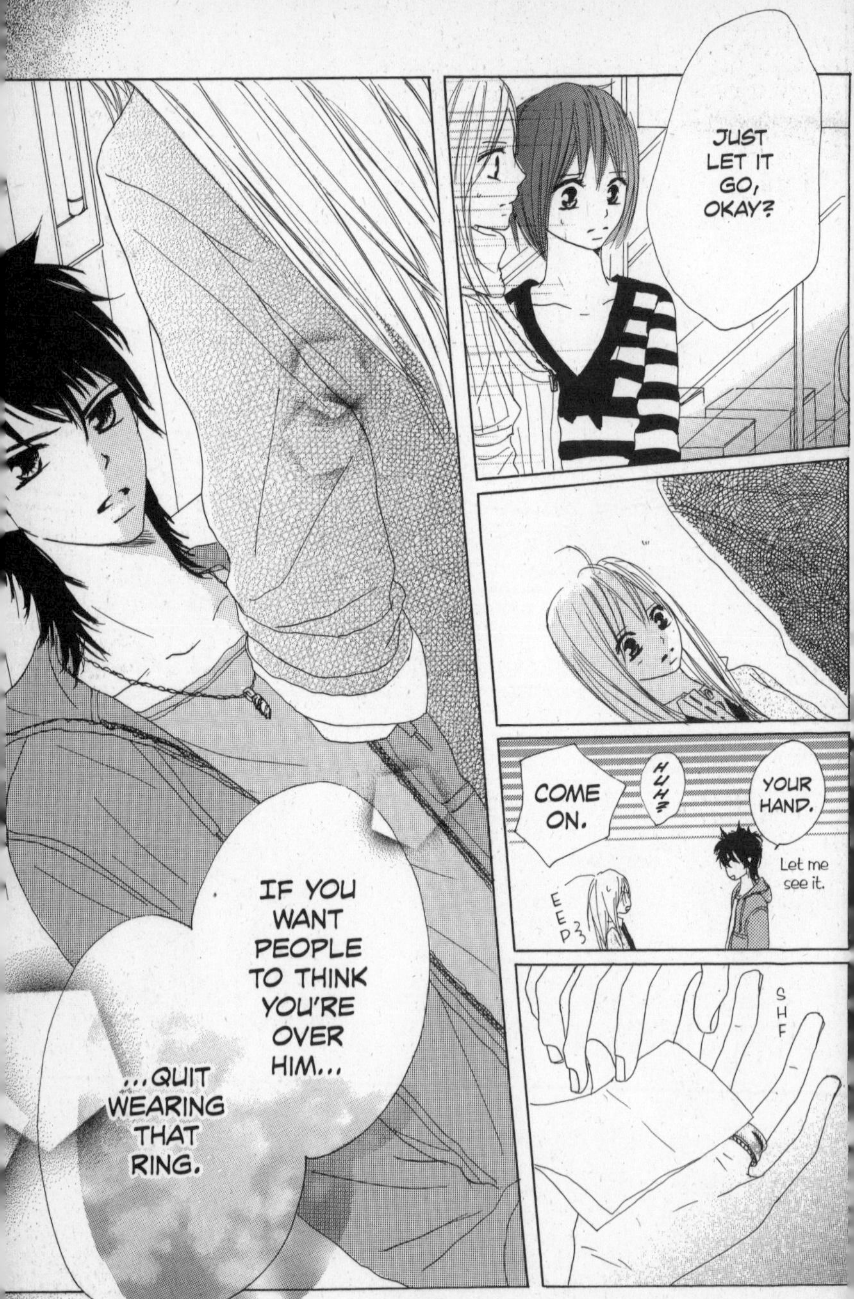
JUST LET IT GO, OKAY?
YOUR HAND.
Let me see it.
HUH?
COME ON.
EEP
SHF
IF YOU WANT PEOPLE TO THINK YOU'RE OVER HIM...
...QUIT WEARING THAT RING.

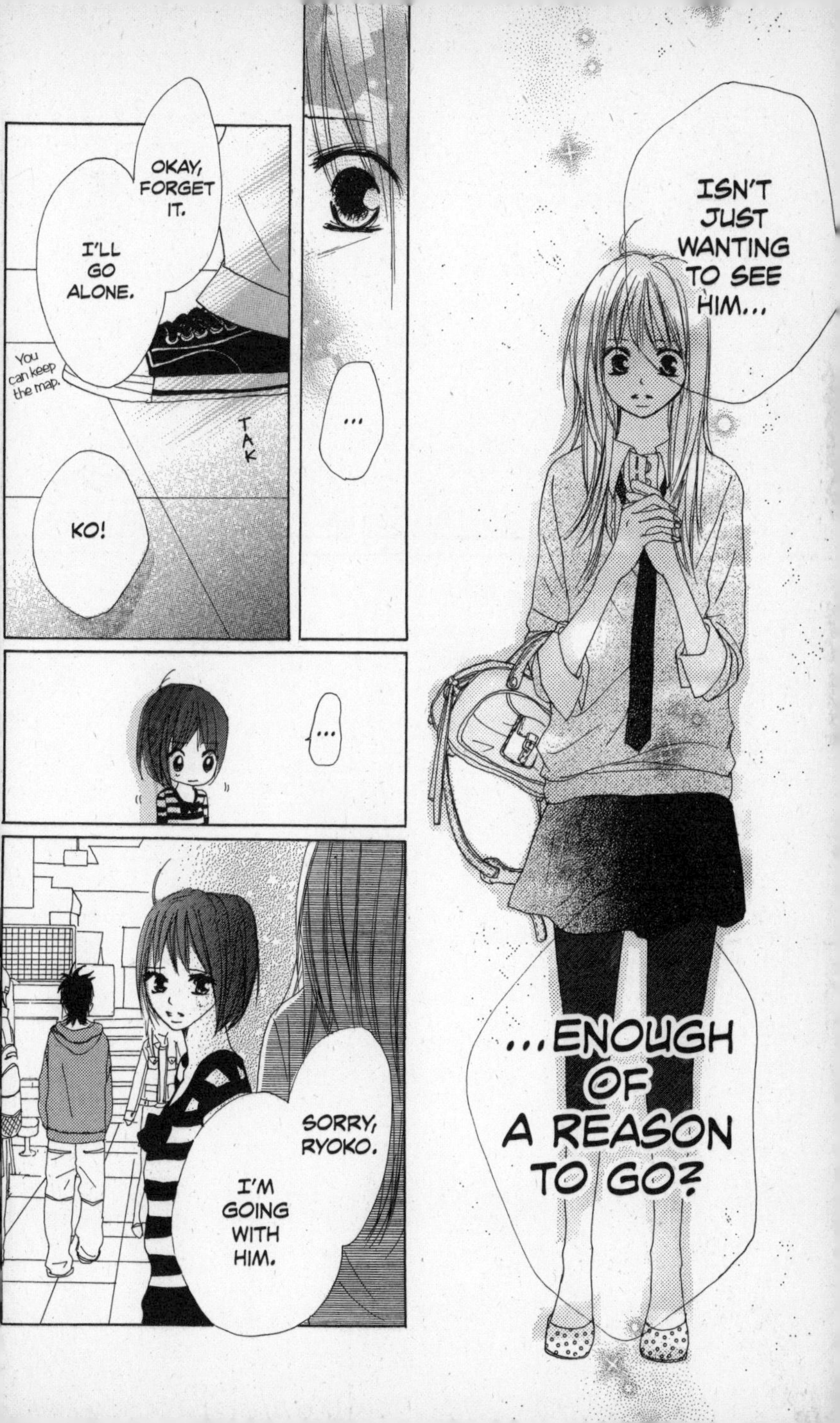
ISN'T JUST WANTING TO SEE HIM...
...ENOUGH OF A REASON TO GO?
...
OKAY, FORGET IT.
I'LL GO ALONE.
You can keep the map.
TAK
KO!
...
SORRY, RYOKO.
I'M GOING WITH HIM.

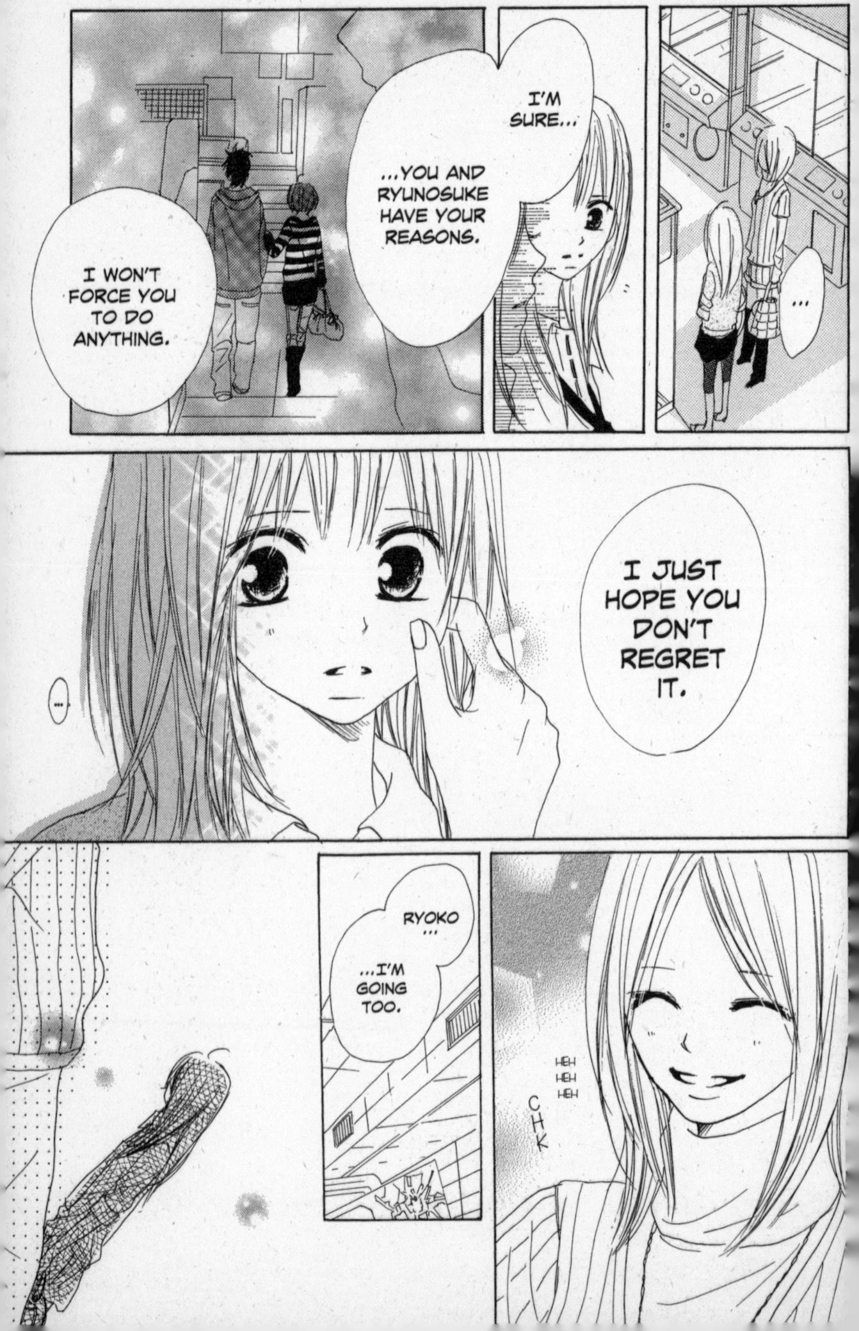
...
I'M SURE...
...YOU AND RYUNOSUKE HAVE YOUR REASONS.
I WON'T FORCE YOU TO DO ANYTHING.
I JUST HOPE YOU DON'T REGRET IT.
...
HEH HEH HEH
CHK
RYOKO...
...I'M GOING TOO.

ISN'T JUST WANTING TO SEE HIM ENOUGH OF A REASON TO GO?

YOU BOTH STILL LIKE EACH OTHER, SO WHY CAN'T YOU BE TOGETHER?

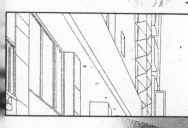

...SEE HIM AGAIN?

WHAT IF YOU NEVER...

I JUST HOPE YOU DON'T REGRET IT.

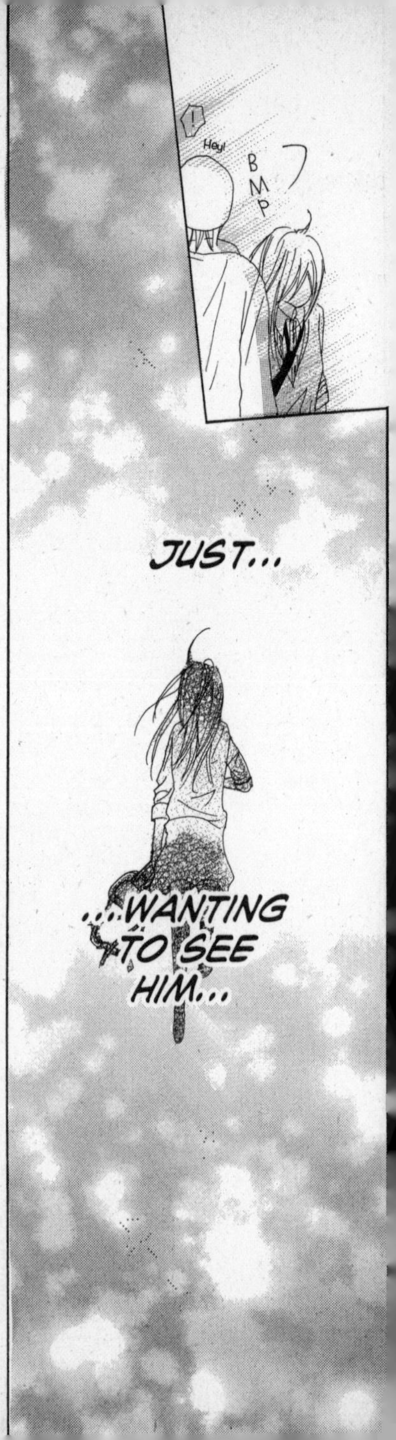
!
Hey!
BMP
JUST...
...WANTING TO SEE HIM...

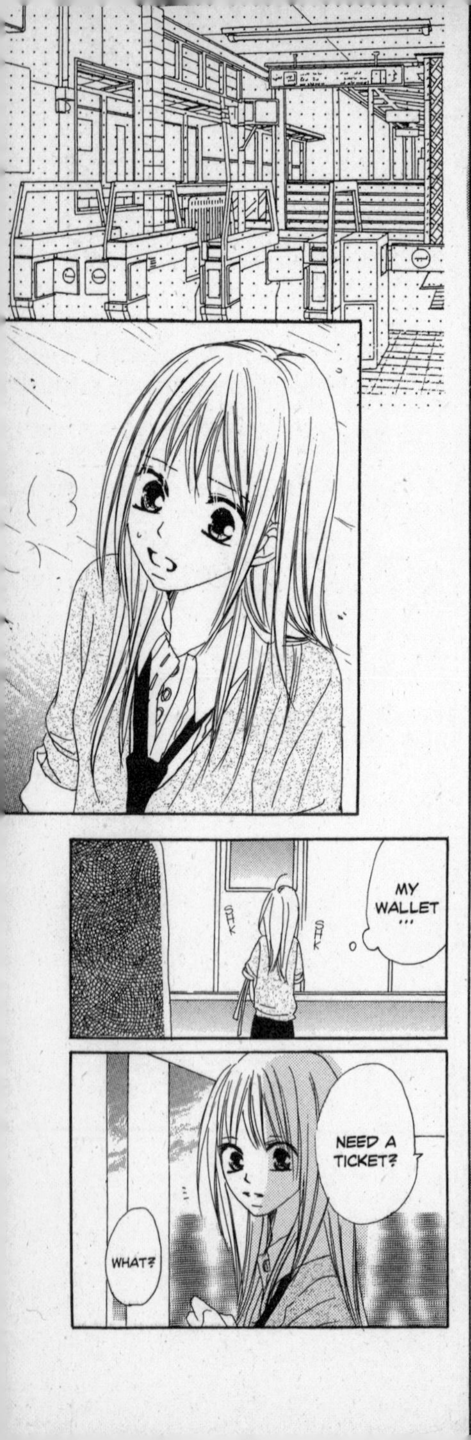
MY WALLET...
SHK
SHK
NEED A TICKET?
WHAT?

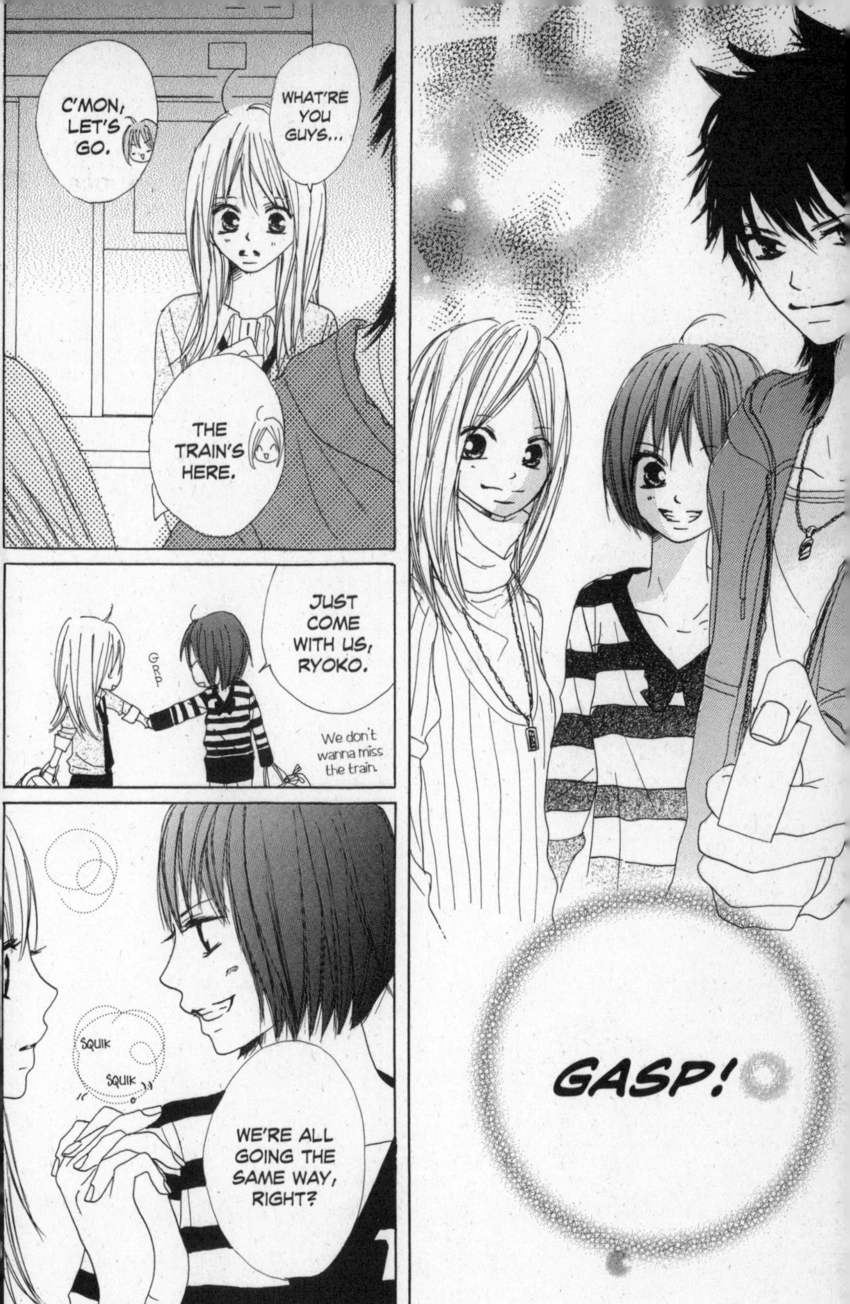
GASP!
WHAT'RE YOU GUYS...
C'MON, LET'S GO.
THE TRAIN'S HERE.
JUST COME WITH US, RYOKO.
GRP
We don't wanna miss the train.
WE'RE ALL GOING THE SAME WAY, RIGHT?
SQUIK
SQUIK

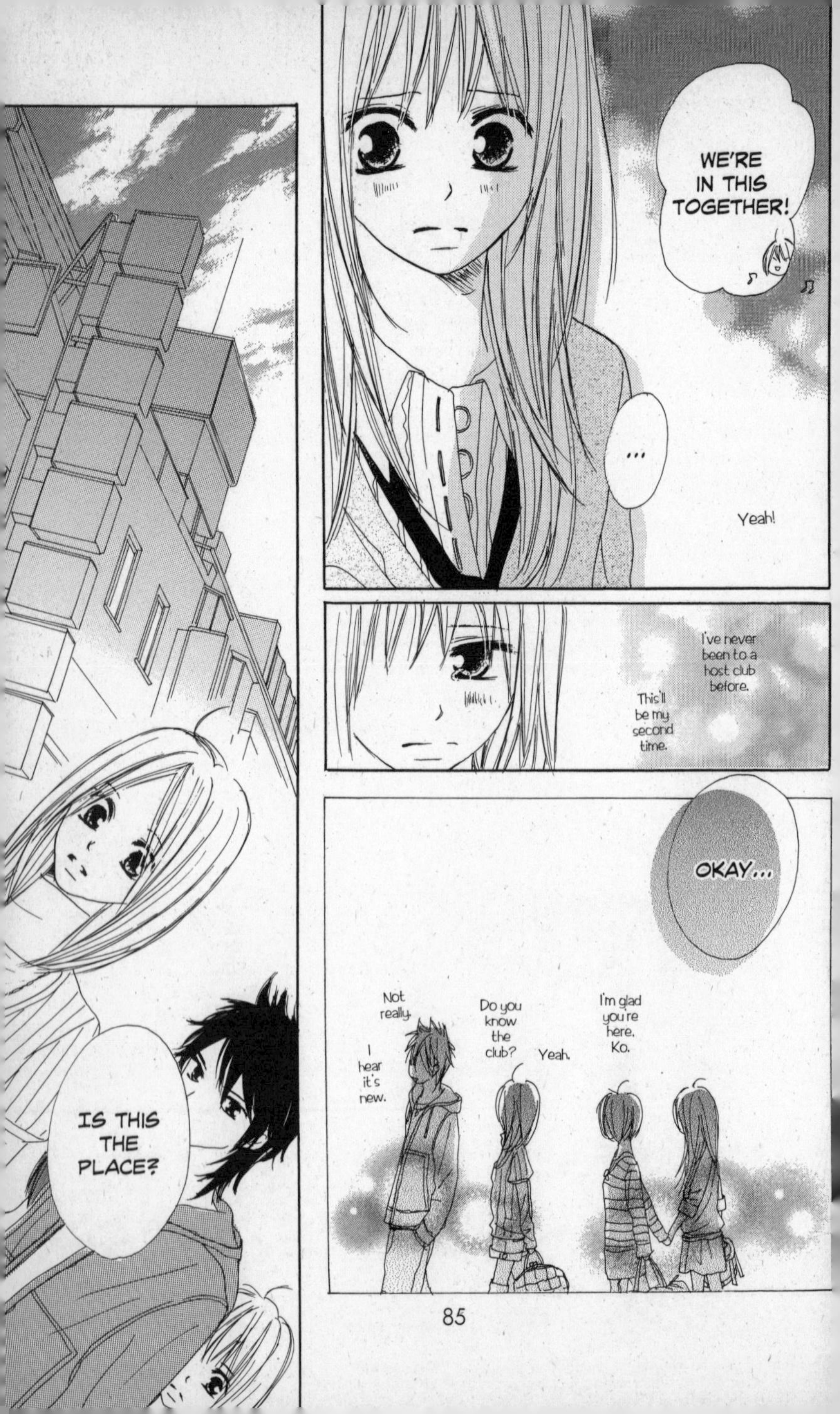
WE'RE IN THIS TOGETHER!
...
Yeah!
I've never been to a host club before.
This'll be my second time.
OKAY...
I'm glad you're here, Ko.
Yeah.
Do you know the club?
Not really.
I hear it's new.
IS THIS THE PLACE?

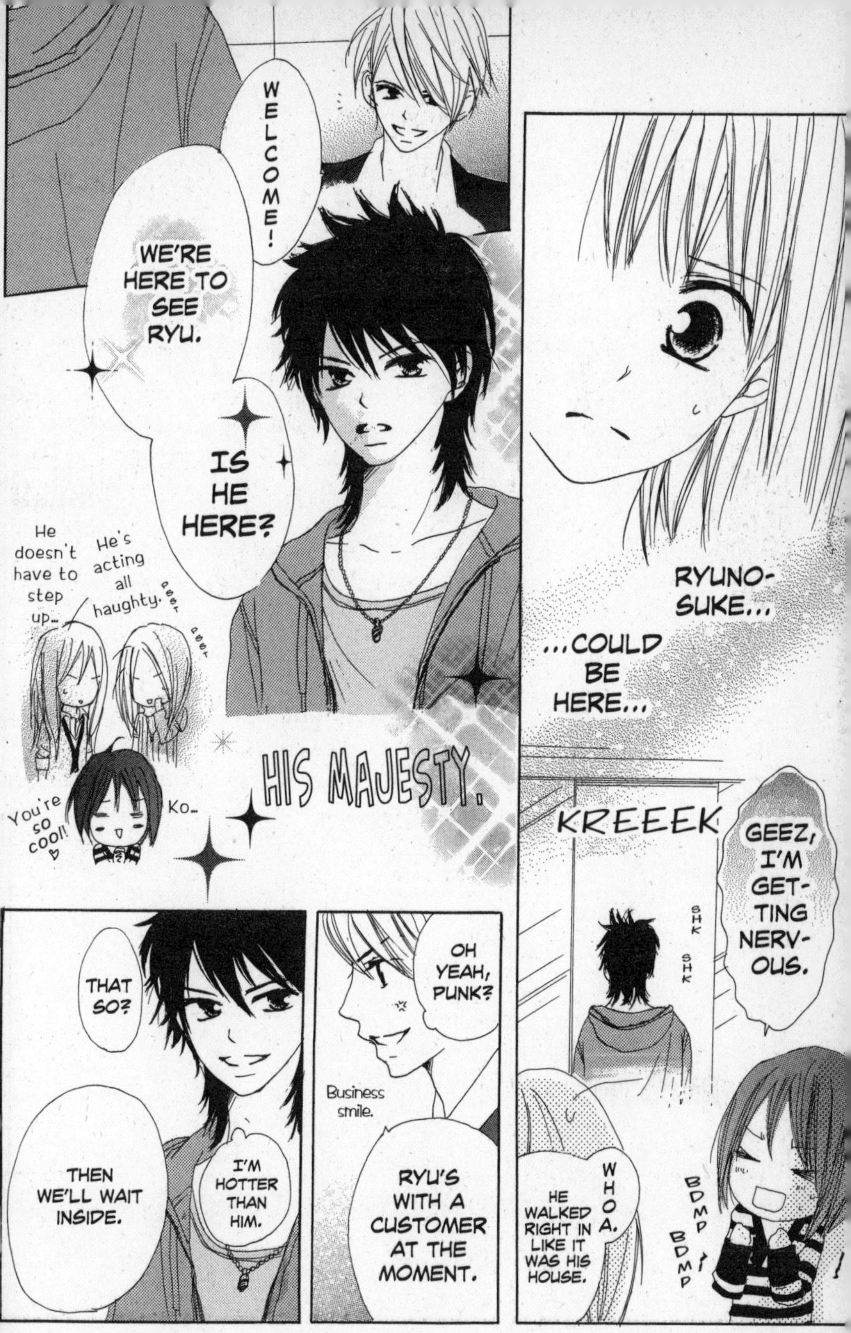
RYUNO-SUKE...
...COULD BE HERE...
KREEEK
GEEZ, I'M GET-TING NERV-OUS.
SHK SHK
WHOA.
HE WALKED RIGHT IN LIKE IT WAS HIS HOUSE.
BDMP BDMP
WELCOME!
WE'RE HERE TO SEE RYU.
IS HE HERE?
He's acting all haughty.
psst psst
He doesn't have to step up...
HIS MAJESTY.
Ko...
You're so cool! ♥
OH YEAH, PUNK?
Business smile.
RYU'S WITH A CUSTOMER AT THE MOMENT.
THAT SO?
I'M HOTTER THAN HIM.
THEN WE'LL WAIT INSIDE.

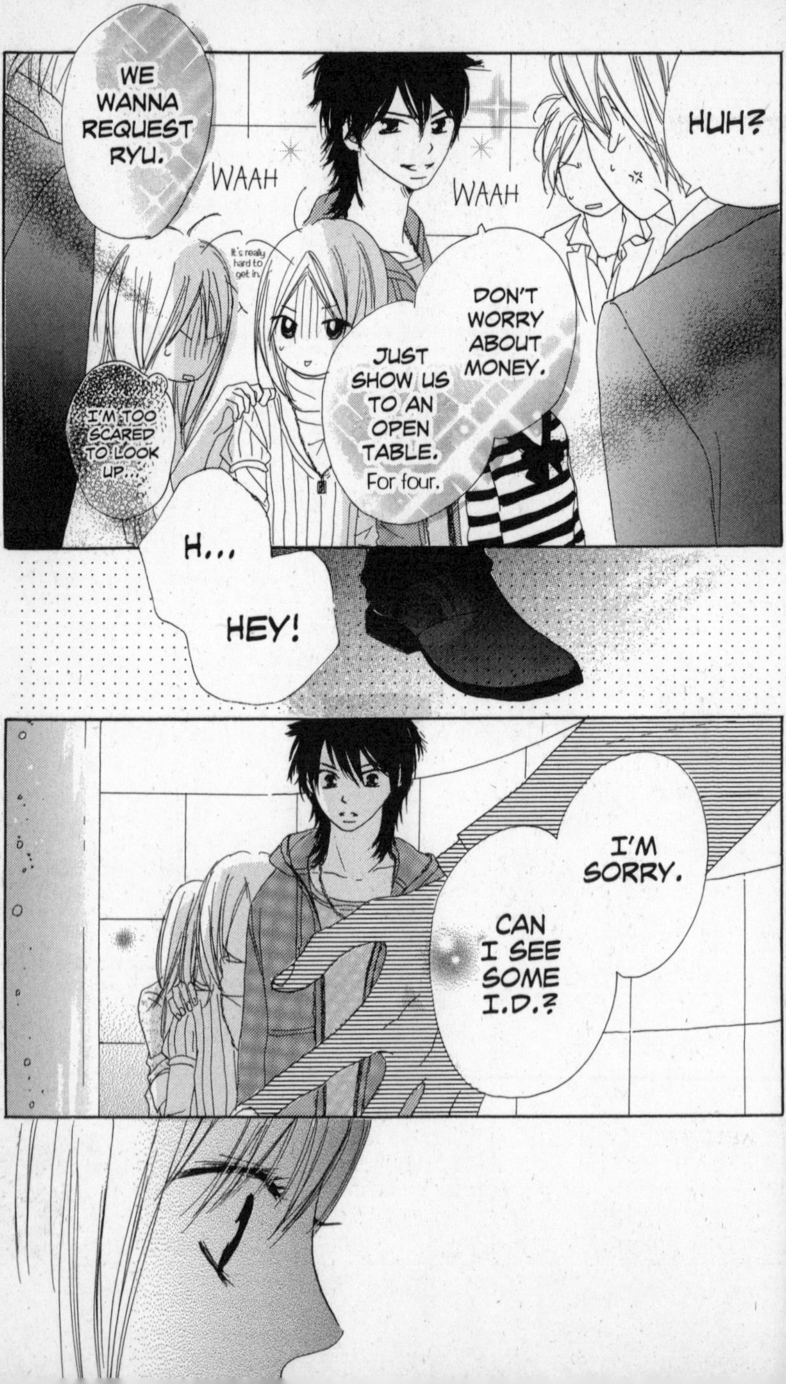
HUH?
WAAH
WE WANNA REQUEST RYU.
WAAH
DON'T WORRY ABOUT MONEY.
JUST SHOW US TO AN OPEN TABLE. For four.
It's really hard to get in.
I'M TOO SCARED TO LOOK UP...
H... HEY!
I'M SORRY.
CAN I SEE SOME I.D.?

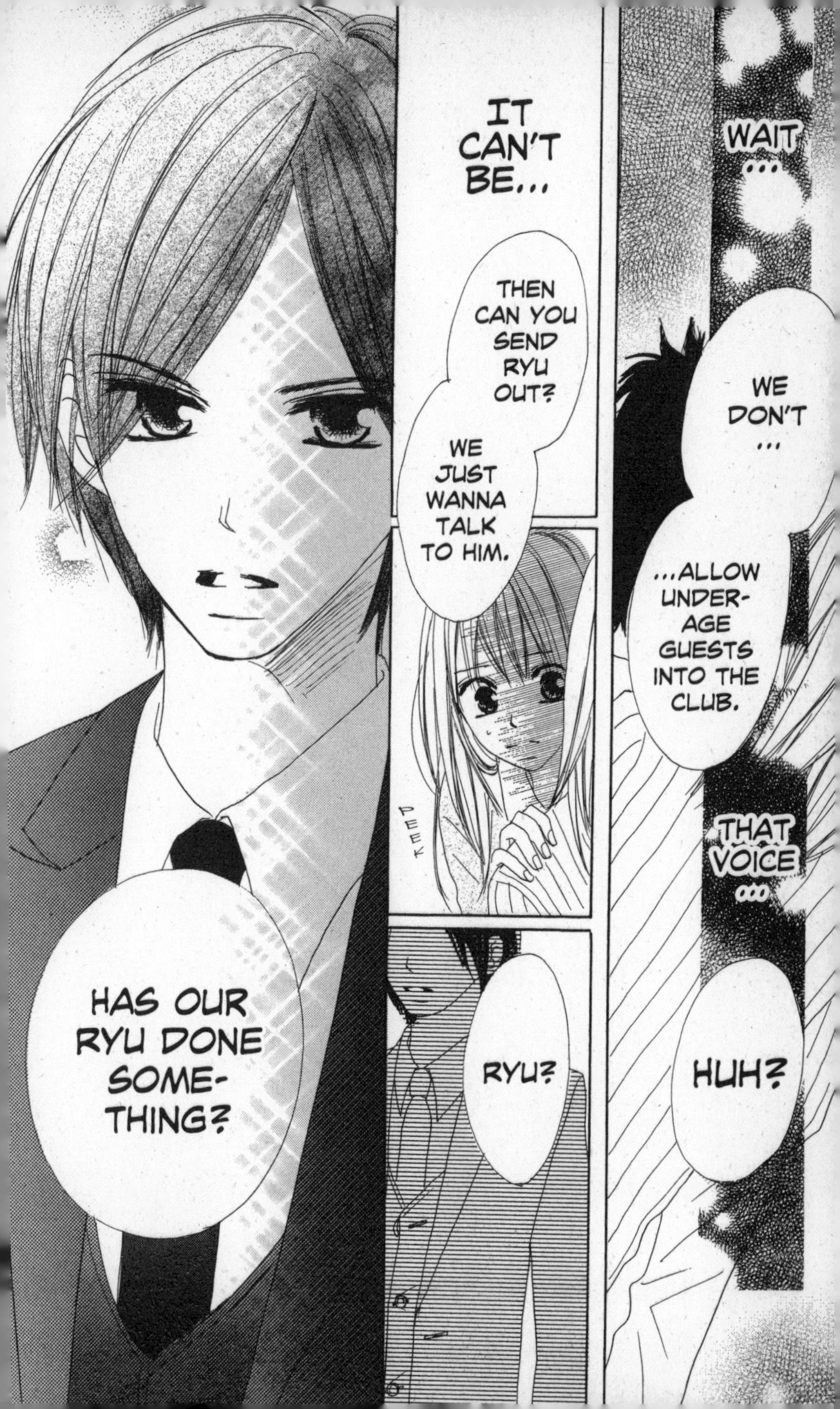
WAIT...
WE DON'T...
...ALLOW UNDER-AGE GUESTS INTO THE CLUB.
THAT VOICE...
HUH?
IT CAN'T BE...
THEN CAN YOU SEND RYU OUT?
WE JUST WANNA TALK TO HIM.
PEEK
RYU?
HAS OUR RYU DONE SOMETHING?

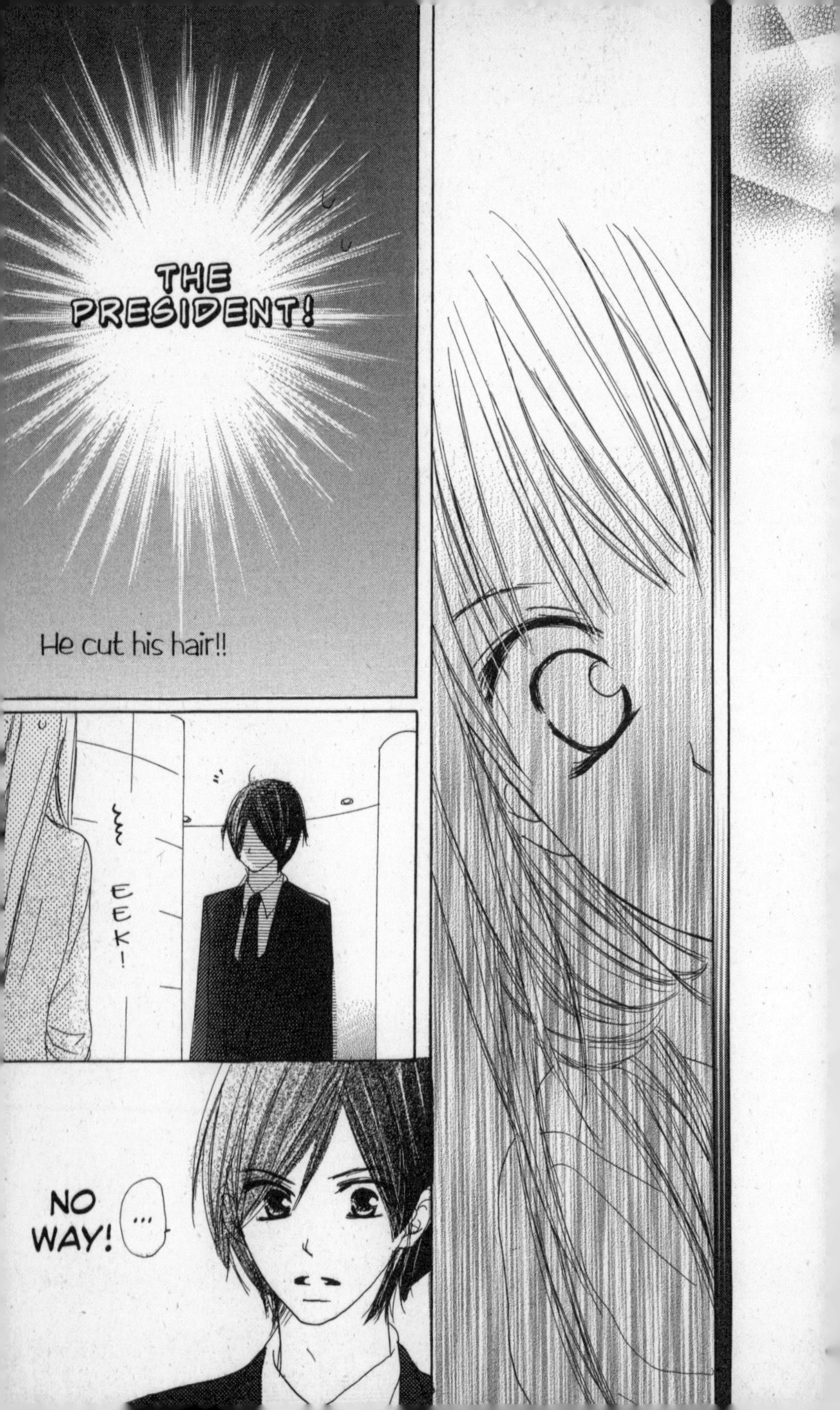
THE PRESIDENT!
He cut his hair!!
EEK!
NO WAY!
...

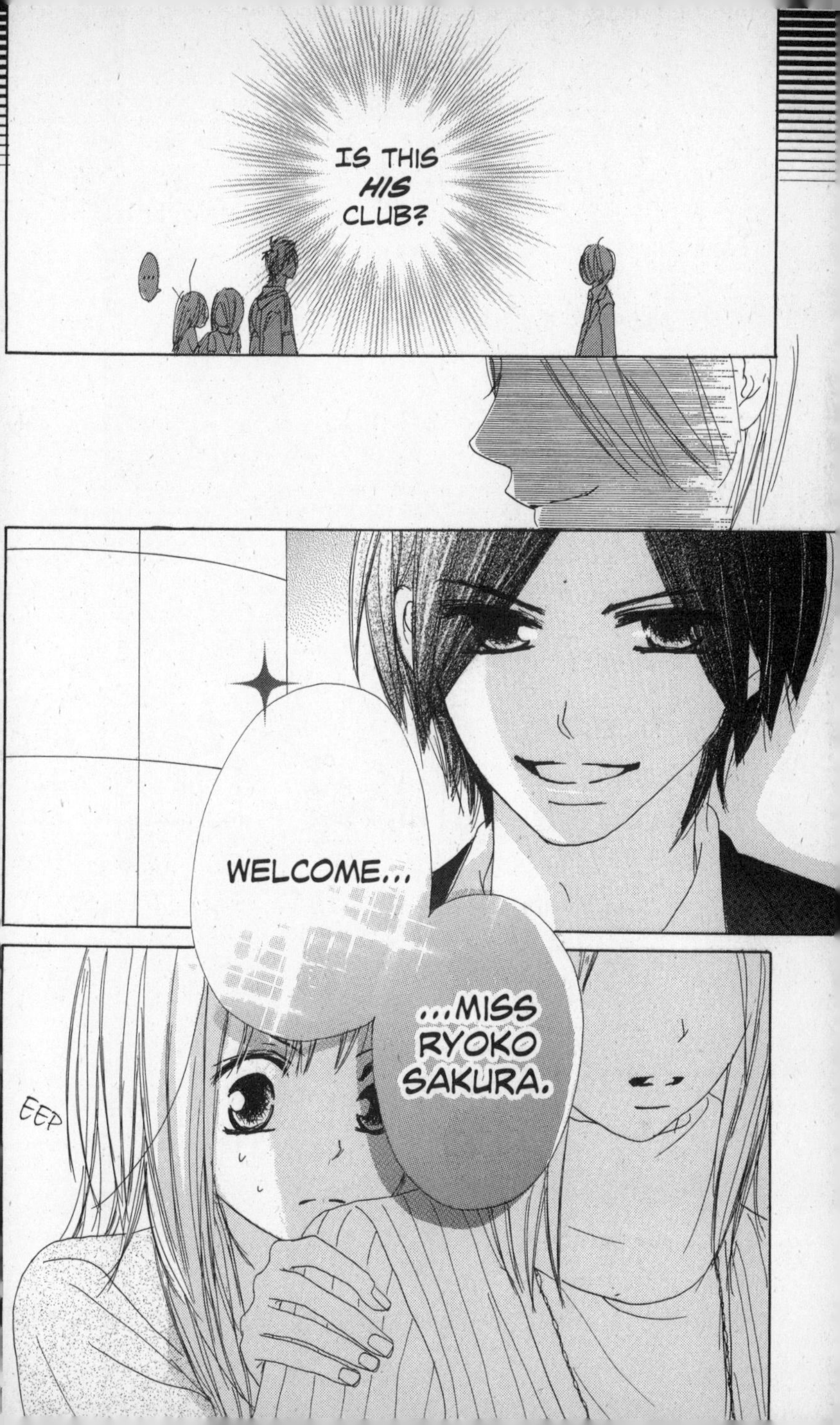
IS THIS *HIS* CLUB?
...
WELCOME...
...MISS RYOKO SAKURA.
EEP

Q&A Corner

I'd like to answer some of the most common questions I receive.

Q1: How do you come up with plots?

Writing the name.

…… …… ……

Cross-legged on chair

Paper and mechanical pencil

Cell

Basic Name Writing Style

A: Like this: I sit at my desk, completely still, and before I know it six hours have gone by. Between bouts of despair, I text Karuho Shiina and say…

"I can't do it!!!"

"This sucks!!"

I scream stuff like that. If that doesn't help, I cry until I feel better.

SNIFFLE

Last-ditch solutions…

I can't do it... anymore...

I won't make it in time...

Force myself to sleep.

Roll around.

OOF

OOF

OOF

Why? Why?

Why can't I do this? Arrgh!

wup wup

Fetal position.

Argh...

I can't do it... I won't make it in time...

How does this help?

How can I put this? ✦ It's not often I can say, "Yay! I've got an idea! It's going so smoothly!" In fact, that almost never happens to me… Maybe once in a while for a one-shot story? Nah… But if I keep thinking and thinking about it, I'll figure out something I can write. Or I'll stare at a blank sheet of paper until I come up with some lines.

When I *do* get an idea, for some reason I get really restless and start pacing around.

TUP

Yes! Aha!

TUP

I only got around to answering one question!!!

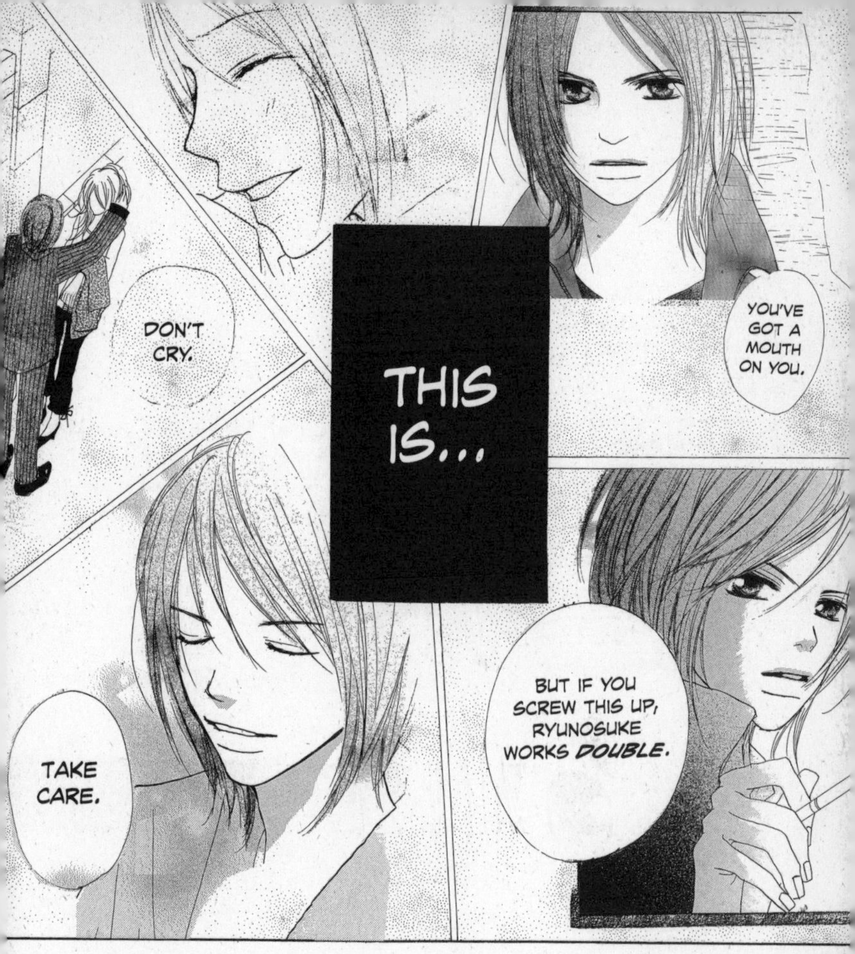
YOU'VE GOT A MOUTH ON YOU.
DON'T CRY.
THIS IS...
BUT IF YOU SCREW THIS UP, RYUNOSUKE WORKS *DOUBLE*.
TAKE CARE.

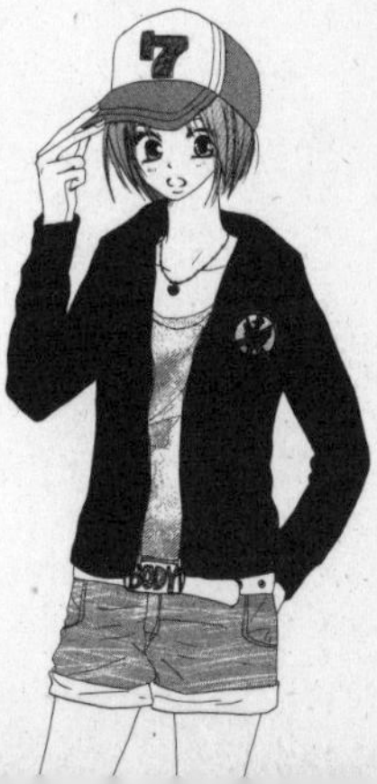

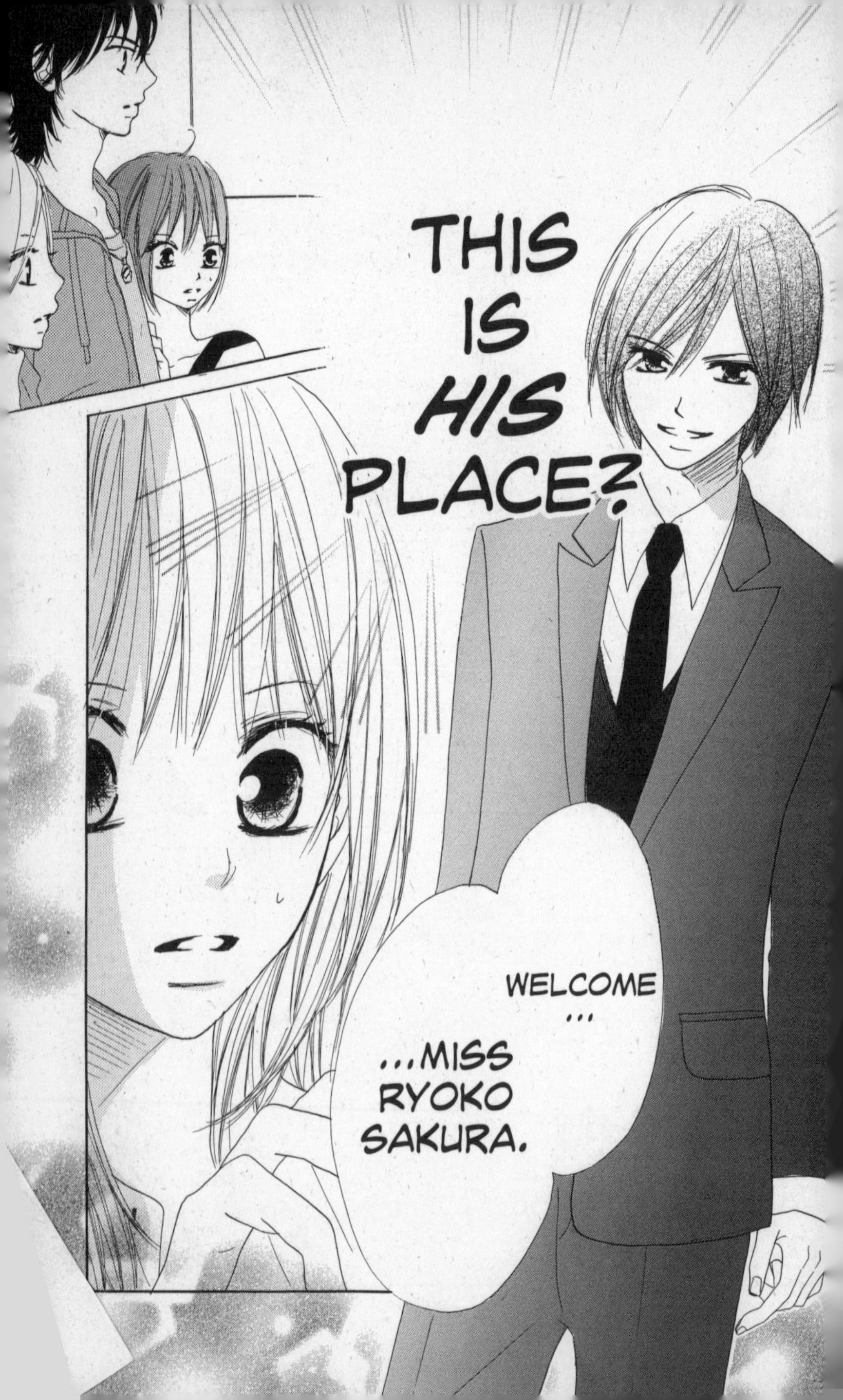
THIS IS HIS PLACE?
WELCOME ...
...MISS RYOKO SAKURA.

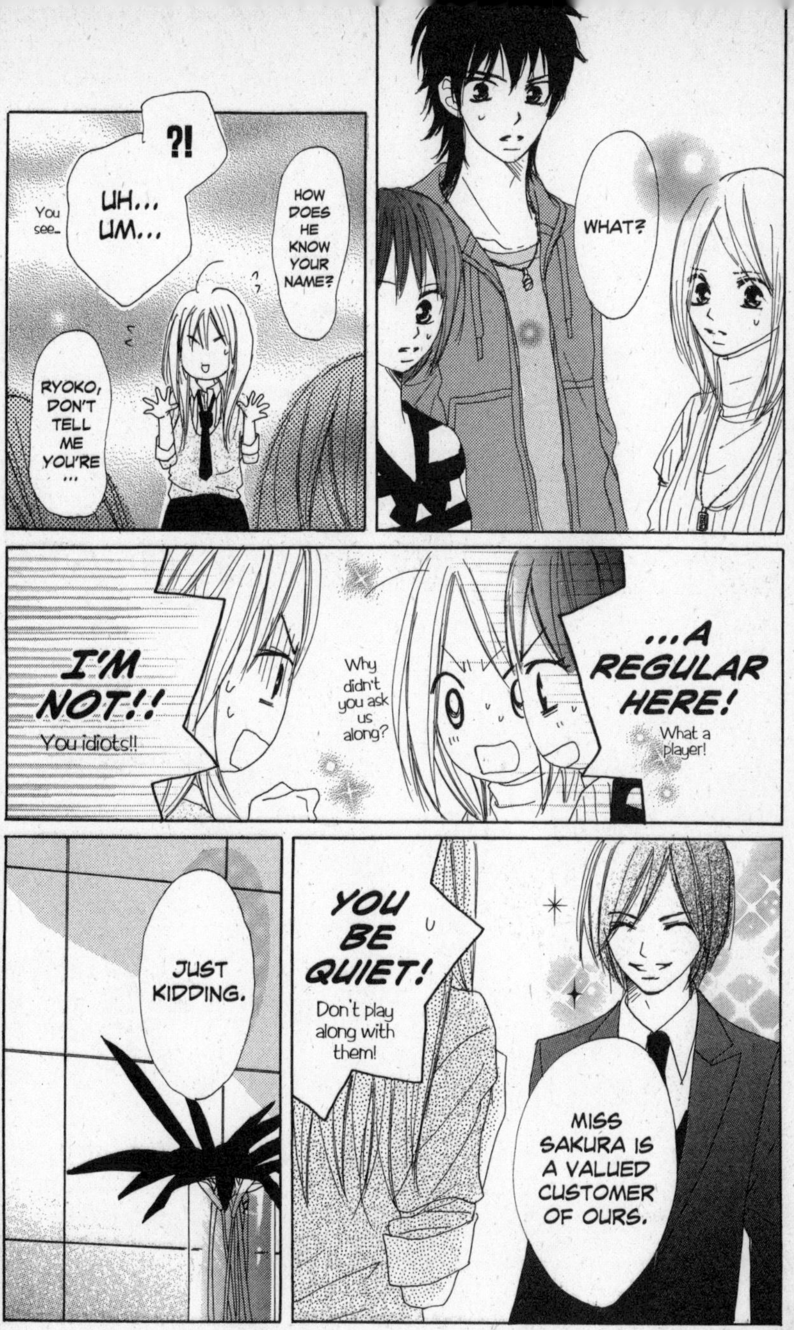
WHAT?
?!
HOW DOES HE KNOW YOUR NAME?
UH... UM...
You see...
RYOKO, DON'T TELL ME YOU'RE ...
...A REGULAR HERE!
What a player!
Why didn't you ask us along?
I'M NOT!!
You idiots!!
MISS SAKURA IS A VALUED CUSTOMER OF OURS.
YOU BE QUIET!
Don't play along with them!
JUST KIDDING.

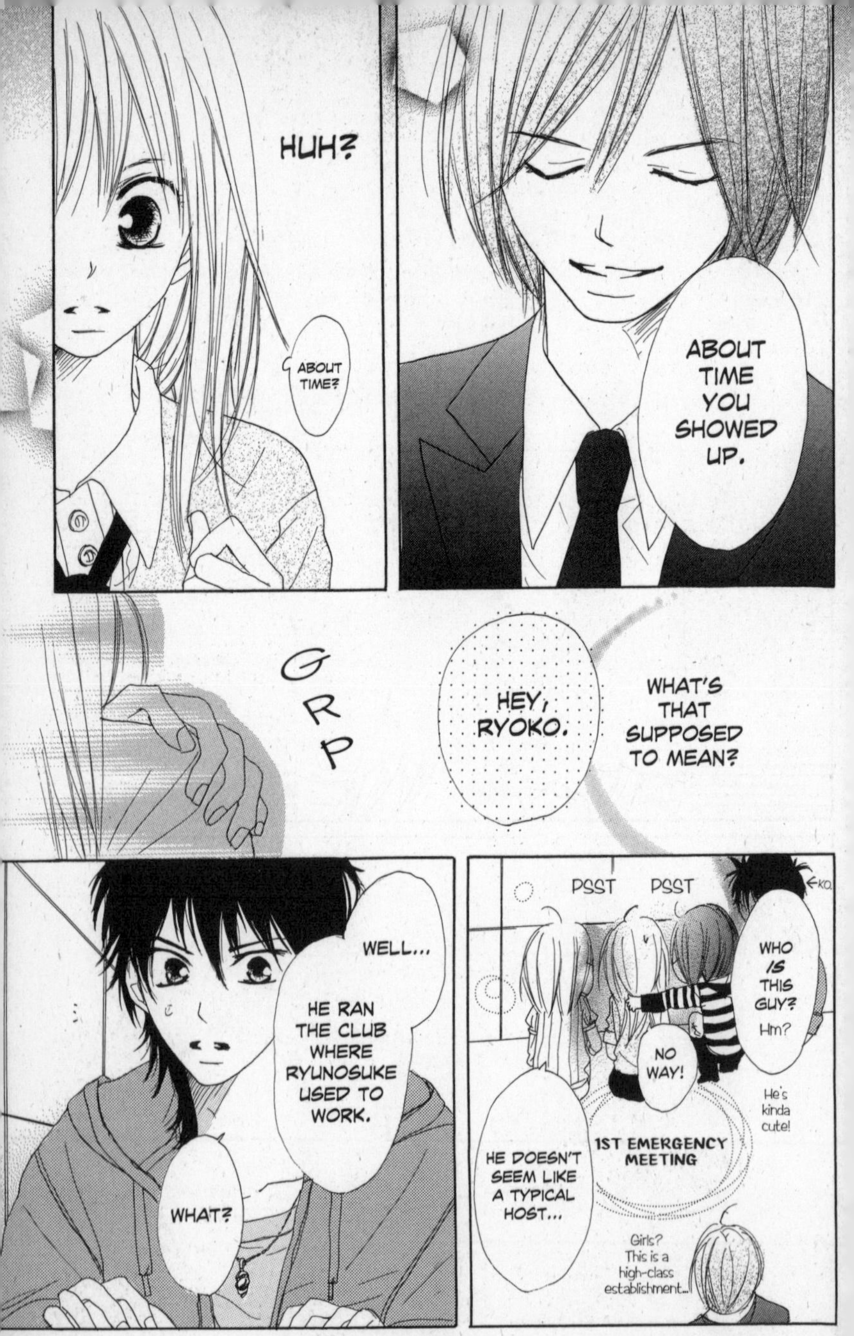
ABOUT TIME YOU SHOWED UP.
HUH?
ABOUT TIME?
WHAT'S THAT SUPPOSED TO MEAN?
HEY, RYOKO.
GRP
PSST
PSST
←KO.
WHO *IS* THIS GUY?
Hm?
NO WAY!
He's kinda cute!
1ST EMERGENCY MEETING
HE DOESN'T SEEM LIKE A TYPICAL HOST...
Girls? This is a high-class establishment...
WELL...
HE RAN THE CLUB WHERE RYUNOSUKE USED TO WORK.
WHAT?

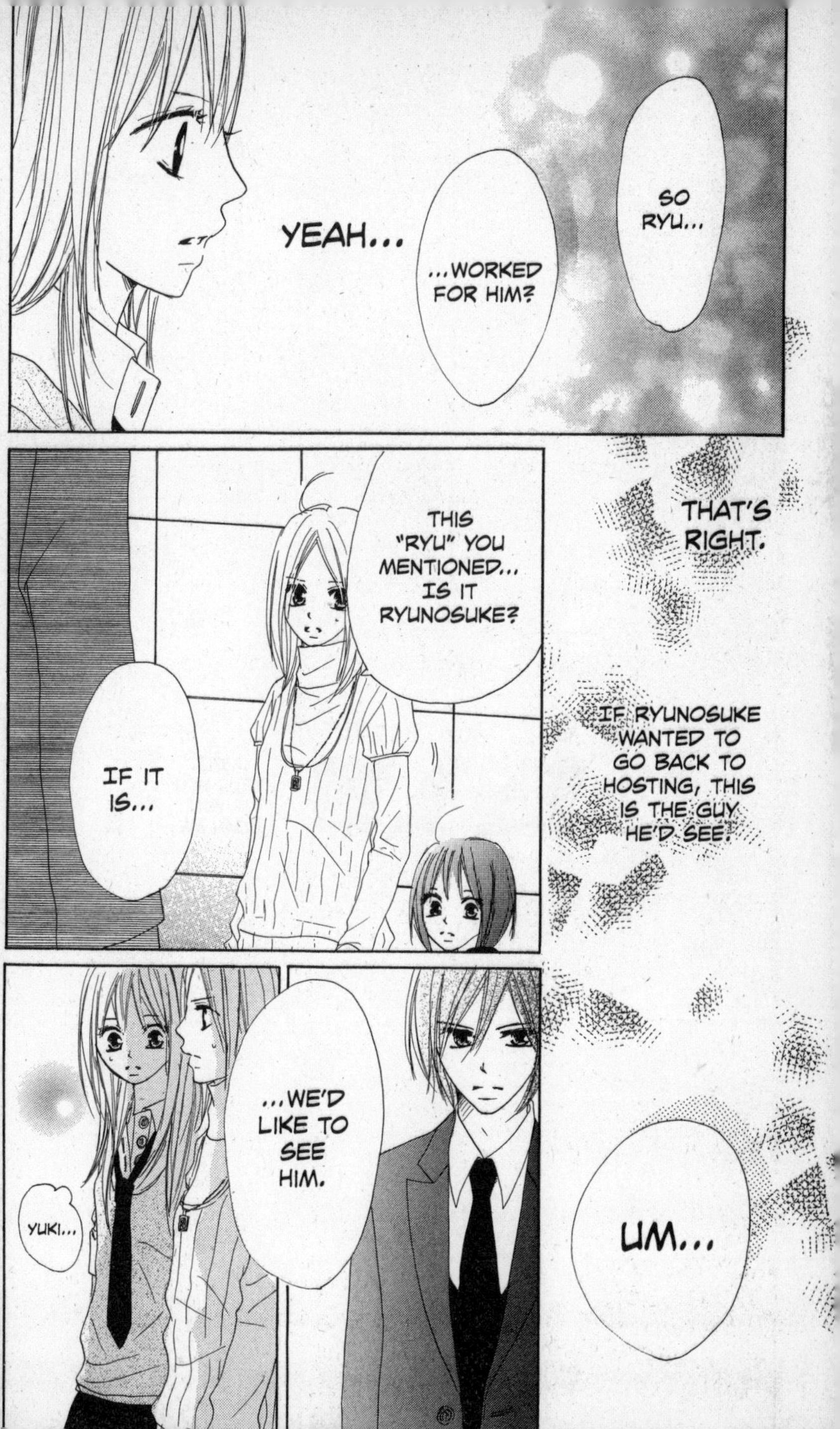
SO RYU...
...WORKED FOR HIM?
YEAH...
THAT'S RIGHT.
IF RYUNOSUKE WANTED TO GO BACK TO HOSTING, THIS IS THE GUY HE'D SEE.
THIS "RYU" YOU MENTIONED... IS IT RYUNOSUKE?
IF IT IS...
UM...
...WE'D LIKE TO SEE HIM.
YUKI...

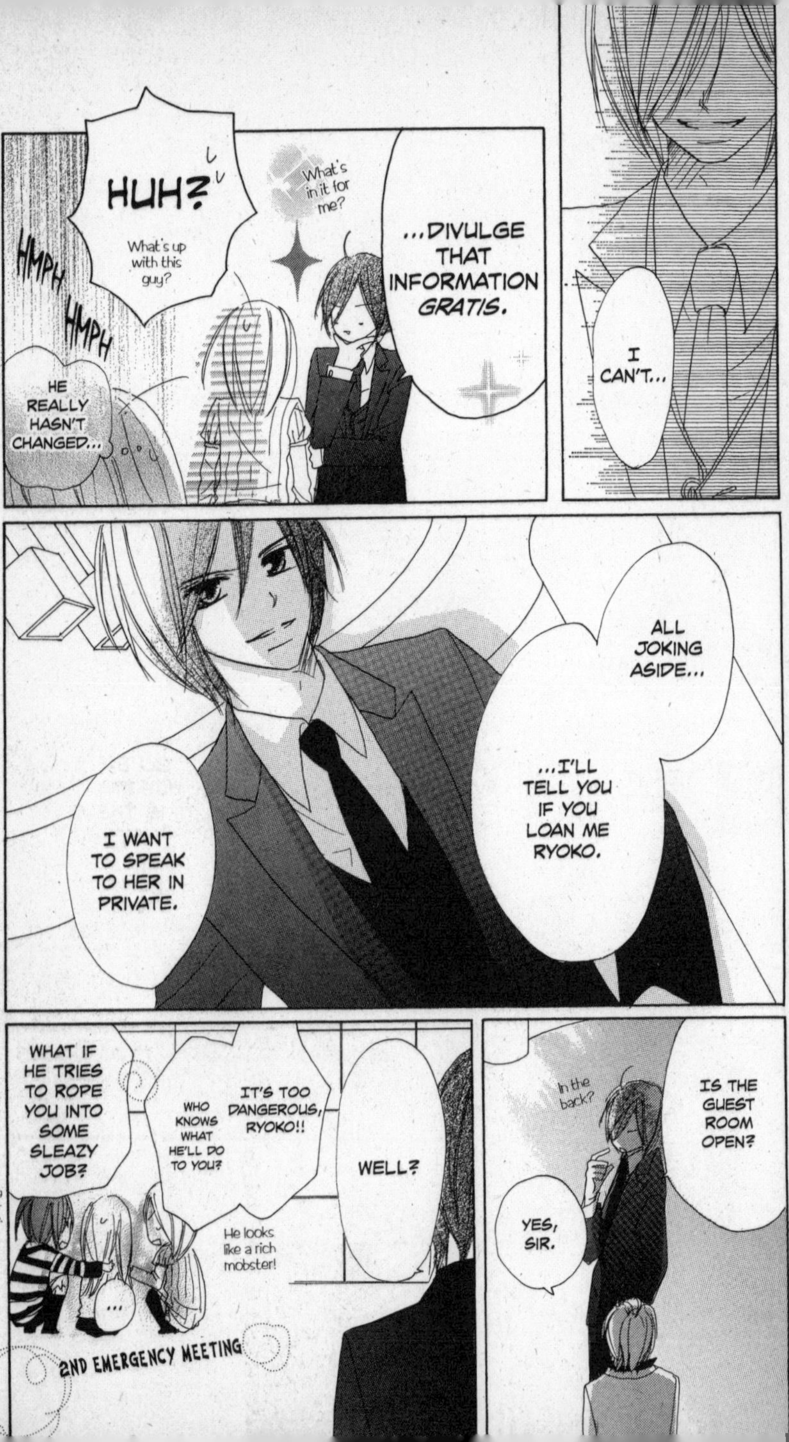
I CAN'T...
...DIVULGE THAT INFORMATION GRATIS.
What's in it for me?
HUH?
What's up with this guy?
HMPH HMPH
HE REALLY HASN'T CHANGED...
ALL JOKING ASIDE...
...I'LL TELL YOU IF YOU LOAN ME RYOKO.
I WANT TO SPEAK TO HER IN PRIVATE.
IS THE GUEST ROOM OPEN?
In the back?
YES, SIR.
WELL?
IT'S TOO DANGEROUS, RYOKO!!
WHO KNOWS WHAT HE'LL DO TO YOU?
WHAT IF HE TRIES TO ROPE YOU INTO SOME SLEAZY JOB?
He looks like a rich mobster!
...
2ND EMERGENCY MEETING
Speaking from experience.

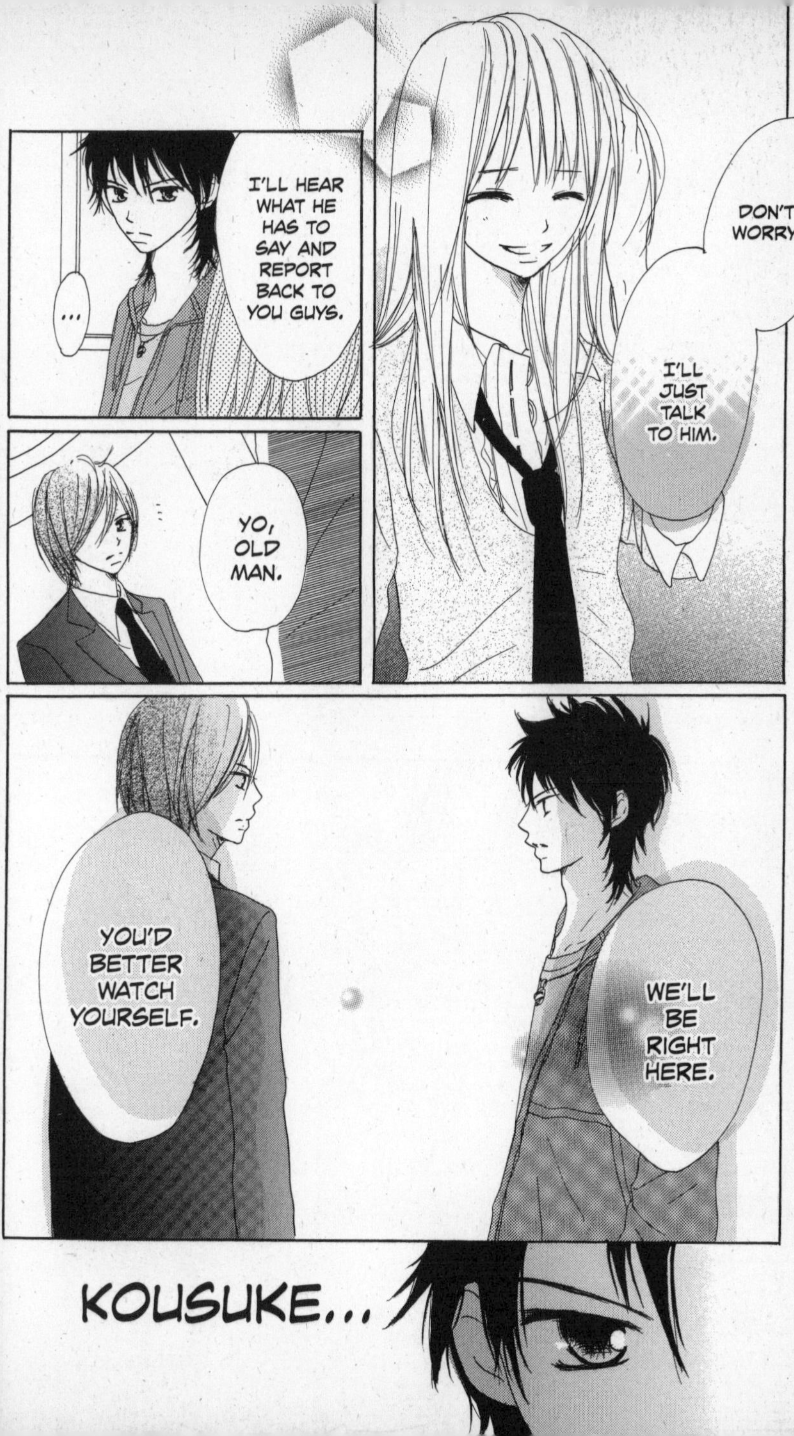
DON'T WORRY.
I'LL JUST TALK TO HIM.
I'LL HEAR WHAT HE HAS TO SAY AND REPORT BACK TO YOU GUYS.
...
YO, OLD MAN.
WE'LL BE RIGHT HERE.
YOU'D BETTER WATCH YOURSELF.
KOUSUKE...

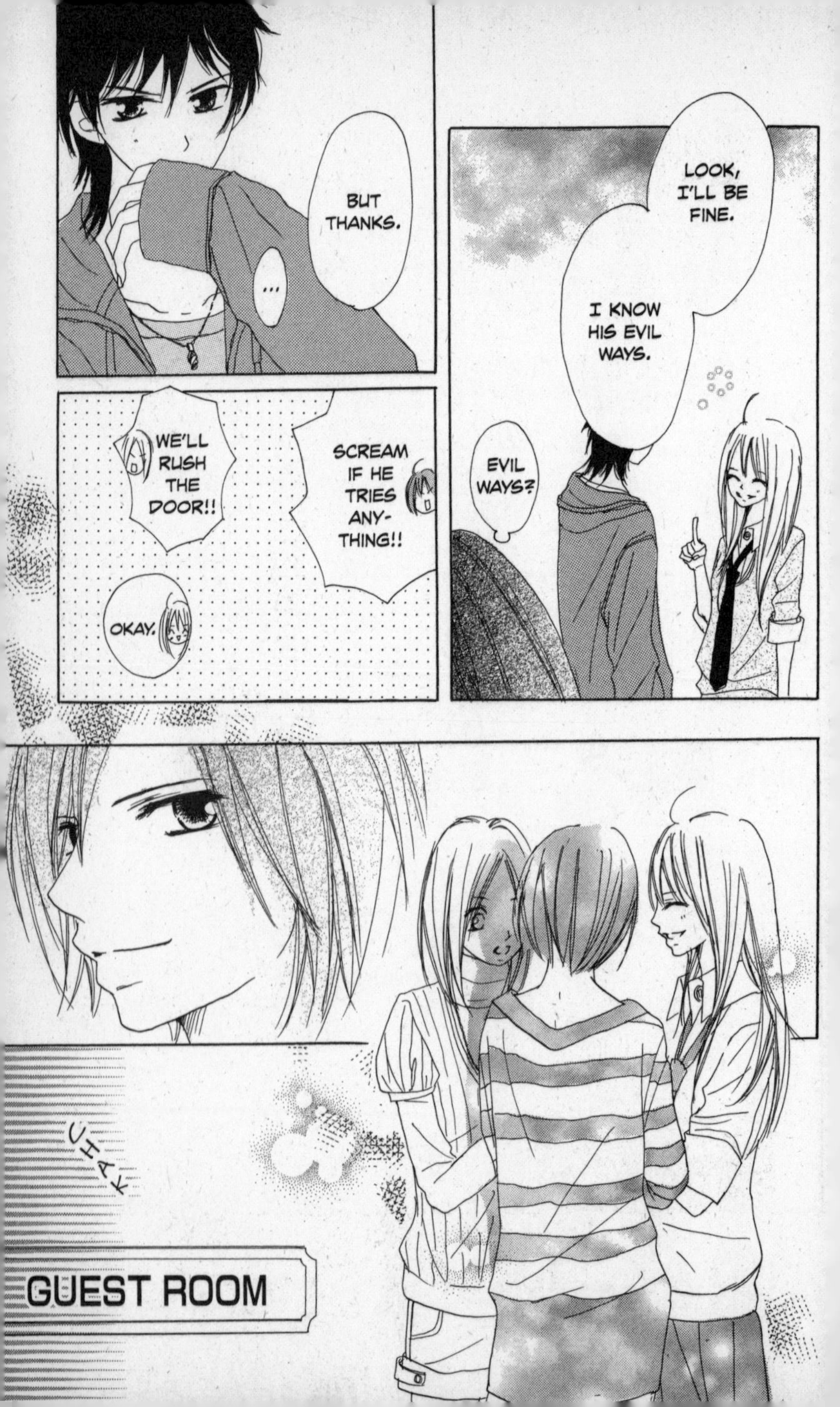
LOOK, I'LL BE FINE.
I KNOW HIS EVIL WAYS.
EVIL WAYS?
BUT THANKS.
...
SCREAM IF HE TRIES ANYTHING!!
WE'LL RUSH THE DOOR!!
OKAY.
CHAK
GUEST ROOM

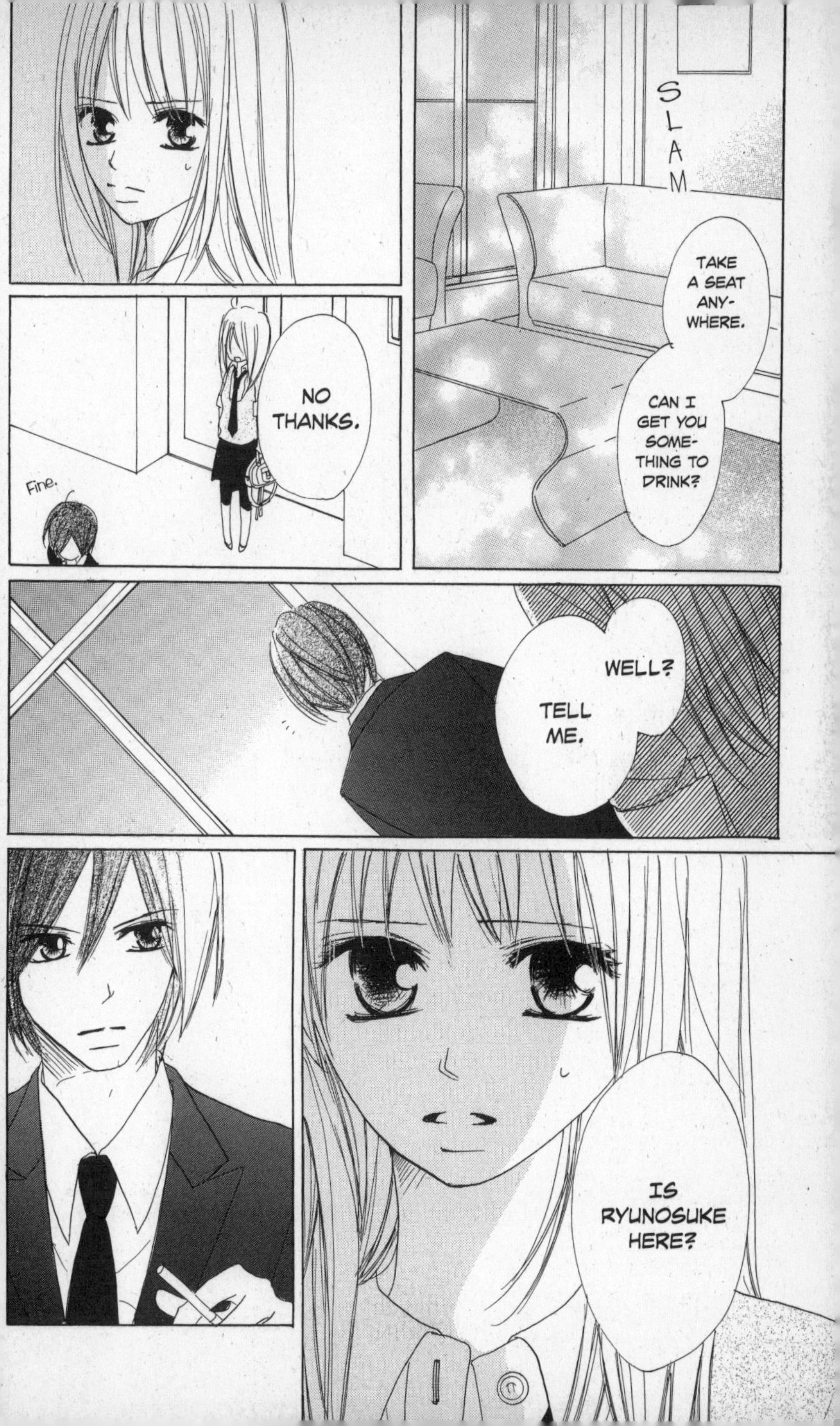
SLAM
TAKE A SEAT ANYWHERE.
CAN I GET YOU SOMETHING TO DRINK?
NO THANKS.
Fine.
WELL?
TELL ME.
IS RYUNOSUKE HERE?

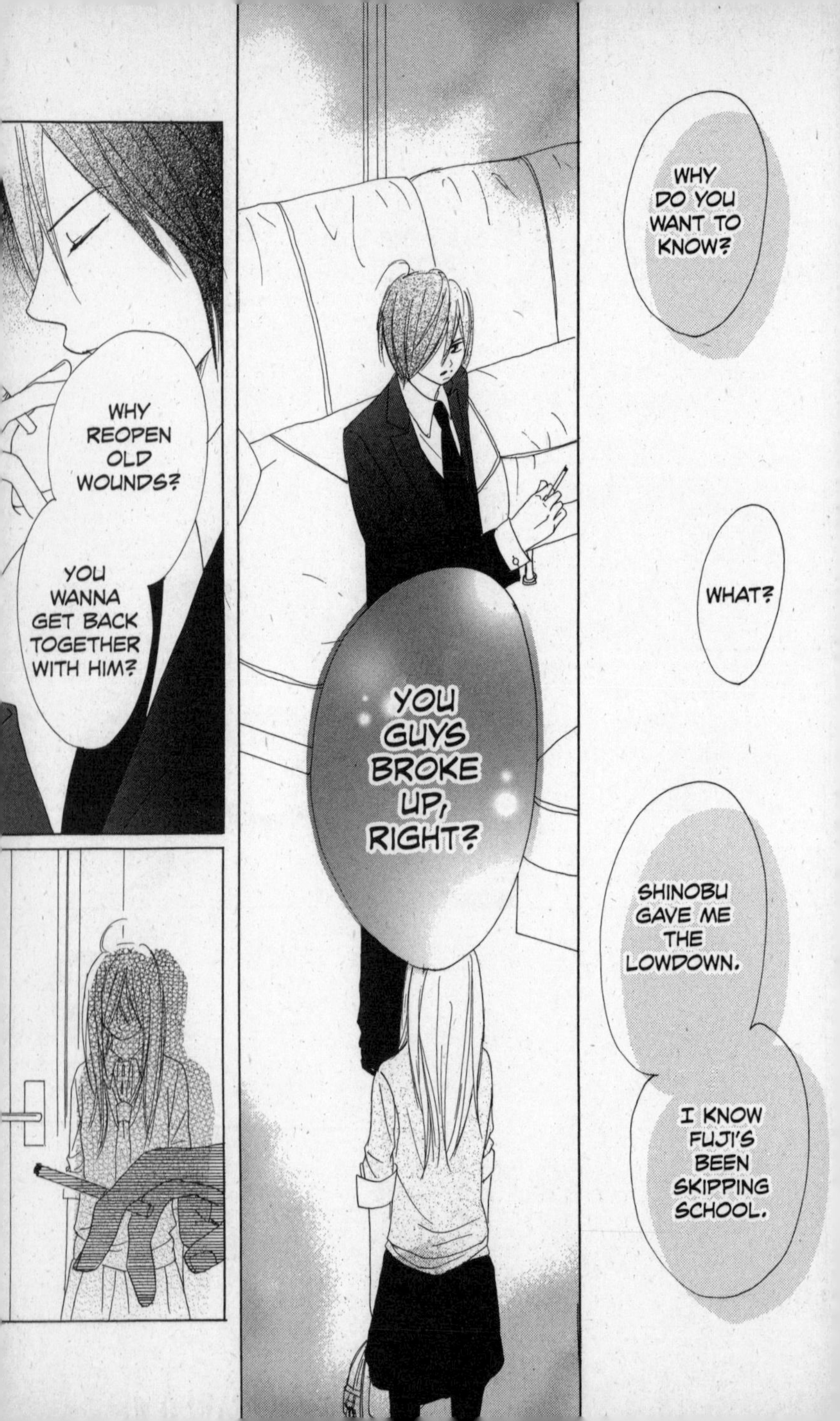
WHY DO YOU WANT TO KNOW?
WHAT?
SHINOBU GAVE ME THE LOWDOWN.
I KNOW FUJI'S BEEN SKIPPING SCHOOL.
YOU GUYS BROKE UP, RIGHT?
WHY REOPEN OLD WOUNDS?
YOU WANNA GET BACK TOGETHER WITH HIM?

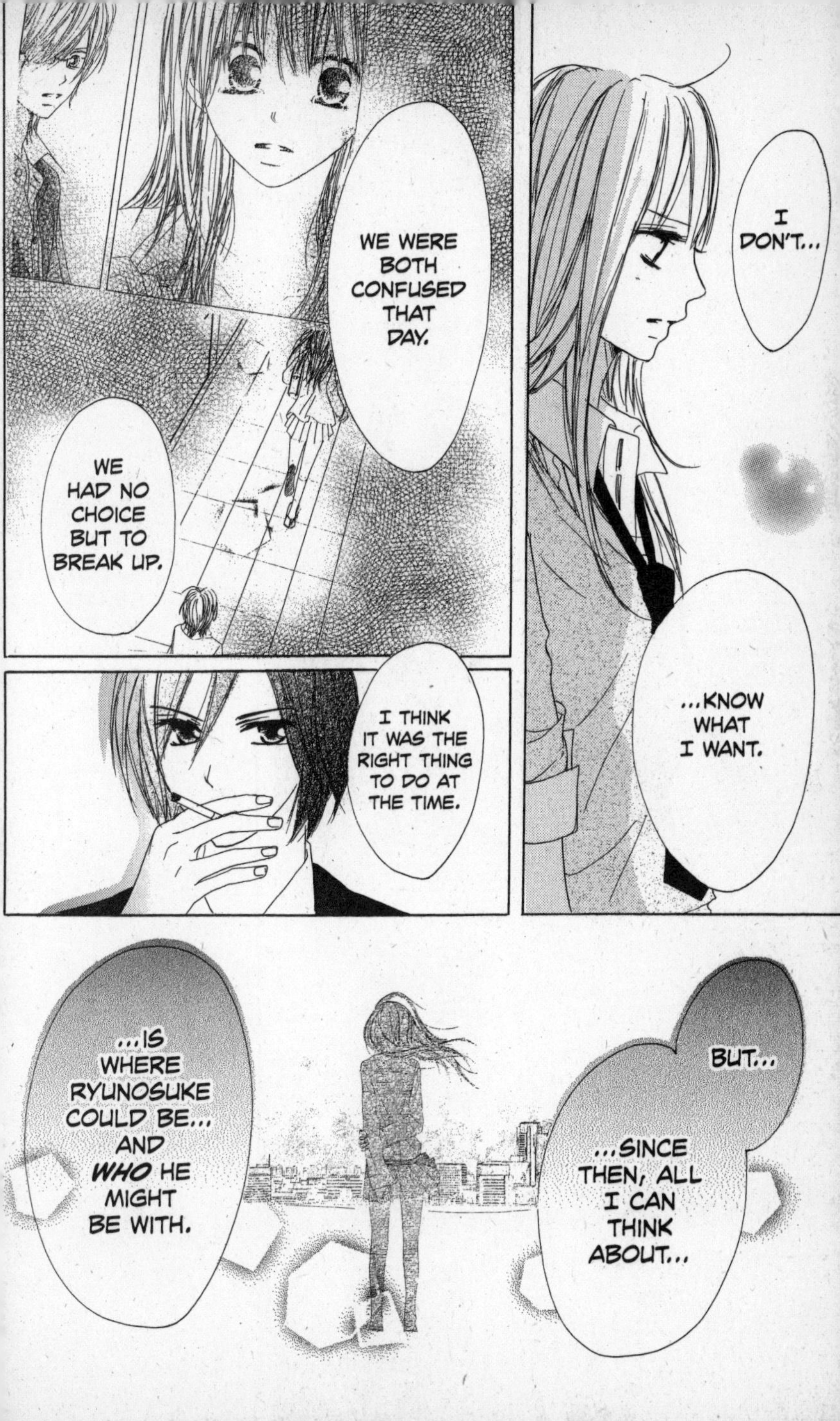
I DON'T...
...KNOW WHAT I WANT.
WE WERE BOTH CONFUSED THAT DAY.
WE HAD NO CHOICE BUT TO BREAK UP.
I THINK IT WAS THE RIGHT THING TO DO AT THE TIME.
BUT...
...SINCE THEN, ALL I CAN THINK ABOUT...
...IS WHERE RYUNOSUKE COULD BE... AND *WHO* HE MIGHT BE WITH.

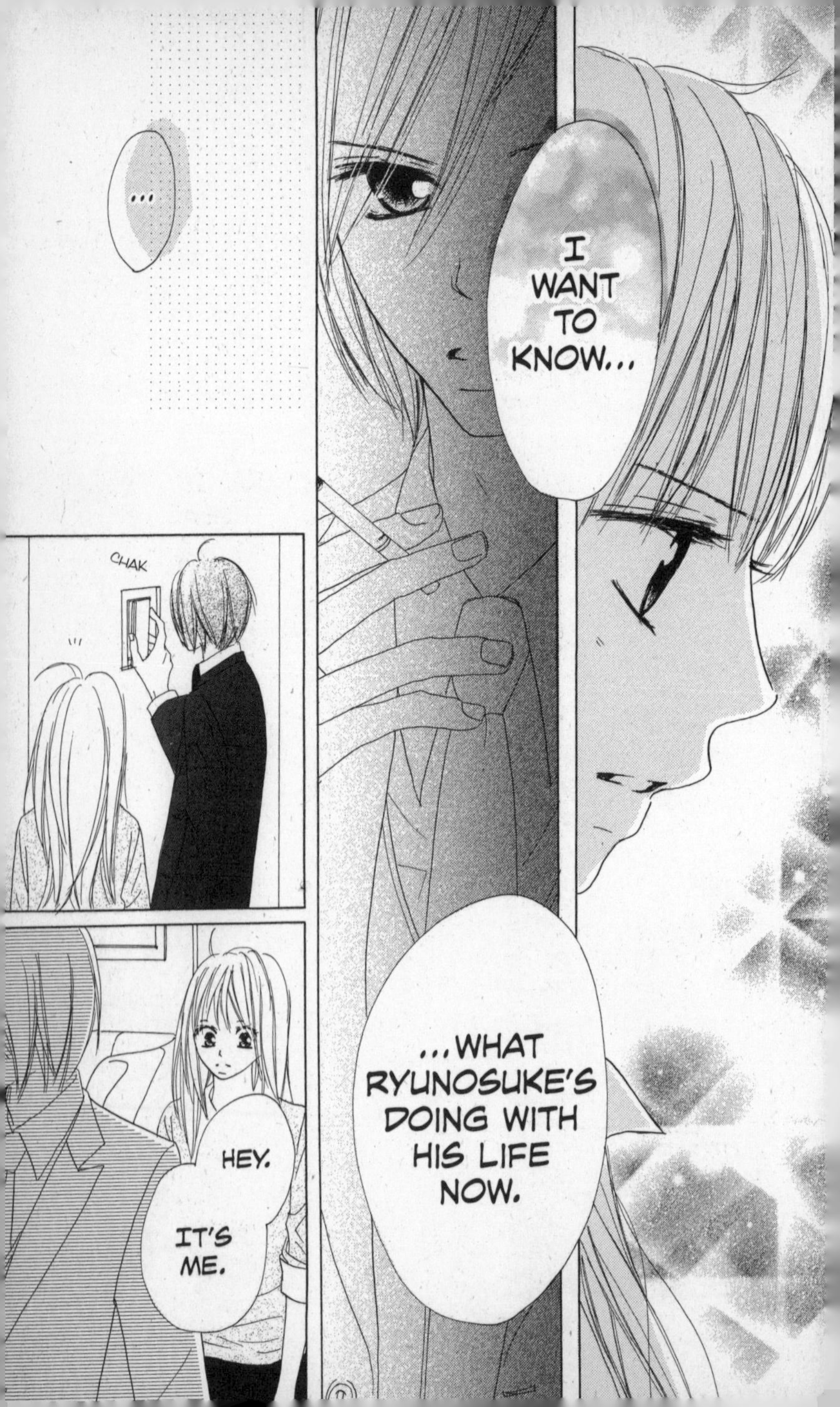

I WANT TO KNOW...
...WHAT RYUNOSUKE'S DOING WITH HIS LIFE NOW.
...
CHAK
HEY.
IT'S ME.

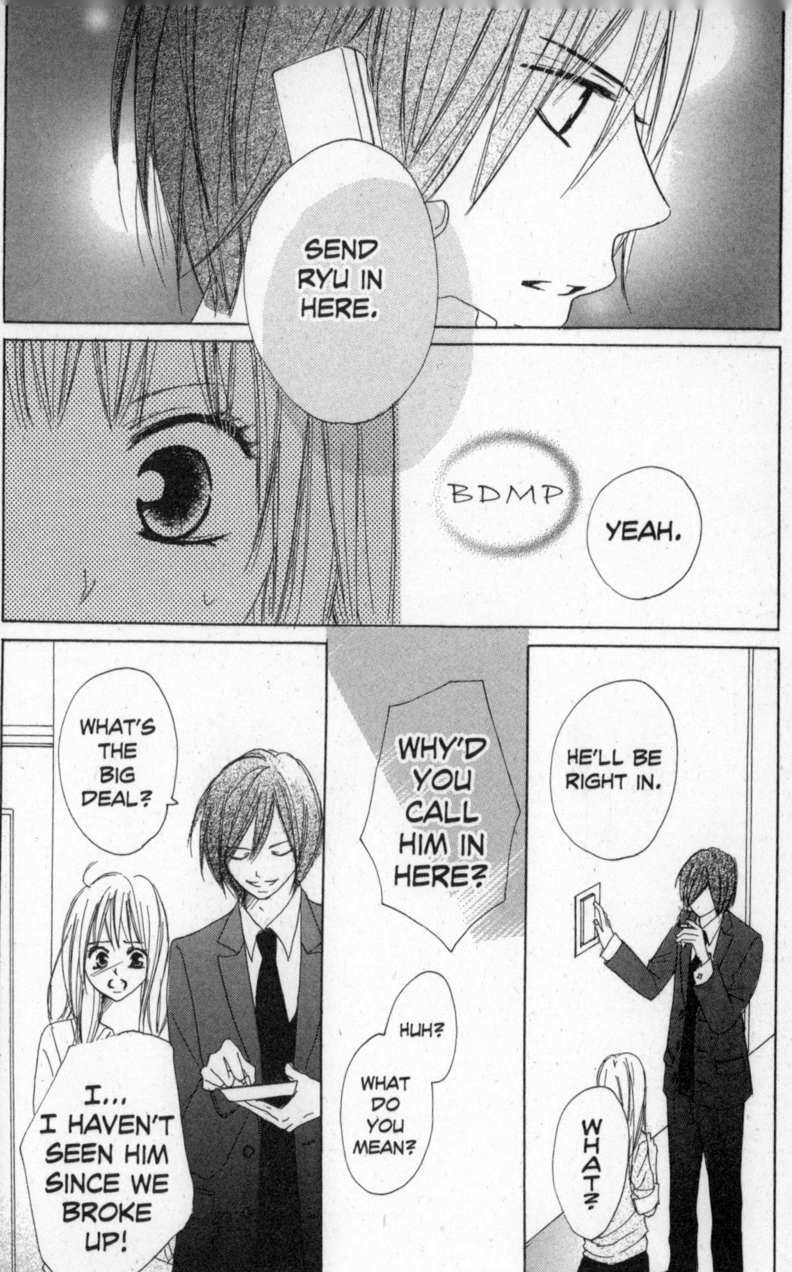
SEND RYU IN HERE.
YEAH.
BDMP
HE'LL BE RIGHT IN.
WHAT?
WHY'D YOU CALL HIM IN HERE?
HUH?
WHAT DO YOU MEAN?
WHAT'S THE BIG DEAL?
I... I HAVEN'T SEEN HIM SINCE WE BROKE UP!

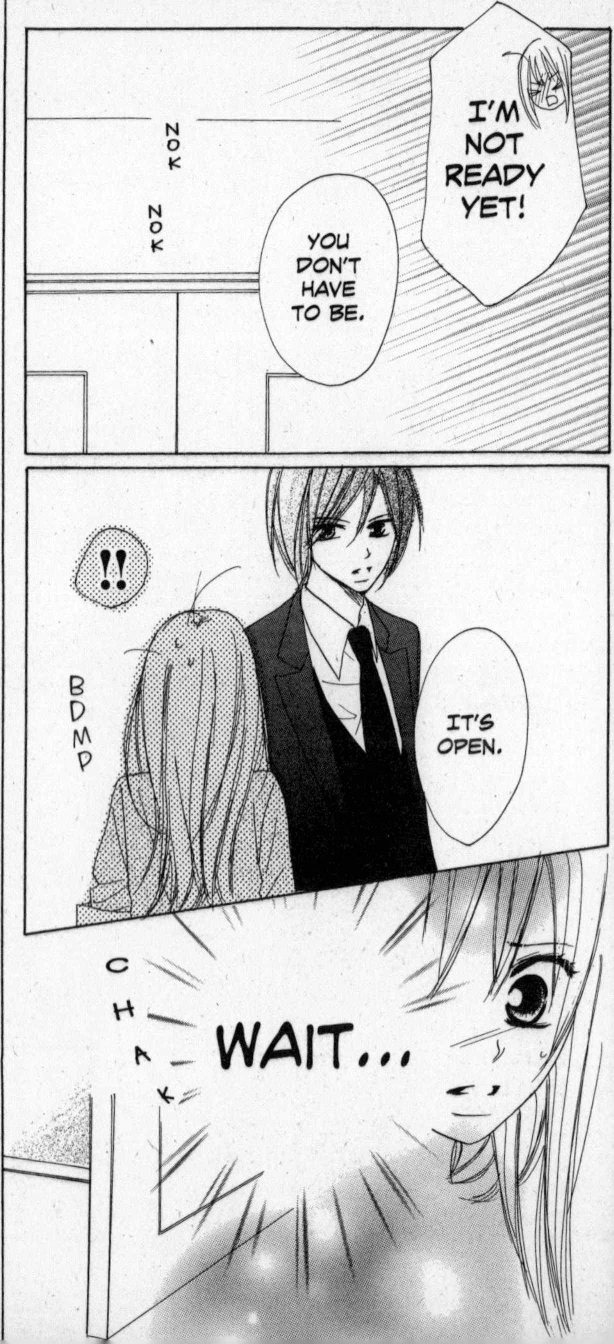
I'M NOT READY YET!
YOU DON'T HAVE TO BE.
NOK NOK
IT'S OPEN.
!!
BDMP
WAIT...
CHAK

③ WUP

I also like the animal documentaries on J:COM. I watch that stuff sometimes too. Boy, I hope everyone understands what I'm talking about.

Another thing I'm into lately is...panties! I collect cute panties.

Six-layer frills

These are six-layer frill panties from my favorite designer!! They come in a bunch of different patterns: bananas, watermelons, cherries, leopard print...it's just too cute.

I'm in love...

Aw... Look at you, all frilly...

And I can't stop buying scrunchies.

Water drop pattern

Insect pattern (It's so cute!)

④ To be continued...

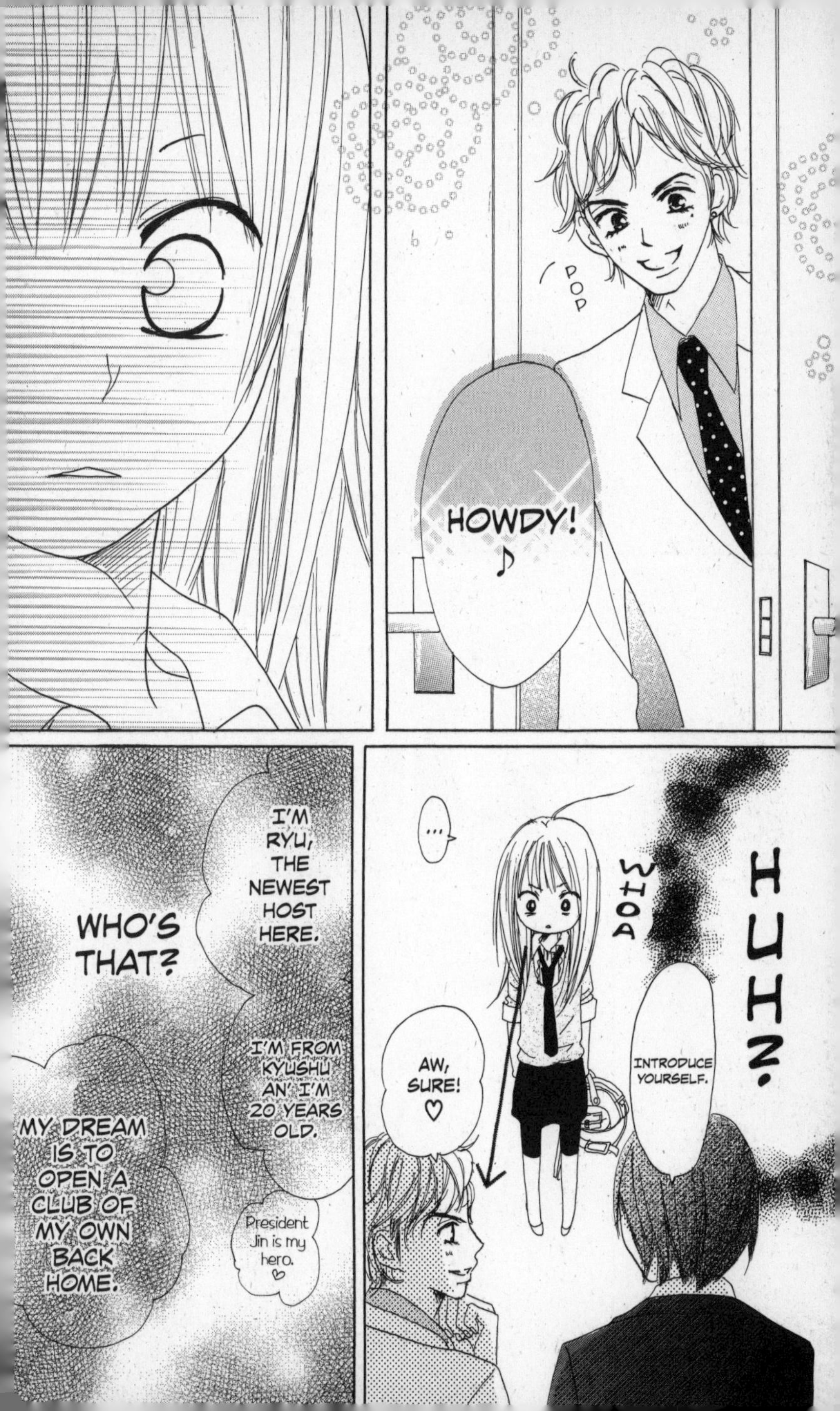
POP
HOWDY! ♪
HUH?
WHOA
...
INTRODUCE YOURSELF.
AW, SURE! ♡
I'M RYU, THE NEWEST HOST HERE.
WHO'S THAT?
I'M FROM KYUSHU AN' I'M 20 YEARS OLD.
President Jin is my hero. ♡
MY DREAM IS TO OPEN A CLUB OF MY OWN BACK HOME.

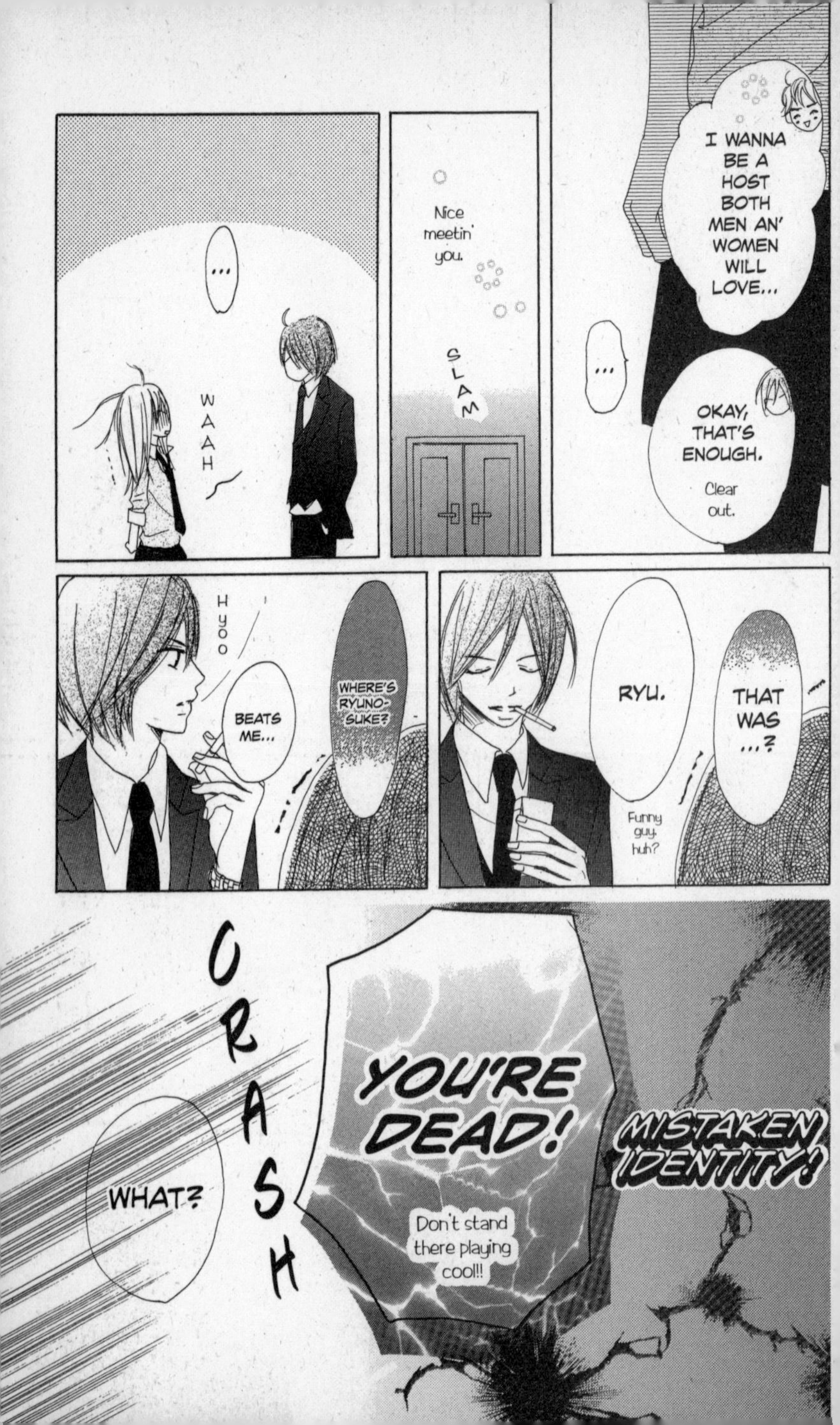
I WANNA BE A HOST BOTH MEN AN' WOMEN WILL LOVE...
...
OKAY, THAT'S ENOUGH.
Clear out.
Nice meetin' you.
SLAM
...
WAAH
THAT WAS ...?
RYU.
Funny guy, huh?
WHERE'S RYUNOSUKE?
BEATS ME...
Hyoo
YOU'RE DEAD!
MISTAKEN IDENTITY!
Don't stand there playing cool!!
CRASH
WHAT?

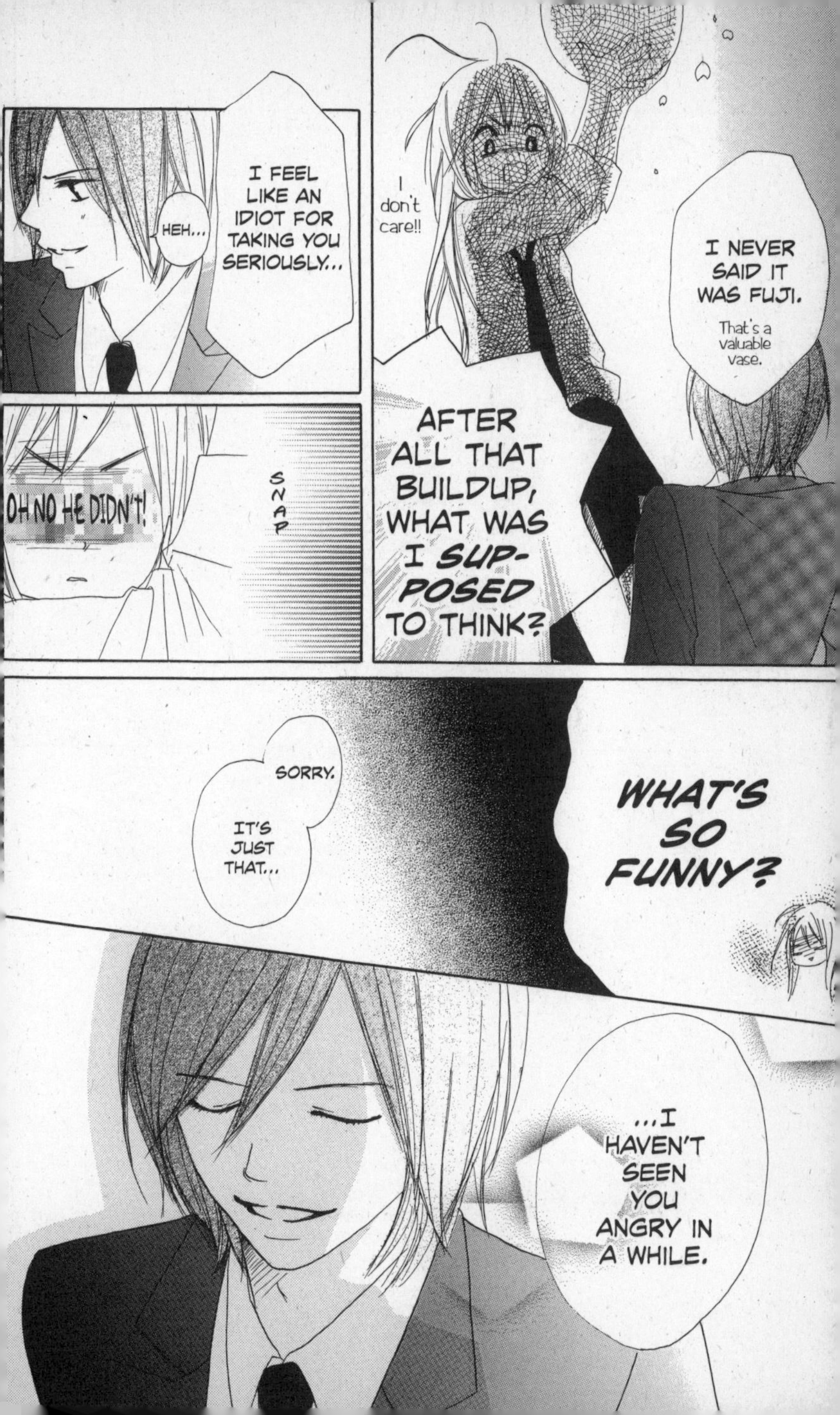
I NEVER SAID IT WAS FUJI.
That's a valuable vase.
I don't care!!
AFTER ALL THAT BUILDUP, WHAT WAS I SUP-POSED TO THINK?
I FEEL LIKE AN IDIOT FOR TAKING YOU SERIOUSLY...
HEH...
SNAP
OH NO HE DIDN'T!
WHAT'S SO FUNNY?
SORRY.
IT'S JUST THAT...
...I HAVEN'T SEEN YOU ANGRY IN A WHILE.

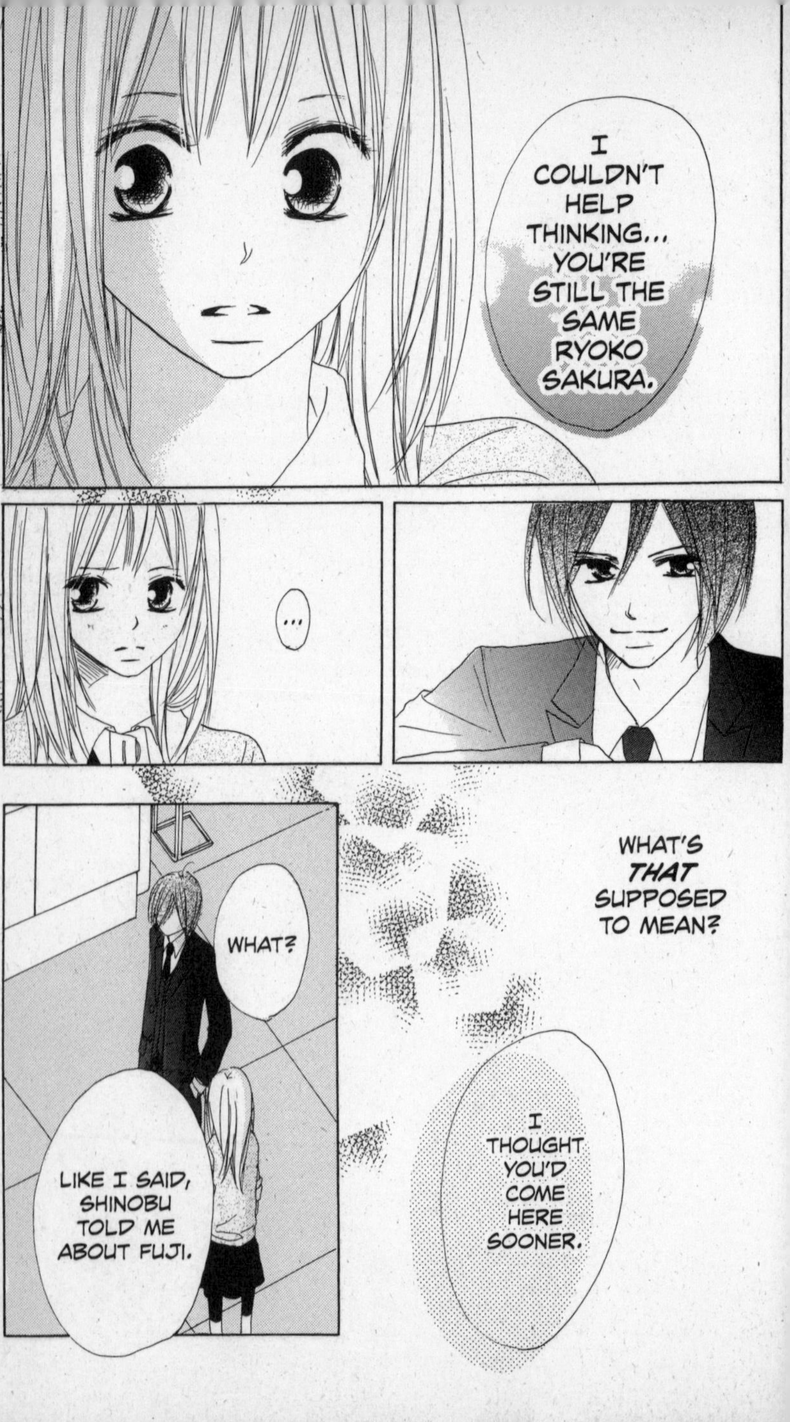

I COULDN'T HELP THINKING... YOU'RE STILL THE SAME RYOKO SAKURA.
...
WHAT'S *THAT* SUPPOSED TO MEAN?
I THOUGHT YOU'D COME HERE SOONER.
WHAT?
LIKE I SAID, SHINOBU TOLD ME ABOUT FUJI.

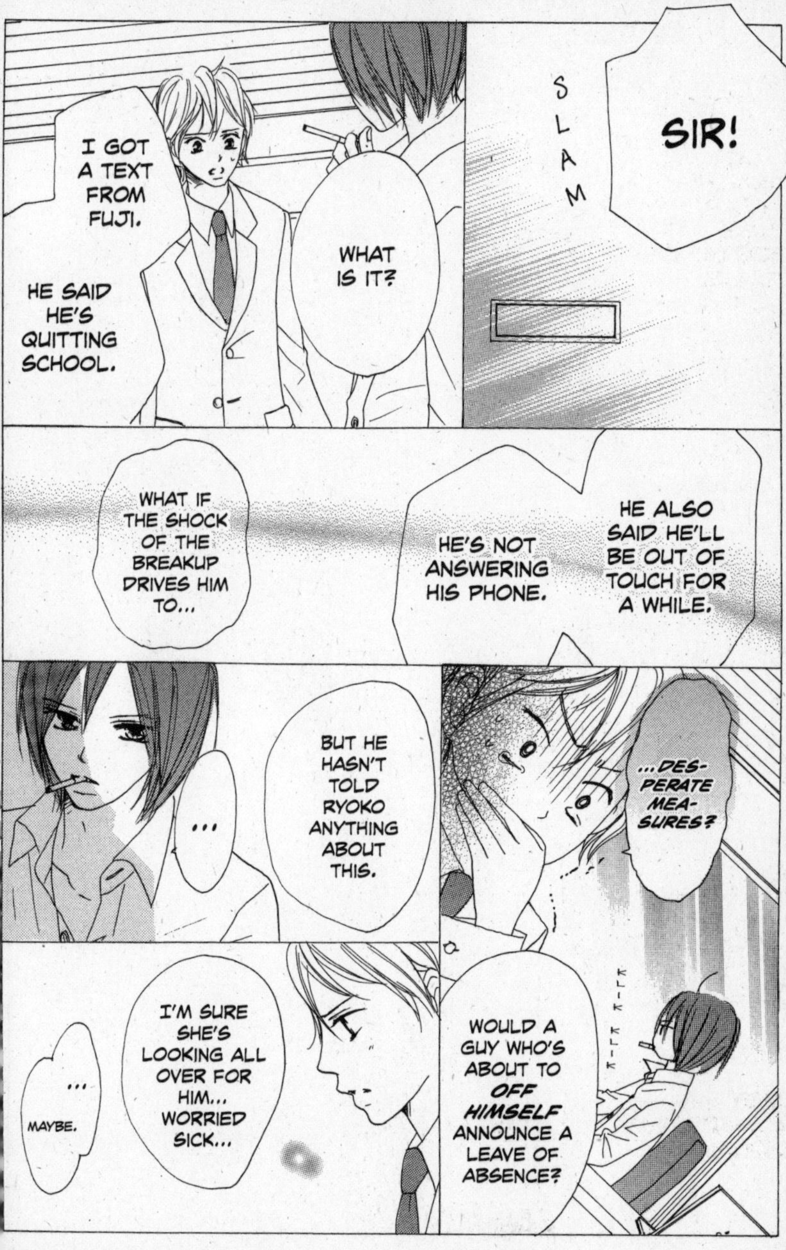
SLAM
SIR!
WHAT IS IT?
I GOT A TEXT FROM FUJI.
HE SAID HE'S QUITTING SCHOOL.
HE ALSO SAID HE'LL BE OUT OF TOUCH FOR A WHILE.
HE'S NOT ANSWERING HIS PHONE.
WHAT IF THE SHOCK OF THE BREAKUP DRIVES HIM TO...
...DES-PERATE MEA-SURES?
KLIK KLIK
WOULD A GUY WHO'S ABOUT TO *OFF HIMSELF* ANNOUNCE A LEAVE OF ABSENCE?
BUT HE HASN'T TOLD RYOKO ANYTHING ABOUT THIS.
...
I'M SURE SHE'S LOOKING ALL OVER FOR HIM... WORRIED SICK...
... MAYBE.

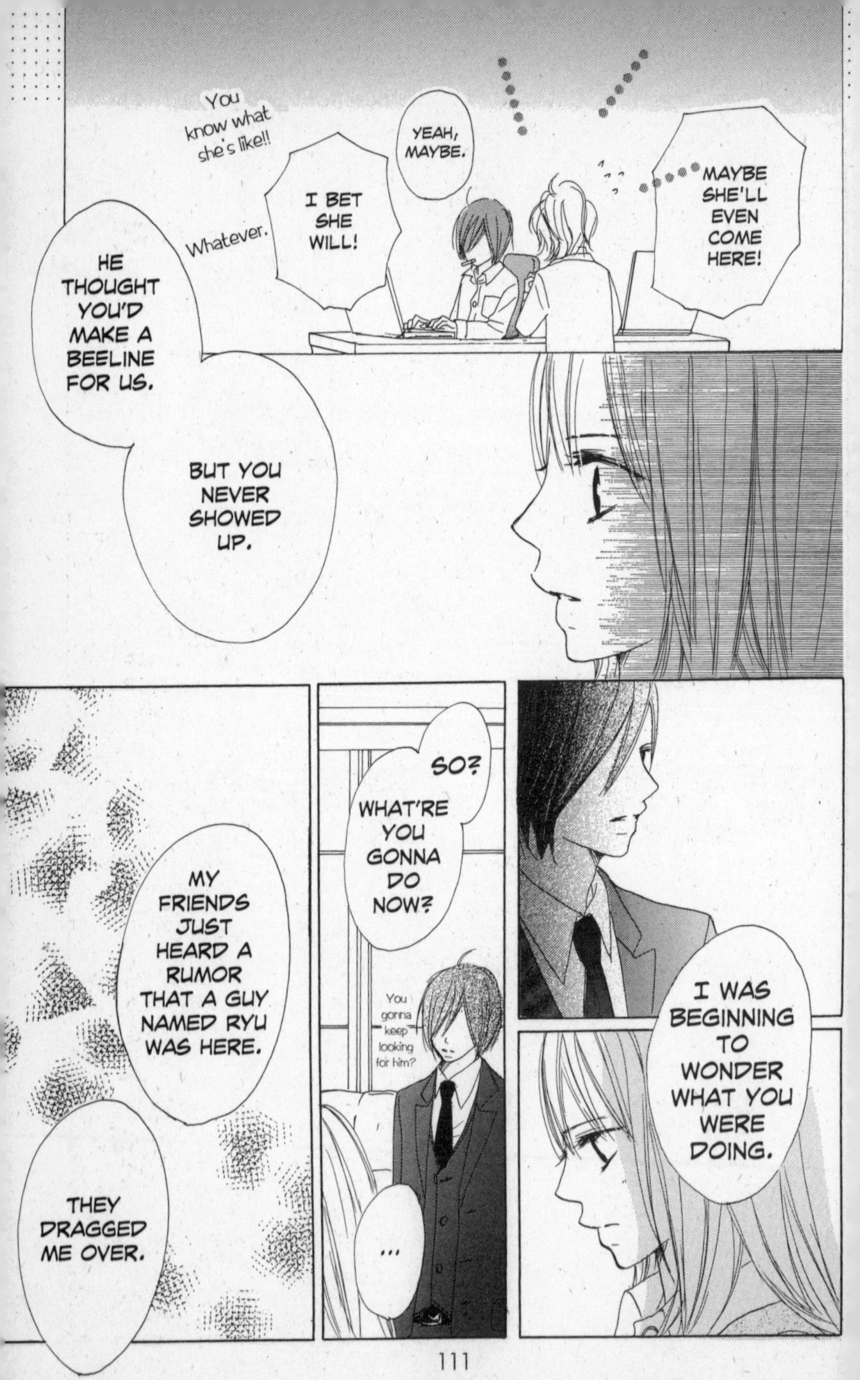

MAYBE SHE'LL EVEN COME HERE!
YEAH, MAYBE.
I BET SHE WILL!
Whatever.
You know what she's like!!
HE THOUGHT YOU'D MAKE A BEELINE FOR US.
BUT YOU NEVER SHOWED UP.
I WAS BEGINNING TO WONDER WHAT YOU WERE DOING.
SO? WHAT'RE YOU GONNA DO NOW?
You gonna keep looking for him?
...
MY FRIENDS JUST HEARD A RUMOR THAT A GUY NAMED RYU WAS HERE.
THEY DRAGGED ME OVER.

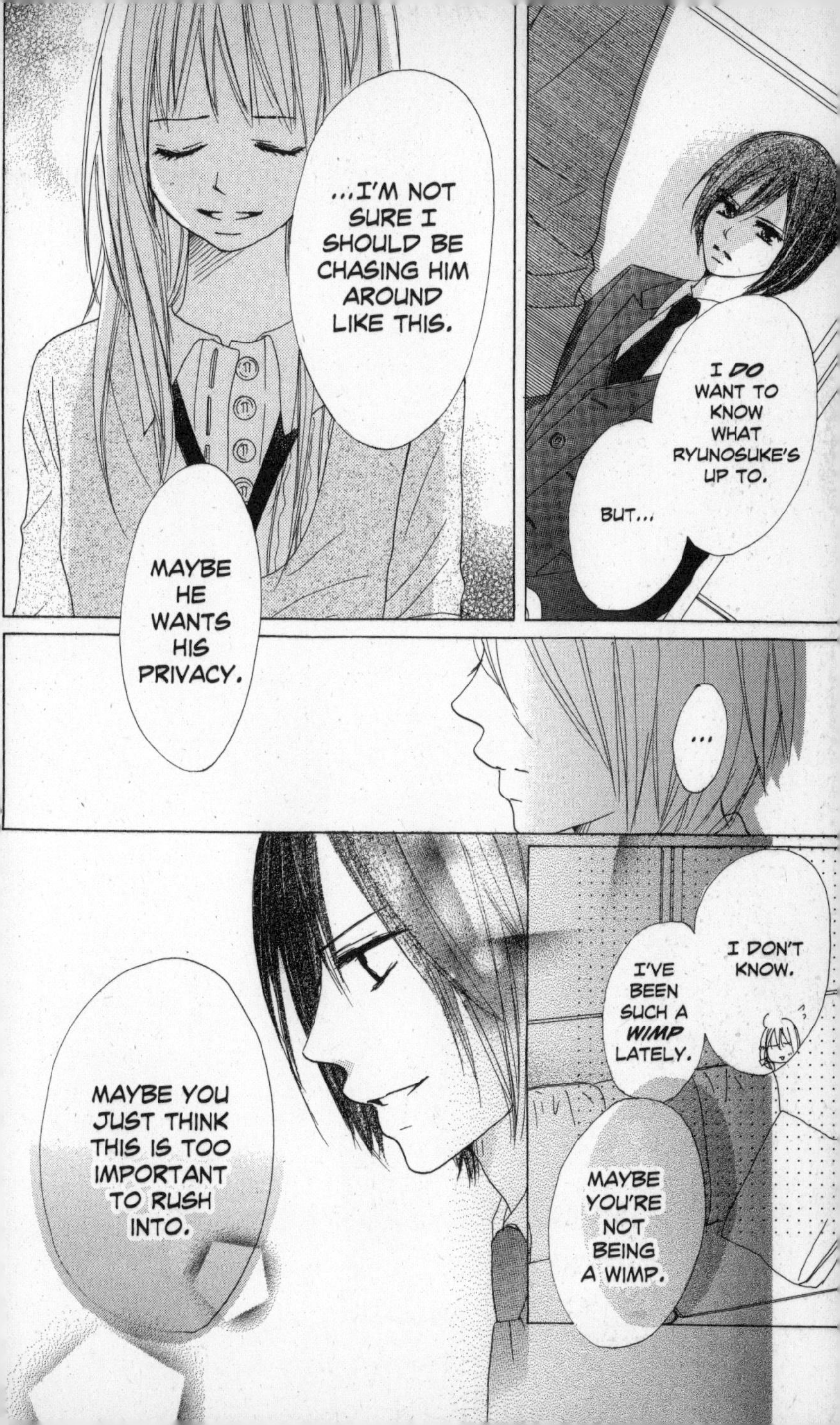
I DO WANT TO KNOW WHAT RYUNOSUKE'S UP TO.
BUT...
...I'M NOT SURE I SHOULD BE CHASING HIM AROUND LIKE THIS.
MAYBE HE WANTS HIS PRIVACY.
...
I DON'T KNOW.
I'VE BEEN SUCH A WIMP LATELY.
MAYBE YOU'RE NOT BEING A WIMP.
MAYBE YOU JUST THINK THIS IS TOO IMPORTANT TO RUSH INTO.

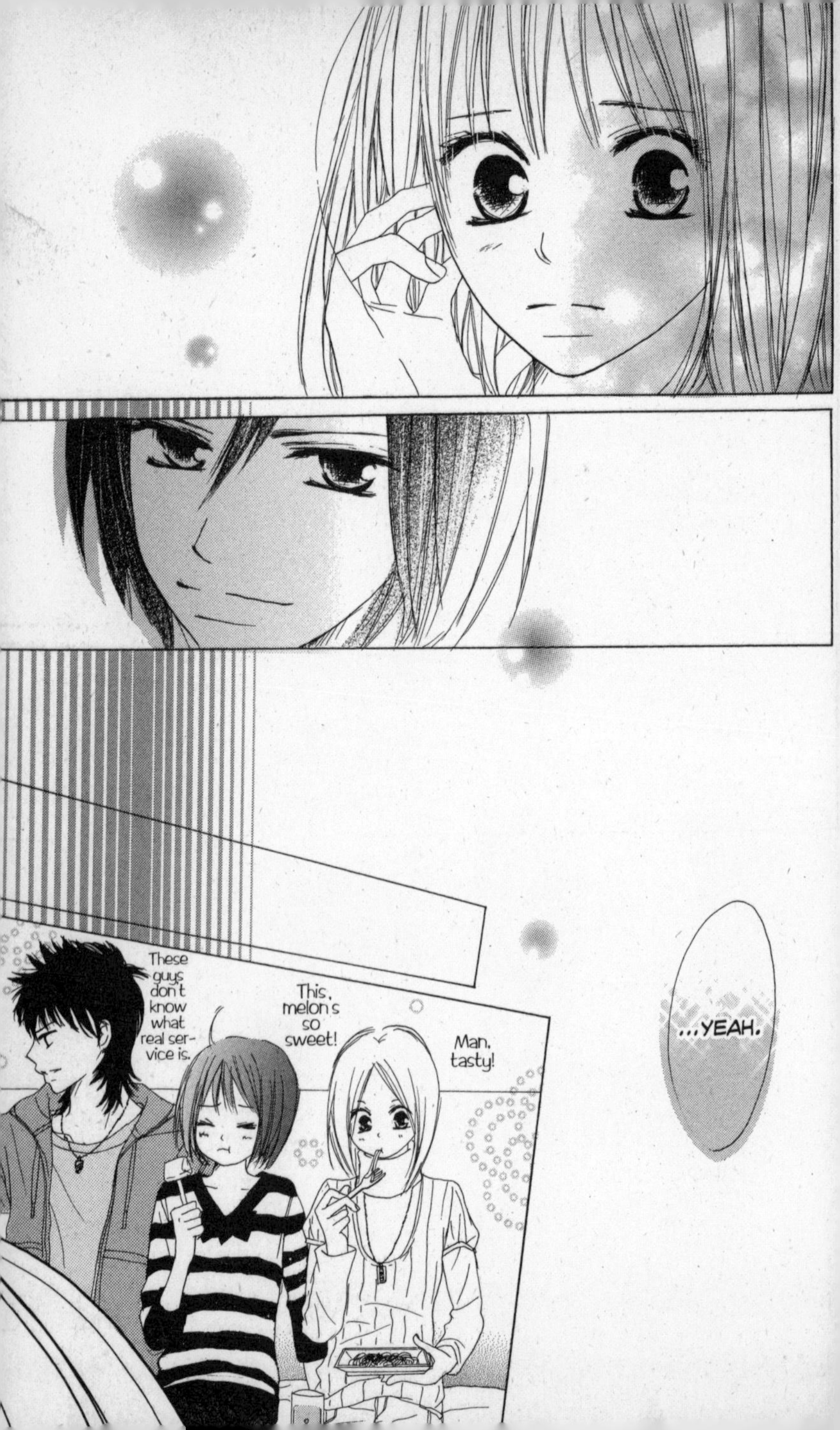
...YEAH.
Man, tasty!
This melon's so sweet!
These guys don't know what real service is.

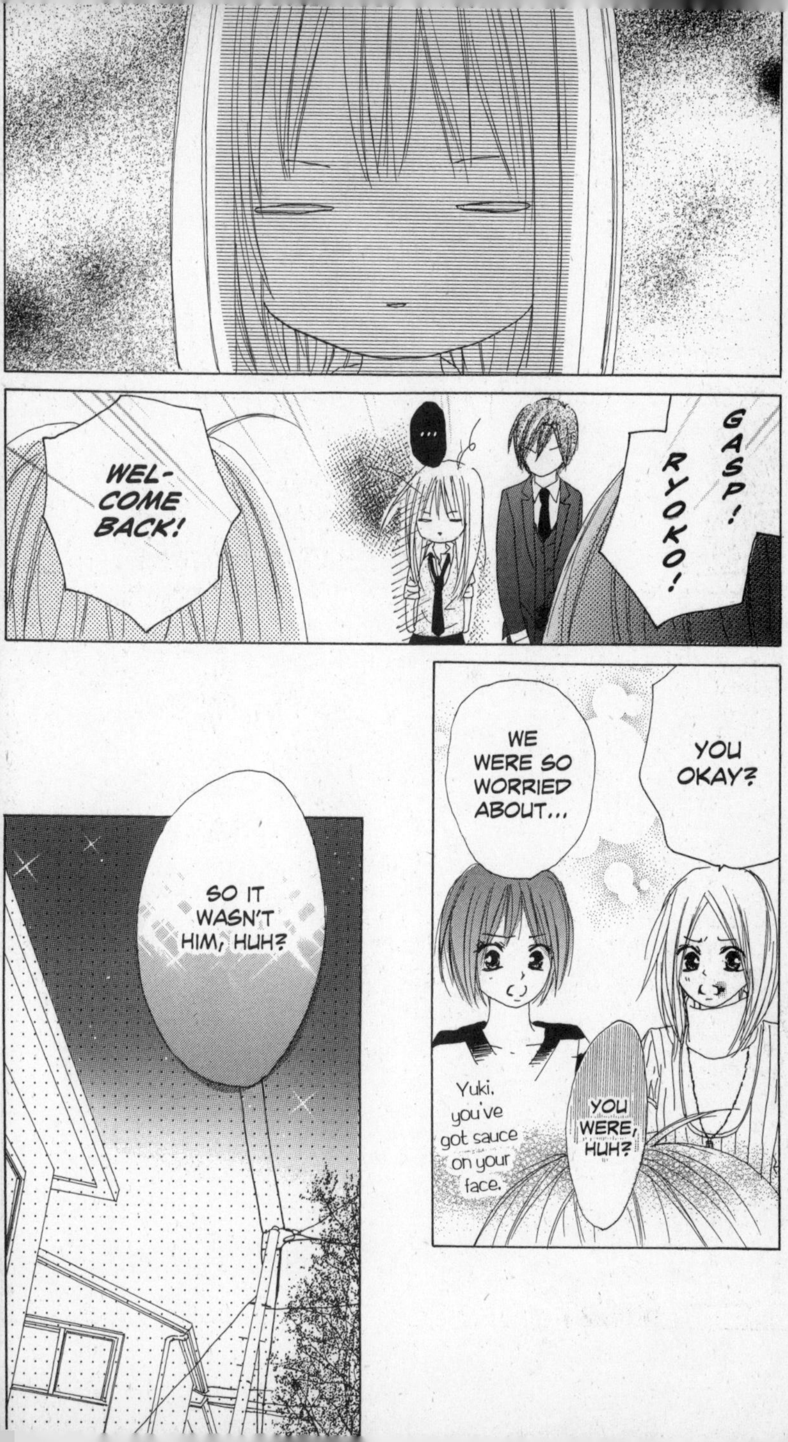
GASP! RYOKO!
...
WEL-COME BACK!
YOU OKAY?
WE WERE SO WORRIED ABOUT...
YOU WERE, HUH?
Yuki, you've got sauce on your face.
SO IT WASN'T HIM, HUH?

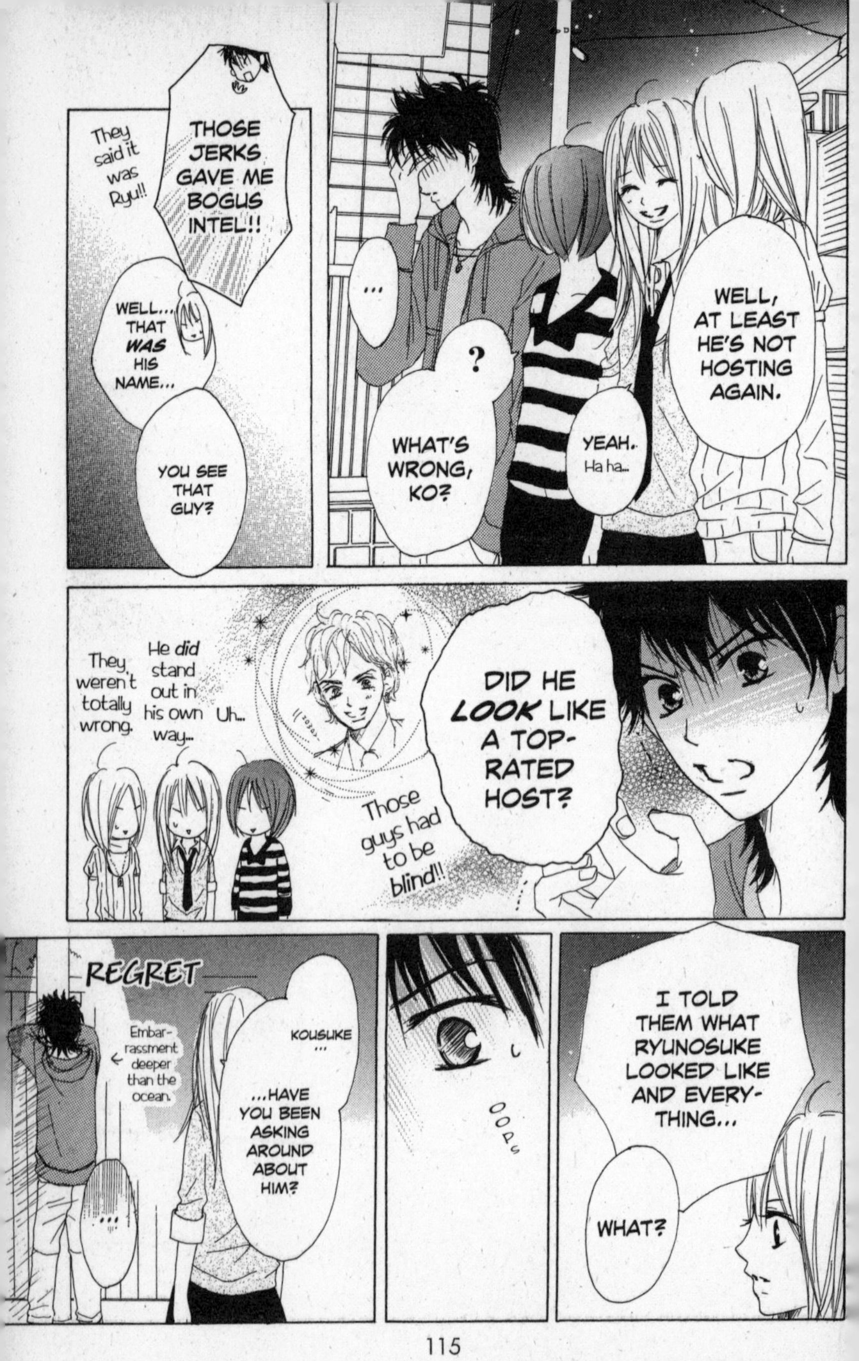
WELL, AT LEAST HE'S NOT HOSTING AGAIN.
YEAH. Ha ha...
...
?
WHAT'S WRONG, KO?
THOSE JERKS GAVE ME BOGUS INTEL!!
They said it was Ryu!!
WELL... THAT *WAS* HIS NAME...
YOU SEE THAT GUY?
DID HE *LOOK* LIKE A TOP-RATED HOST?
Those guys had to be blind!!
Uh...
He *did* stand out in his own way...
They weren't totally wrong.
I TOLD THEM WHAT RYUNOSUKE LOOKED LIKE AND EVERYTHING...
WHAT?
OOPS
REGRET
KOUSUKE ...
...HAVE YOU BEEN ASKING AROUND ABOUT HIM?
Embarrassment deeper than the ocean.
...!!

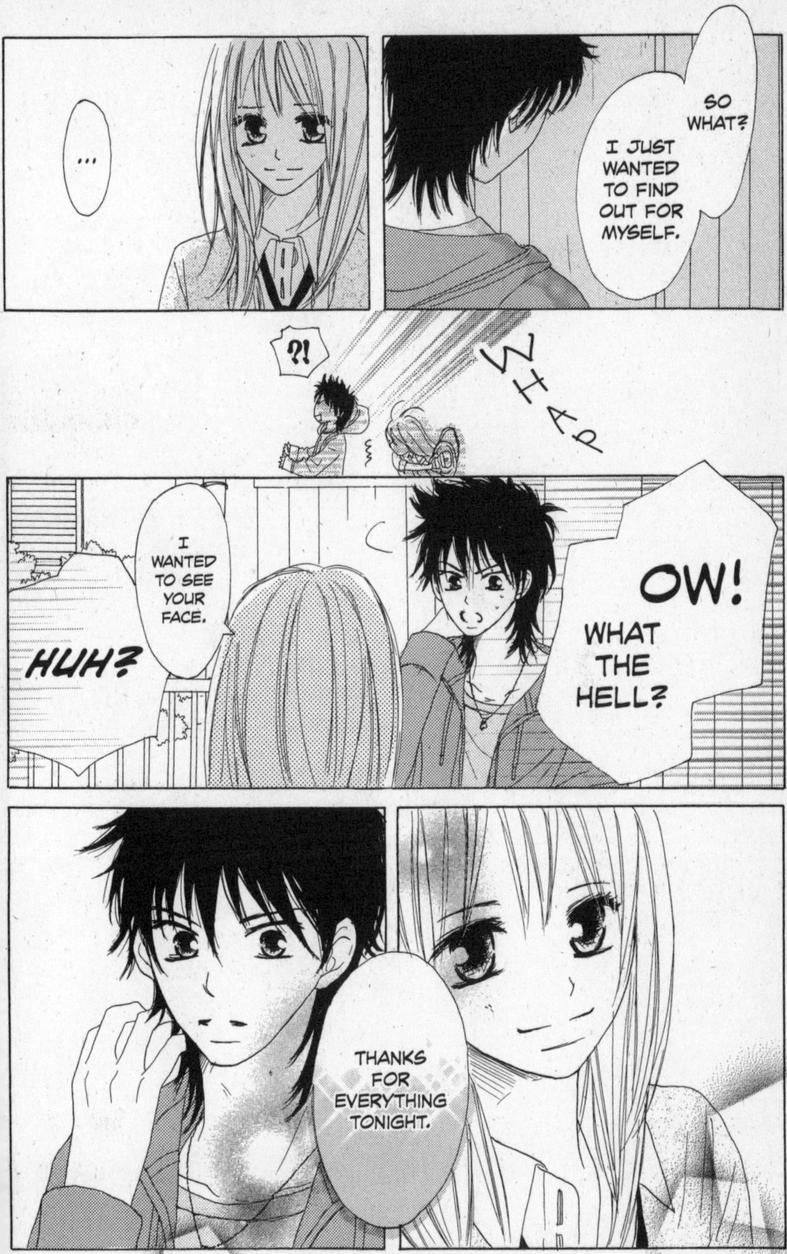
SO WHAT?
I JUST WANTED TO FIND OUT FOR MYSELF.
...
WHAP
?!
OW!
WHAT THE HELL?
I WANTED TO SEE YOUR FACE.
HUH?
THANKS FOR EVERYTHING TONIGHT.

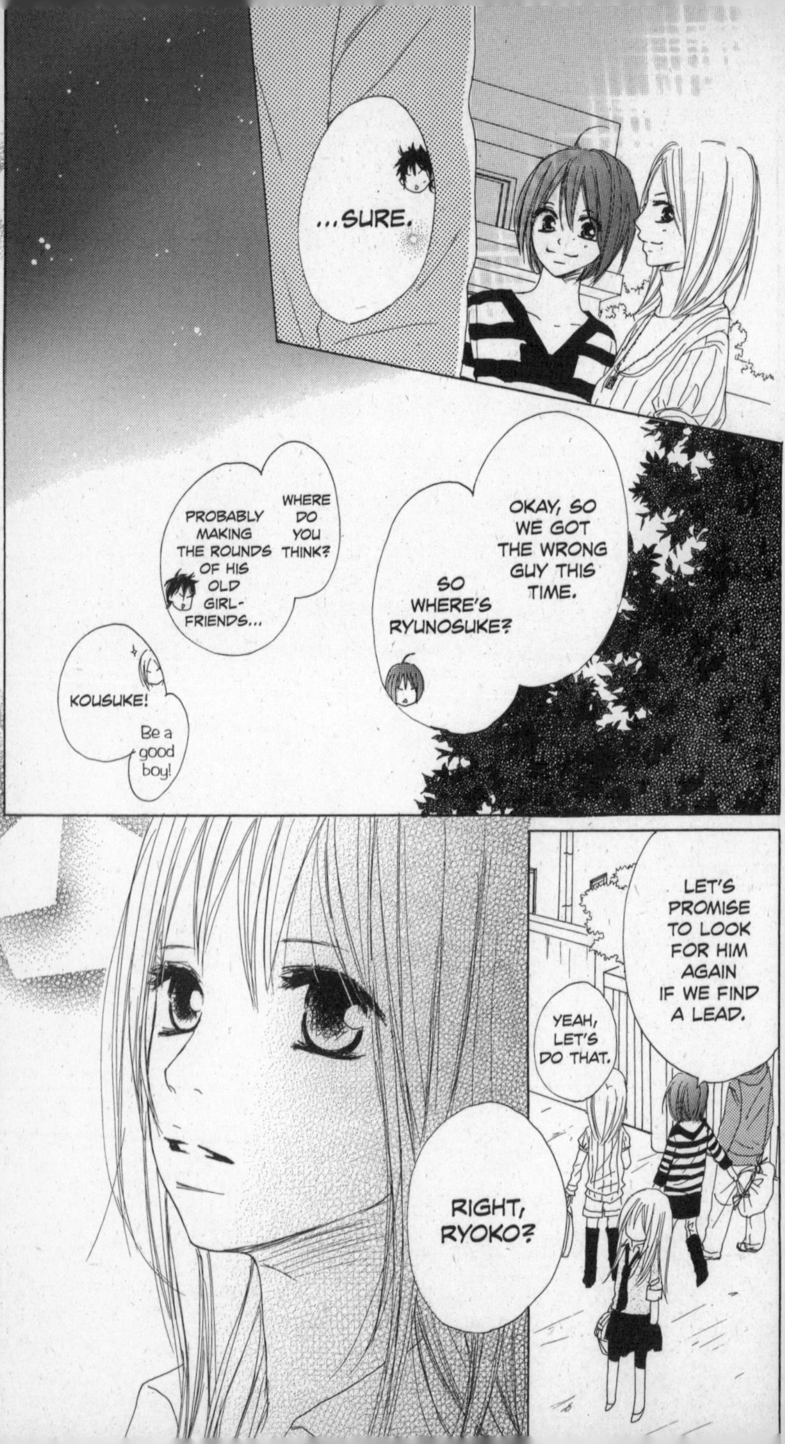
...SURE.
OKAY, SO WE GOT THE WRONG GUY THIS TIME.
SO WHERE'S RYUNOSUKE?
WHERE DO YOU THINK?
PROBABLY MAKING THE ROUNDS OF HIS OLD GIRLFRIENDS...
KOUSUKE!
Be a good boy!
LET'S PROMISE TO LOOK FOR HIM AGAIN IF WE FIND A LEAD.
YEAH, LET'S DO THAT.
RIGHT, RYOKO?

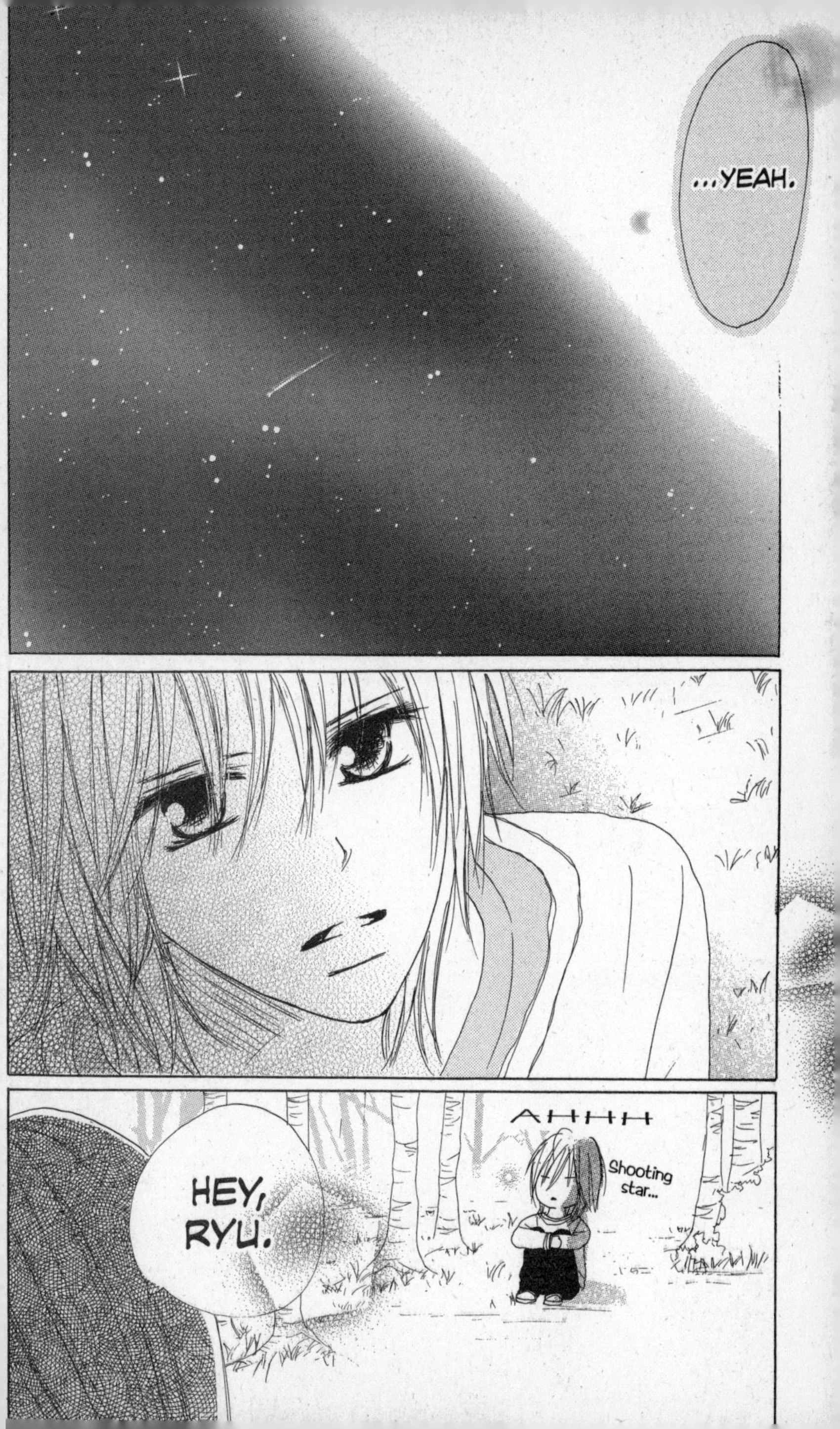
...YEAH.
AHHH
Shooting star...
HEY, RYU.

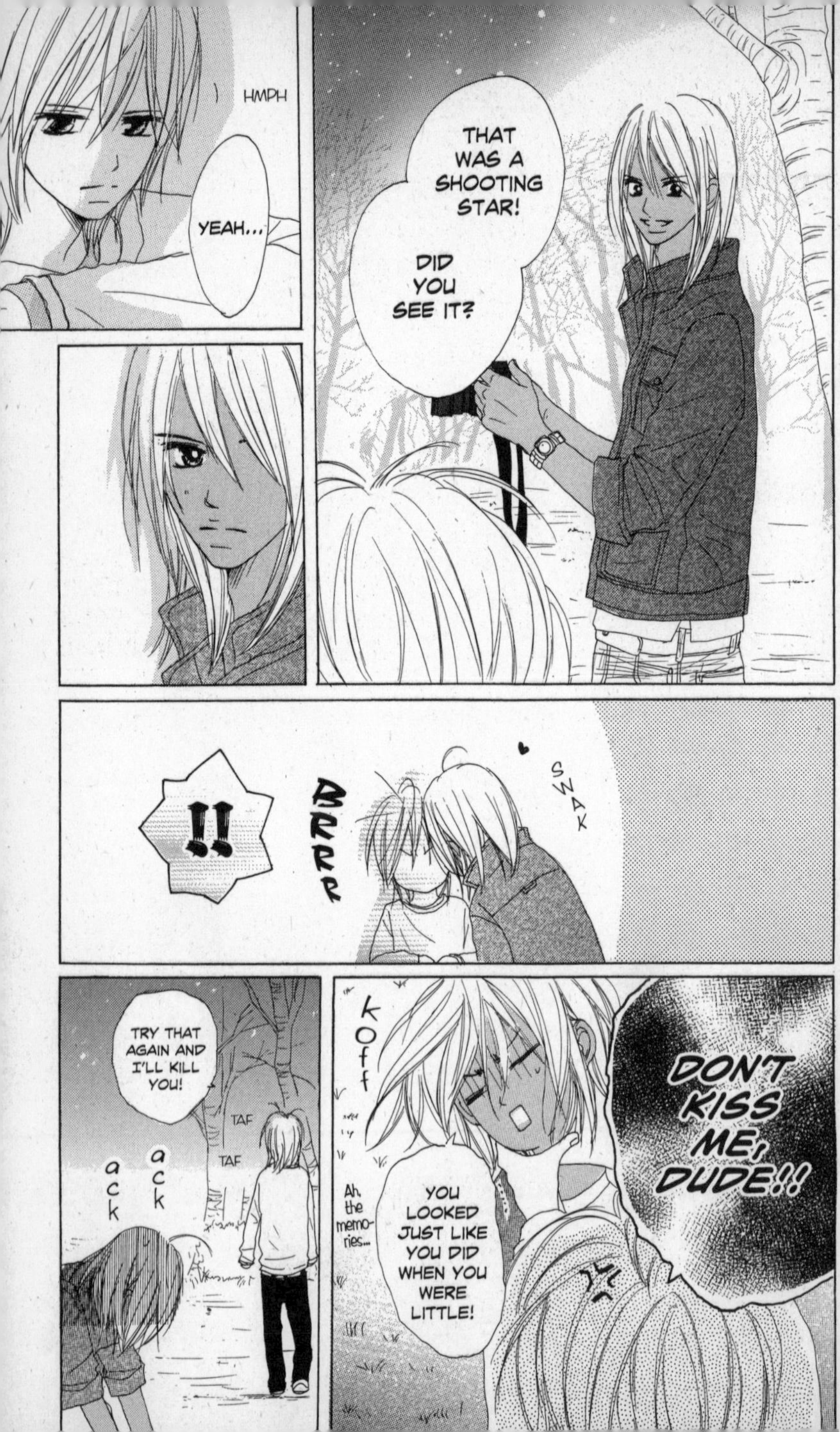
THAT WAS A SHOOTING STAR!
DID YOU SEE IT?
HMPH
YEAH...
SWAK
BRRR
!!
DON'T KISS ME, DUDE!!
KOFF
YOU LOOKED JUST LIKE YOU DID WHEN YOU WERE LITTLE!
Ah, the memories...
TRY THAT AGAIN AND I'LL KILL YOU!
TAF
TAF
ack
ack

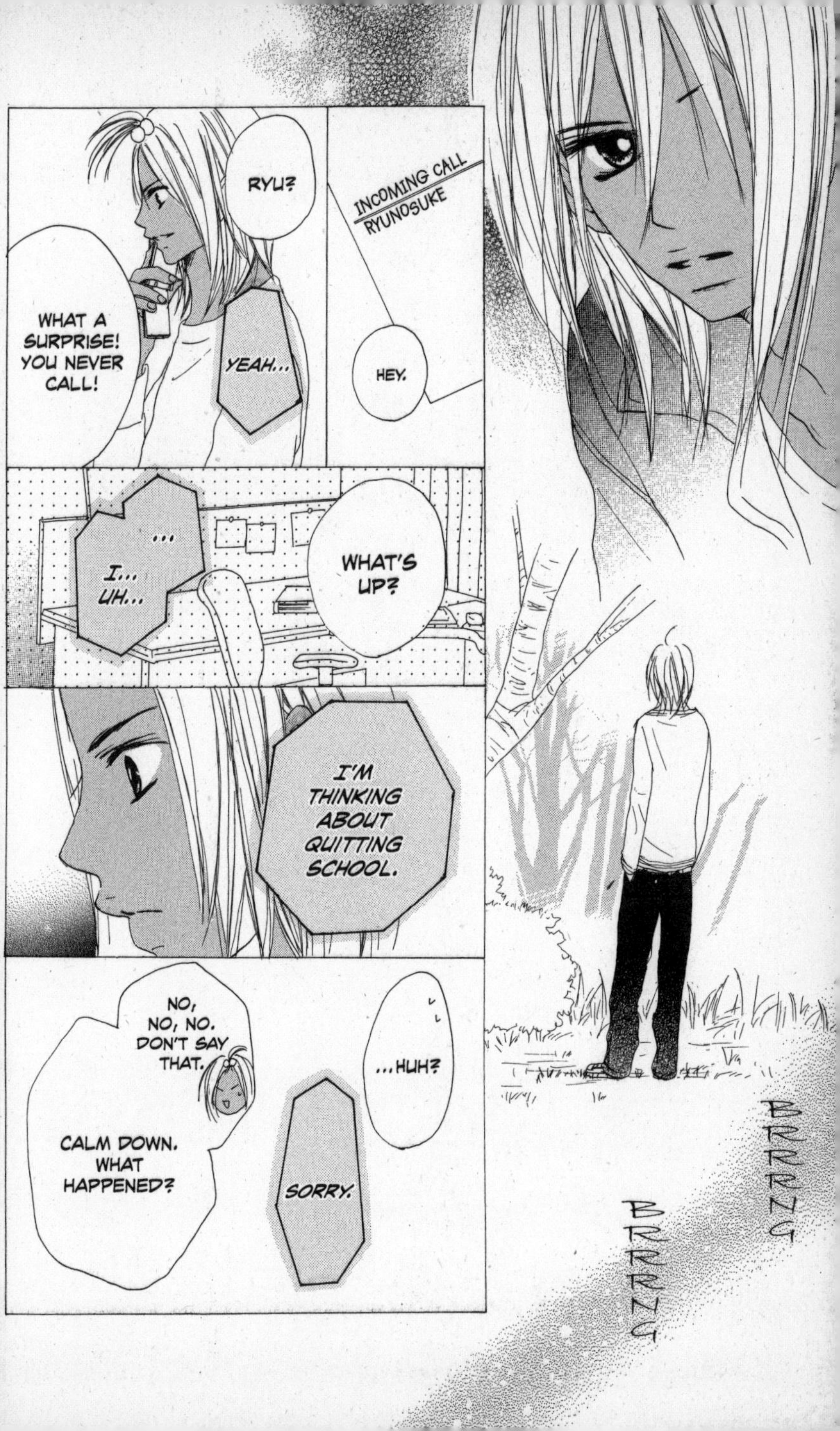
BRRRNG
BRRRNG
INCOMING CALL
RYUNOSUKE
HEY.
RYU?
YEAH...
WHAT A SURPRISE! YOU NEVER CALL!
WHAT'S UP?
...
I... UH...
I'M THINKING ABOUT QUITTING SCHOOL.
...HUH?
SORRY.
NO, NO, NO. DON'T SAY THAT.
CALM DOWN. WHAT HAPPENED?

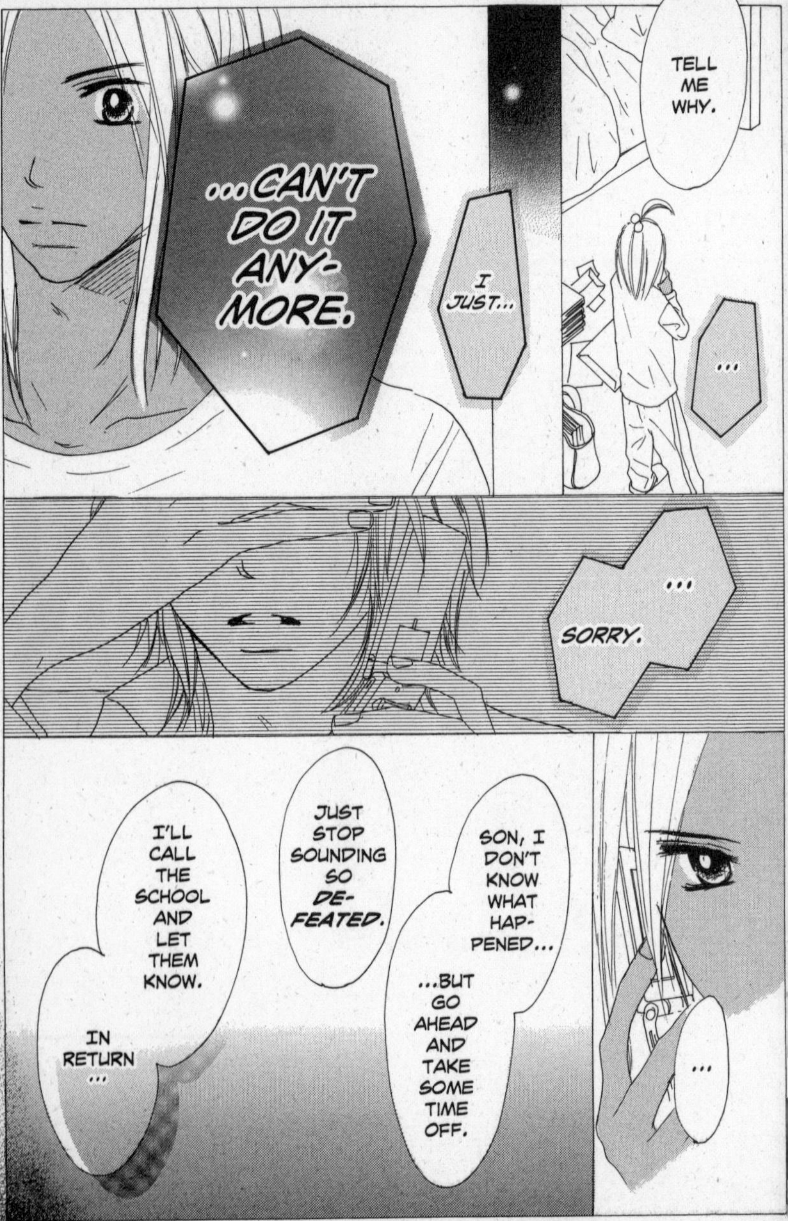
TELL ME WHY.
...
I JUST...
...CAN'T DO IT ANYMORE.
... SORRY.
...
SON, I DON'T KNOW WHAT HAPPENED...
...BUT GO AHEAD AND TAKE SOME TIME OFF.
JUST STOP SOUNDING SO *DEFEATED.*
I'LL CALL THE SCHOOL AND LET THEM KNOW.
IN RETURN...

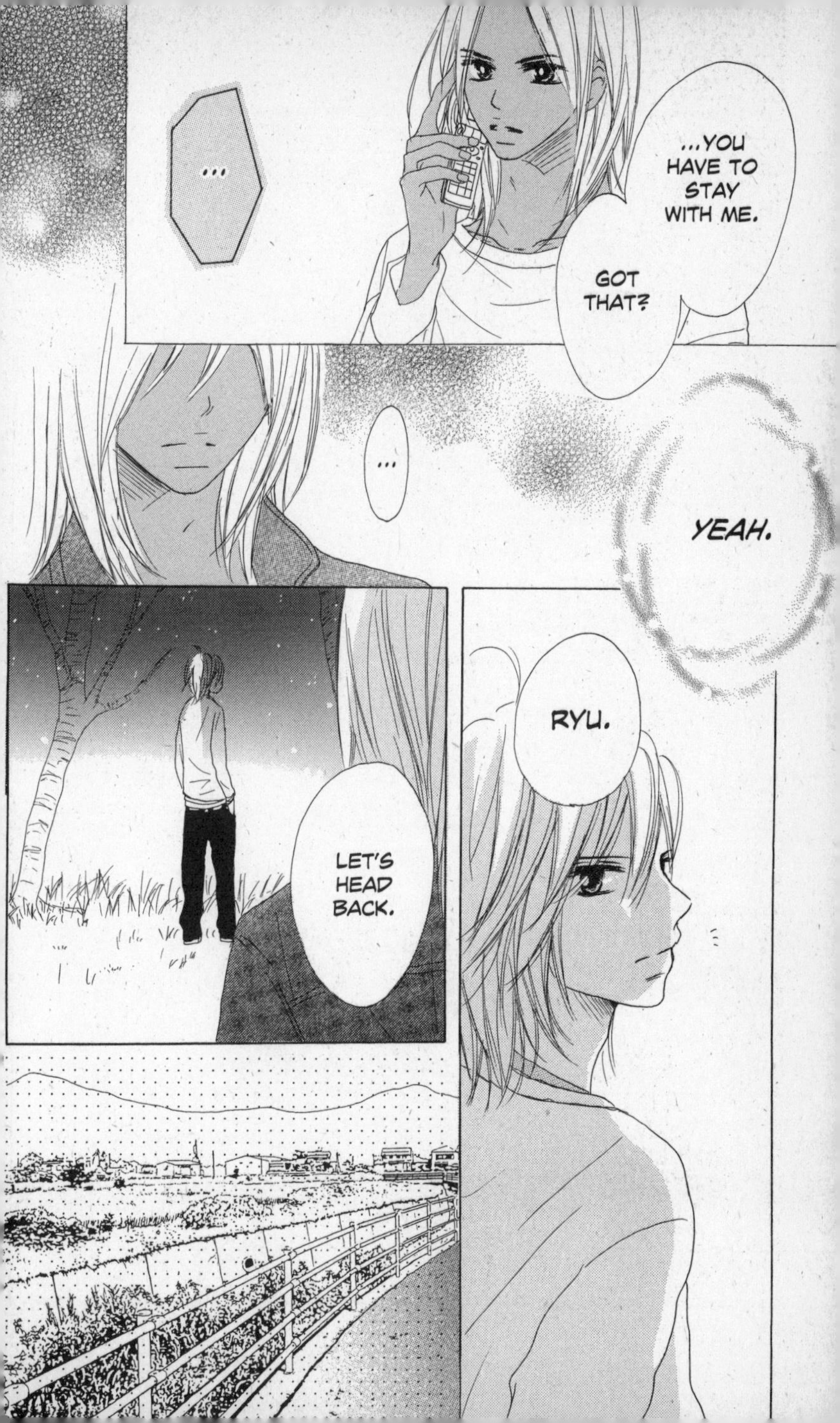
...YOU HAVE TO STAY WITH ME.
GOT THAT?
...
...
YEAH.
RYU.
LET'S HEAD BACK.

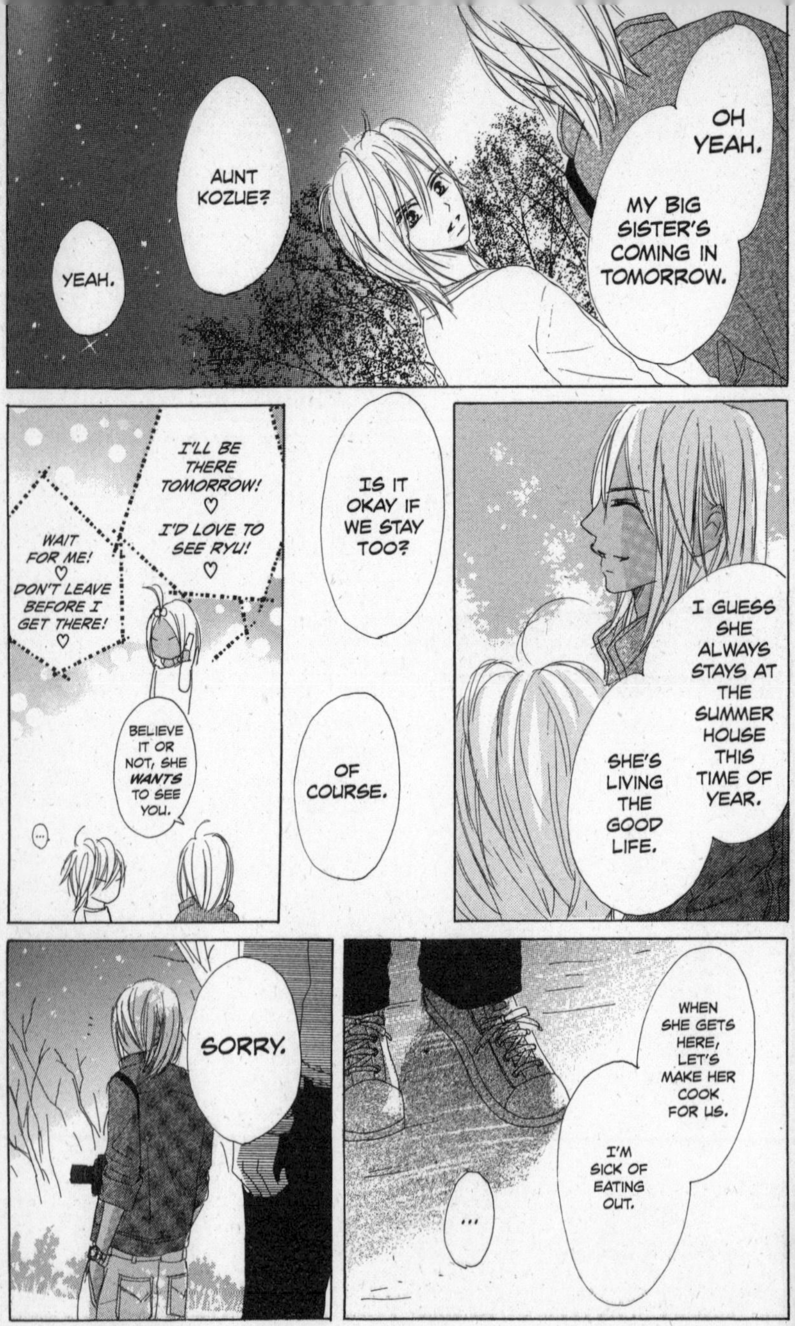
OH YEAH.
MY BIG SISTER'S COMING IN TOMORROW.
AUNT KOZUE?
YEAH.
I GUESS SHE ALWAYS STAYS AT THE SUMMER HOUSE THIS TIME OF YEAR.
SHE'S LIVING THE GOOD LIFE.
IS IT OKAY IF WE STAY TOO?
OF COURSE.
I'LL BE THERE TOMORROW! ♡ I'D LOVE TO SEE RYU! ♡
WAIT FOR ME! ♡ DON'T LEAVE BEFORE I GET THERE! ♡
BELIEVE IT OR NOT, SHE *WANTS* TO SEE YOU.
...
WHEN SHE GETS HERE, LET'S MAKE HER COOK FOR US.
I'M SICK OF EATING OUT.
...
SORRY.

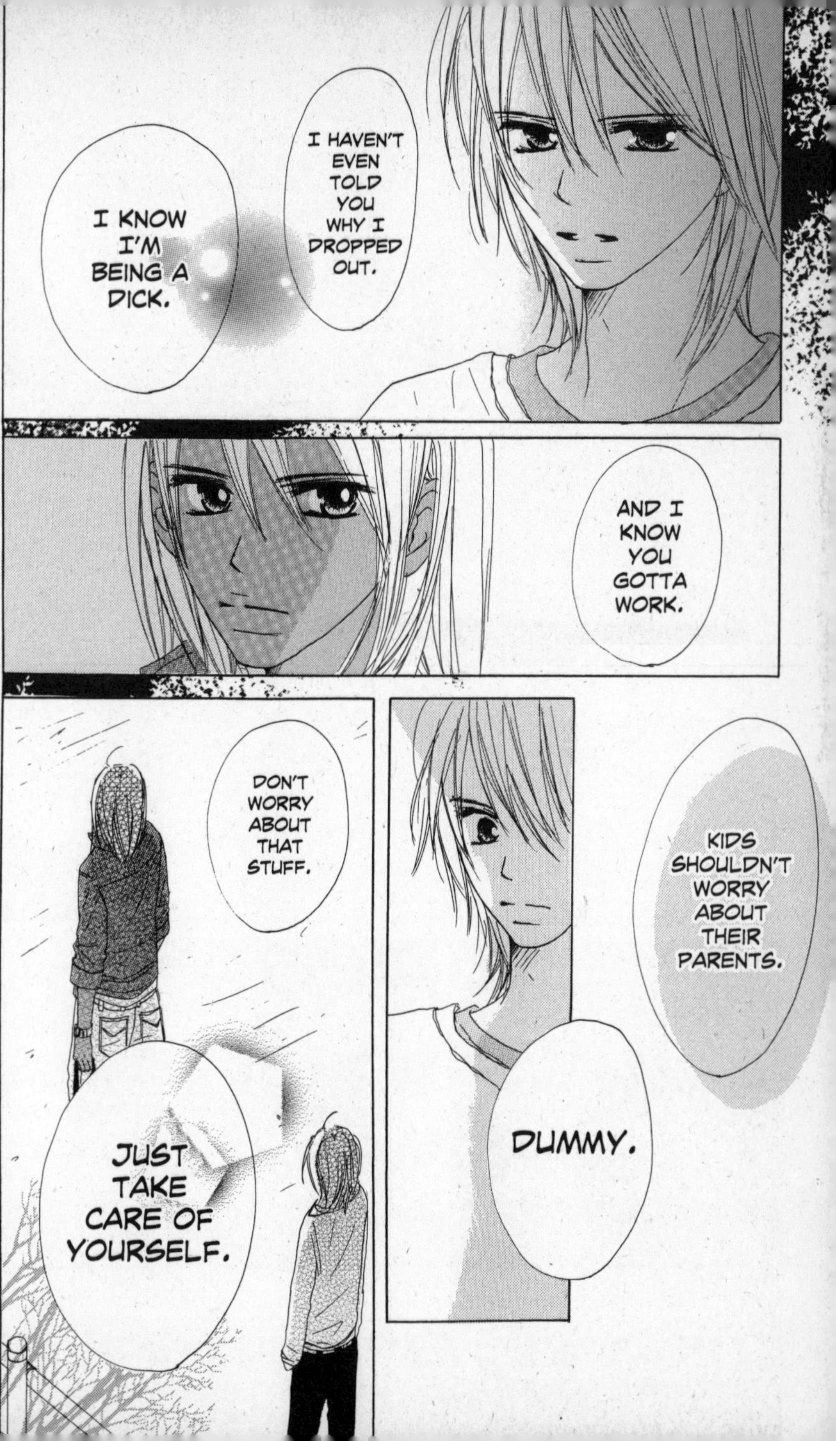
I HAVEN'T EVEN TOLD YOU WHY I DROPPED OUT.
I KNOW I'M BEING A DICK.
AND I KNOW YOU GOTTA WORK.
KIDS SHOULDN'T WORRY ABOUT THEIR PARENTS.
DUMMY.
DON'T WORRY ABOUT THAT STUFF.
JUST TAKE CARE OF YOURSELF.

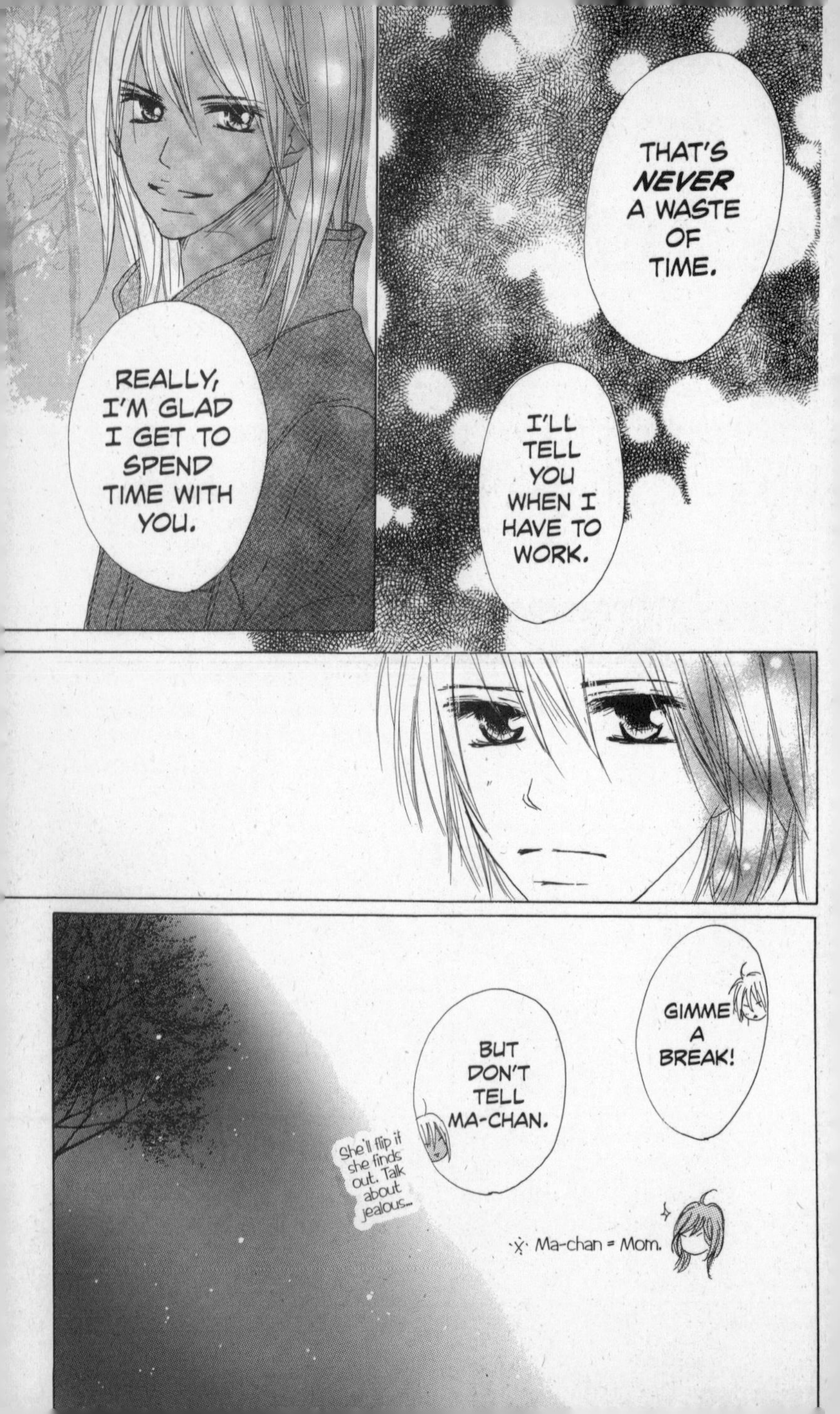
THAT'S *NEVER* A WASTE OF TIME.
I'LL TELL YOU WHEN I HAVE TO WORK.
REALLY, I'M GLAD I GET TO SPEND TIME WITH YOU.
GIMME A BREAK!
BUT DON'T TELL MA-CHAN.
She'll flip if she finds out. Talk about jealous...
※ Ma-chan = Mom.

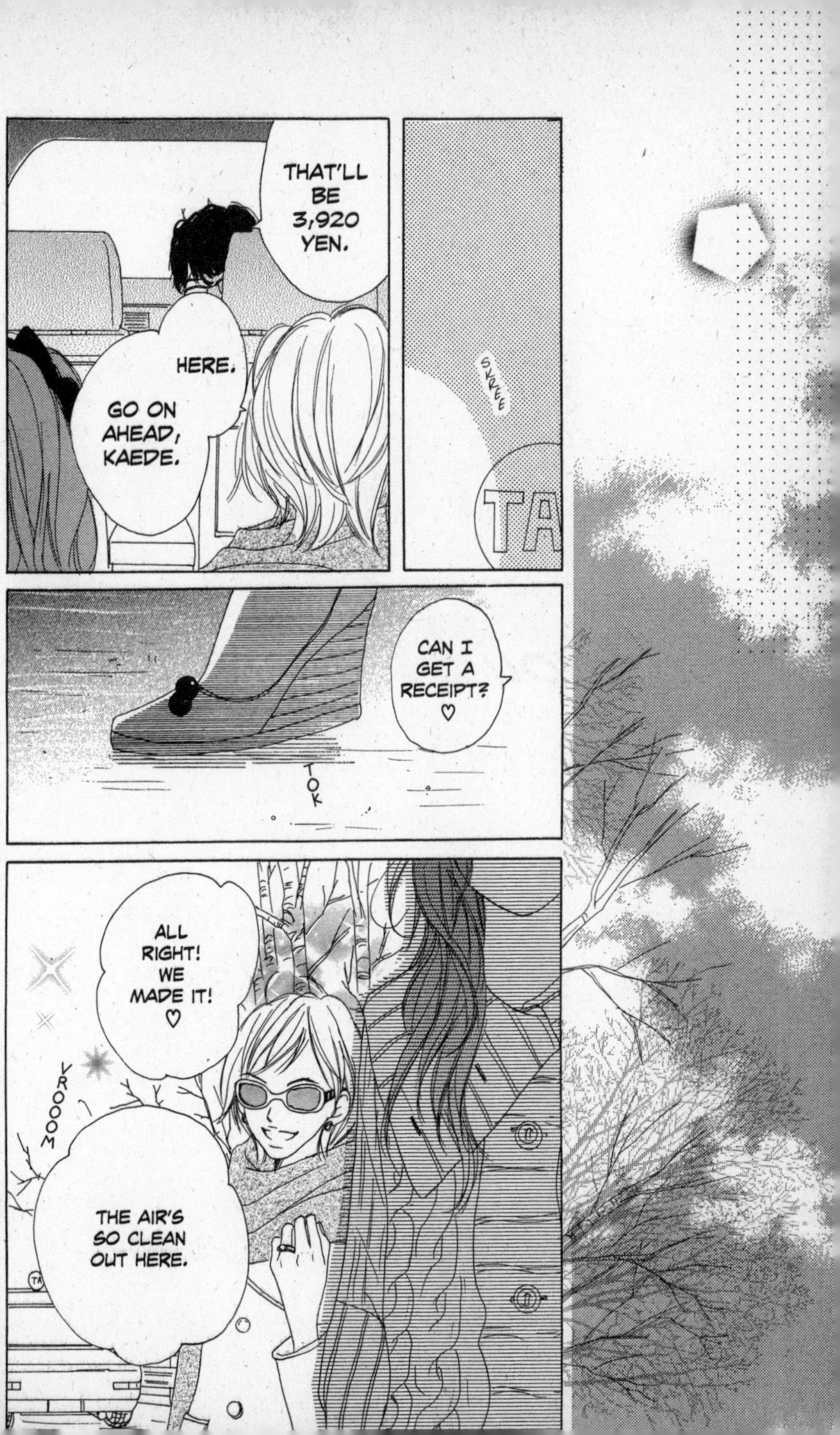
SKREE
TA
THAT'LL BE 3,920 YEN.
HERE.
GO ON AHEAD, KAEDE.
CAN I GET A RECEIPT? ♡
TOK
ALL RIGHT! WE MADE IT! ♡
VROOOM
THE AIR'S SO CLEAN OUT HERE.
TA

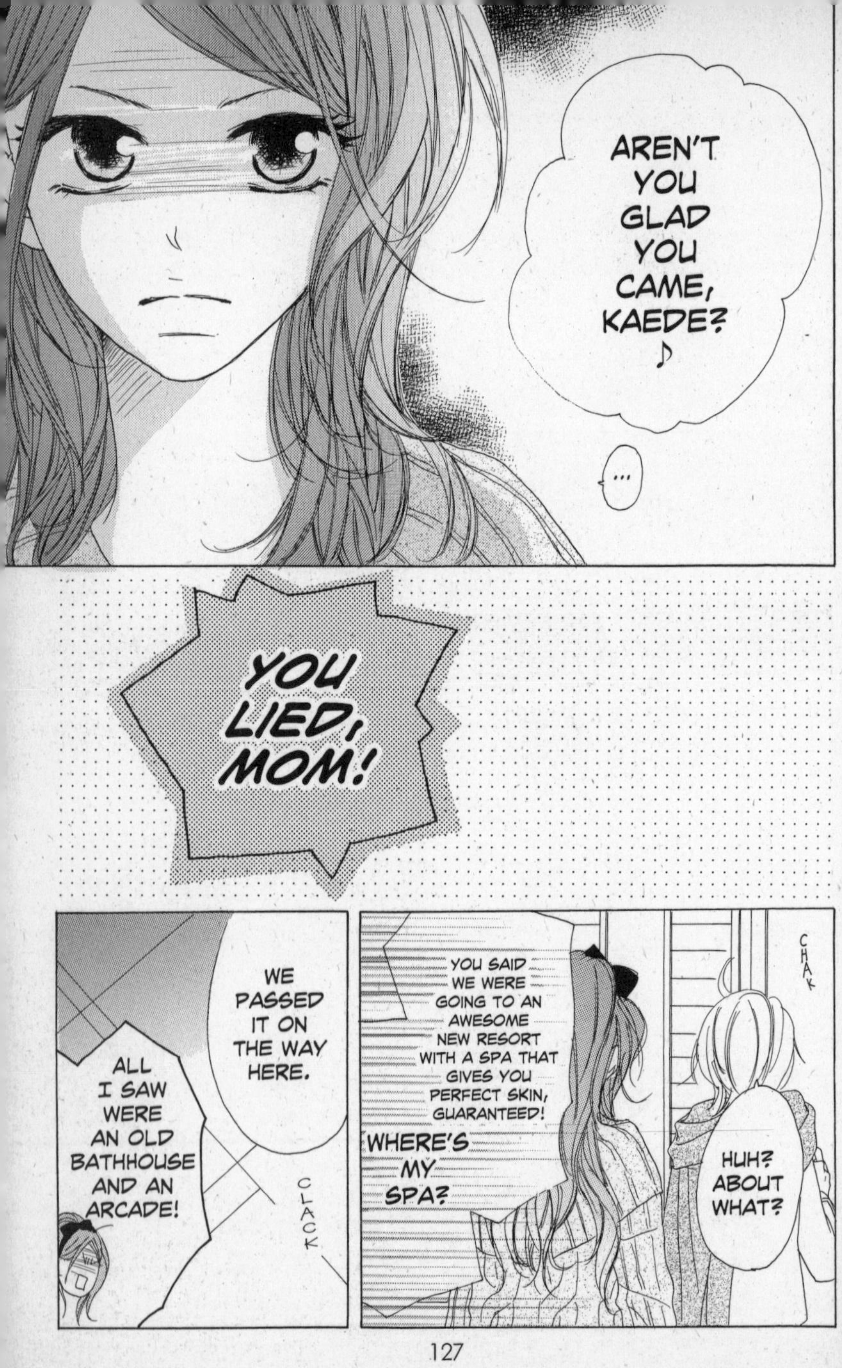
AREN'T YOU GLAD YOU CAME, KAEDE? ♪
...
YOU LIED, MOM!
CHAK
HUH? ABOUT WHAT?
YOU SAID WE WERE GOING TO AN AWESOME NEW RESORT WITH A SPA THAT GIVES YOU PERFECT SKIN, GUARANTEED!
WHERE'S MY SPA?
WE PASSED IT ON THE WAY HERE.
CLACK
ALL I SAW WERE AN OLD BATHHOUSE AND AN ARCADE!

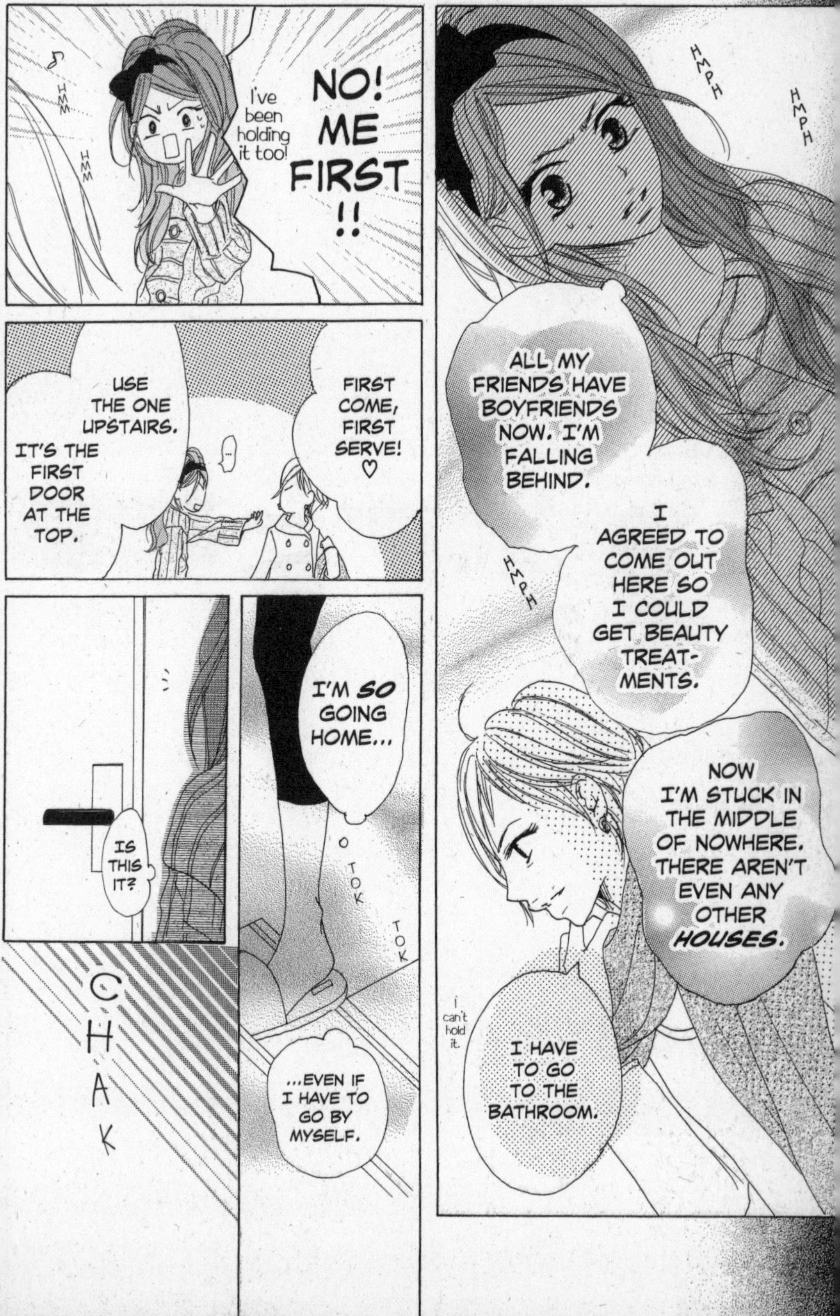
HMPH
HMPH
ALL MY FRIENDS HAVE BOYFRIENDS NOW. I'M FALLING BEHIND.
HMPH
I AGREED TO COME OUT HERE SO I COULD GET BEAUTY TREATMENTS.
NOW I'M STUCK IN THE MIDDLE OF NOWHERE. THERE AREN'T EVEN ANY OTHER *HOUSES*.
I can't hold it.
I HAVE TO GO TO THE BATHROOM.
NO! ME FIRST!!
I've been holding it too!
♪
HMM
HMM
FIRST COME, FIRST SERVE! ♡
...
USE THE ONE UPSTAIRS.
IT'S THE FIRST DOOR AT THE TOP.
I'M *SO* GOING HOME...
TOK
TOK
...EVEN IF I HAVE TO GO BY MYSELF.
IS THIS IT?
CHAK

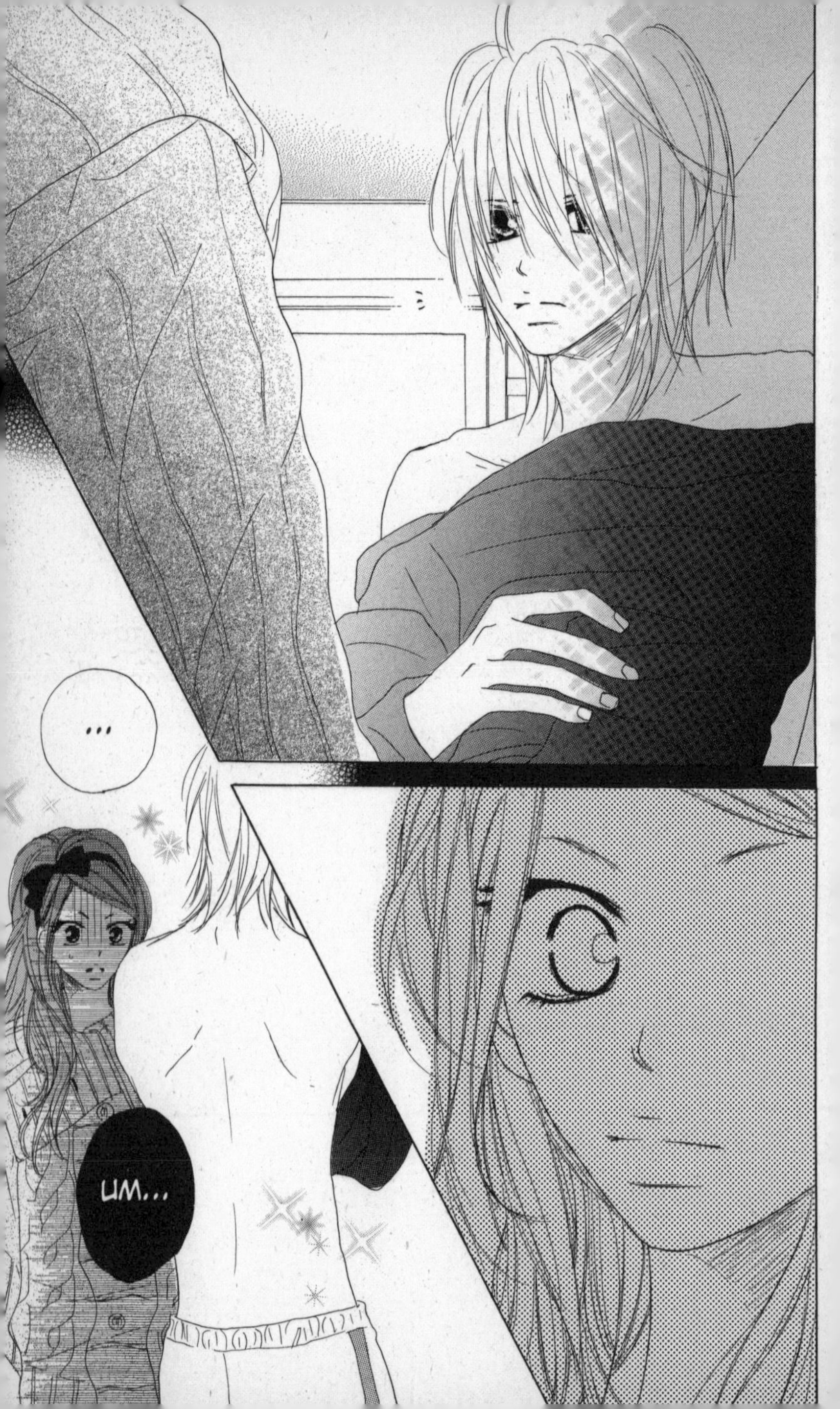
...
UM...

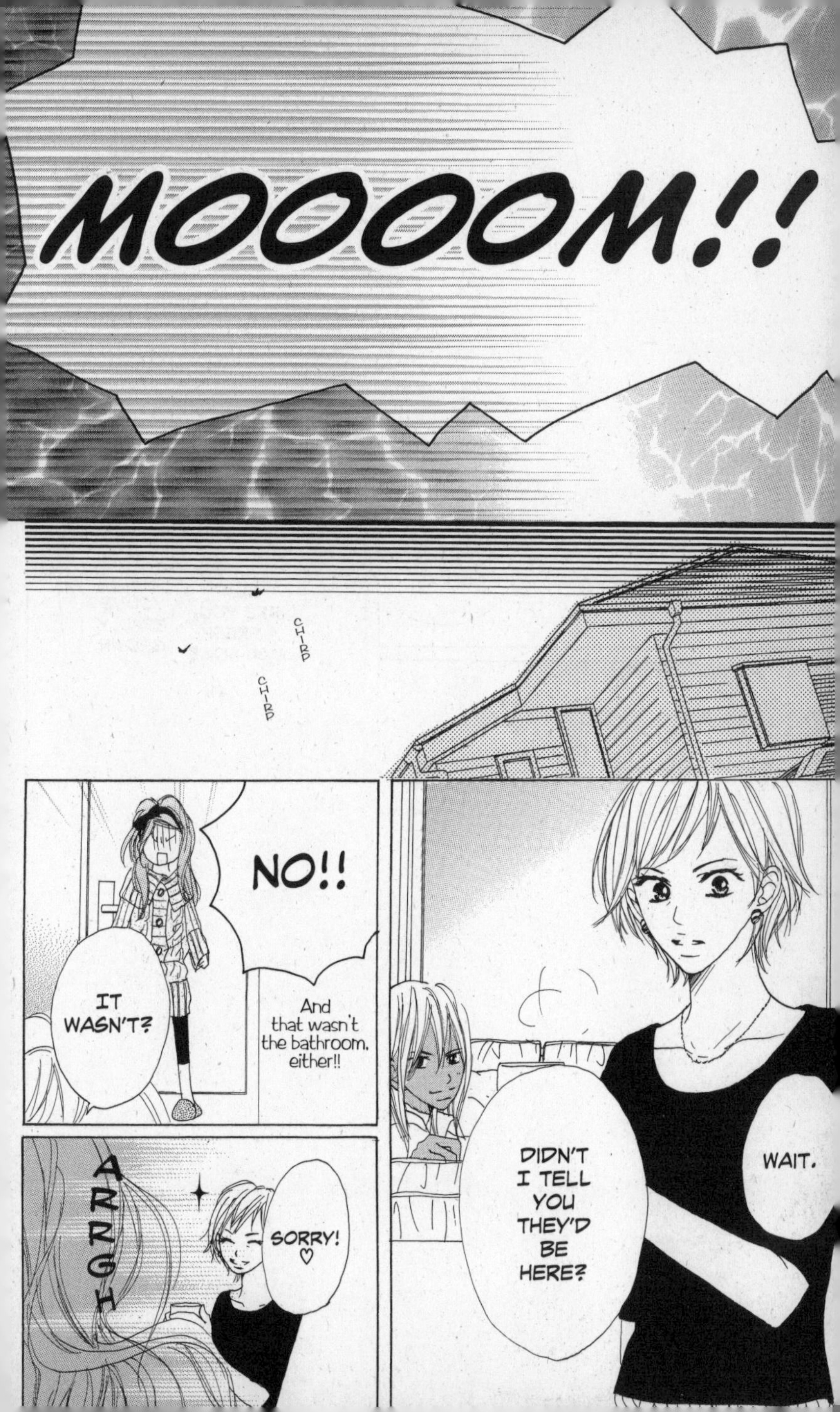
MOOOM!!
CHIRP
CHIRP
WAIT.
DIDN'T I TELL YOU THEY'D BE HERE?
NO!!
And that wasn't the bathroom, either!!
IT WASN'T?
SORRY! ♥
ARRGH

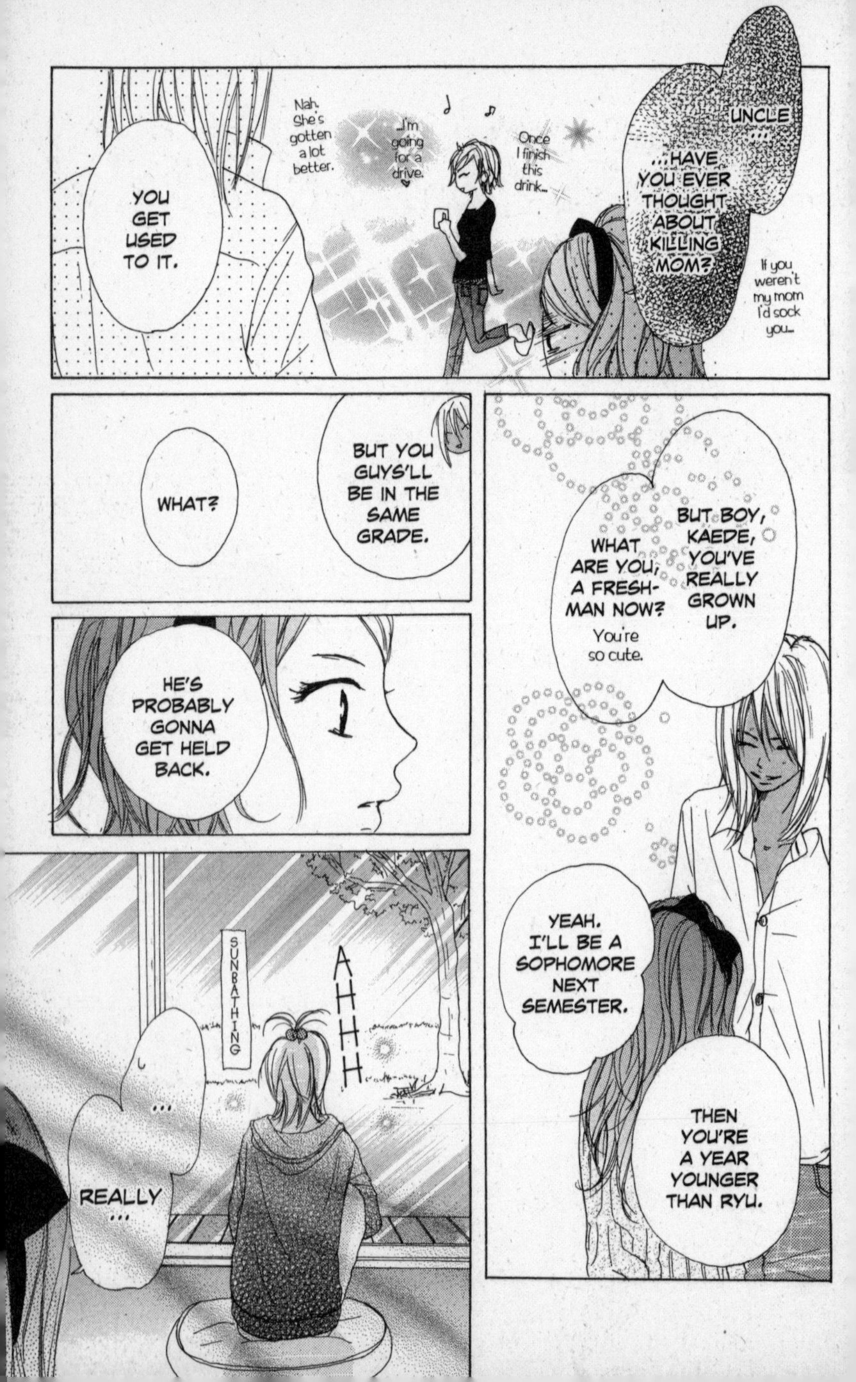
UNCLE ...
...HAVE YOU EVER THOUGHT ABOUT KILLING MOM?
If you weren't my mom I'd sock you...
Once I finish this drink...
...I'm going for a drive.
Nah. She's gotten a lot better.
YOU GET USED TO IT.
BUT BOY, KAEDE, YOU'VE REALLY GROWN UP.
WHAT ARE YOU, A FRESH-MAN NOW?
You're so cute.
YEAH. I'LL BE A SOPHOMORE NEXT SEMESTER.
THEN YOU'RE A YEAR YOUNGER THAN RYU.
BUT YOU GUYS'LL BE IN THE SAME GRADE.
WHAT?
HE'S PROBABLY GONNA GET HELD BACK.
SUNBATHING
AHHH
...
REALLY ...

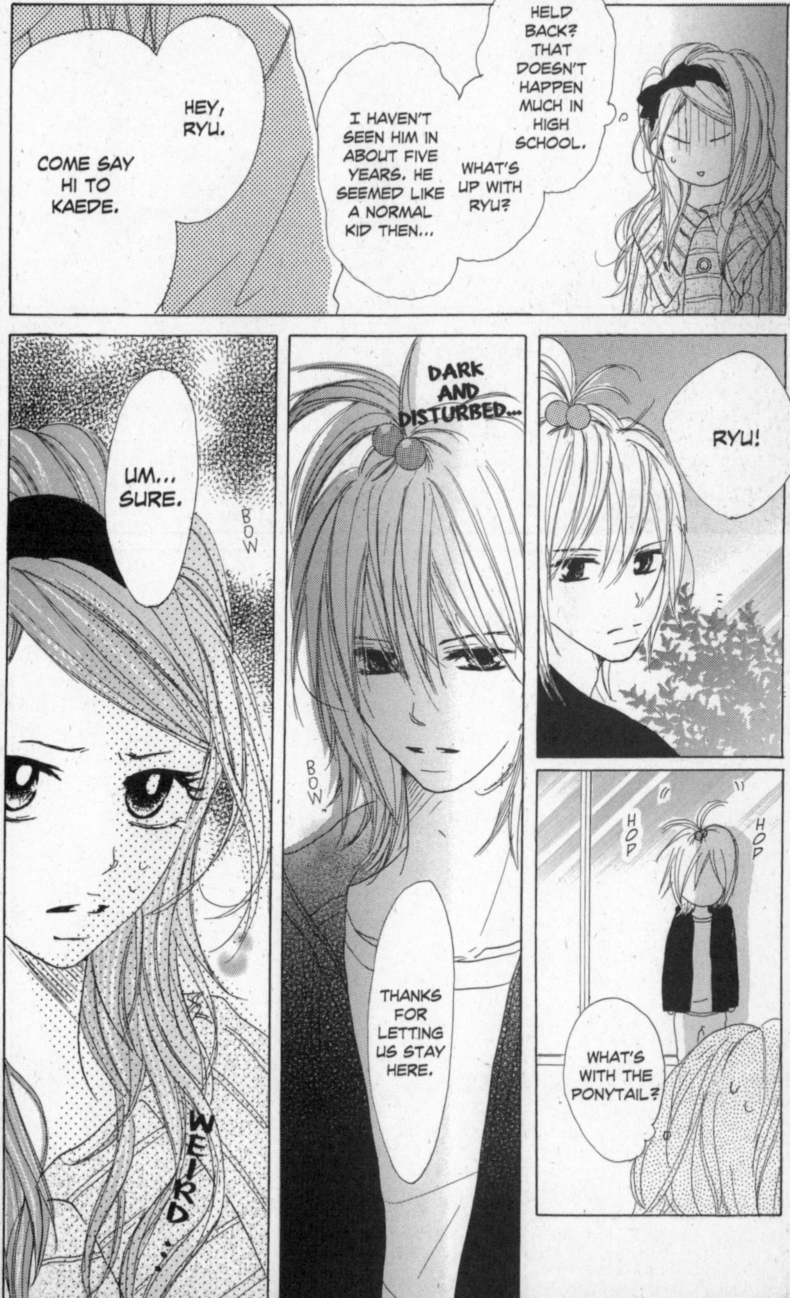
HELD BACK? THAT DOESN'T HAPPEN MUCH IN HIGH SCHOOL.
WHAT'S UP WITH RYU?
I HAVEN'T SEEN HIM IN ABOUT FIVE YEARS. HE SEEMED LIKE A NORMAL KID THEN...
HEY, RYU.
COME SAY HI TO KAEDE.
RYU!
HOP
HOP
WHAT'S WITH THE PONYTAIL?
DARK AND DISTURBED...
BOW
THANKS FOR LETTING US STAY HERE.
UM... SURE.
BOW
WEIRD...

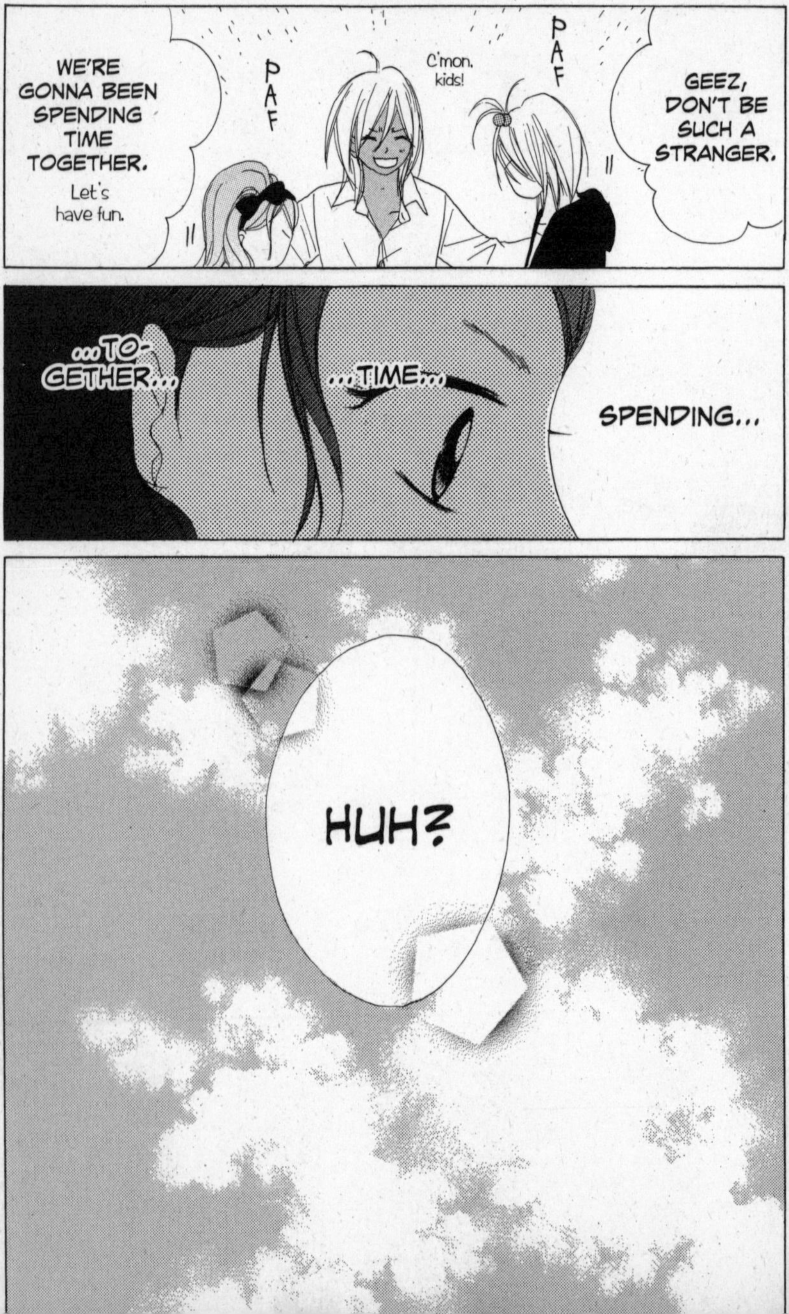
GEEZ, DON'T BE SUCH A STRANGER.
PAF
C'mon. kids!
PAF
WE'RE GONNA BEEN SPENDING TIME TOGETHER.
Let's have fun.
SPENDING...
...TIME...
...TO-GETHER...
HUH?

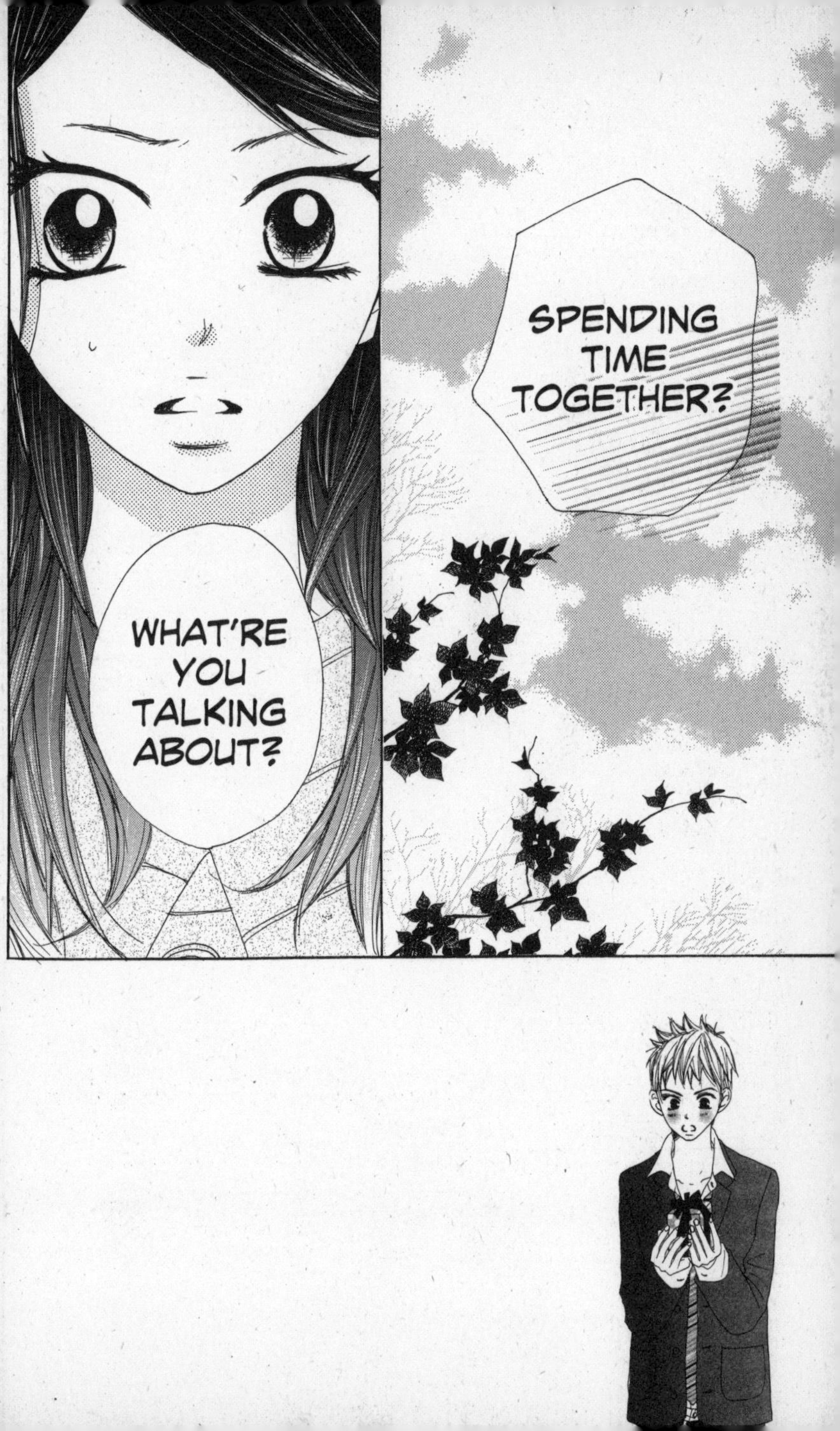
SPENDING TIME TOGETHER?
WHAT'RE YOU TALKING ABOUT?

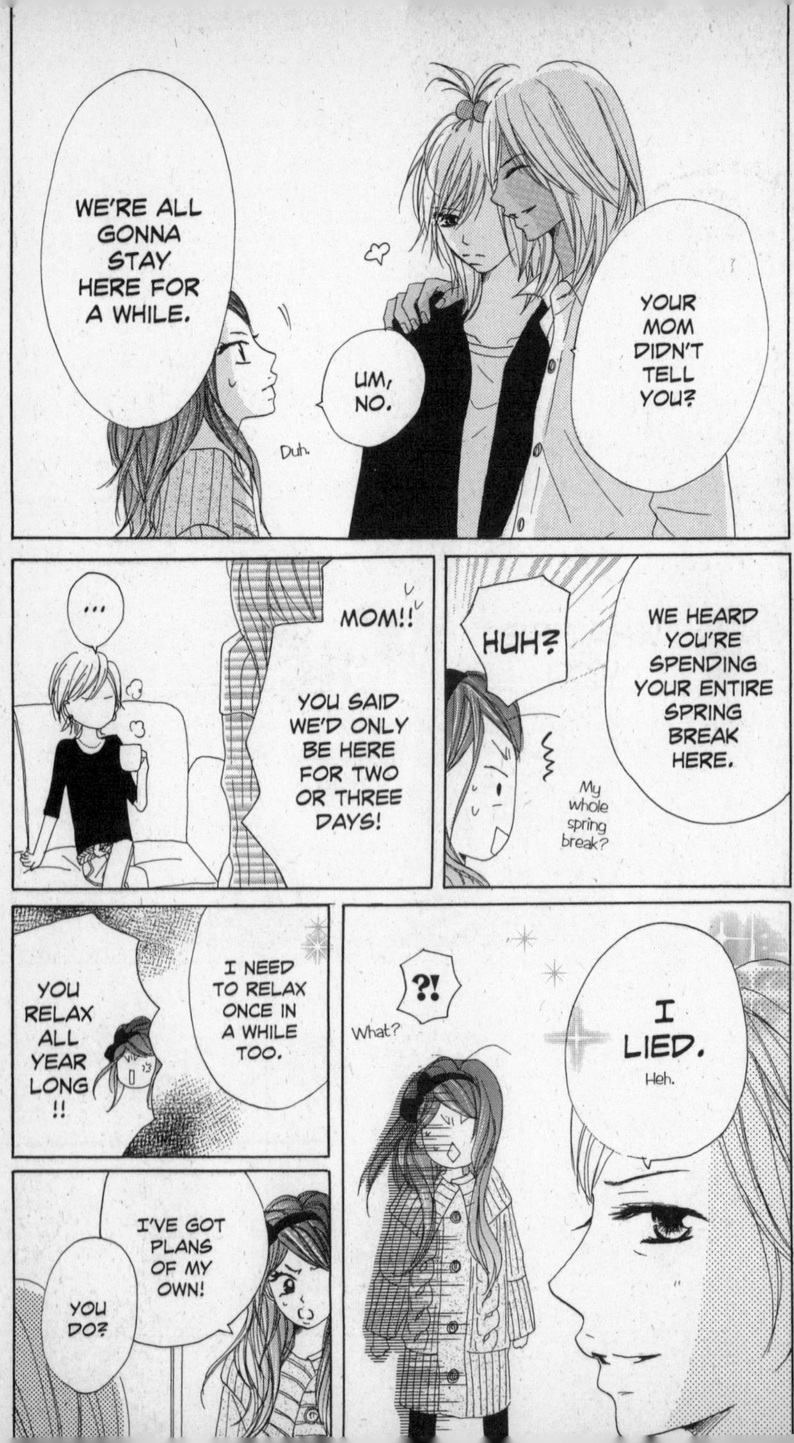
WE'RE ALL GONNA STAY HERE FOR A WHILE.
YOUR MOM DIDN'T TELL YOU?
UM, NO.
Duh.
WE HEARD YOU'RE SPENDING YOUR ENTIRE SPRING BREAK HERE.
HUH?
My whole spring break?
MOM!!
YOU SAID WE'D ONLY BE HERE FOR TWO OR THREE DAYS!
...
I LIED.
Heh.
?!
What?
I NEED TO RELAX ONCE IN A WHILE TOO.
YOU RELAX ALL YEAR LONG!!
I'VE GOT PLANS OF MY OWN!
YOU DO?

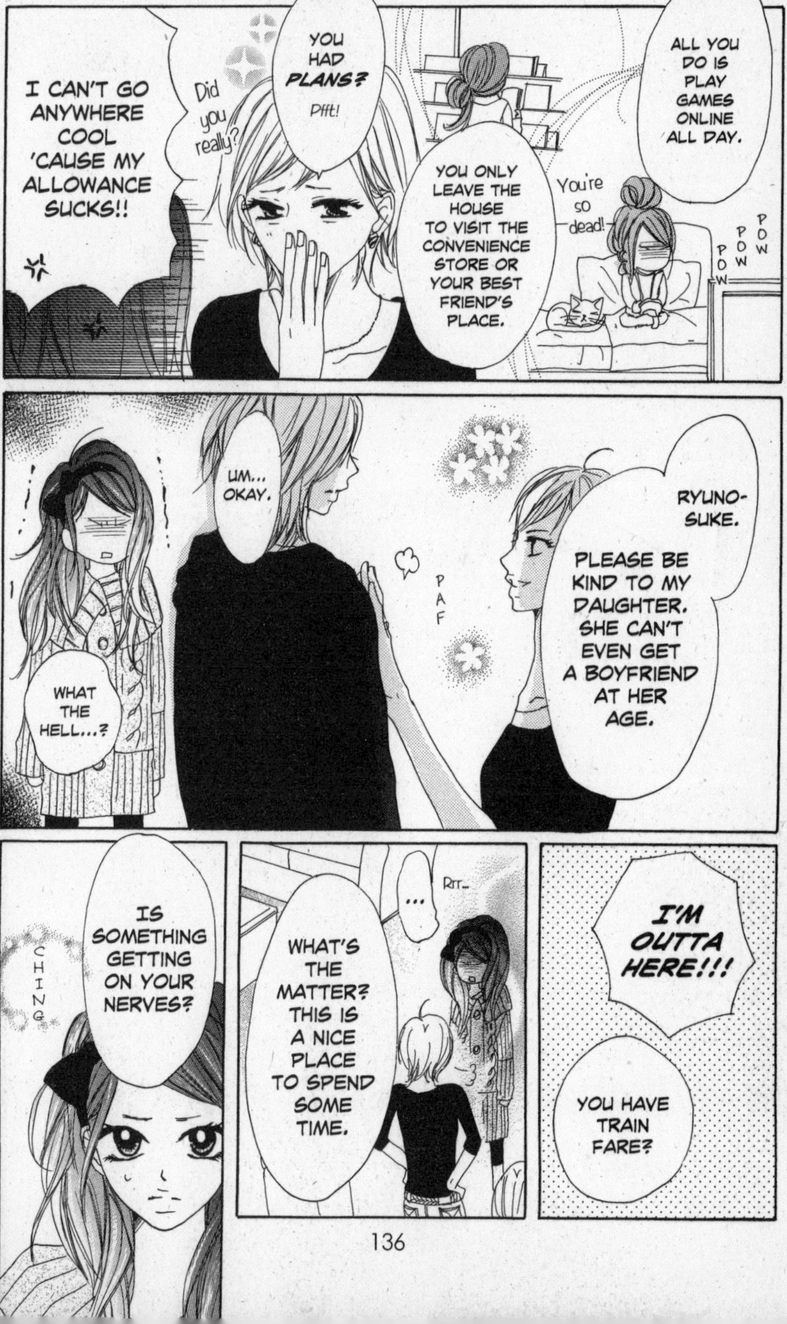
ALL YOU DO IS PLAY GAMES ONLINE ALL DAY.
You're so dead!
POW POW POW
YOU ONLY LEAVE THE HOUSE TO VISIT THE CONVENIENCE STORE OR YOUR BEST FRIEND'S PLACE.
YOU HAD PLANS?
Pfft!
Did you really?
I CAN'T GO ANYWHERE COOL 'CAUSE MY ALLOWANCE SUCKS!!
RYUNOSUKE.
PLEASE BE KIND TO MY DAUGHTER. SHE CAN'T EVEN GET A BOYFRIEND AT HER AGE.
PAF
UM... OKAY.
WHAT THE HELL...?
I'M OUTTA HERE!!!
YOU HAVE TRAIN FARE?
...
Rit..
WHAT'S THE MATTER? THIS IS A NICE PLACE TO SPEND SOME TIME.
CHING
IS SOMETHING GETTING ON YOUR NERVES?

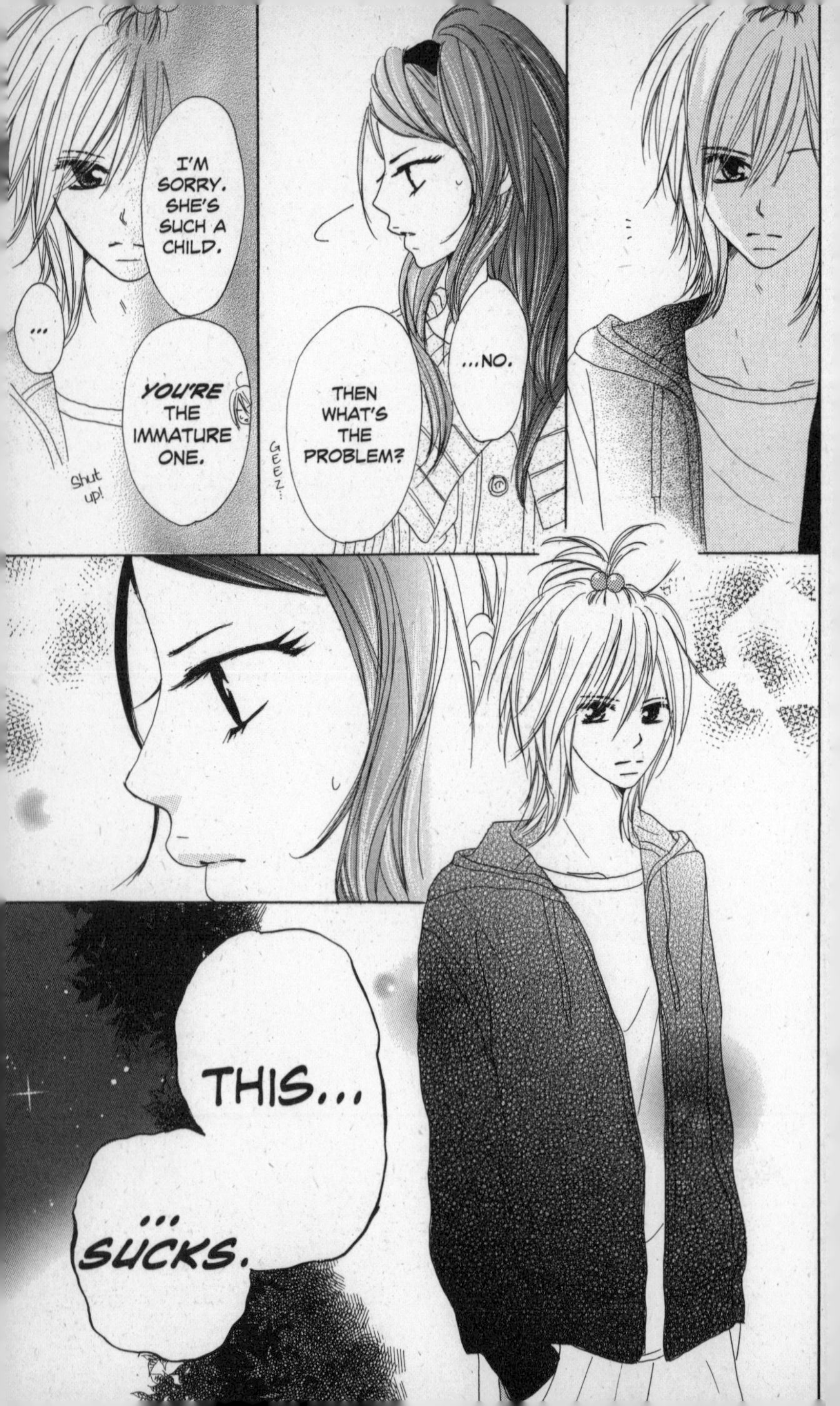
...NO.
THEN WHAT'S THE PROBLEM?
GEEZ...
I'M SORRY. SHE'S SUCH A CHILD.
...
YOU'RE THE IMMATURE ONE.
Shut up!
THIS...
...SUCKS.

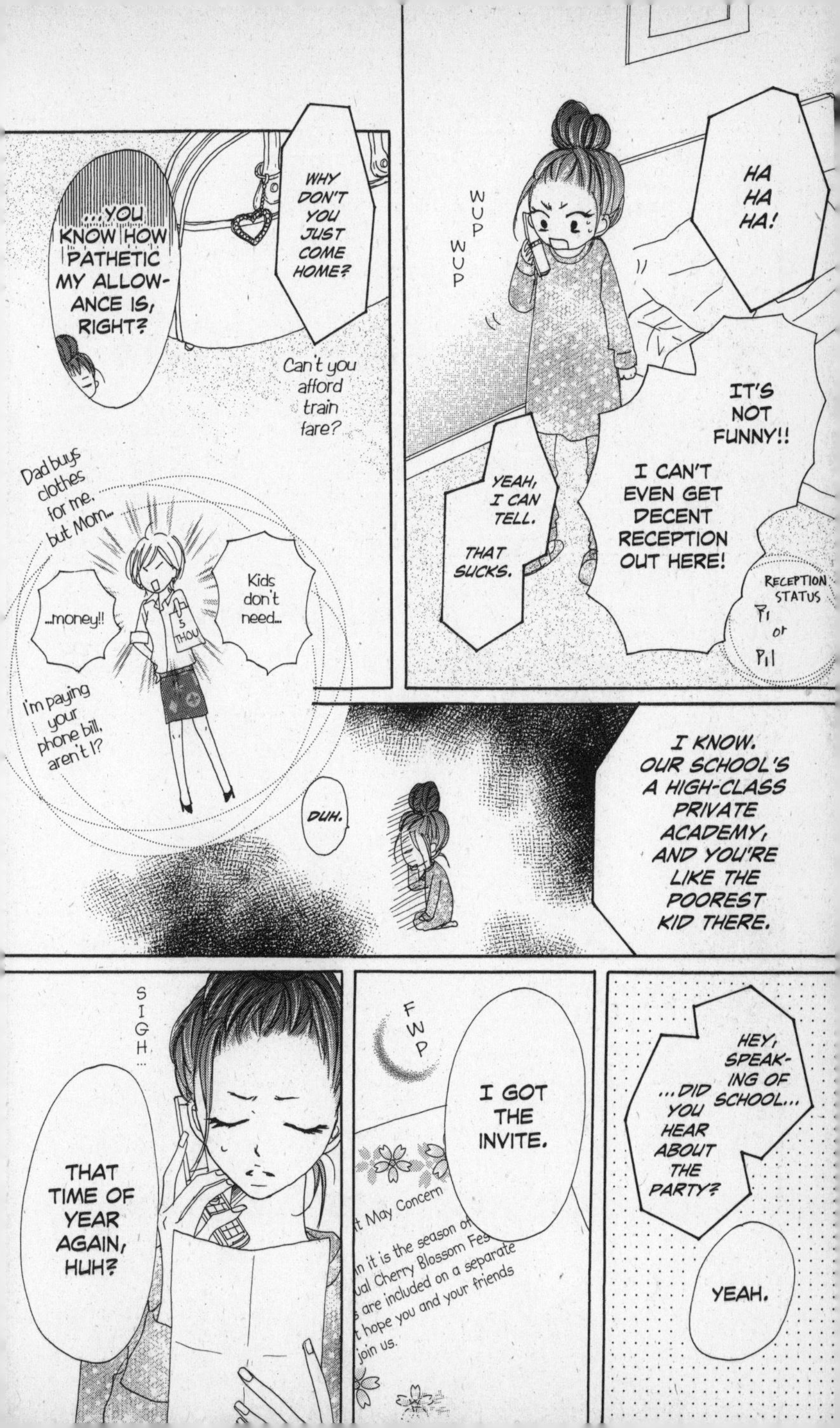
HA HA HA!
WUP WUP
IT'S NOT FUNNY!!
I CAN'T EVEN GET DECENT RECEPTION OUT HERE!
RECEPTION STATUS
or
YEAH, I CAN TELL.
THAT SUCKS.
WHY DON'T YOU JUST COME HOME?
...YOU KNOW HOW PATHETIC MY ALLOWANCE IS, RIGHT?
Can't you afford train fare?
Dad buys clothes for me, but Mom...
Kids don't need...
...money!!
5 THOU
I'm paying your phone bill, aren't I?
I KNOW. OUR SCHOOL'S A HIGH-CLASS PRIVATE ACADEMY, AND YOU'RE LIKE THE POOREST KID THERE.
DUH.
HEY, SPEAKING OF SCHOOL...
...DID YOU HEAR ABOUT THE PARTY?
YEAH.
FWP
I GOT THE INVITE.
t May Concern
n it is the season of
ual Cherry Blossom Fes
s are included on a separate
t hope you and your friends
join us.
SIGH...
THAT TIME OF YEAR AGAIN, HUH?

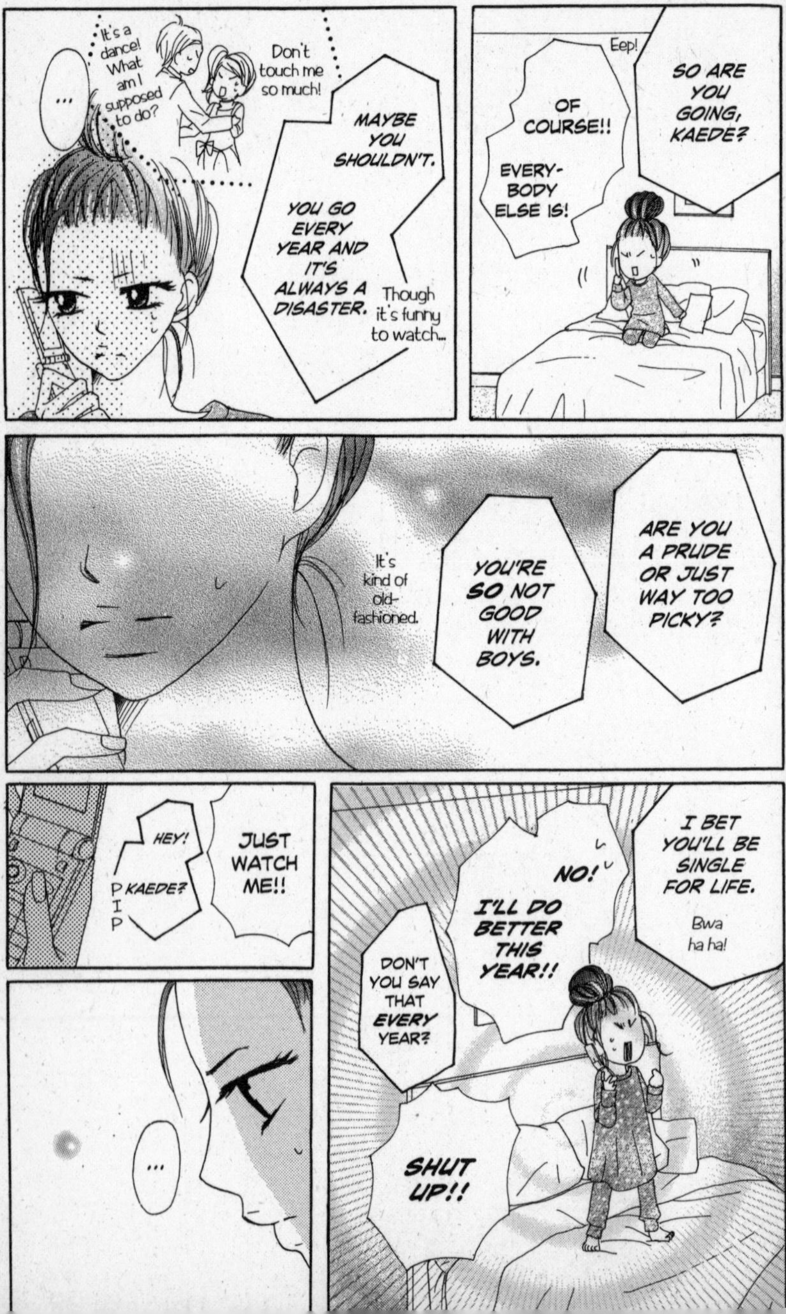
SO ARE YOU GOING, KAEDE?
Eep!
OF COURSE!!
EVERY-BODY ELSE IS!
MAYBE YOU SHOULDN'T.
YOU GO EVERY YEAR AND IT'S ALWAYS A DISASTER.
Don't touch me so much!
It's a dance! What am I supposed to do?
...
Though it's funny to watch...
ARE YOU A PRUDE OR JUST WAY TOO PICKY?
YOU'RE SO NOT GOOD WITH BOYS.
It's kind of old-fashioned.
I BET YOU'LL BE SINGLE FOR LIFE.
Bwa ha ha!
NO!
I'LL DO BETTER THIS YEAR!!
DON'T YOU SAY THAT EVERY YEAR?
SHUT UP!!
JUST WATCH ME!!
HEY!
KAEDE?
PIP
...

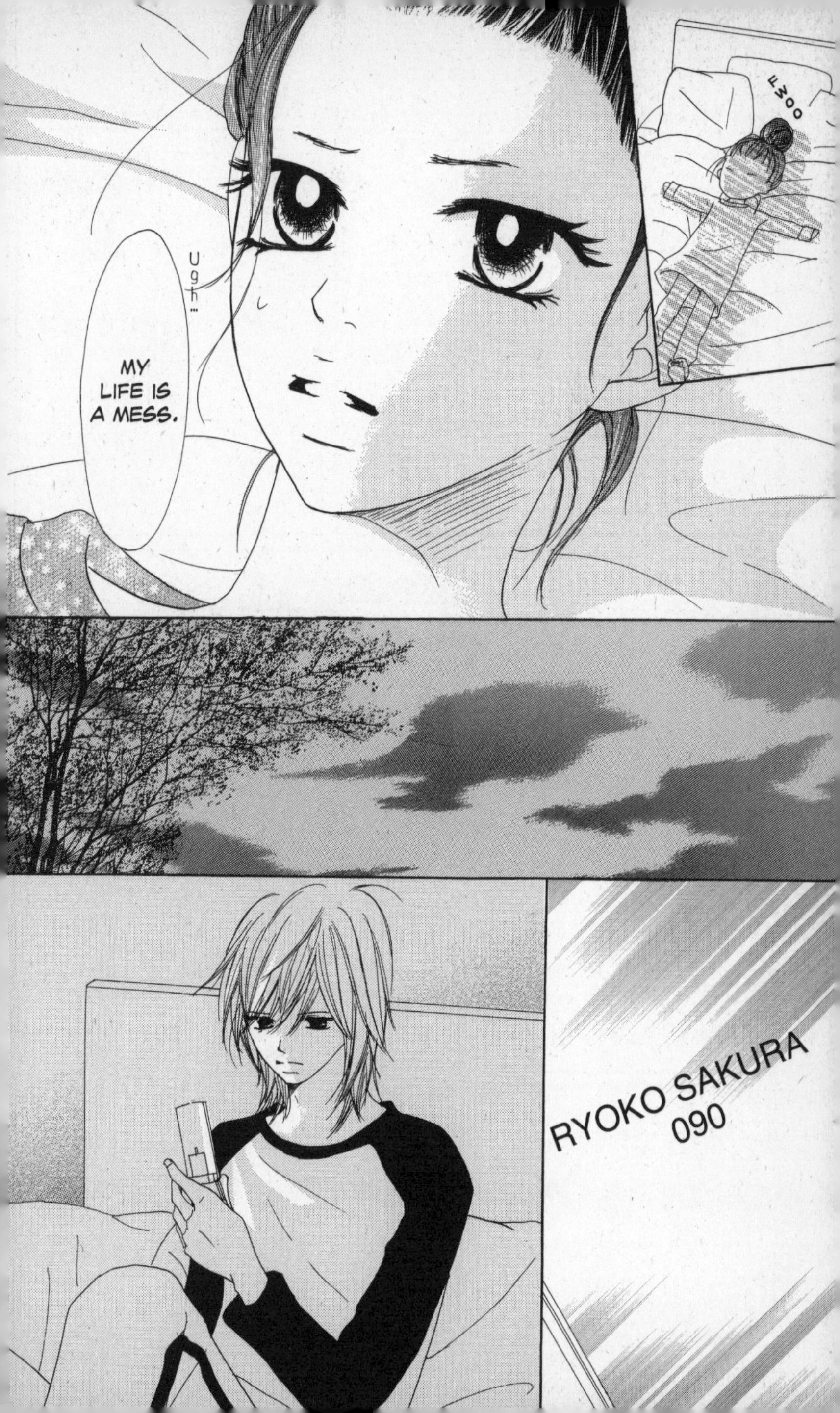

FWOO
Ugh...
MY LIFE IS A MESS.
RYOKO SAKURA 090

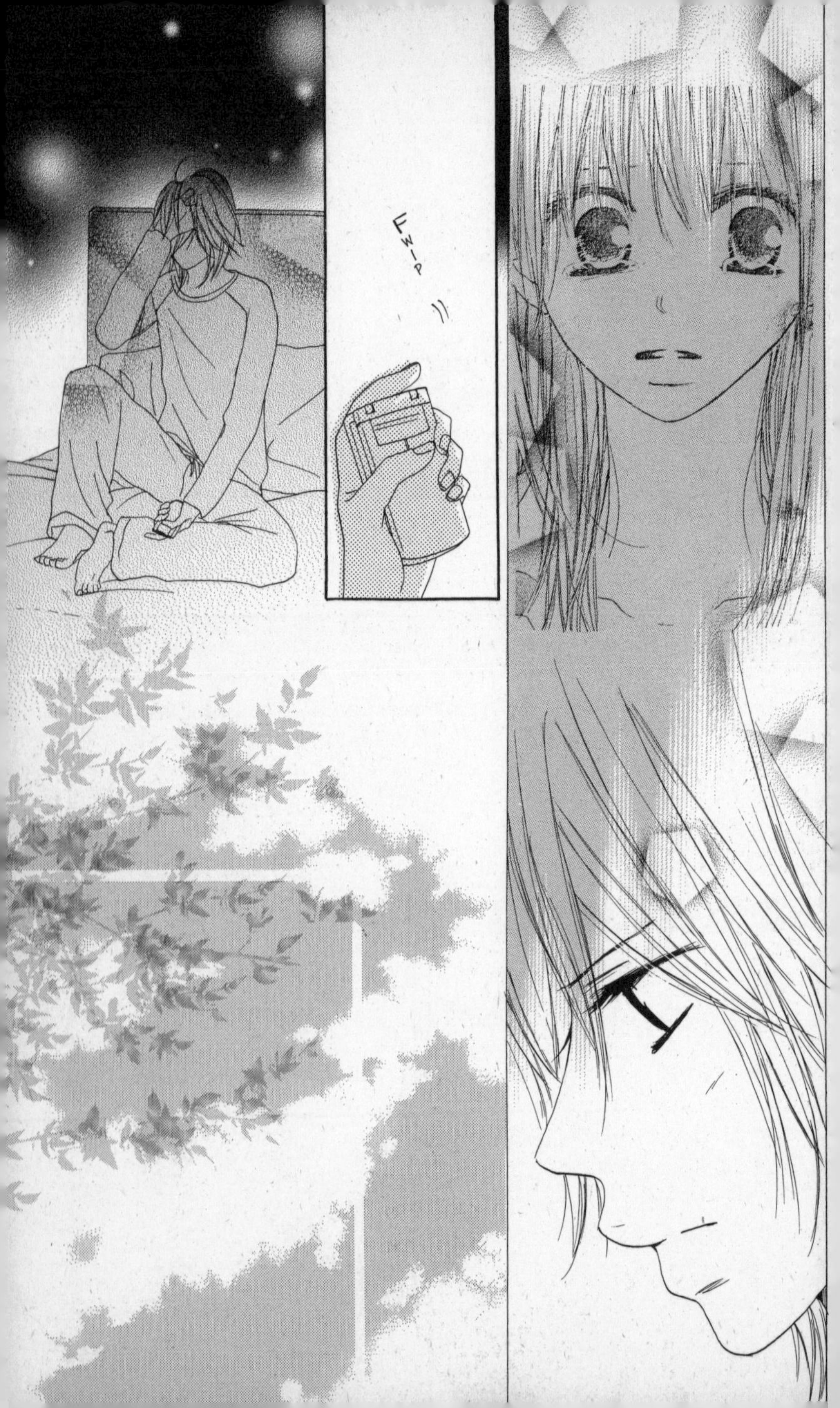
FWIP

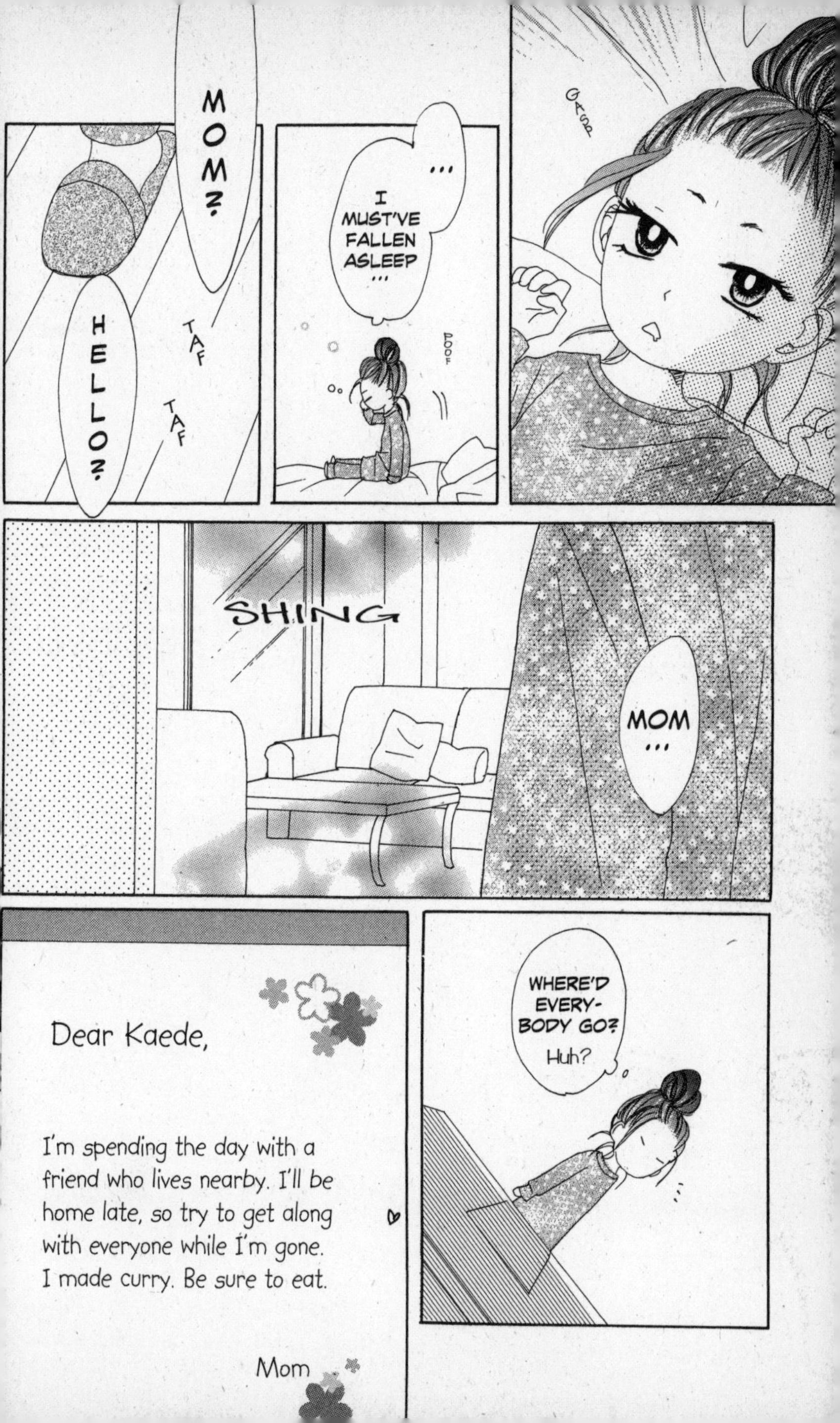
GASP
...
I MUST'VE FALLEN ASLEEP...
POOF
MOM?
HELLO?
TAF
TAF
MOM...
SHING
WHERE'D EVERY-BODY GO?
Huh?
Dear Kaede,
I'm spending the day with a friend who lives nearby. I'll be home late, so try to get along with everyone while I'm gone. I made curry. Be sure to eat.
Mom

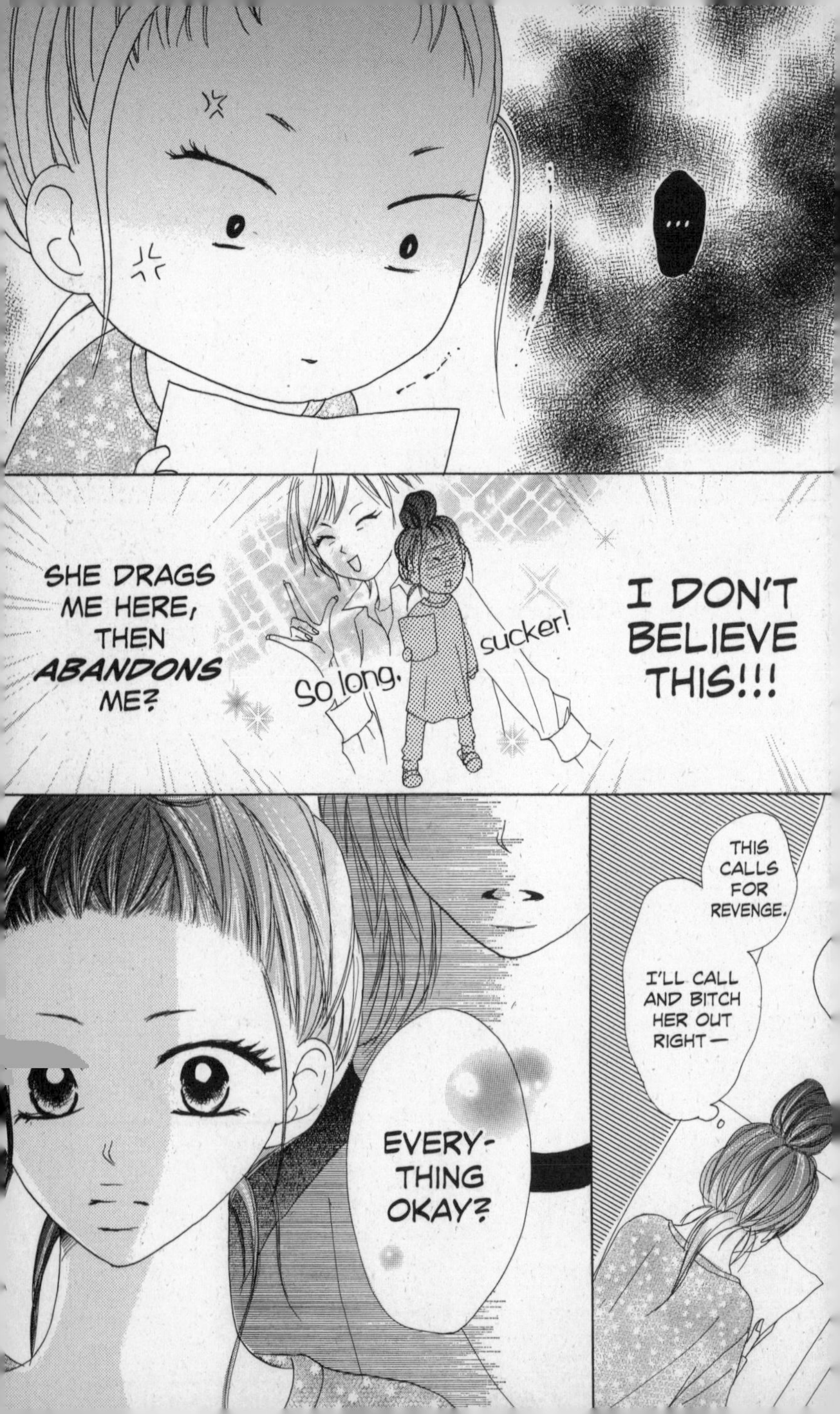
...
I DON'T BELIEVE THIS!!!
sucker!
So long.
SHE DRAGS ME HERE, THEN *ABANDONS* ME?
THIS CALLS FOR REVENGE.
I'LL CALL AND BITCH HER OUT RIGHT—
EVERY-THING OKAY?

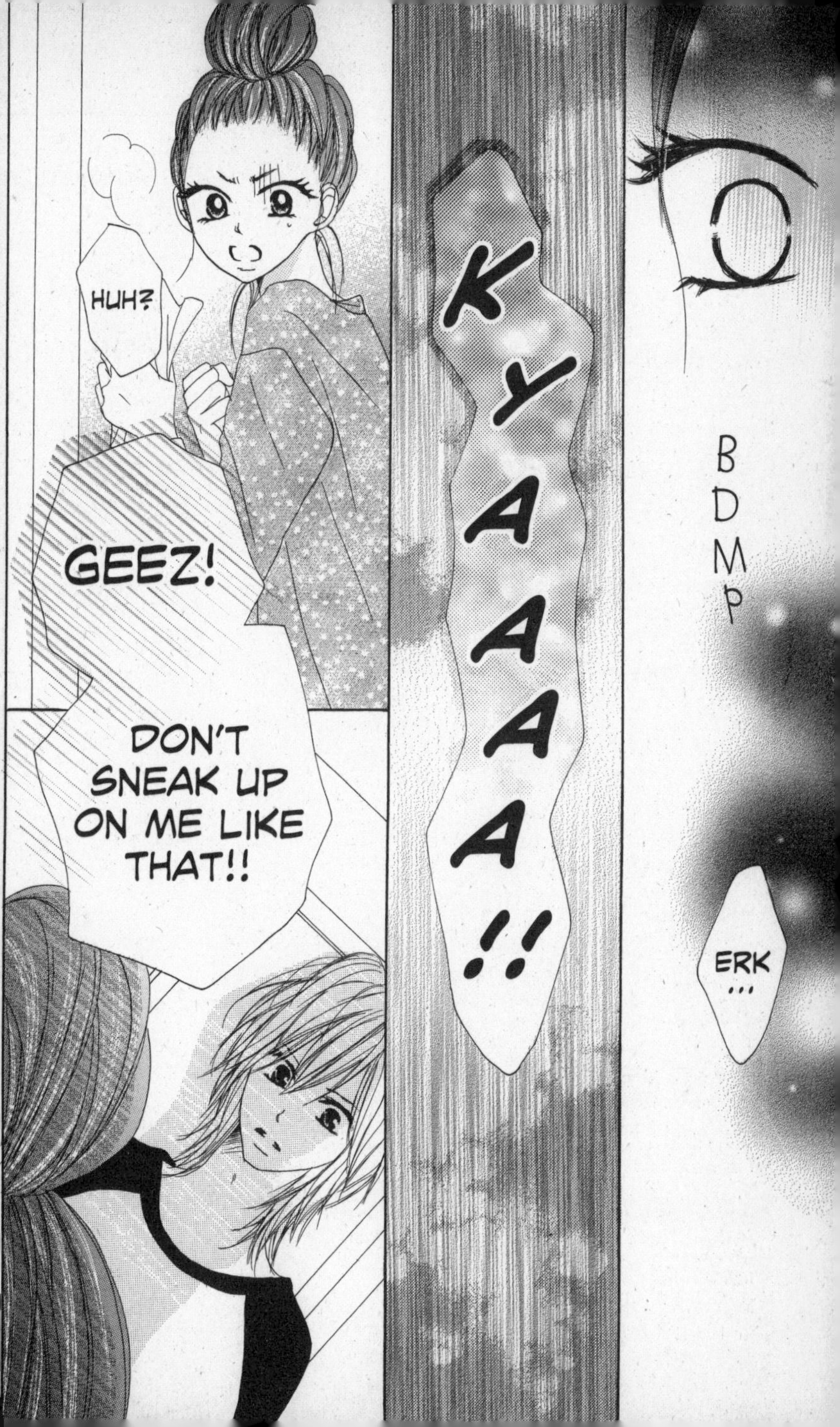
BDMP
ERK...
KYAAAA!!
HUH?
GEEZ!
DON'T SNEAK UP ON ME LIKE THAT!!

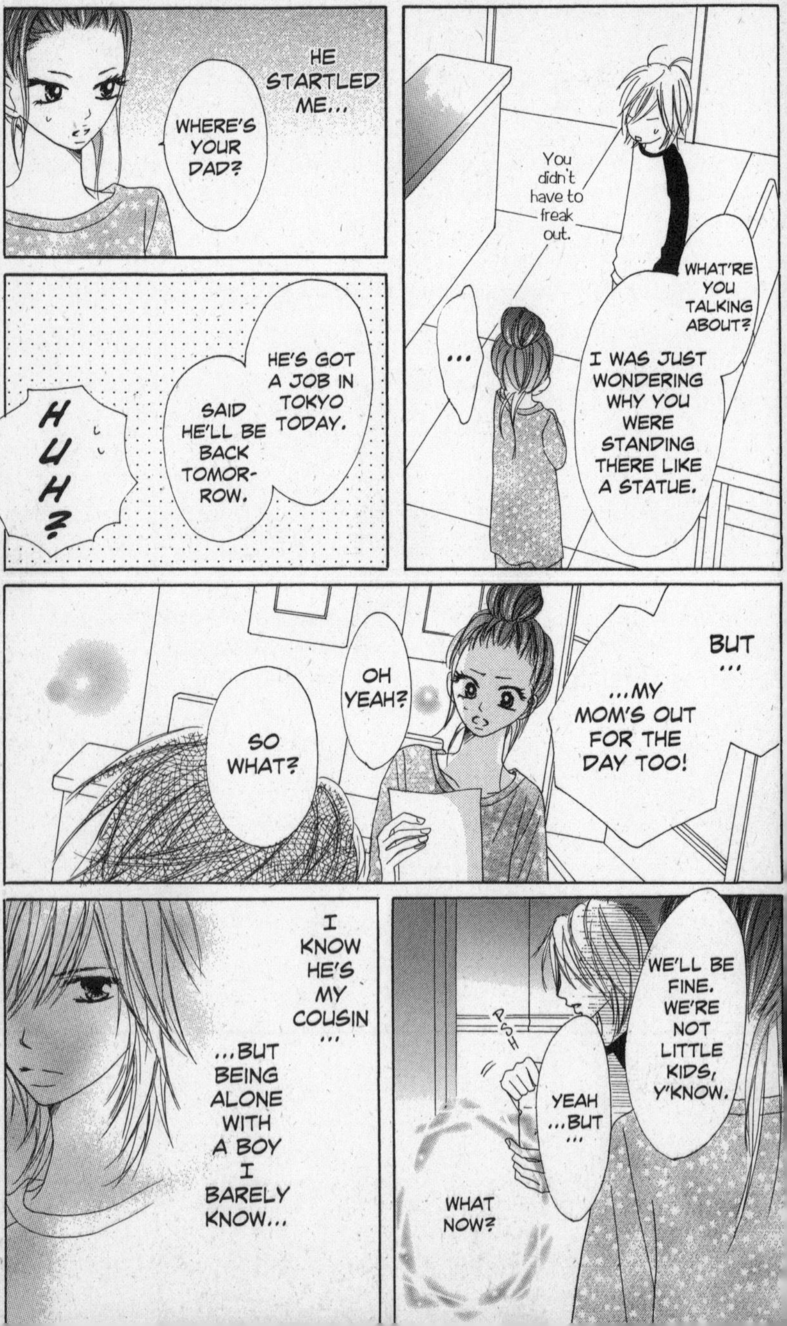
You didn't have to freak out.
...
WHAT'RE YOU TALKING ABOUT?
I WAS JUST WONDERING WHY YOU WERE STANDING THERE LIKE A STATUE.
HE STARTLED ME...
WHERE'S YOUR DAD?
HE'S GOT A JOB IN TOKYO TODAY.
SAID HE'LL BE BACK TOMORROW.
HUH?
BUT...
...MY MOM'S OUT FOR THE DAY TOO!
OH YEAH?
SO WHAT?
WE'LL BE FINE. WE'RE NOT LITTLE KIDS, Y'KNOW.
PSH
YEAH ...BUT ...
WHAT NOW?
I KNOW HE'S MY COUSIN...
...BUT BEING ALONE WITH A BOY I BARELY KNOW...

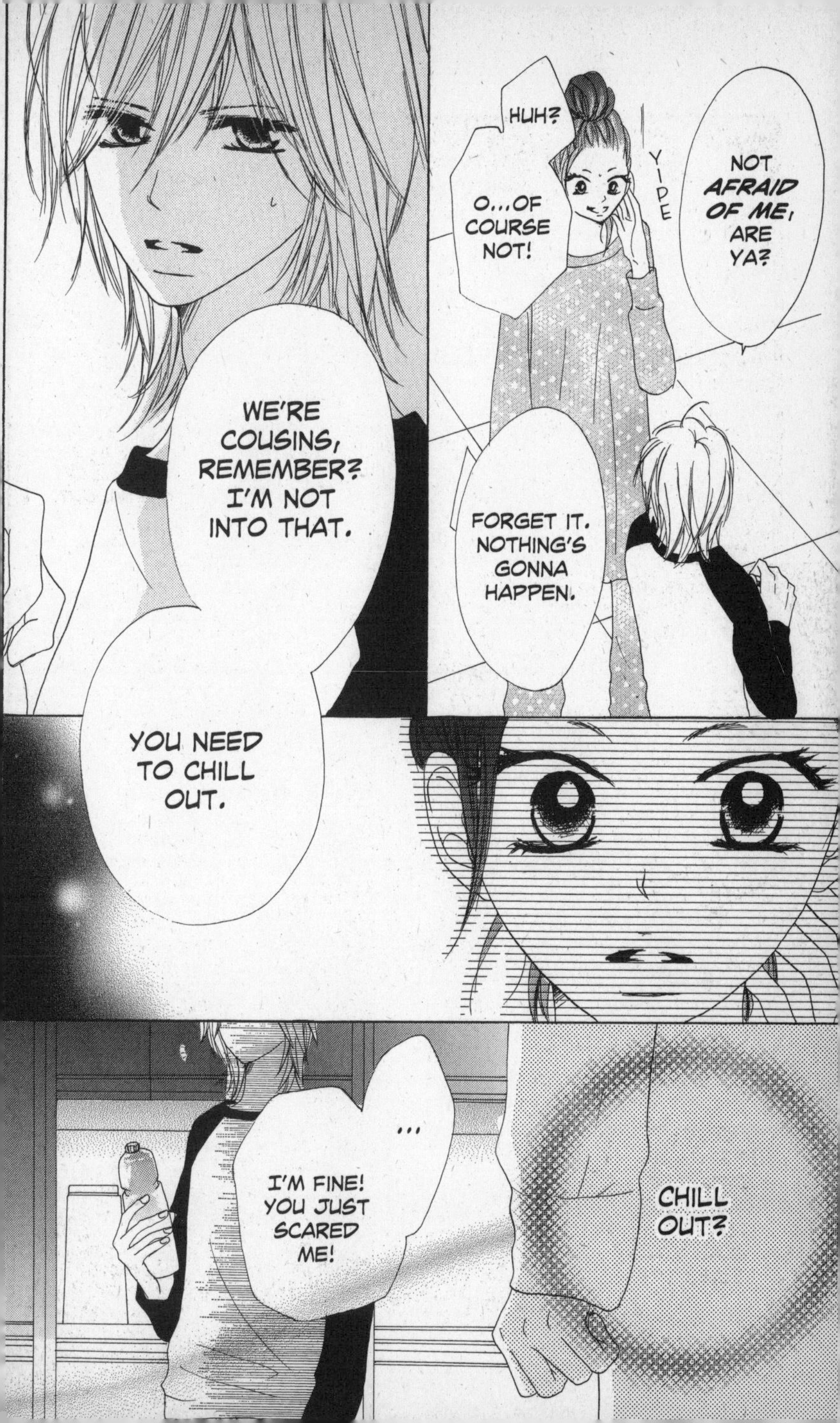
NOT AFRAID OF ME, ARE YA?
YIPE
HUH?
O...OF COURSE NOT!
FORGET IT. NOTHING'S GONNA HAPPEN.
WE'RE COUSINS, REMEMBER? I'M NOT INTO THAT.
YOU NEED TO CHILL OUT.
CHILL OUT?
...
I'M FINE! YOU JUST SCARED ME!

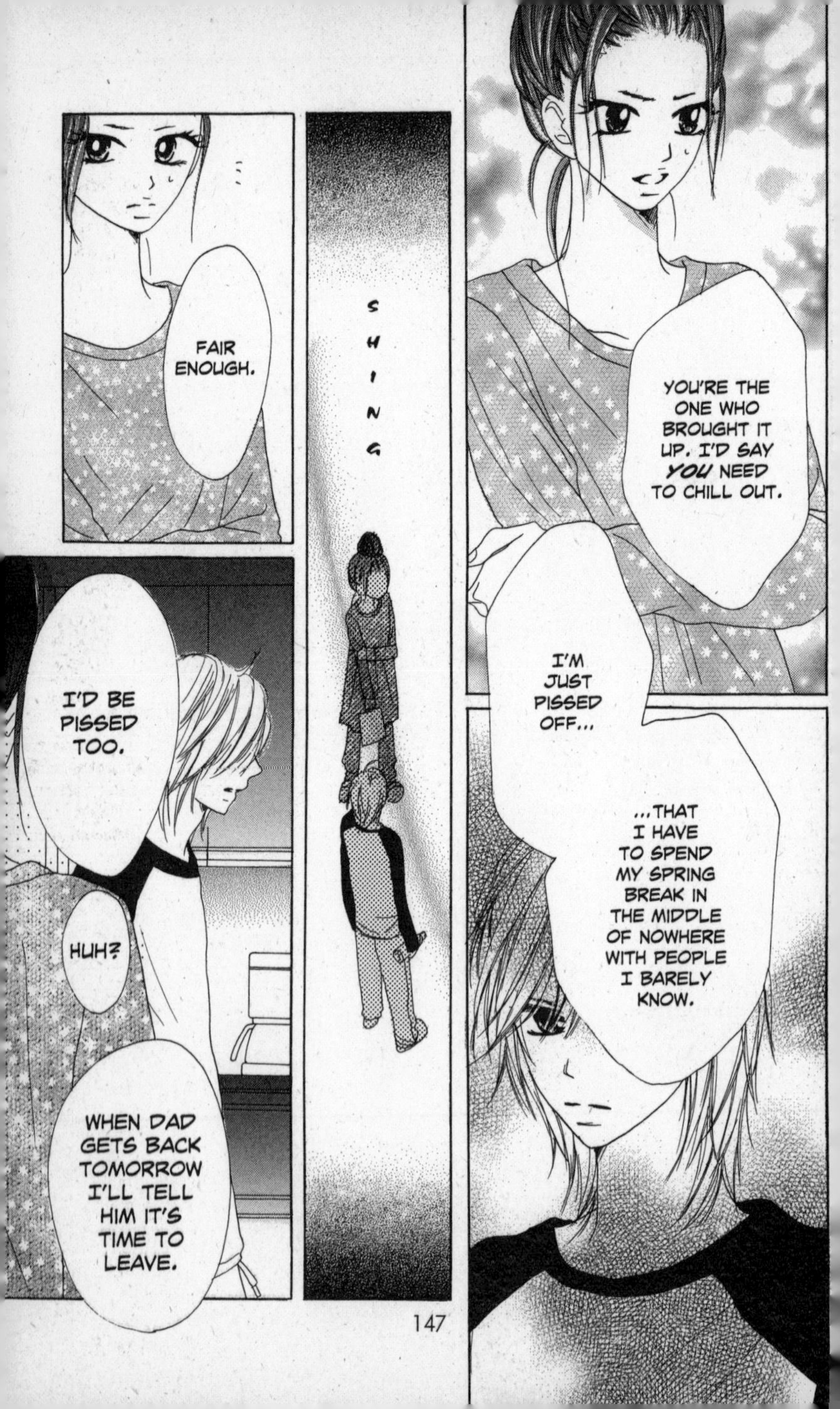
YOU'RE THE ONE WHO BROUGHT IT UP. I'D SAY *YOU* NEED TO CHILL OUT.
I'M JUST PISSED OFF...
...THAT I HAVE TO SPEND MY SPRING BREAK IN THE MIDDLE OF NOWHERE WITH PEOPLE I BARELY KNOW.
SHING
FAIR ENOUGH.
I'D BE PISSED TOO.
HUH?
WHEN DAD GETS BACK TOMORROW I'LL TELL HIM IT'S TIME TO LEAVE.

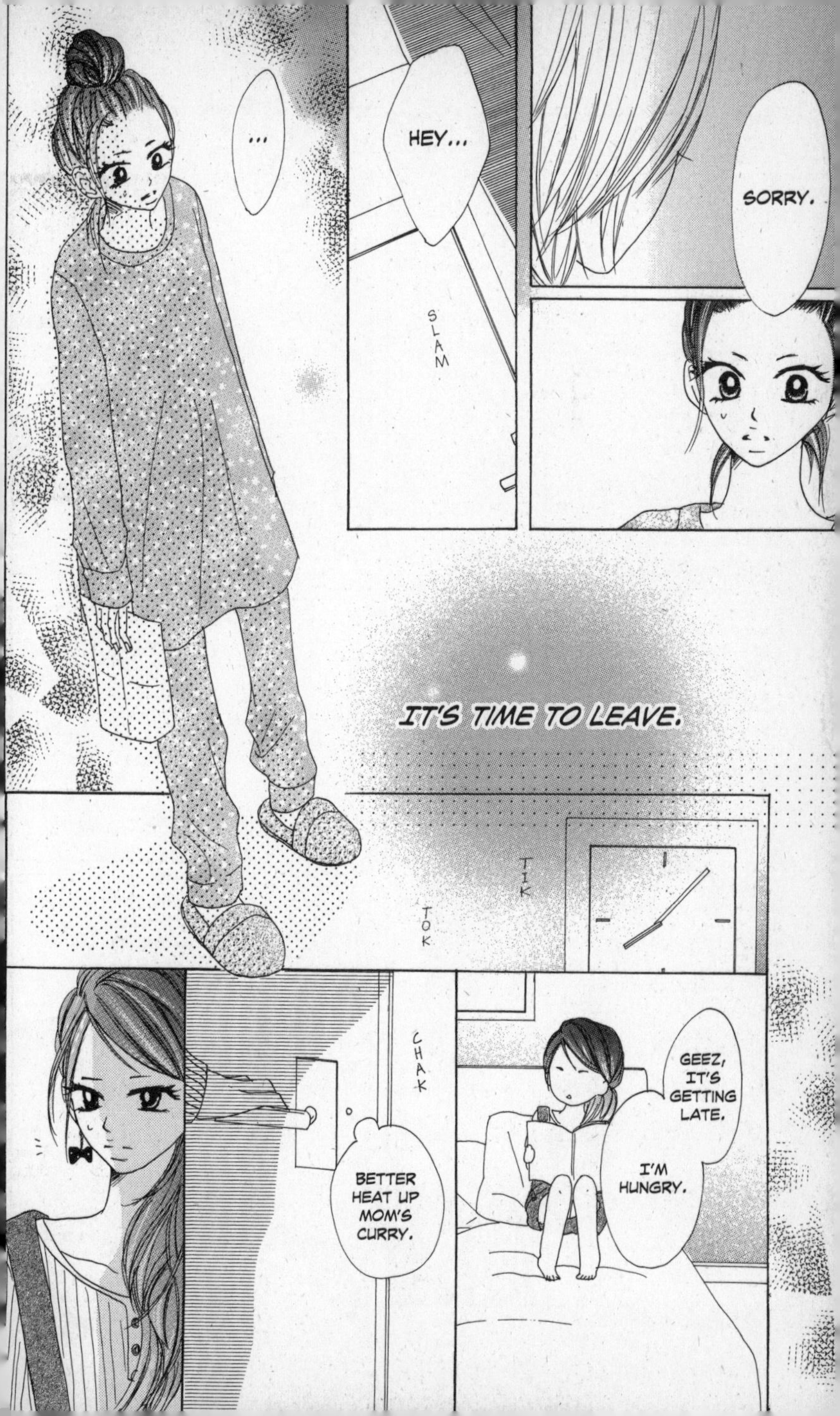
SORRY.
HEY...
SLAM
...
IT'S TIME TO LEAVE.
TIK
TOK
GEEZ, IT'S GETTING LATE.
I'M HUNGRY.
CHAK
BETTER HEAT UP MOM'S CURRY.

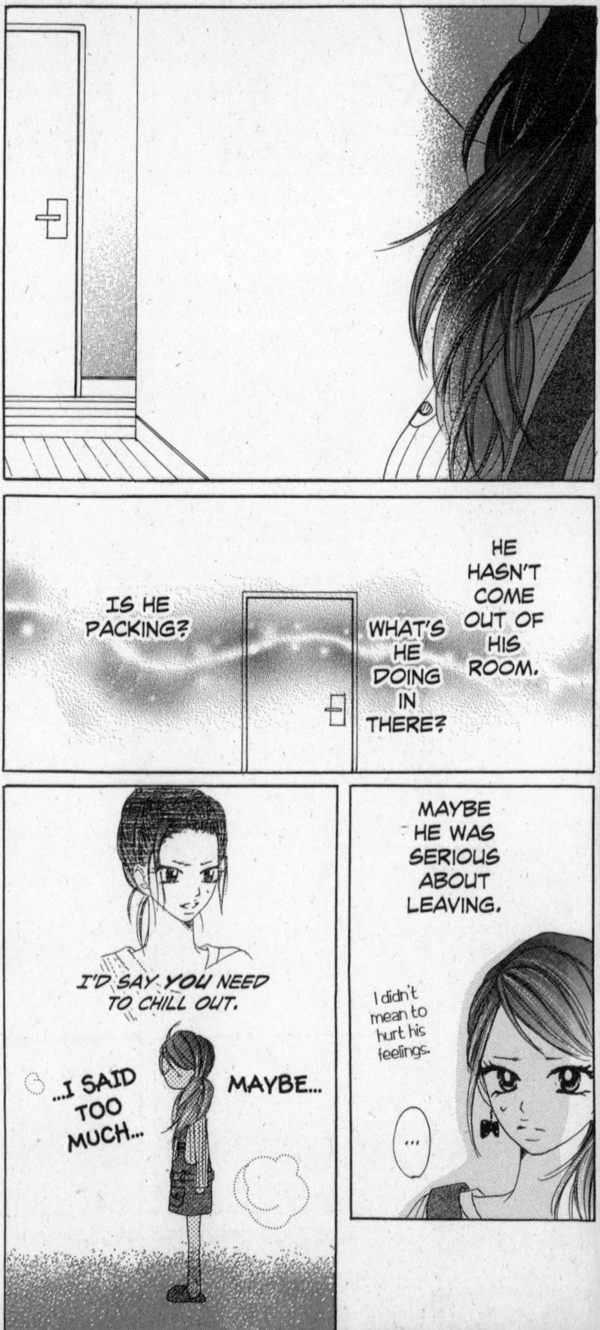
HE HASN'T COME OUT OF HIS ROOM.
WHAT'S HE DOING IN THERE?
IS HE PACKING?
MAYBE HE WAS SERIOUS ABOUT LEAVING.
I didn't mean to hurt his feelings.
...
I'D SAY YOU NEED TO CHILL OUT.
MAYBE...
...I SAID TOO MUCH...

④ Final Note

HEY!

I plan on wearing a lot of one-pieces this summer. ♡ It's a personal fad of mine to dress more girly. Not that I have many opportunities to dress up... I'm basically always in my pajamas!! I love pajamas!!

I enjoy shopping for the softest, most comfortable pajamas I can afford. I like cute ones that have a certain amount of ugliness to them... It's better if they're not too cute!! The droopy, comfortable ones are the best!! ♡

Whew...I got a little excited there...and now I'm out of space. But that was fun. I'm sure you're all wondering what was fun about it. Thanks for putting up with me.

Thank you!

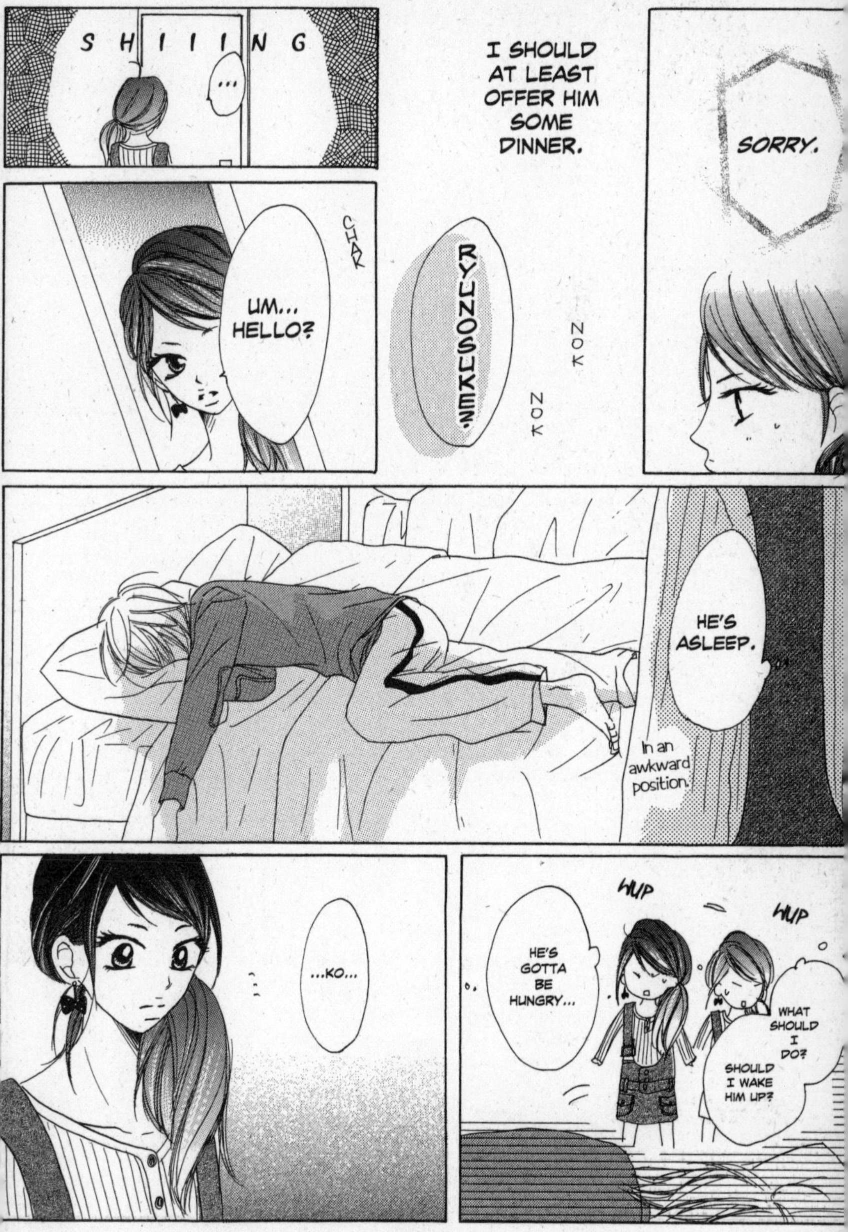

SORRY.
I SHOULD AT LEAST OFFER HIM SOME DINNER.
SHIIING
...
NOK NOK
RYUNOSUKE.
CHAK
UM... HELLO?
HE'S ASLEEP.
In an awkward position.
WUP WUP
WHAT SHOULD I DO?
SHOULD I WAKE HIM UP?
HE'S GOTTA BE HUNGRY...
...KO...

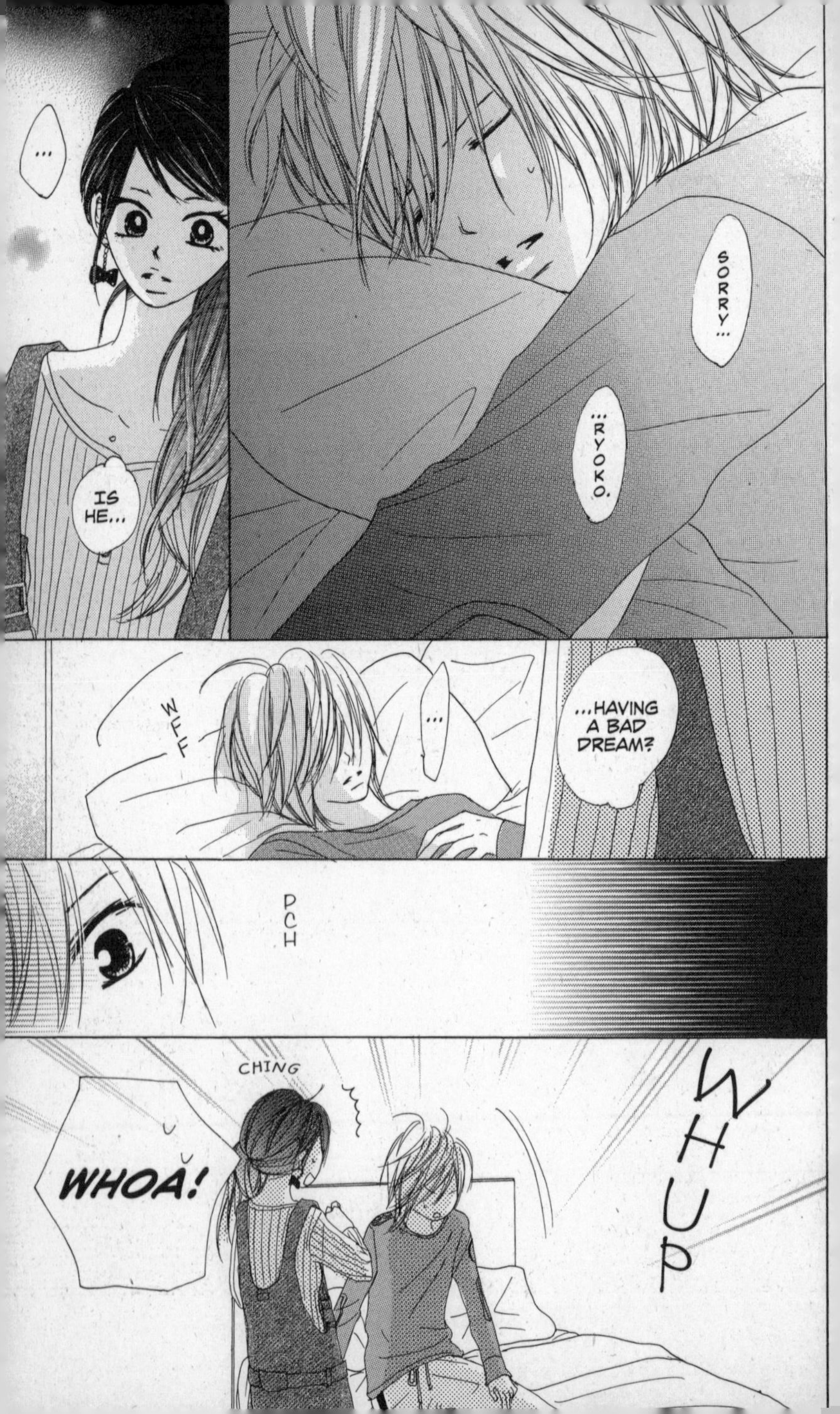
SORRY...
...RYOKO.
...
IS HE...
...HAVING A BAD DREAM?
...
WFF
PCH
WHUP
CHING
WHOA!

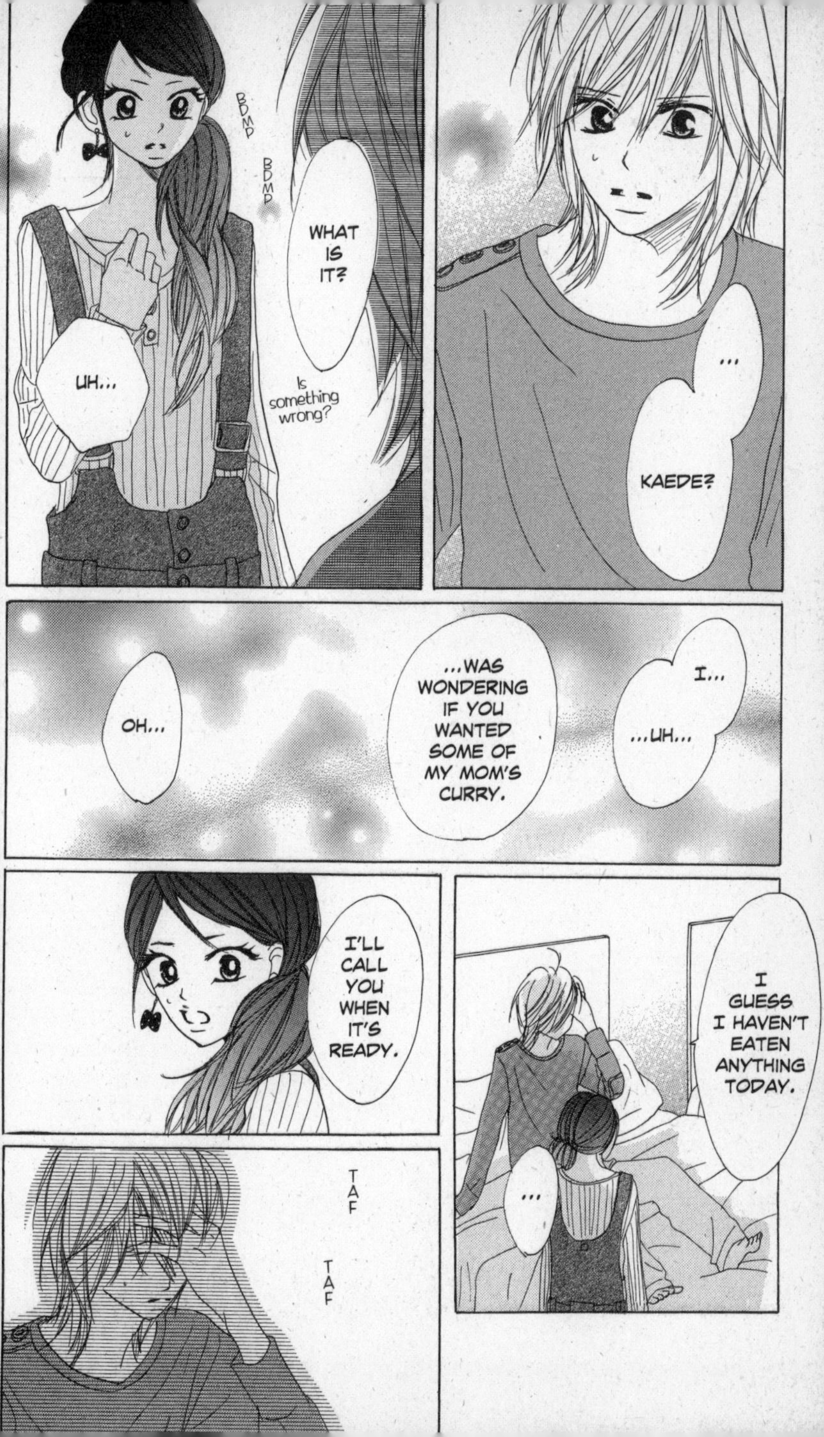
...
KAEDE?
WHAT IS IT?
BDMP
BDMP
Is something wrong?
UH...
I...
...UH...
...WAS WONDERING IF YOU WANTED SOME OF MY MOM'S CURRY.
OH...
I GUESS I HAVEN'T EATEN ANYTHING TODAY.
...
I'LL CALL YOU WHEN IT'S READY.
TAF
TAF

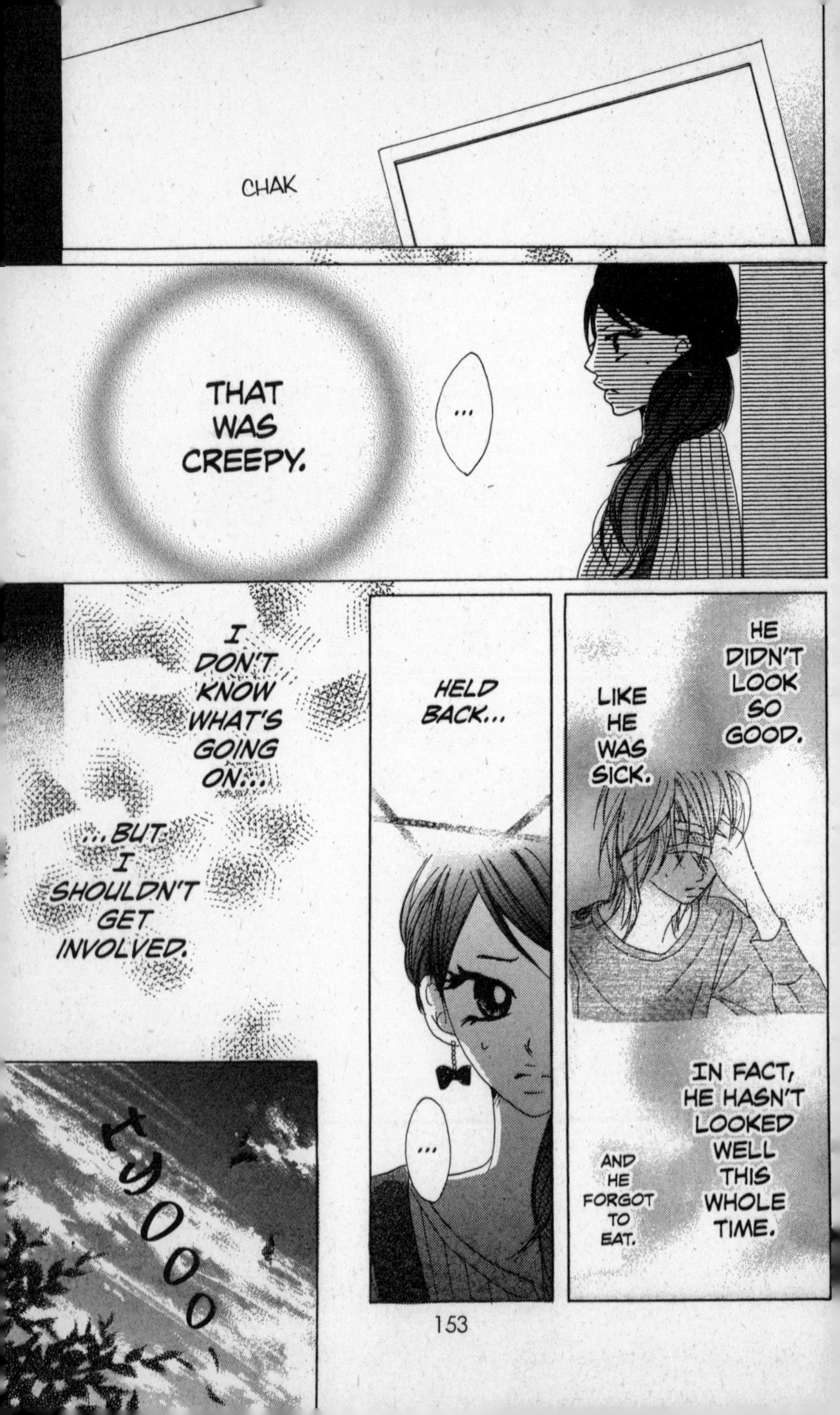
CHAK
...
THAT WAS CREEPY.
HE DIDN'T LOOK SO GOOD.
LIKE HE WAS SICK.
IN FACT, HE HASN'T LOOKED WELL THIS WHOLE TIME.
AND HE FORGOT TO EAT.
HELD BACK...
...
I DON'T KNOW WHAT'S GOING ON...
...BUT I SHOULDN'T GET INVOLVED.

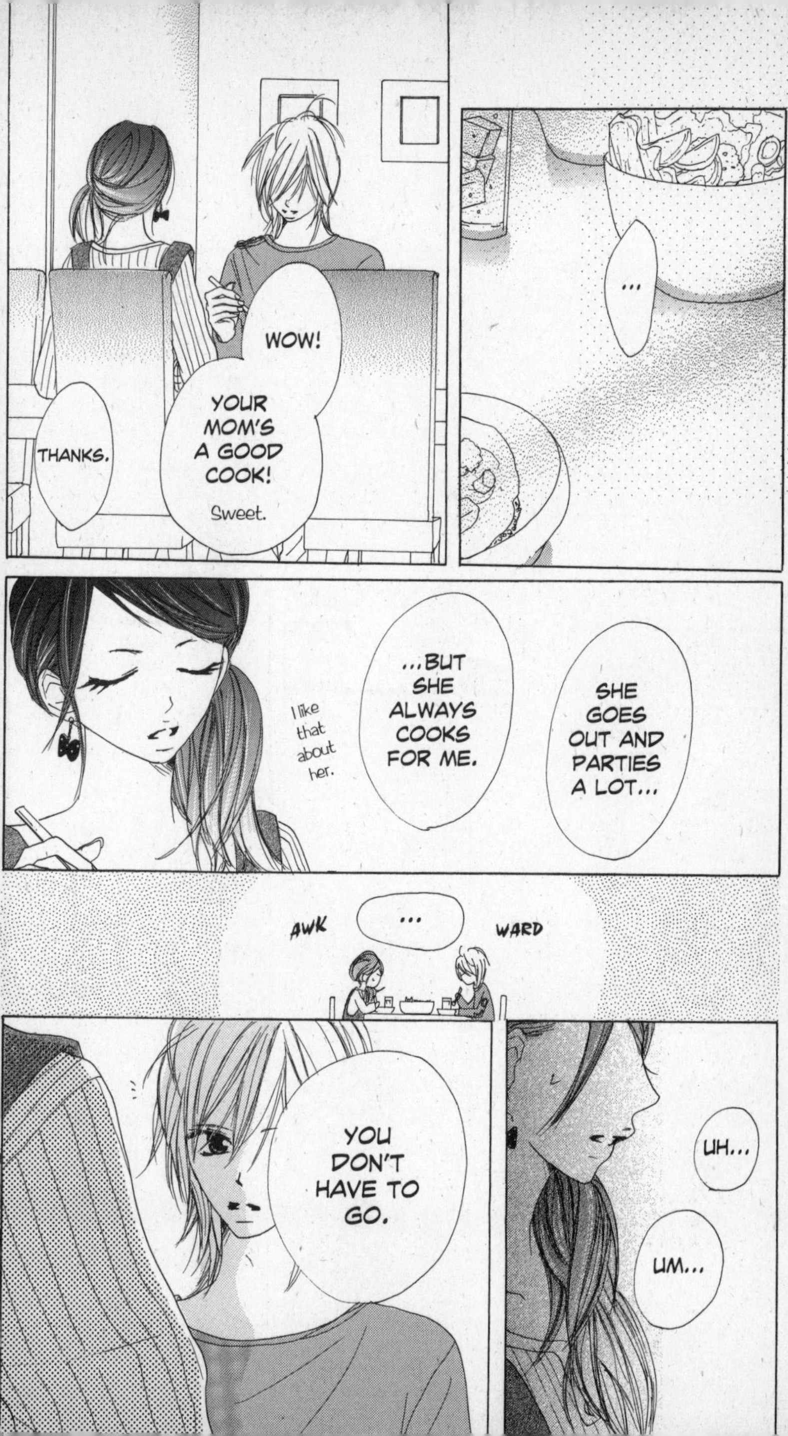
...
WOW!
YOUR MOM'S A GOOD COOK!
Sweet.
THANKS.
SHE GOES OUT AND PARTIES A LOT...
...BUT SHE ALWAYS COOKS FOR ME.
I like that about her.
AWK
...
WARD
UH...
UM...
YOU DON'T HAVE TO GO.

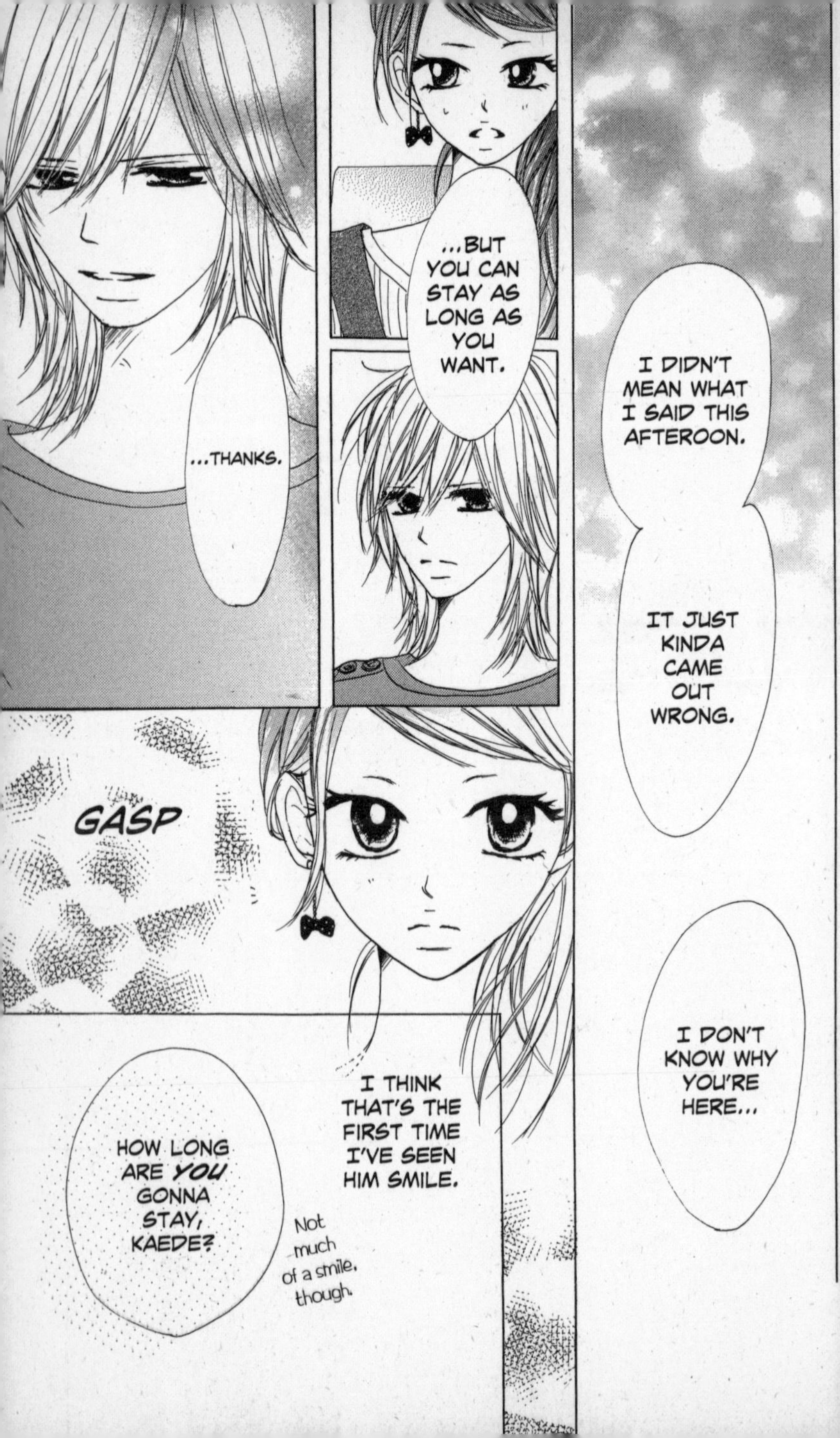
I DIDN'T MEAN WHAT I SAID THIS AFTEROON.
IT JUST KINDA CAME OUT WRONG.
I DON'T KNOW WHY YOU'RE HERE...
...BUT YOU CAN STAY AS LONG AS YOU WANT.
...THANKS.
GASP
I THINK THAT'S THE FIRST TIME I'VE SEEN HIM SMILE.
Not much of a smile, though.
HOW LONG ARE YOU GONNA STAY, KAEDE?

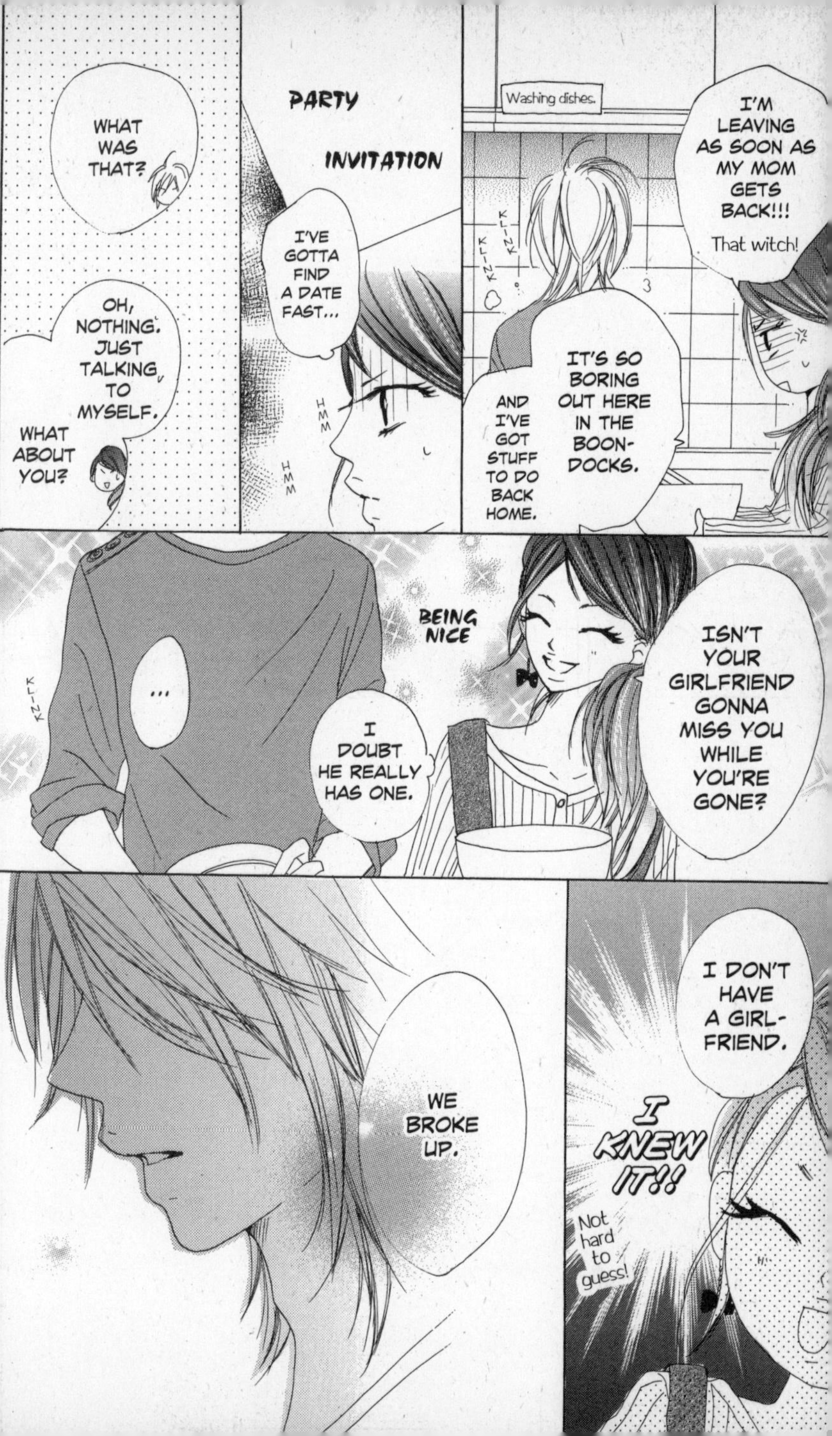
Washing dishes.
I'M LEAVING AS SOON AS MY MOM GETS BACK!!!
That witch!
KLINK KLINK
IT'S SO BORING OUT HERE IN THE BOONDOCKS.
AND I'VE GOT STUFF TO DO BACK HOME.
PARTY INVITATION
I'VE GOTTA FIND A DATE FAST...
HMM HMM
WHAT WAS THAT?
OH, NOTHING. JUST TALKING TO MYSELF.
WHAT ABOUT YOU?
ISN'T YOUR GIRLFRIEND GONNA MISS YOU WHILE YOU'RE GONE?
BEING NICE
I DOUBT HE REALLY HAS ONE.
...
KLINK
I DON'T HAVE A GIRLFRIEND.
I KNEW IT!!
Not hard to guess!
WE BROKE UP.

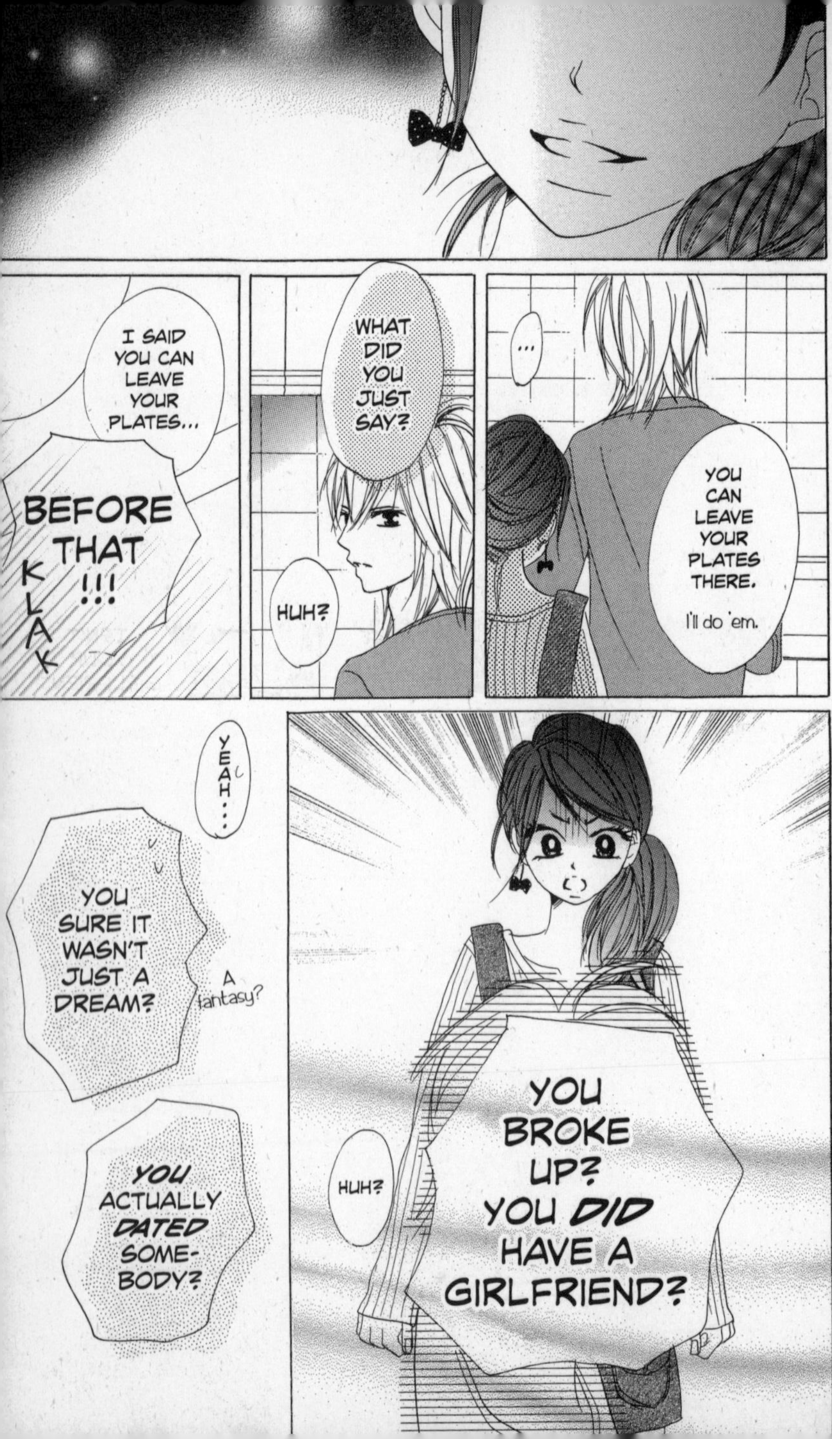
...
YOU CAN LEAVE YOUR PLATES THERE.
I'll do 'em.
WHAT DID YOU JUST SAY?
HUH?
I SAID YOU CAN LEAVE YOUR PLATES...
BEFORE THAT!!!
KLAK
YOU BROKE UP? YOU DID HAVE A GIRLFRIEND?
HUH?
YEAH...
YOU SURE IT WASN'T JUST A DREAM?
A fantasy?
YOU ACTUALLY DATED SOMEBODY?

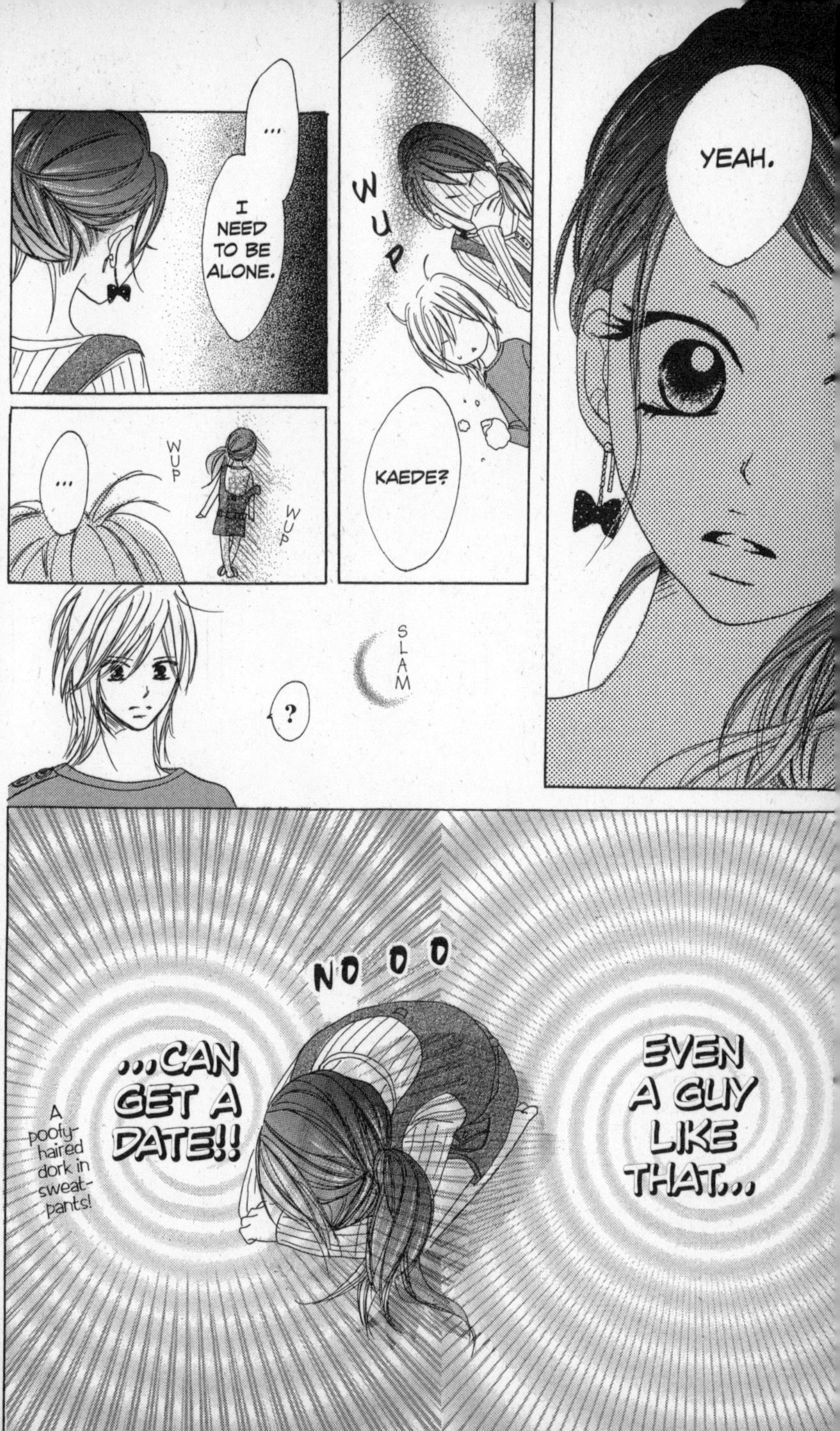
YEAH.
WUP
KAEDE?
...
I NEED TO BE ALONE.
...
WUP
WUP
SLAM
?
EVEN A GUY LIKE THAT...
NOOO
...CAN GET A DATE!!
A poofy-haired dork in sweat-pants!

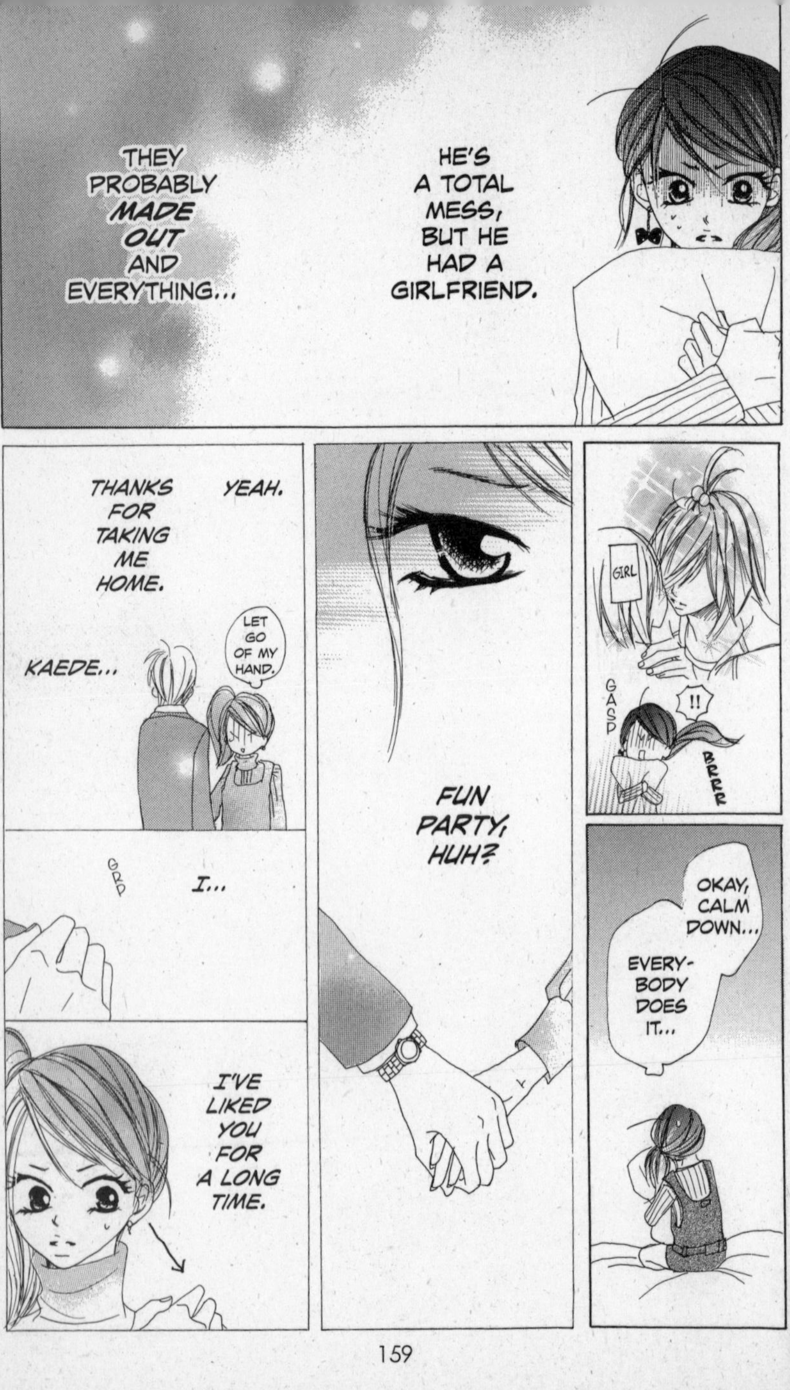
HE'S A TOTAL MESS, BUT HE HAD A GIRLFRIEND.
THEY PROBABLY MADE OUT AND EVERYTHING...
GIRL
!!
GASP
BRRR
OKAY, CALM DOWN...
EVERY-BODY DOES IT...
FUN PARTY, HUH?
YEAH.
THANKS FOR TAKING ME HOME.
LET GO OF MY HAND.
KAEDE...
GRP
I...
I'VE LIKED YOU FOR A LONG TIME.

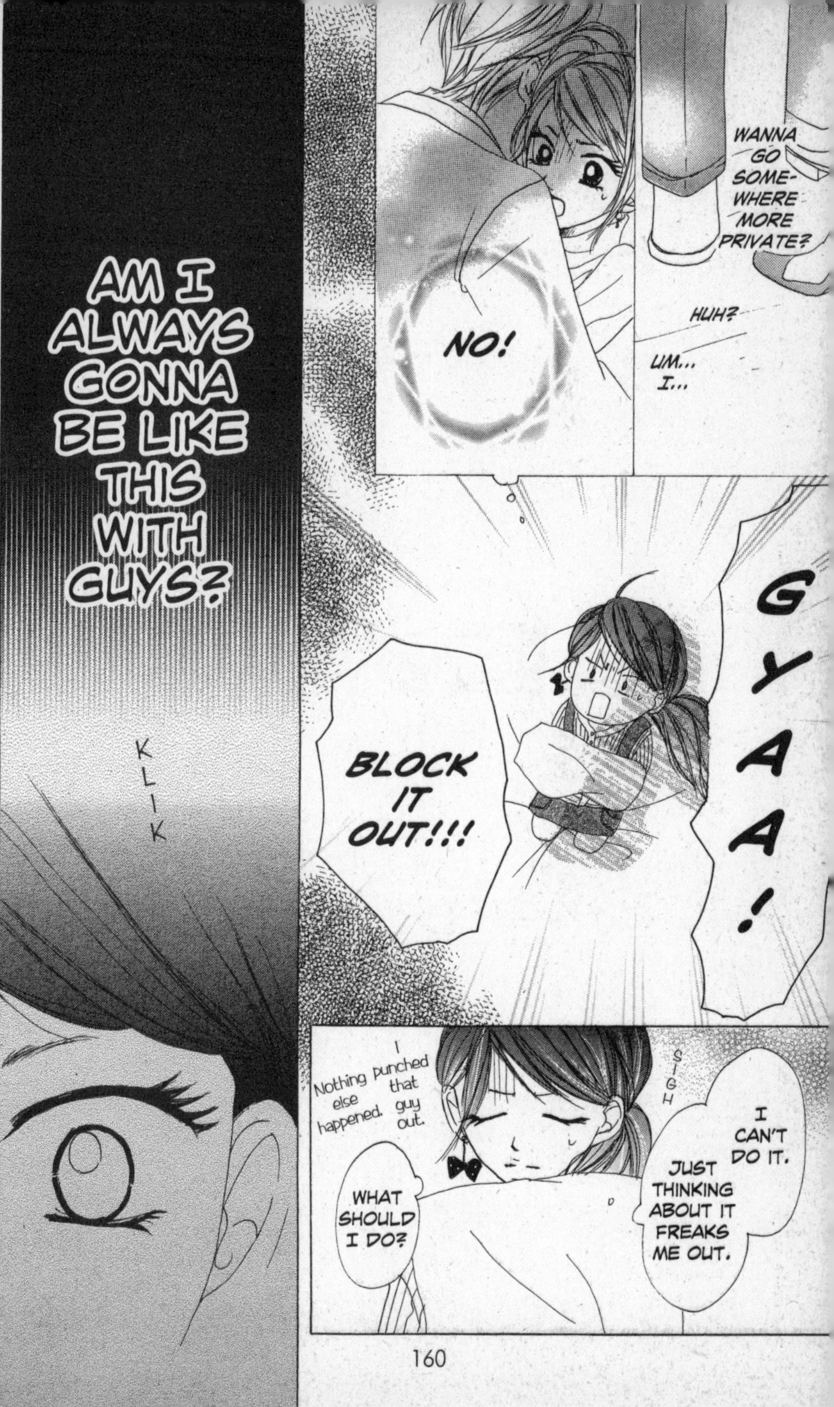
WANNA GO SOME-WHERE MORE PRIVATE?
HUH?
UM... I...
NO!
GYAAA!
BLOCK IT OUT!!!
I punched that guy out.
Nothing else happened.
SIGH
I CAN'T DO IT.
JUST THINKING ABOUT IT FREAKS ME OUT.
WHAT SHOULD I DO?
AM I ALWAYS GONNA BE LIKE THIS WITH GUYS?
KLIK

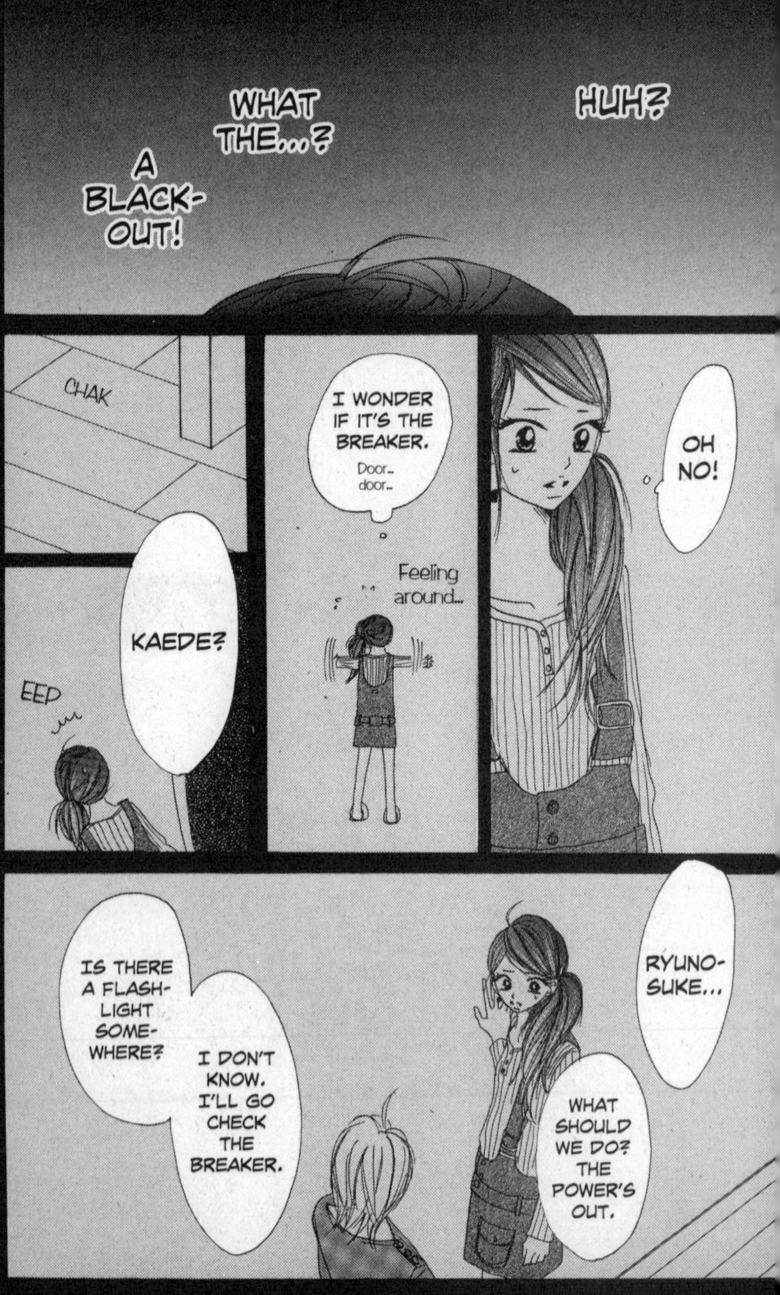
HUH?
WHAT THE...?
A BLACK-OUT!
OH NO!
I WONDER IF IT'S THE BREAKER.
Door... door...
Feeling around...
CHAK
KAEDE?
EEP
RYUNO-SUKE...
WHAT SHOULD WE DO? THE POWER'S OUT.
IS THERE A FLASH-LIGHT SOME-WHERE?
I DON'T KNOW. I'LL GO CHECK THE BREAKER.

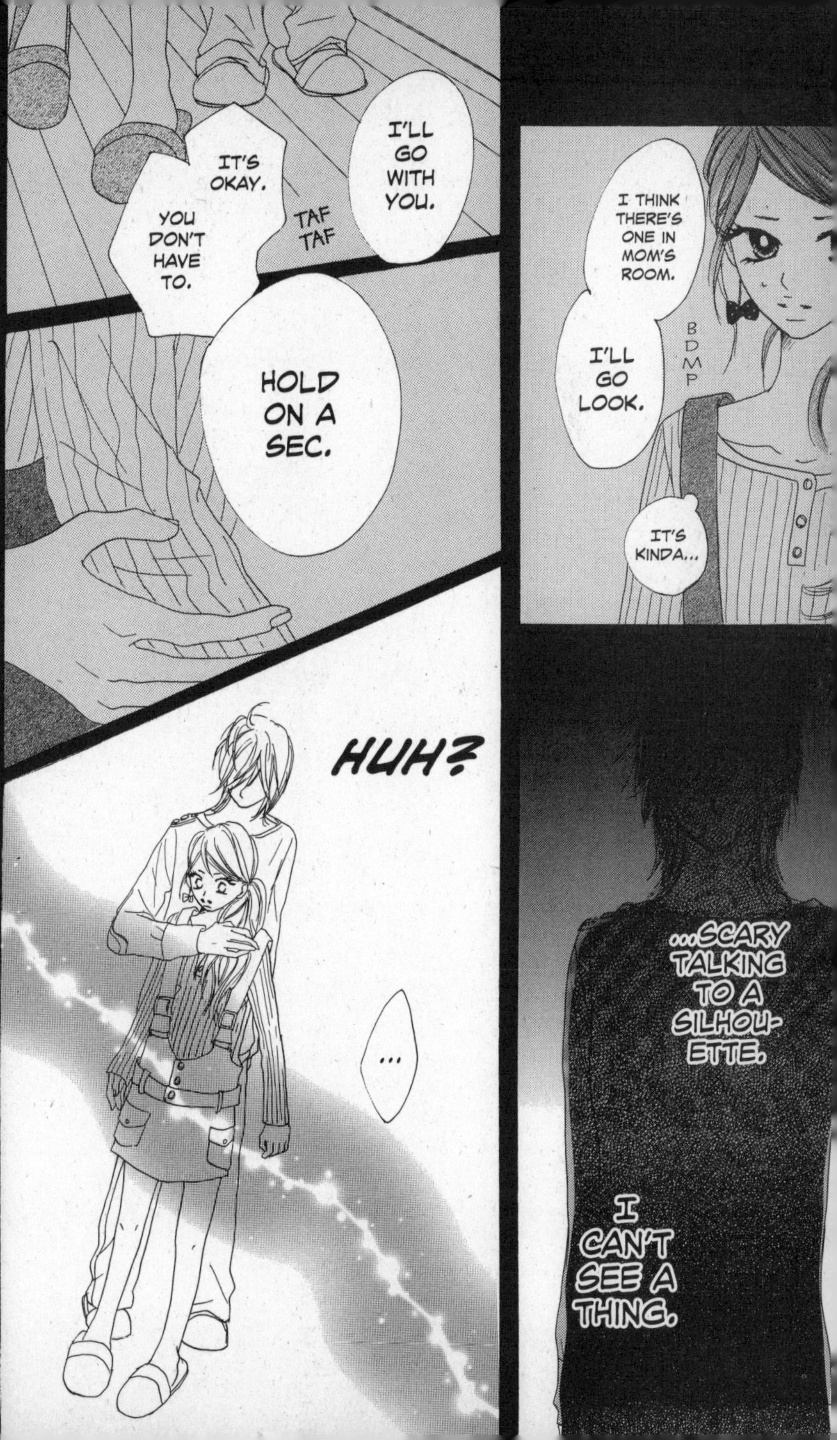
I THINK THERE'S ONE IN MOM'S ROOM.
BDMP
I'LL GO LOOK.
IT'S KINDA...
...SCARY TALKING TO A SILHOU-ETTE.
I CAN'T SEE A THING.
I'LL GO WITH YOU.
IT'S OKAY.
YOU DON'T HAVE TO.
TAF TAF
HOLD ON A SEC.
HUH?
...

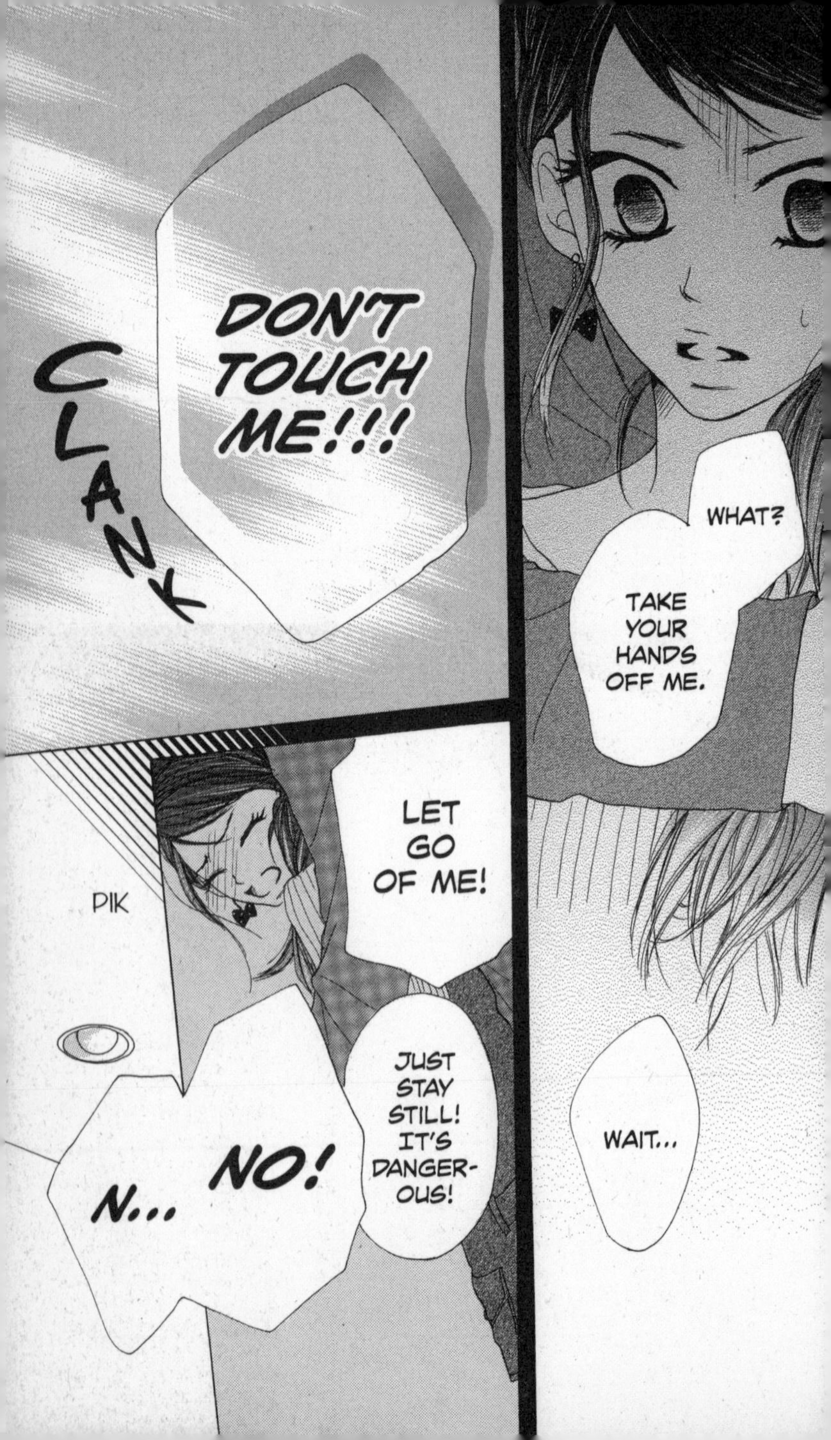
WHAT?
TAKE YOUR HANDS OFF ME.
DON'T TOUCH ME!!!
CLANK
WAIT...
LET GO OF ME!
PIK
JUST STAY STILL! IT'S DANGER-OUS!
N... NO!

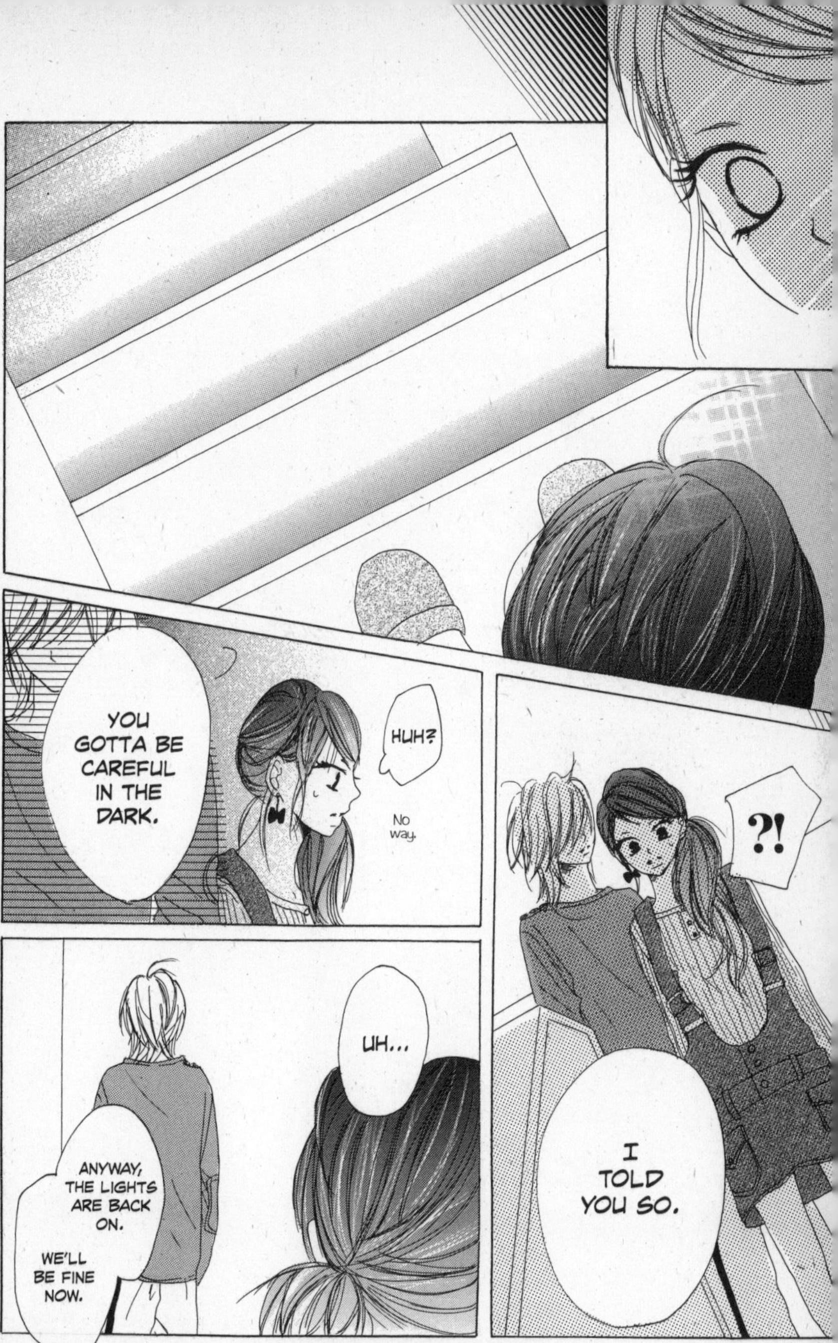
?!
I TOLD YOU SO.
YOU GOTTA BE CAREFUL IN THE DARK.
HUH?
No way.
UH...
ANYWAY, THE LIGHTS ARE BACK ON.
WE'LL BE FINE NOW.

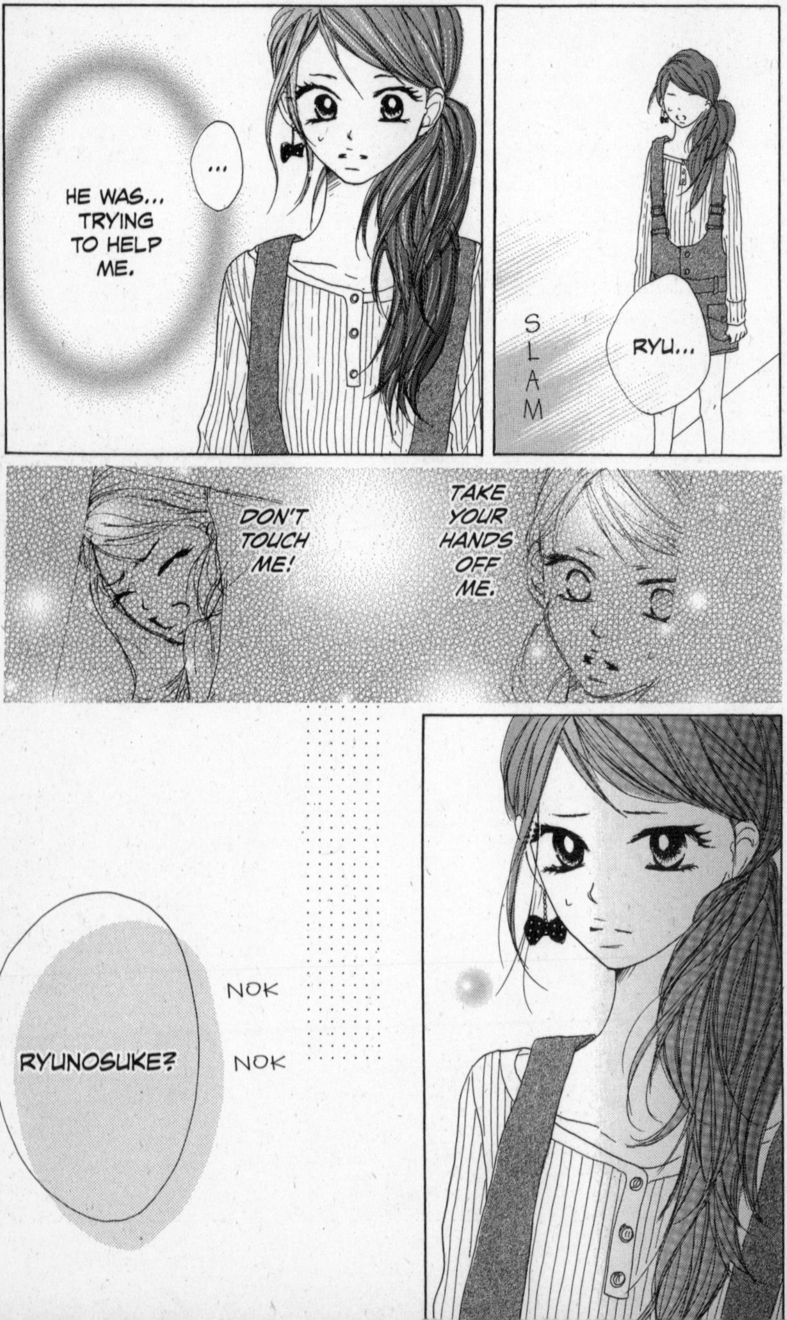
SLAM
RYU...
...
HE WAS... TRYING TO HELP ME.
TAKE YOUR HANDS OFF ME.
DON'T TOUCH ME!
NOK
NOK
RYUNOSUKE?

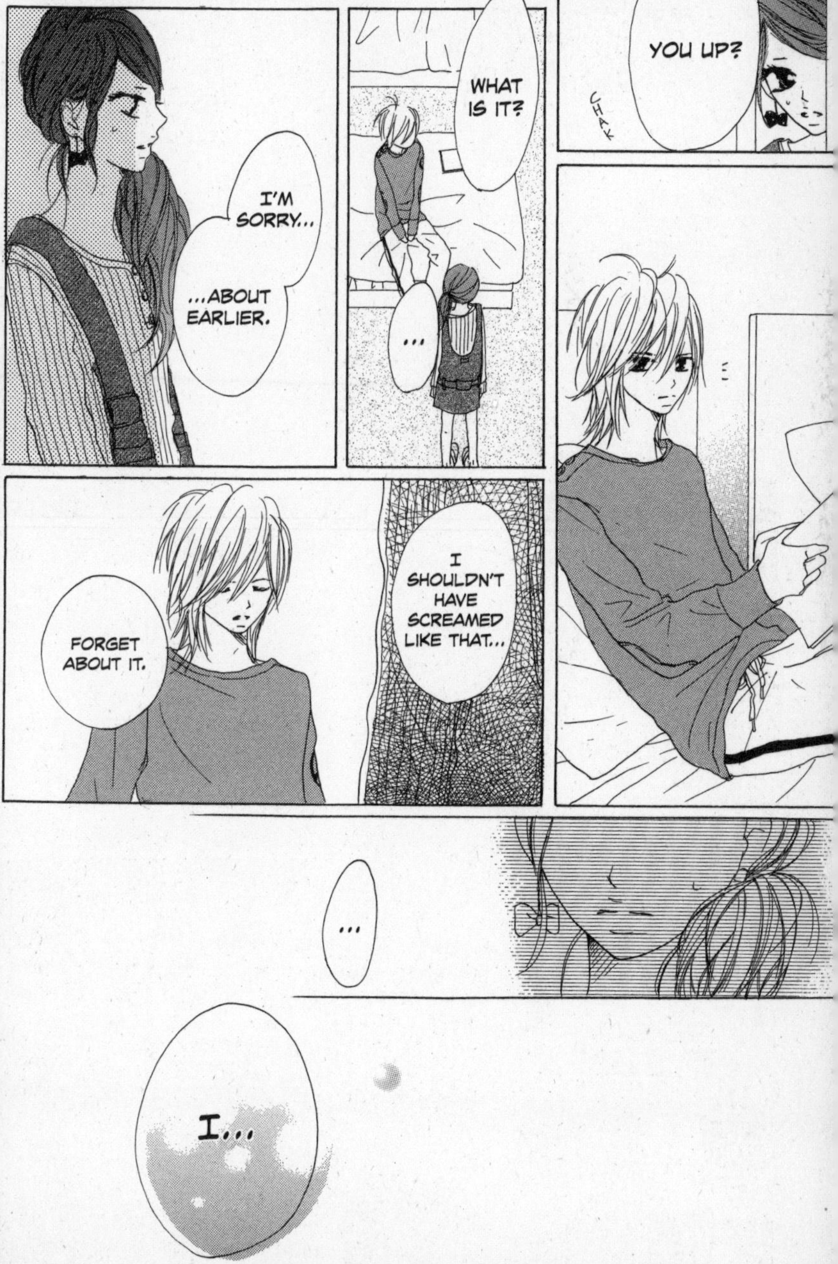
CHAK
YOU UP?
WHAT IS IT?
...
I'M SORRY...
...ABOUT EARLIER.
I SHOULDN'T HAVE SCREAMED LIKE THAT...
FORGET ABOUT IT.
...
I...

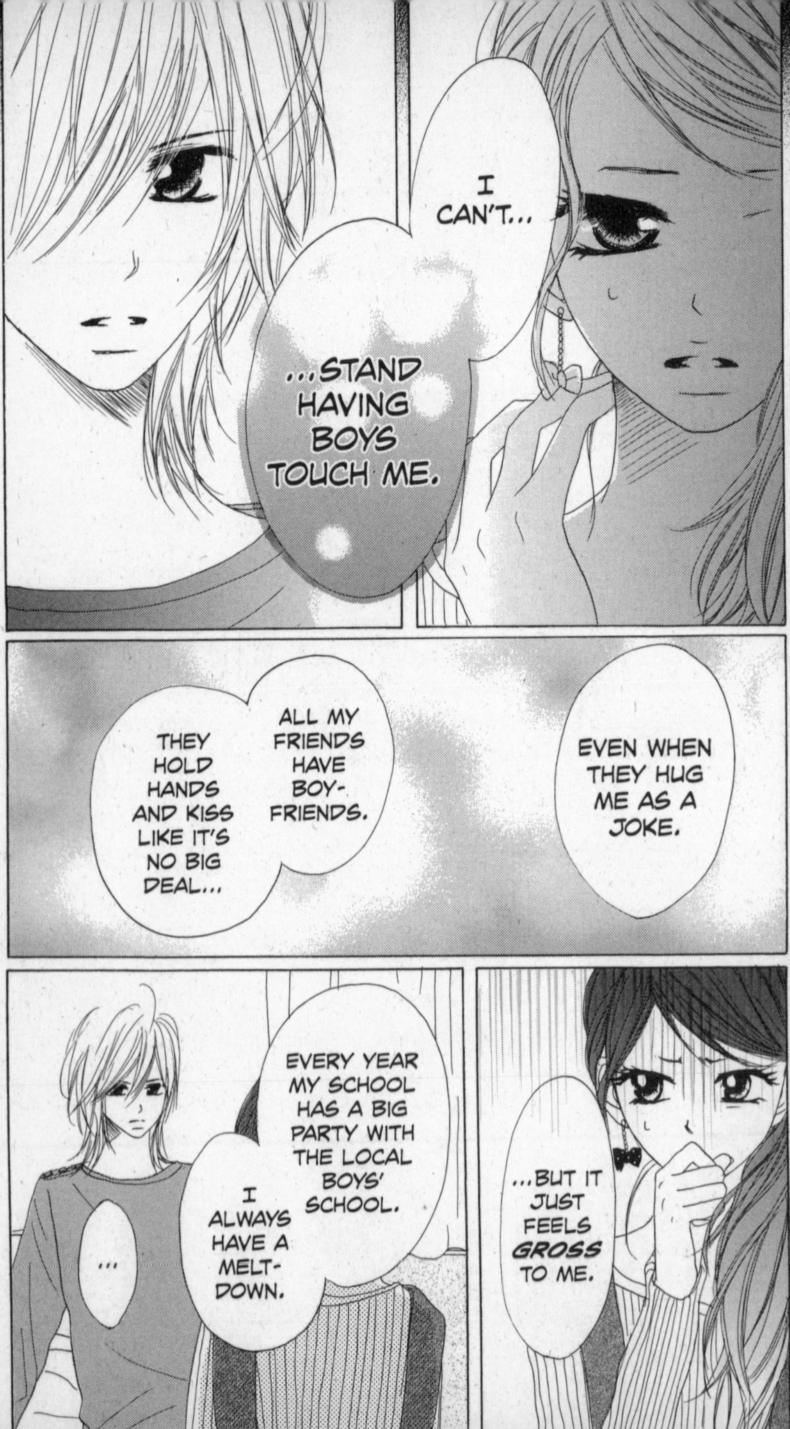
I CAN'T...
...STAND HAVING BOYS TOUCH ME.
EVEN WHEN THEY HUG ME AS A JOKE.
ALL MY FRIENDS HAVE BOY-FRIENDS.
THEY HOLD HANDS AND KISS LIKE IT'S NO BIG DEAL...
...BUT IT JUST FEELS **GROSS** TO ME.
EVERY YEAR MY SCHOOL HAS A BIG PARTY WITH THE LOCAL BOYS' SCHOOL.
I ALWAYS HAVE A MELT-DOWN.
...

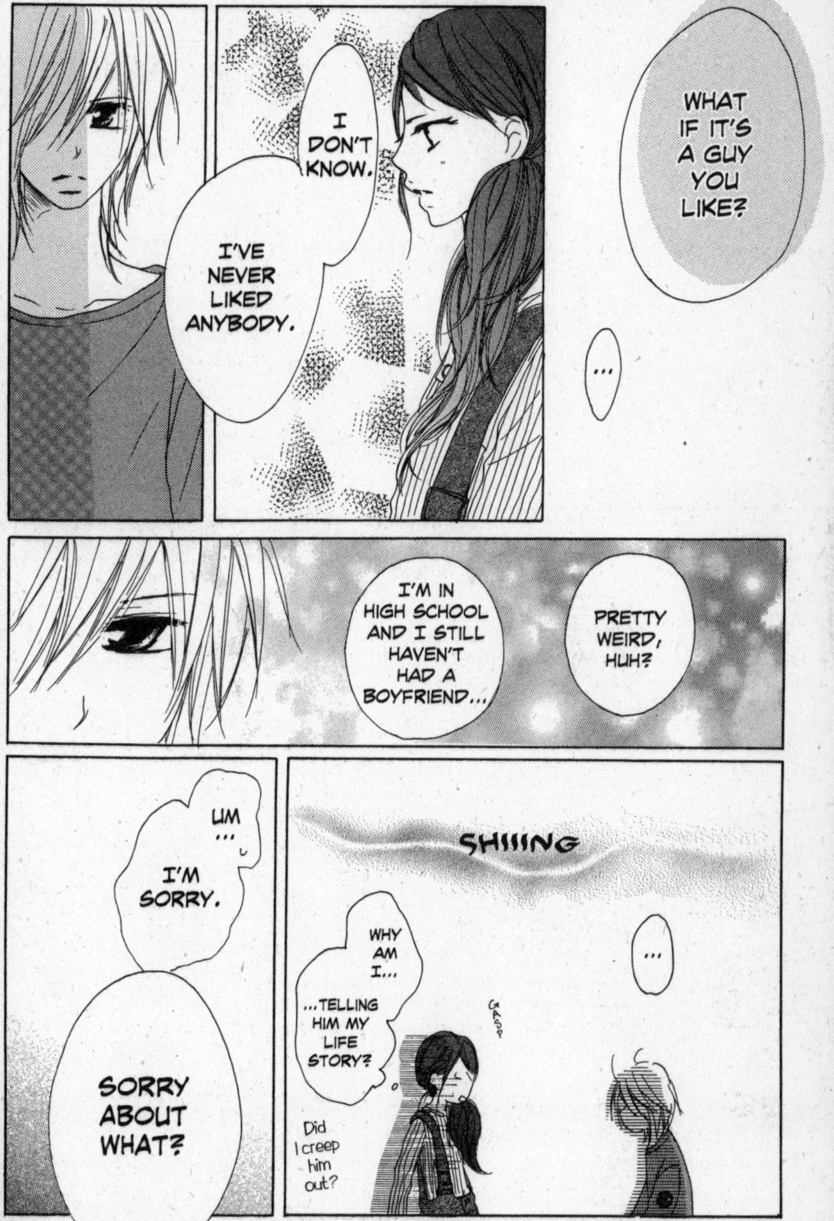
WHAT IF IT'S A GUY YOU LIKE?
...
I DON'T KNOW.
I'VE NEVER LIKED ANYBODY.
PRETTY WEIRD, HUH?
I'M IN HIGH SCHOOL AND I STILL HAVEN'T HAD A BOYFRIEND...
SHIIING
...
WHY AM I...
...TELLING HIM MY LIFE STORY?
GASP
Did I creep him out?
UM ... I'M SORRY.
SORRY ABOUT WHAT?

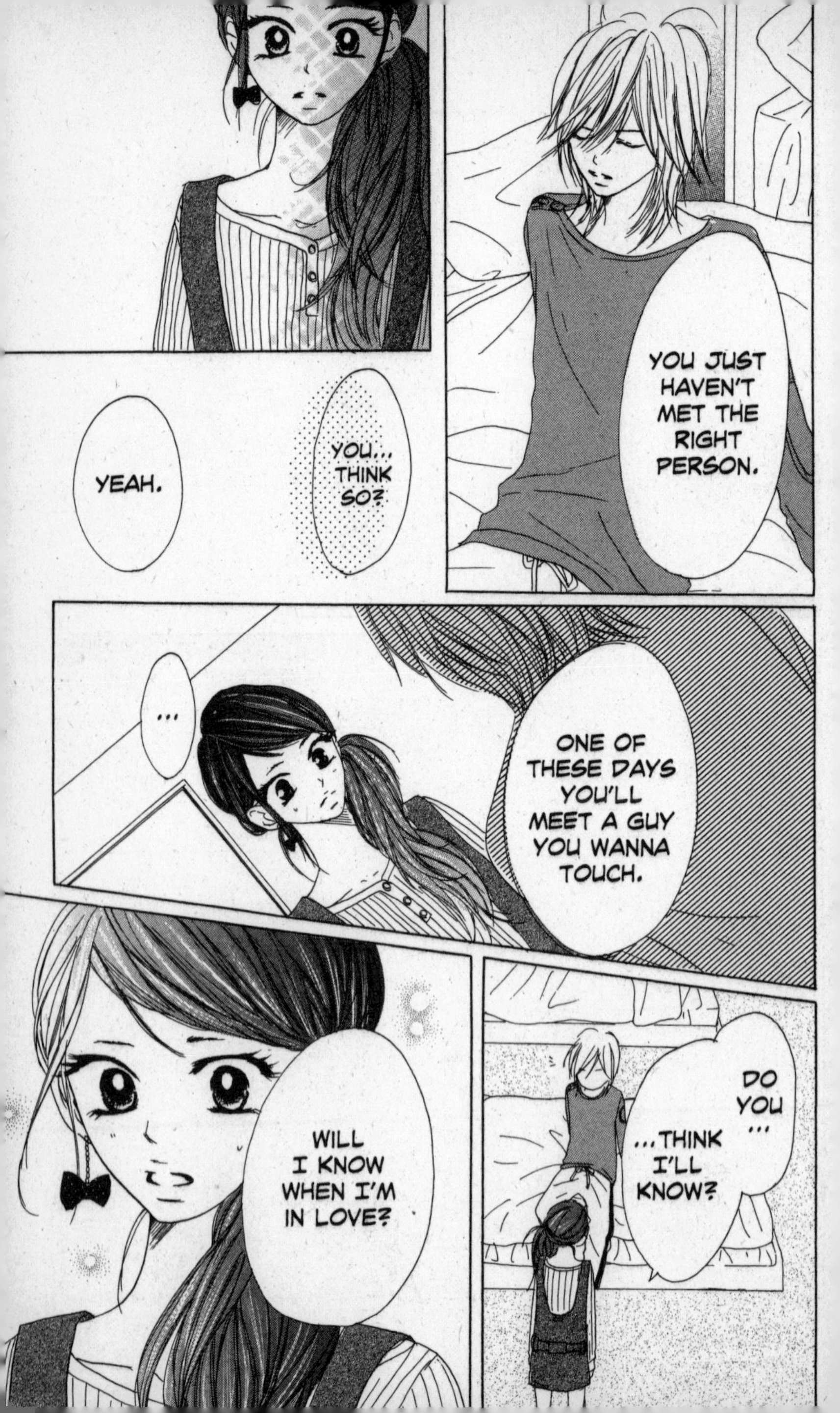
YOU JUST HAVEN'T MET THE RIGHT PERSON.
YOU... THINK SO?
YEAH.
ONE OF THESE DAYS YOU'LL MEET A GUY YOU WANNA TOUCH.
...
DO YOU...
...THINK I'LL KNOW?
WILL I KNOW WHEN I'M IN LOVE?

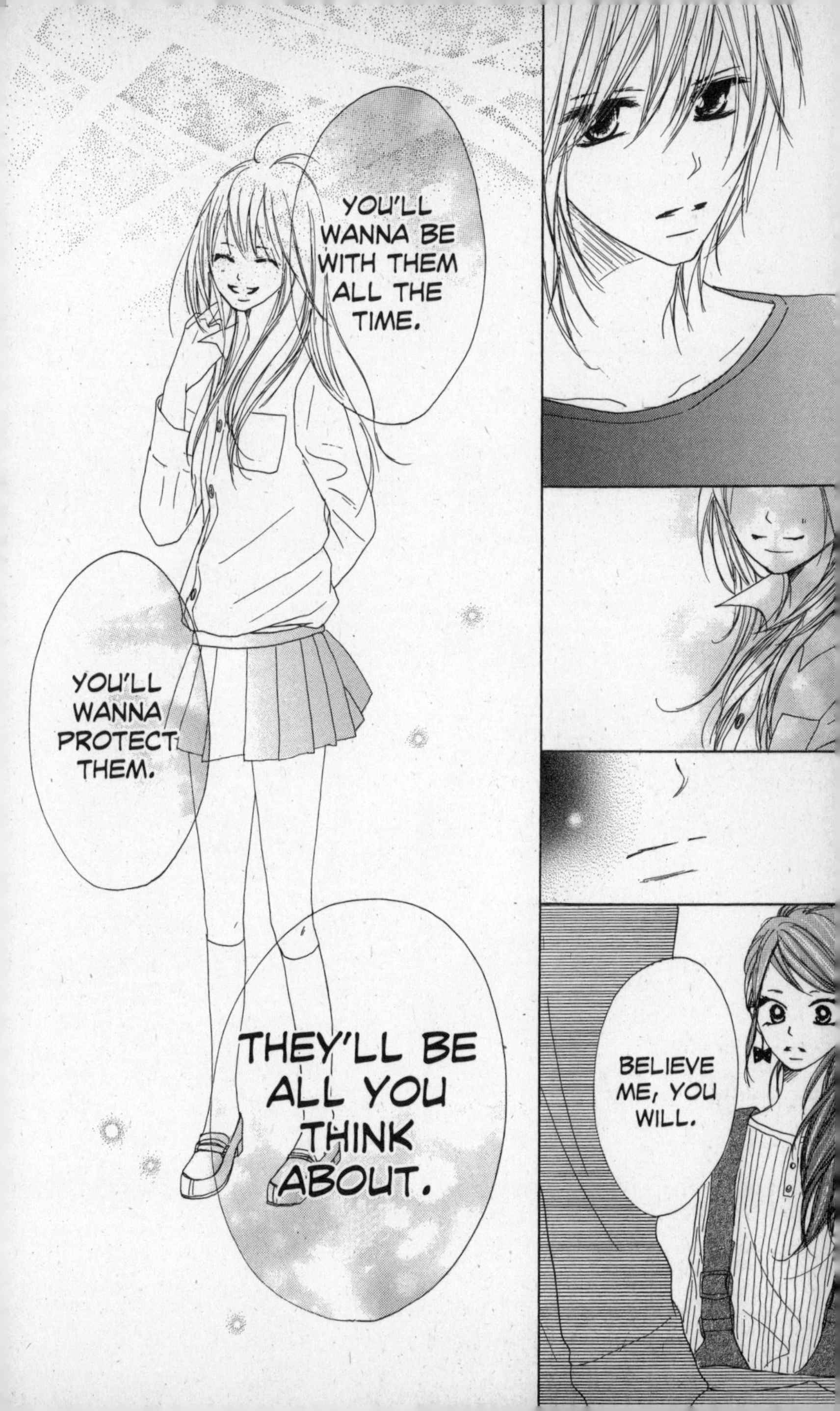
BELIEVE ME, YOU WILL.
YOU'LL WANNA BE WITH THEM ALL THE TIME.
YOU'LL WANNA PROTECT THEM.
THEY'LL BE ALL YOU THINK ABOUT.

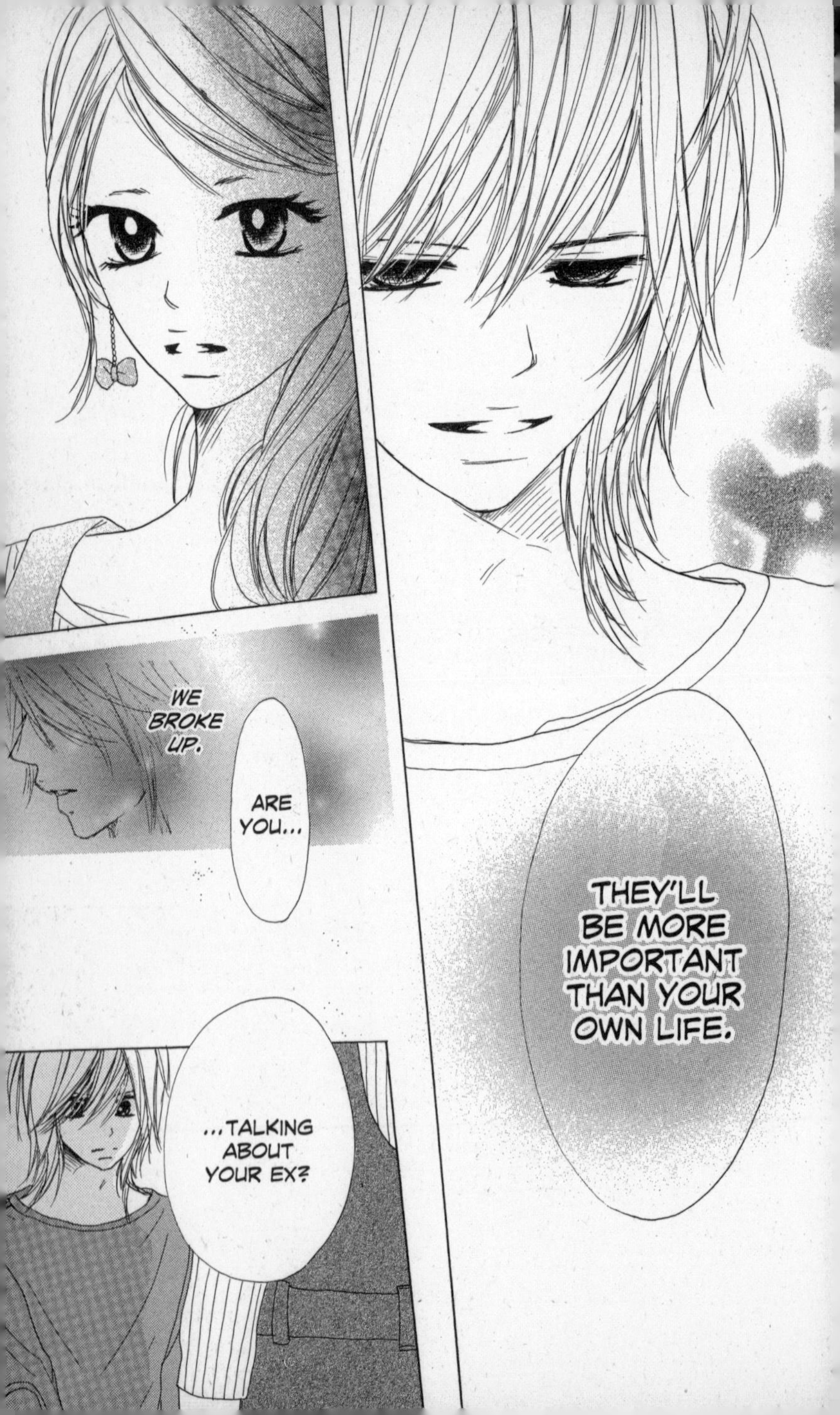
THEY'LL BE MORE IMPORTANT THAN YOUR OWN LIFE.
WE BROKE UP.
ARE YOU...
...TALKING ABOUT YOUR EX?

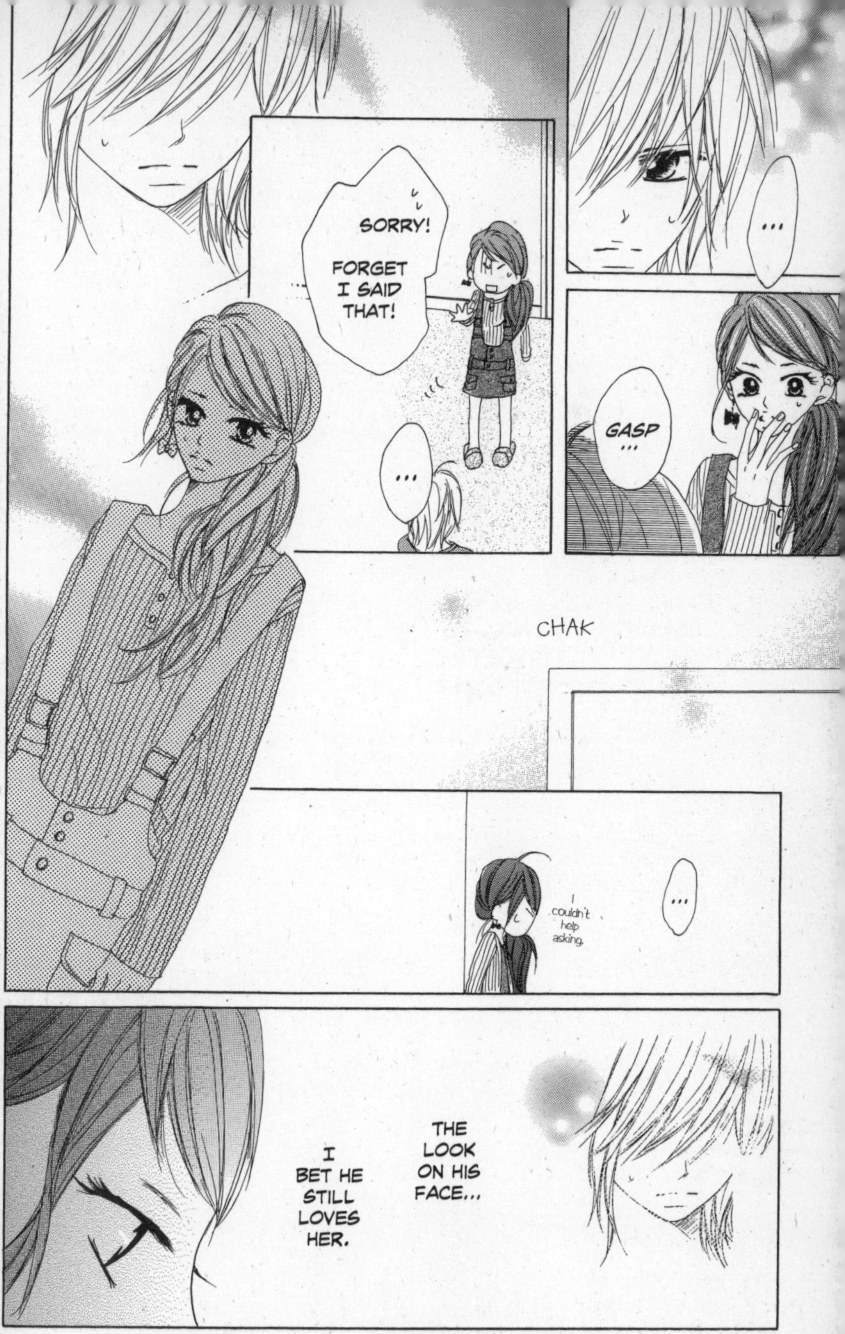
...
SORRY!
FORGET I SAID THAT!
...
GASP ...
CHAK
...
I couldn't help asking.
THE LOOK ON HIS FACE...
I BET HE STILL LOVES HER.

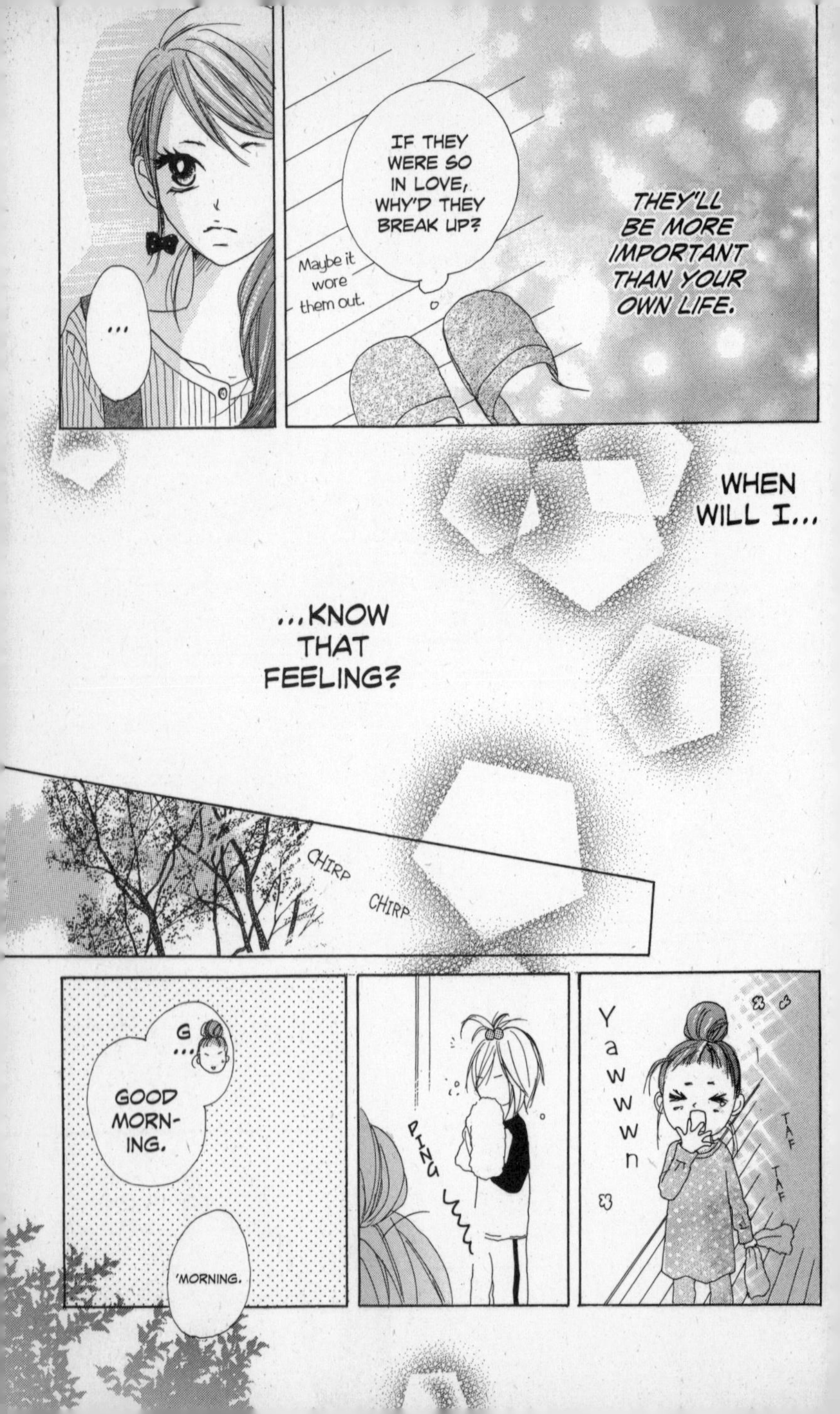
THEY'LL BE MORE IMPORTANT THAN YOUR OWN LIFE.
IF THEY WERE SO IN LOVE, WHY'D THEY BREAK UP?
Maybe it wore them out.
...
WHEN WILL I...
...KNOW THAT FEELING?
CHIRP
CHIRP
Yawwwn
TAF
TAF
PING
G...
GOOD MORNING.
'MORNING.

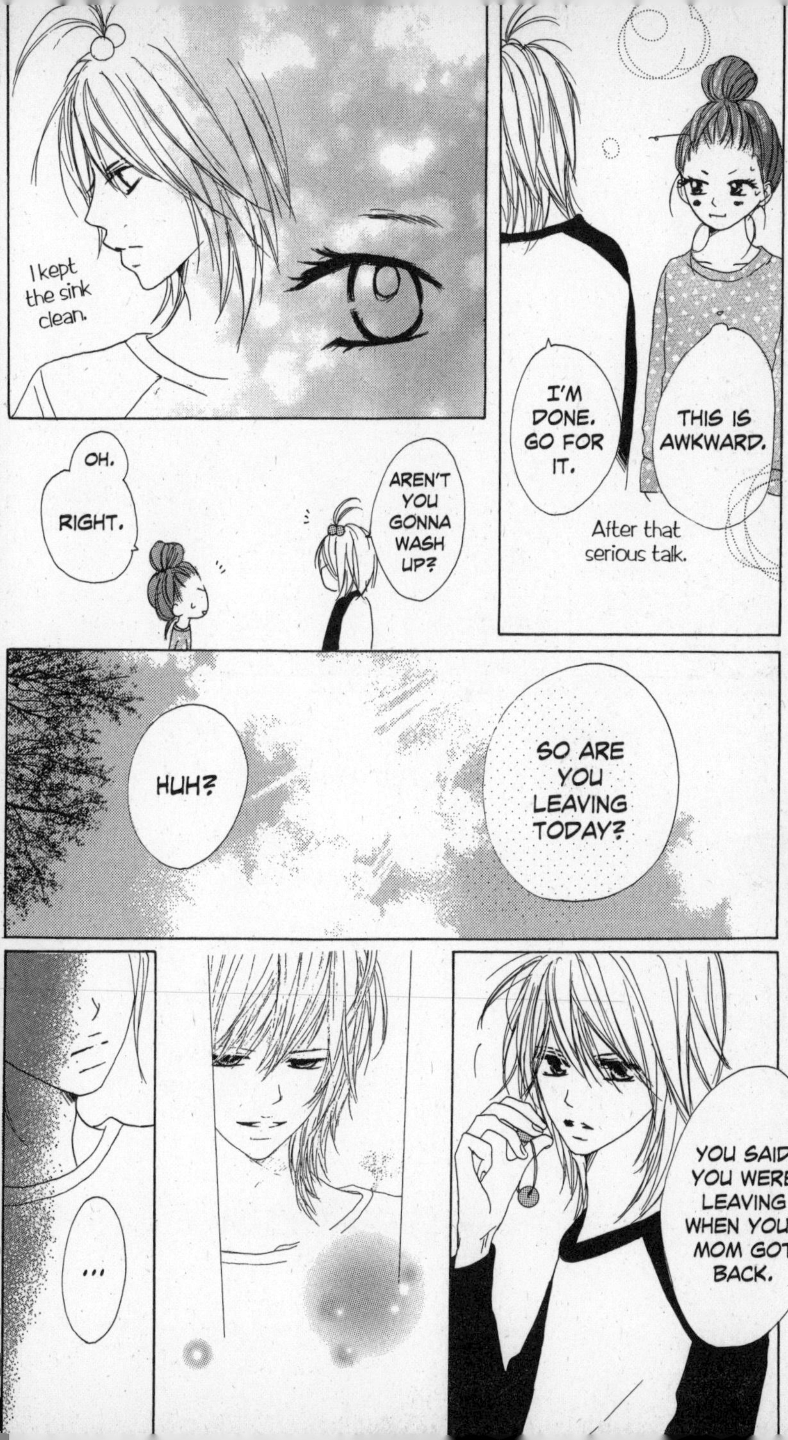
THIS IS AWKWARD.
I'M DONE. GO FOR IT.
After that serious talk.
I kept the sink clean.
AREN'T YOU GONNA WASH UP?
OH. RIGHT.
SO ARE YOU LEAVING TODAY?
HUH?
YOU SAID YOU WERE LEAVING WHEN YOUR MOM GOT BACK.
...

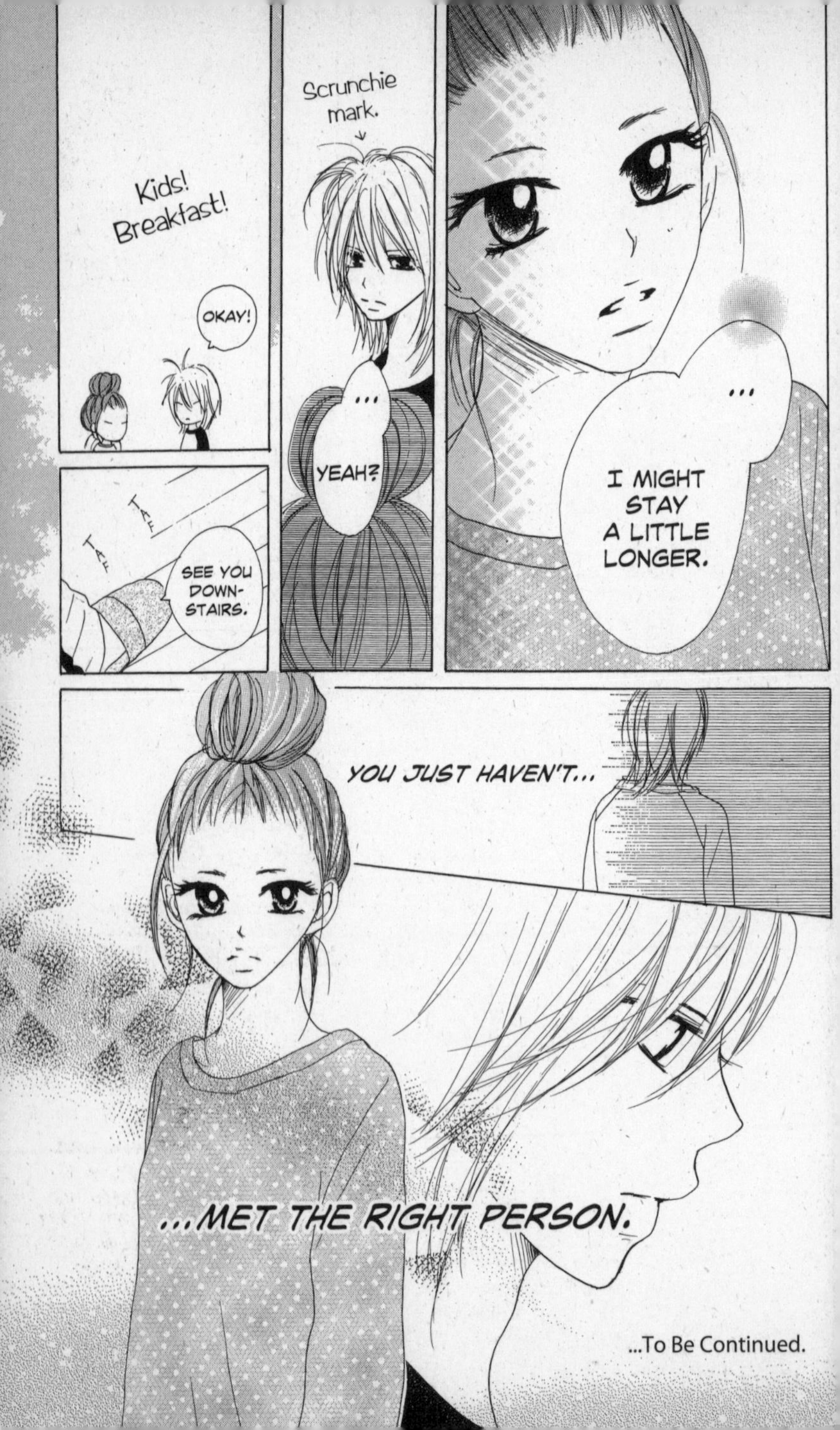
...
I MIGHT STAY A LITTLE LONGER.
Scrunchie mark.
...
YEAH?
Kids! Breakfast!
OKAY!
TAF
TAF
SEE YOU DOWN-STAIRS.
YOU JUST HAVEN'T...
...MET THE RIGHT PERSON.
...To Be Continued.

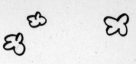

Drawing Upside Down

This is another game that evolved at Karuho Shiina's studio. One day I received sketches of Kazehaya and Sadako (the main characters in her manga *Kimi ni Todoke*) from Karuho.

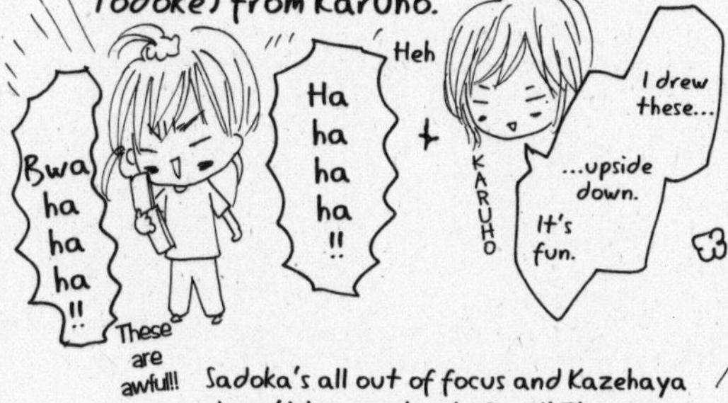
Heh
I drew these...
...upside down.
It's fun.
KARUHO
Ha ha ha ha!!
Bwa ha ha ha!!
These are awful!!

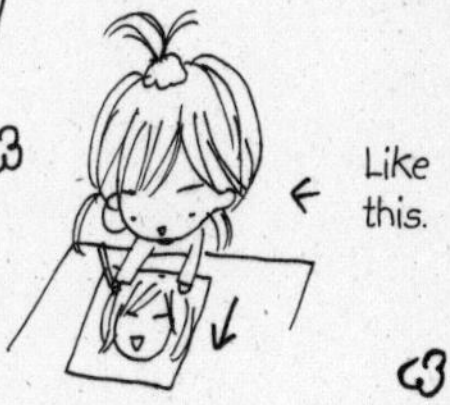
Like this.

Sadoka's all out of focus and Kazehaya doesn't have a shred of cool! They were so funny I had her fax them to me and had myself another laugh.

Then I tried it myself!!!

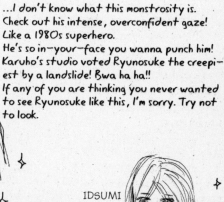

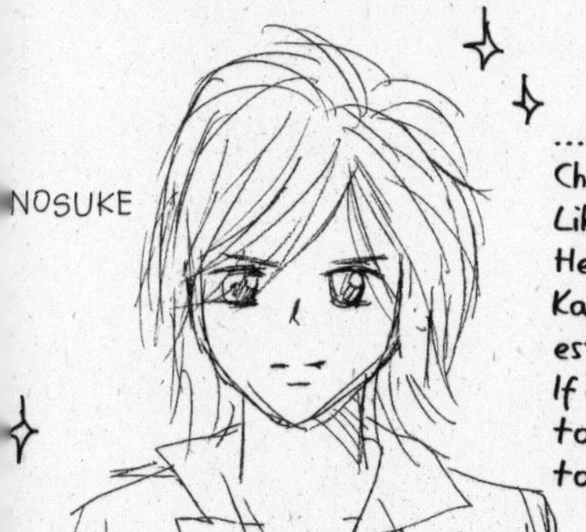
NOSUKE

...I don't know what this monstrosity is. Check out his intense, overconfident gaze! Like a 1980s superhero.
He's so in-your-face you wanna punch him! Karuho's studio voted Ryunosuke the creepiest by a landslide! Bwa ha ha!!
If any of you are thinking you never wanted to see Ryunosuke like this, I'm sorry. Try not to look.

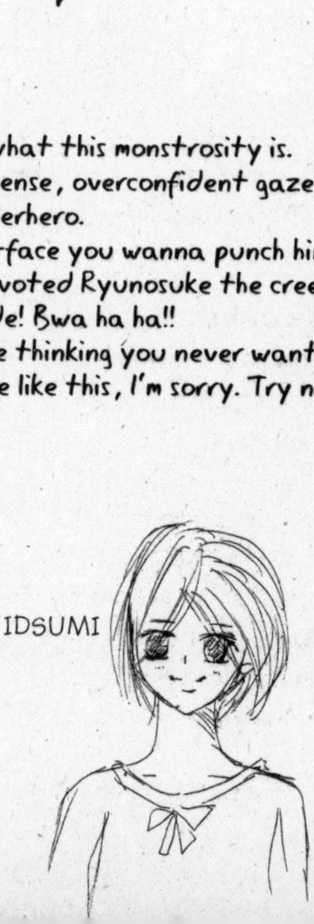
IDSUMI

Izumi is...awful, but not that funny.
Also, I misspelled her name.

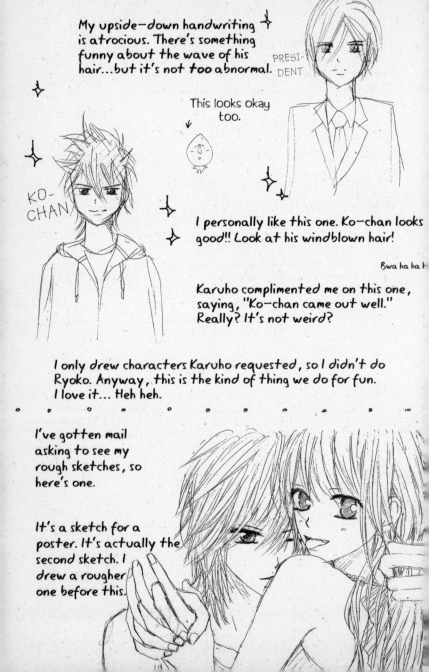

My upside-down handwriting is atrocious. There's something funny about the wave of his hair...but it's not too abnormal.

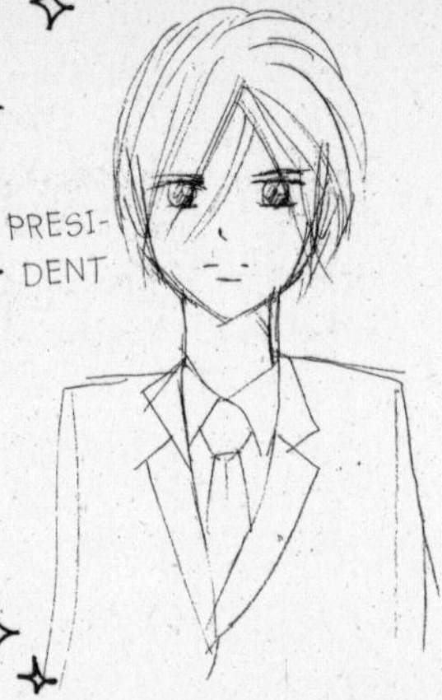
PRESI-
DENT

This looks okay too.

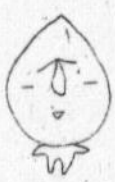

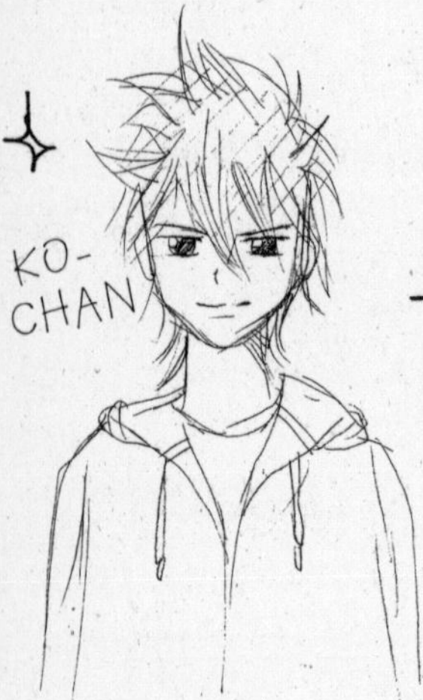
KO-
CHAN

I personally like this one. Ko-chan looks good!! Look at his windblown hair!

Bwa ha ha h

Karuho complimented me on this one, saying, "Ko-chan came out well." Really? It's not weird?

I only drew characters Karuho requested, so I didn't do Ryoko. Anyway, this is the kind of thing we do for fun. I love it... Heh heh.

I've gotten mail asking to see my rough sketches, so here's one.

It's a sketch for a poster. It's actually the second sketch. I drew a rougher one before this.

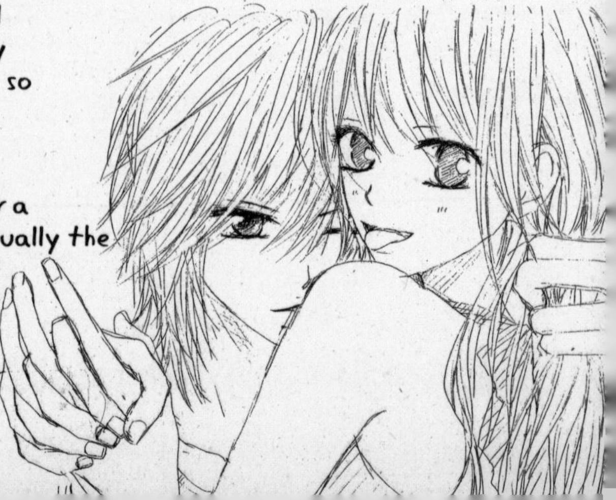

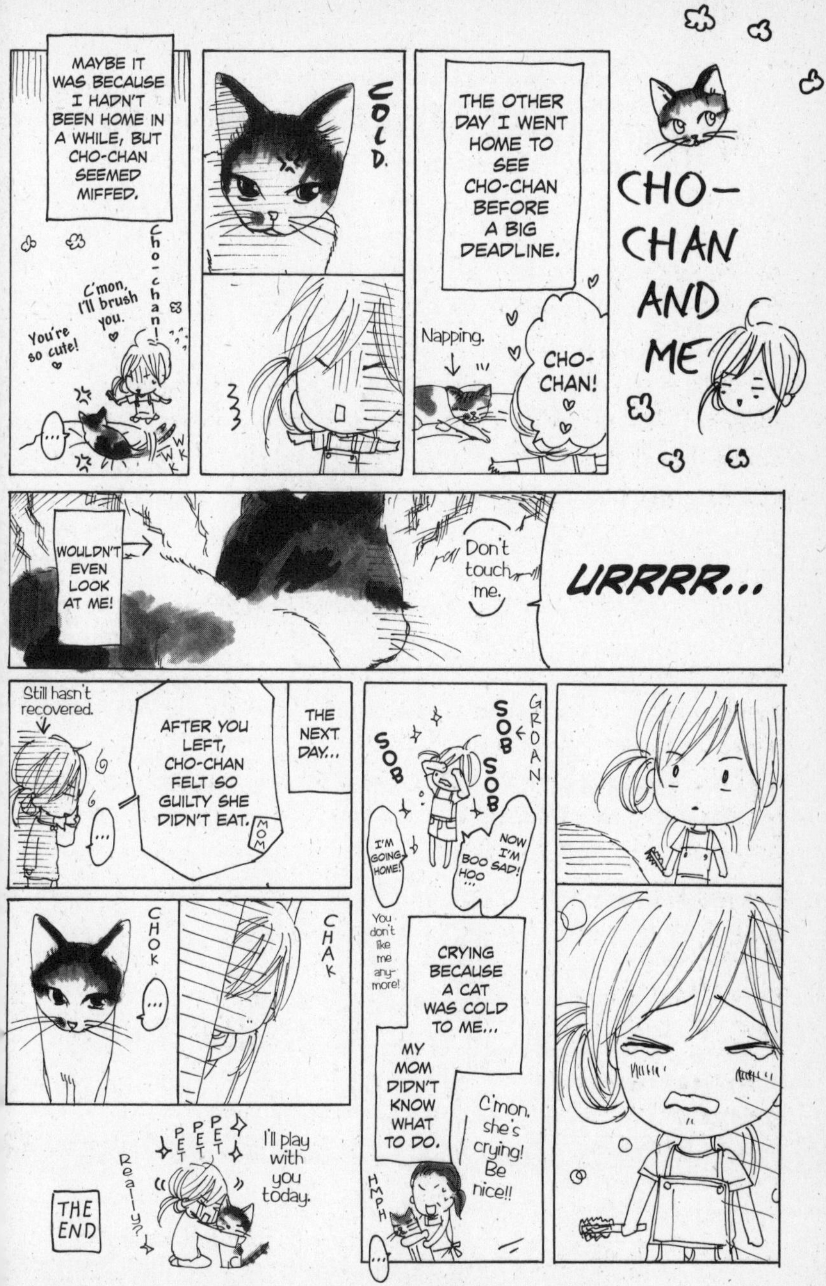

CHO-CHAN AND ME
THE OTHER DAY I WENT HOME TO SEE CHO-CHAN BEFORE A BIG DEADLINE.
Napping.
CHO-CHAN!
COLD.
MAYBE IT WAS BECAUSE I HADN'T BEEN HOME IN A WHILE, BUT CHO-CHAN SEEMED MIFFED.
Cho-chan!
C'mon, I'll brush you.
You're so cute!
...
WK WK
URRRR...
Don't touch me.
WOULDN'T EVEN LOOK AT ME!
SOB
SOB
SOB
GROAN
NOW I'M SAD!
BOO HOO ...
I'M GOING HOME!
THE NEXT DAY...
AFTER YOU LEFT, CHO-CHAN FELT SO GUILTY SHE DIDN'T EAT.
MOM
Still hasn't recovered.
...
You don't like me anymore!
CRYING BECAUSE A CAT WAS COLD TO ME...
MY MOM DIDN'T KNOW WHAT TO DO.
C'mon, she's crying! Be nice!!
HMPH
...
CHAK
CHOK
...
PET PET PET
I'll play with you today.
Really?
THE END

What did you think?

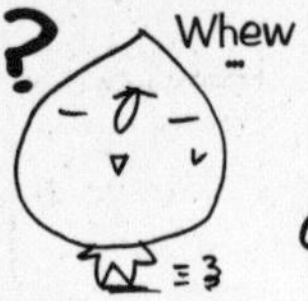
Whew

We're already on the last page! I got responses to the "what would you like Ryunosuke to do?" poll from volume 9. Thank you!!! I'll share the results in volume 11. So hold on! Maybe I'll keep writing about a certain video game too... Oh!!! That's right!!! I finally received a photograph from AlXce!!

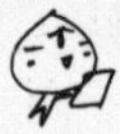
I have to put it up somewhere!
Yay!!
Yay!!

Well, that's about it for volume 10. It's been so long since Jin or Shirai have appeared!! Bwa ha ha!! But I always wanted them to show up again, so I'm glad I got to write them in. Will they appear again once in a while? I'm not sure. I'll do my best on volume 11, so I hope you'll stop by again.

Send letters to

B.O.D.Y.
c/o VIZ Media, LLC
P.O. Box 77010
San Francisco,
CA 94107

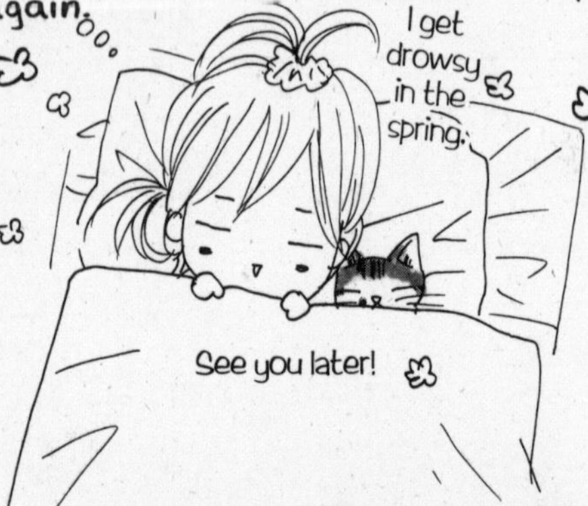
I get drowsy in the spring.
See you later!

2007.5.17 Ao Mimori

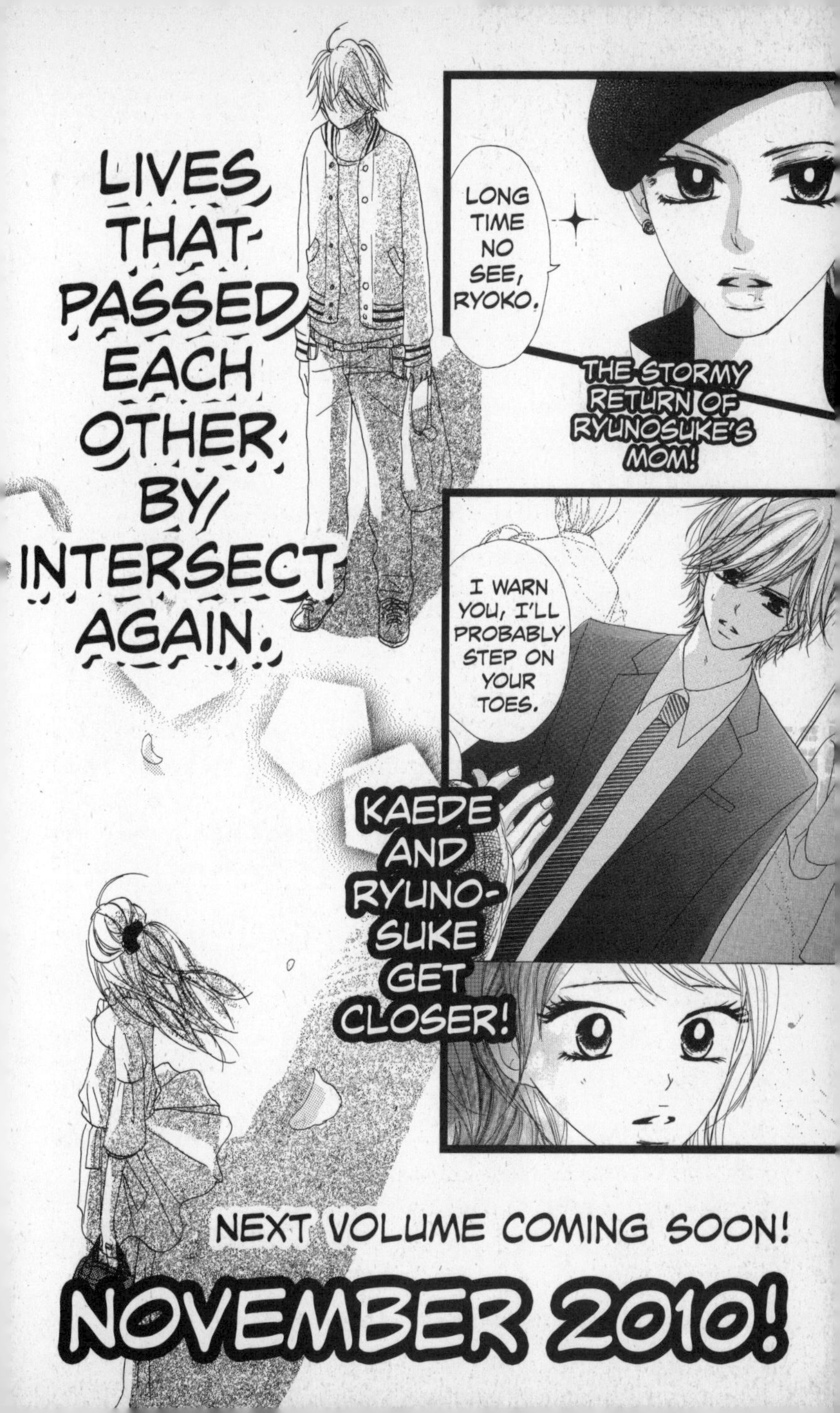
LONG TIME NO SEE, RYOKO.
THE STORMY RETURN OF RYUNOSUKE'S MOM!
LIVES THAT PASSED EACH OTHER BY INTERSECT AGAIN.
I WARN YOU, I'LL PROBABLY STEP ON YOUR TOES.
KAEDE AND RYUNO-SUKE GET CLOSER!
NEXT VOLUME COMING SOON!
NOVEMBER 2010!

NEXT VOLUME...

TWO HEART-POUNDING STORIES AT ONCE! THINGS ARE HEATING UP!

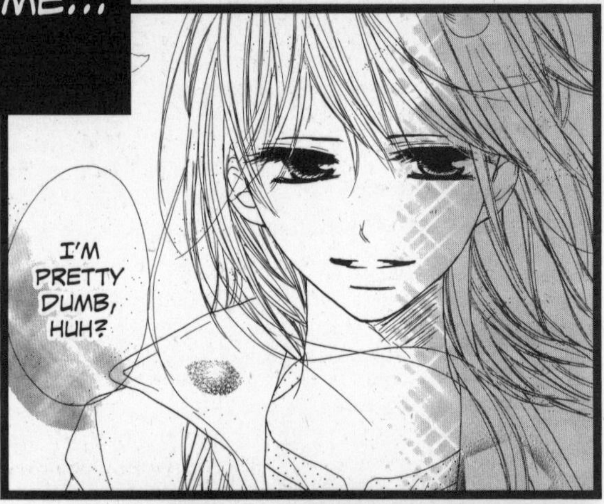
I'M PRETTY DUMB, HUH?

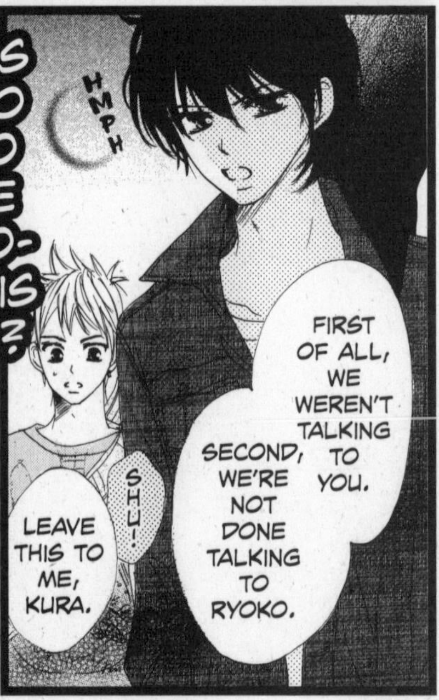
WHAT'S RYOKO UP TO WHILE RYUNOSUKE IS GONE?
HMPH
FIRST OF ALL, WE WEREN'T TALKING TO YOU.
SECOND, WE'RE NOT DONE TALKING TO RYOKO.
SHU!
LEAVE THIS TO ME, KURA.

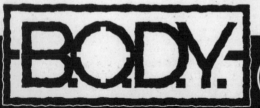

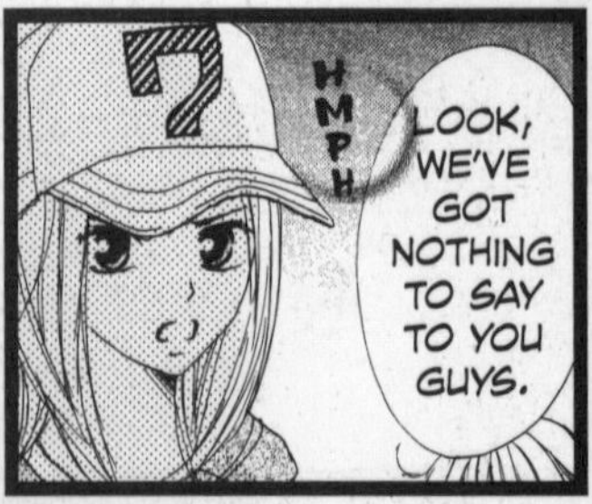
HMPH
LOOK, WE'VE GOT NOTHING TO SAY TO YOU GUYS.

B.O.D.Y. 11

B.O.D.Y. Language

Page 15, Author's Note: J:COM
A Japanese cable TV provider.

Page 15, Author's Note: AXN
A cable TV channel owned by Sony Pictures and available in many parts of the world, including Japan. AXN Japan shows a lot of American programming; it's probably where Mimori watches *Lost*.

Page 71, Author's Note: Tamama
Private Tamama, a character in the manga and anime *Sgt. Frog*.

Page 91, Author's Note: Karuho Shiina
Shojo manga artist and creator of *Kimi ni Todoke: From Me to You*.

Page 91, Author's Note: name
Manga-industry terminology for the rough draft or thumbnail of a manga chapter.

Page 126, panel 3: 3,920 yen
About $40.

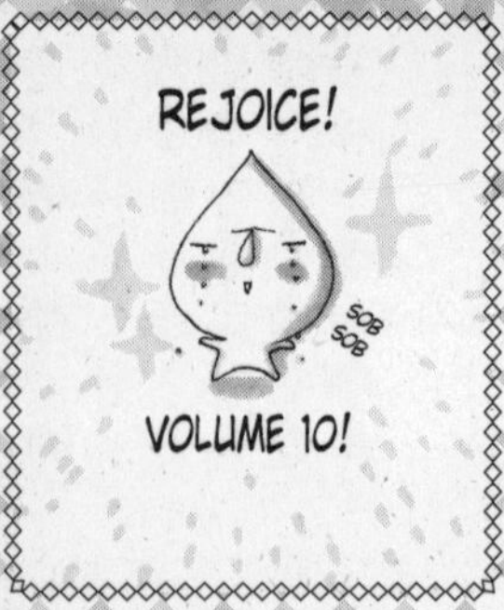
REJOICE!
SOB SOB
VOLUME 10!

Author's Commentary

Thanks to your support, we've reached volume 10! I can't believe a manga that was originally scheduled to run for eight chapters has come this far. What path with Ryoko and Ryunosuke take next? I hope you'll stick around to find out.♡

Ao Mimori began creating manga during her junior year of college, and her work debuted when she was only 23. *B.O.D.Y.*, her third series, was first published in *Bessatsu Margaret* in 2003 and is also available in Japanese as an audio CD. Her other work includes *Sonnano Koi Jyanai* (That's Not Love), *Anta Nanka Iranai* (I Don't Need You), *Dakishimetaiyo Motto* (I Want to Hold You More), *I LOVE YOU* and *Kamisama no Iu Toori* (As the God of Death Dictates).

Shojo Beat

B.O.D.Y. VOL
Shojo Beat Edition

STORY & ART BY
AO MIMORI

Translation/Joe Yamazaki
Touch-up Art & Lettering/HudsonYards
Design/Sean Lee
Editor/Shaenon K. Garrity

VP, Production/Alvin Lu
VP, Sales & Product Marketing/Gonzalo Ferreyra
VP, Creative/Linda Espinosa
Publisher/Hyoe Narita

Printed in Canada

Published by VIZ Media, LLC
P.O. Box 77010
San Francisco, CA 94107

10 9 8 7 6 5 4 3 2 1
First printing, August 2010

viz media
w.viz.com www.shojobeat.com

RATED T+ FOR OLDER TEEN

PARENTAL ADVISORY
B.O.D.Y. is rated T+ for Older Teen and is recommended for ages 16 and up. This volume contains mature themes.
ratings.viz.com

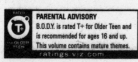